Strategies for Educating Students with Severe Handicaps

Strategies for Educating Students with Severe Handicaps

Robert J. Gaylord-Ross
San Francisco State University

Jennifer F. Holvoet
University of Kansas

Little, Brown and Company
Boston Toronto

Library of Congress Cataloging in Publication Data

Gaylord-Ross, Robert.
Strategies for educating students with severe handicaps.

Includes index.
1. Handicapped children—Education. 2. Handicapped—Education. 3. Ability—Testing. I. Holvoet, Jennifer F. II. Title.
LC4015.G36 1985 371.9 84–25022
ISBN 0–316–30547–2

Library of Congress Catalog Card Number 84–25022

ISBN 0-316-30547-2

9 8 7 6 5 4 3 2 1

MV

Published simultaneously in Canada by Little, Brown & Company (Canada) Limited

Printed in the United States of America

Excerpt, page 295: Adapted from C. T. Michaelis, *Home and School Partnerships in Exceptional Education*. Copyright © 1980 Aspen Systems Corporation. Used by permission of Aspen Systems Corporation, Rockville, Md.

Portions of Chapter 3 have appeared previously in J. Holvoet, M. Mulligan, N. Schussler, L. Lacy, and D. Guess, *The KICS Model: Sequencing Learning Experiences for Severely Handicapped Children and Youth*, a report funded in part by the U.S. Department of Education, Office of Special Education, Division for Innovation and Development, 1982. The opinions expressed, however, do not necessarily reflect the position or policy of the U.S. Department of Education; and no official endorsement by the Department should be inferred.

Foreword

For some time now, our approach to the education of learners with severe handicapping conditions has been grounded in learning theory and systematic instructional practices. Behavioral principles have been applied to meeting the instructional needs of these students, and this movement has been fundamentally helpful in solving difficulties in teaching and learning. Yet, until now, practitioners working with this population have had to refer to applied guidelines on behavior analysis written for use in clinics and classrooms. Many of the students with whom we work are still kept isolated from the community and their nondisabled peers; too many children are required to attend "special schools" which are far from their home neighborhoods and which make it impossible for them to begin the task of learning to perform in a normalized environment, with other people. In contrast, today's "most promising practices" clearly advocate that our instructional strategies must be appropriate for implementation in the real world—in the community. How then do we structure systematic learning trials and contingently respond to the behavior of students with severe needs, in the presence of natural, infinitely varying stimuli and environmental consequences?

We need a "second generation" of behavior modification: principles translated into workable strategies for the community and for interactions with persons in the community. This is one of the first volumes to give practitioners such guidelines. It is unique in its comprehensive and accurate approach to meeting our needs as teachers, parents, psychologists, and therapists in attempting to apply new recommendations to our work with students. First, principles and strategies of behavior analysis are presented here in a manner which serves both as an introduction and a handbook for professionals and caregivers *and* which continuously relates this material to meeting the needs of students with severe disabilities. Second, the authors never let us forget that our technology is no substitute for serious, individualized decisions on what we are teaching. It is no longer enough to be pleased that we have taught something; we must be able to defend our choice of what we teach by showing that, somehow, the learner's quality of life and the reactions of others to that person are improved as a result of our efforts. Third, our technology must be moved out of artificial, segregated clinic and classroom environments and into the community where students will live, recreate, and work. We can no longer expect persons with severe disabilities to live out their school careers (and lives!) in isolated environments to allow us to more easily control antecedents and consequences. There is no doubt that instruction in the confusion and complexity of the real world will be more difficult for us. But after a solid foundation of nearly two decades of applications of behavioral analysis in controlled settings, these authors and many of their peers feel that we are ready to get down to business. Now we must demonstrate that our methods can work without lessening respect for the rights of these individuals to live and learn under normalized conditions.

Gaylord-Ross and Holvoet have provided the field with an important and crucial framework for clinical and educational practices with children and adults who have severe disabilities. Their recommendations are consistent with both our values and our dedication to structured and systematic intervention. This is a competent and dramatic work, and the authors are to be congratulated for helping us to synthesize principles and normalized practices while maintaining our commitment to effectiveness. Our programs should make a difference, and this book will make it easier to move in the right direction.

Luanna H. Meyer, Ph.D.
Syracuse University
Syracuse, New York

Preface

Since the early 1960s we have seen increased interest in providing meaningful educational services and experiences for persons with severe handicaps. That attention has brought about improvements in our manner of instruction. In this textbook on methods of instruction we have set out to create an approach to teaching individuals with severe handicaps that is based on research and is practical. Our efforts are intended for both teachers in training and those already working in schools.

We begin our coverage with a chapter on assessment and on selecting educational goals. The next two chapters deal with instructional design and making curriculum natural and functional. In Chapter 4 we look at measurement and in Chapter 5 we discuss behavior management. An analysis of curriculum for persons with severe handicaps is the topic of Chapter 6. Classroom organization and home-school instruction are covered in the following two chapters. In Chapter 9 we consider the many facets of teaching, and in the last chapter we describe the trends and directions of the field.

Strategies for Educating Students with Severe Handicaps comprehensively covers teaching methods. We present a model for instruction describing systematic instructional procedures based on the principles of applied behavior analysis. Implicit in our approach is the need to select functional curricular goals and activities that are keyed to the student's present and subsequent environments. Rather than focusing merely on a student's deficits, we call on the teacher to identify critical skills that severely handicapped persons need to learn in order to succeed in natural settings in the community. The model stresses that instruction should take place in multiple natural settings. In these, the student will be better able to transfer newly acquired skills to different situations.

We use a format presenting and demonstrating many concepts with case examples. In these we show how the concepts can be used with persons and how teachers can enlarge upon various strategies. Such modeling of educational practice, we believe, will lead to better comprehension of those concepts, and set the stage for further applications.

To further enhance the designing and implementing of instructional programs, we include illustrations. Some, such as recording sheets, are aids that teachers can use with students. Others display exemplary curricula that are commercially available. The illustrations also present findings from research, model programs, and new developments in educational technology.

In the Epilogue, we include practicum exercises that can be used as a base for in-class work or for independent study.

In developing our model of instruction and in writing this book we were influenced by varied forces. First, we drew upon our own experience with severely disabled individuals. Second, the thinking of colleagues has affected our work, including Harvey Switzky, Doug Guess, Lou Brown, Herb Handley, Salomon Rettig, Cap Peck, Vicki Casella, Marci Hanson, Luce Schuler, Martin Miller, Howard Cohen, Ed Helmstetter, Tom Haring, Wayne Sailor, Ian Pumpian, and Bill Wilson. Third, we acknowledge our debt of gratitude to our colleagues who read all or parts of our manuscript and generously shared their ideas and recommendations for improving the chapters: Tamara Adams, University of New Hampshire; John Filler, California State University, Hayward; Bonnie Utley, University of Kansas; Luanna Meyer, Syracuse University; and Barbara Wilcox, University of Oregon. Fourth, we appreciate the many hours that our typist, Jackie Pomies, devoted to the several drafts. We would also like to acknowledge the photographer, Dolores Jenkin. Finally, we would like to thank our spouses, Cory and Charles, for giving us that special support so needed during a writing project. Without their belief in our work, this volume would never have been completed.

Brief Contents

Prologue xix
Chapter 1 Assessment and Target Selection 1
Chapter 2 Instructional Design for Skill Acquisition 41
Chapter 3 Making the Curriculum Natural and Functional 89
Chapter 4 Measurement 125
Chapter 5 Behavior Management 165
Chapter 6 Curriculum 197
Chapter 7 Environmental and Classroom Organization 223
Chapter 8 Home-School Interactions 251
Chapter 9 The Many Facets of Being a Teacher 281
Chapter 10 Past, Present, and Future Directions 307
Epilogue 333

Contents

Prologue xix

Chapter 1
Assessment and Target Selection 1

Assessment for Screening Purposes 2
Characteristics of Good Screening Instruments 3
Parameters of Screening Instruments 4
The Teacher's Role in Screening 5
Representative Screening Instruments 5
Diagnostic Testing 5
Three Components 6
The Controversy over Diagnostic Testing 7
Criteria for Diagnostic Assessment Instruments 8
Types of Diagnostic Assessment Instruments 9
Intelligence Tests 10
Tests of Adaptive Behavior 11
Other Diagnostic Procedures 13
Assessment for Educational Decision Making 17
Determining What to Teach 17
Criteria for Educational Decision-Making Assessments 18
Representative Developmental Instruments 19
Environmental Assessments 20
Determining Learning Styles 22
Attentional Control 23
Modality Preference 23
Level of Processing 25
Impulsivity and Reflectivity 27
Grouping Preferences 28
Reinforcement Preferences 29
Representative Learning Style Instruments 30
Recognizing Sensorimotor Deficits 31
Sensory Assessments 32

Representative Instruments 32
The Assessment Process 33
Discussion of Assessment with Parents 33
Preassessment Preparation 34
Conducting the Assessment 36
Interpreting the Results and Making Decisions 36
Summary 39

Chapter 2
Instructional Design for Skill Acquisition 41
An Instructional Model for Teaching Students with Severe Handicaps 42
Discrete-Trial Learning 44
Defining a Response 44
Defining a Stimulus 45
Presenting a Reinforcer 46
Intertrial Interval 47
Consistency 48
Selecting Positive Reinforcers 50
Prompt Strategies 52
Verbal Prompts 55
Observational Prompts 57
Physical Prompts 58
Sequencing Prompts 58
Time Delay of Prompts 60
Operant Fading, Thinning, and Chaining 61
Fading of Stimuli 61
Thinning of Reinforcement 64
Shaping of Responses 70
Chaining and Task Analysis 72
Related Topics in Instructional Design 77
Attending and Learning 77
Response Adaptations 78
Prosthetic Devices 79
Partial Participation 80
Forward and Backward Chaining 81
Token Economies 83
Designing Instructional Program 86
Summary 88

Chapter 3
Making the Curriculum Natural and Functional 89
Bases for Developing a Curriculum 90
Students' Lack of Stimulus Generalization 90

Students' Inability to Learn Quickly *91*
Students' Inability to Know When and Where to Use Skills *92*
Eight Components of the Functional Curriculum 92
Selecting Functional Skills *93*
Environmental Inventories 94
Educational Assessment Scales 94
Functional Objectives 94
Functional Materials 95
Teach in Functional Settings Using Natural Cues *96*
Analysis of Settings and Cues 96
Importance of Verbal Cues 97
Using Varied Materials *98*
Object-Specific and Generic Materials 99
Students' Choice of Materials 100
Incorporating Communication Programs into the Daily Routine *101*
The Gap between Theory and Practice 101
A Functional Communication System 102
Incorporating Motor Programs into the Daily Routine *106*
Motor Programs 106
Massed Practice 106
Distributed Practice 109
Sequencing Skills in a Logical and Normative Manner *110*
Incorporating Behavioral Programs into the Daily Routine *112*
Basic Components 112
Behavior Checks 114
Teaching in Groups *115*
Control of Motivational Variables 116
Opportunity to Respond to and Learn from Peers 116
Opportunity to Learn Group Skills 118
Organizing a Functional Group 118
Summary 124

Chapter 4
Measurement 125

The Importance of Measurement 126
Developing a Recording System 129
Trial-by-Trial System *129*
Recording Performance 129
Recording Devices 131
Multiple-Response Measurement *131*
Concurrent Chains 132
Functional Skills Sequences 133

Multiple Student Measurements 136
Recording Prompts 137
Rate Data 140
Recording Intervals 142
Time Sampling 144
Duration of Responses 145
Determining Reliability 146
Observer Agreement Check 147
Define Behavior to Be Recorded 147
Total Agreement 150
Partition Agreement 150
Occurrence Agreement 152
Graphing and Taking Reliability Data 152
Interpreting the Data 153
First Judgments 154
The Quarter-Intersect Trend Line 155
The Aim Star Procedure 157
Other Aspects of Graphing 158
Organizing a Data Management System 159
Basic Steps 160
Data Entries and Decisions 160
How Much Information Is Enough? 161
Summary 164

Chapter 5
Behavior Management 165

Distinguishing Characteristics of Persons with Severe Handicaps 166
Types of Problem Behaviors 168
Generic Problems 168
A Case Study: Tommy 169
Targeting Behaviors for Treatment 170
Analyzing Behavior 171
The Example of Tommy 172
Strategies for Treatment 174
Assessment 175
Biomedical Factors 175
Functional Analysis 176
Characteristics of the Participants 177
Ecological and Curricular Variables 180
Ecological Factors 181
Curricular Factors 184
Reinforcement 186
Extinction 187

Differential Reinforcement of Alternative Behaviors 187
Differential Reinforcement of Other Behavior 188
Punishment 190
Aversive Stimuli 190
Withdrawal of Positive Stimuli 192
Overcorrection and Contingent Restraint 193
The Treatment of Tommy 194
Summary 196

Chapter 6
Curriculum 197

Selecting Curricula 199
Guidelines 199
Commercially Available Curricula 202
Language Training 202
Self-Care Skills 207
Vocational Training 209
Leisure Skills 214
Adapting Curricula 218
Branching 219
Prosthetic Devices 219
Partial Participation 220
Summary 221
Appendix: Commercially Available Curricula 221

Chapter 7
Environmental and Classroom Organization 223

The Environment 224
Past Lessons 225
Instruction in Multiple Settings 225
The Physical Environment 226
Institutions 226
Community Placement 228
The School Environment 229
Segregated Schools 229
Integrated Classes 230
Off Campus Activities 231
An Example of Multiple-Setting Instruction 232
Designing the Classroom 234
Areas and Zones 234
Decor 237
The Social Environment 238
Scheduling 239

Dividing the School Day 240
Key Factors 241
Group Instruction 241
Social Integration 243
Social Play 244
Types of Social Interactions 245
Contexts for Social Interaction 248
Summary 250

Chapter 8
Home-School Interactions 251

Being a Parent 252
Parental Demands 253
The Brighter Side 253
Communication 254
Interpersonal Dynamics 254
Establishing a Communication System 255
The Initial Contact 255
Building on Parents' Roles 256
Using Demonstrations 257
Maintaining Parent Involvement 259
The Daily Log 259
Parent Visits 261
Setting Goals 263
Parenting Skills 265
Stimulation 265
Physical Stimulation 265
Social Environment 266
Behavior Management 267
Delivering Instructions and Reinforcers 268
Delivering Aversive Consequences 269
Data Collection 270
The Parental Involvement Model 271
Coordinating Home and School Endeavors 271
Providing a Support System 274
An Example: The Jones Family 276
Summary 279

Chapter 9
The Many Facets of Being a Teacher 281

Specific Roles 282
Educator 283
Parental Liaison 284

Supervisor of Paraprofessionals *285*
Member of a Multidisciplinary Team *289*
Occupational Therapist 289
Physical Therapist 290
Speech and Language Therapist 290
Psychologist 290
Nurse 291
Other Educational Specialists 291
Audiologist 291
Administrator 291
Parents 292
Advocate for Persons with Severe Handicaps *294*
The Personal Level 294
The School Level 294
The Community Level 298
Key Skills 300
Attentive and Responsive Listening *300*
Some Guidelines 301
Conducting Meetings *303*
Steps to Improve Meetings 303
Negotiating *305*
Summary 306

Chapter 10
Past, Present, and Future Directions 307
Past History 308
Normalization *309*
Mainstreaming *309*
Model Programs 310
The Madison Preschool Program *310*
The Madison Secondary Program *312*
Sensorimotor Programming: The Akron Program *314*
Research 317
Behavior Modification and Instruction *317*
Social Integration *322*
New Educational Developments 327
Microcomputers *327*
Adaptive Devices *328*
Summary 331
Epilogue 333
References 337
Index 349

Prologue

Society's view of persons with severe handicaps has changed dramatically in recent years. In the not too distant past, pejorative labels such as imbecile and retardate were used by professionals and laypersons alike to refer to these individuals. Professionals in particular emphasized the deficiencies and problems of persons with severe handicaps; consequently, very low expectations were set for their growth and development. Because of this devalued status, the services provided consisted mainly of basic medical care and residential comfort. Little attention was given to the human qualities of the individuals or their potential for employment and community life. It is not surprising that persons with severe handicaps were likely to be placed in large institutions away from the mainstream of society. In such residences the focus was on caretaking rather than on educating individuals so that they could cope with and succeed in society.

Fortunately, in the past 20 years there has been a radical change in our perceptions of persons with severe handicaps. We have seen how disabled persons can grow intellectually, overcome physical and sensory impairments, live independently in community residences, and obtain employment in nonsheltered work settings. These accomplishments are the result of a service delivery model that emphasizes the maximization of human potential through life-span educational programming.

Although many individuals helped develop this comprehensive educational model, two professionals have played leading roles. Professor Ivaar Lovaas of UCLA convincingly demonstrated how children with severe handicaps can learn in an impressive fashion. Drawing from the principles of applied behavior analysis, Lovaas showed how children can acquire a system of communication and eliminate serious behavior problems such as self-injury. Lovaas and others who followed demonstrated the power of positive reinforcement, task analysis, and cueing techniques in teaching students who previously had shown little interest or ability in learning.

If Lovaas led the way in showing *how* severely handicapped students could be taught, Professor Lou Brown of the University of Wisconsin–Madison was instrumental in developing an approach to *what* should be taught and *where* instruction should take place. Brown advanced a functional skills model based on the contention that the skills to be taught should be keyed to the subsequent adult environment in which disabled persons must function and that the skills should be taught in those settings. The task of educating students with severe handicaps thus evolved into an attempt to teach skills that will enable them to adjust successfully in the major environments of home, school, work, community, and leisure.

This functional skills model superseded the developmental approach to defining curriculum. The developmental approach recommends that the diagnosis and curriculum for students with handicaps should be keyed to "normal" child development. For example, if a 10-year-old mentally retarded child displays the behaviors and abilities of a normal 3-year-old, the 10-year-old should be diagnosed at the 3-year developmental level, and the tasks taught and the general curriculum should be set at the 3-year-old level. In contrast, the functional skills view looks ahead rather than looking back; it projects ahead for the handicapped student to the critical skills needed for success in subsequent and adult environments.

An effective educational model appeared in response to significant legislation that mandated and funded services to this previously unserved population. The Education for All Handicapped Act (Public Law 94-142) established that all school-aged persons, no matter how severe their disabilities, are entitled to a free and appropriate education. Besides providing a school program for the first time for many handicapped students, P.L. 94-142 shifted the focus from providing basic care for severely disabled persons to offering educational services that would help develop each individual's potential to the fullest.

In order to implement a far-reaching educational program for a newly served population, it was necessary to train a cadre of teachers and related professionals. A number of preservice and in-service personnel training efforts have been conducted by institutions of higher education and local educational agencies. An effective teacher training program should include classroom exposure to materials on educational practices as well as a strong practicum component in which trainees conduct hands-on instruction. Until the present, the majority of books on teaching students with severe handicaps have been edited volumes, i.e., collections of readings or chapters. Although such collections offer varied and specialized contributions, they tend to lack a conceptual theme that runs through the book.

Strategies for Educating Students with Severe Handicaps presents a comprehensive model for educating students with severe handicaps. In demonstrating how instructional units must be prepared carefully if substantive learning is to occur, this book reflects the strong behavior analytic influence of Lovaas. The book also includes Brown's ideas by stressing the teaching of functional skills in multiple environmental settings such as restaurants, businesses, and apartments. Our approach to instructional design subsumes both simple, discrete trial formats and more complex, functional sequencing approaches to response chaining. We offer examples of validated, commercially available curricula as well as guidelines for selecting and developing one's own curriculum. In addition, a comprehensive approach to involving parents in a child's educational program is emphasized. We analyze the role of the teacher in implementing programs for students with severe handicaps, and we describe selected model programs, research, and emerging technologies. Thus, a comprehensive educational model is created that emphasizes a powerful instructional technology delivered in relevant environmental settings. The primary aim of this book is to help teachers and related professionals implement this educational model in a meaningful way in their classrooms and educational programs. Undoubtedly, the model will have to be modified to fit the characteristics of each local setting.

As a result of our emphasis on implementing a model, certain ambiguities and issues in the field as a whole have been given short shrift. For example, there is far from complete agreement in defining just who is severely handicapped. An older, particularistic view focused on the different subgroups that constitute the severely handicapped population: severe mental retardation, autism, trainable mentally retarded, severe multiply handicapped, and specific biological disorders such as Down syndrome. Rather than surveying the characteristics of each group, we have concentrated on commonalities across groups. Because persons with severe handicaps are a low-incidence population, in most school districts there will be heterogeneous groupings of persons with different types of disabling conditions. Emphasis should be placed, therefore, on developing the most effective service delivery model rather than dwelling on the individual differences among disabled students.

Despite the fact that there are commonalities across groups, there is a wide range of students covered by the label "severely handicapped." A student who is quadraplegic, nonverbal, and cognitively functioning at the profound level of mental retardation is quite different from a moderately mentally retarded student who is ambulatory and has an expressive vocabulary of 500 words, even though both students may be labeled severely handicapped. *Strategies for Educating Students with Severe Handicaps* attempts to describe an educational model that can educate students effectively across this wide range of disabilities. Examples are presented of instructional programs for preschool, primary, and secondary students. Emphasis is placed on program characteristics and implementation rather than on age or other individual differences. Hopefully, educators will be able to take our model for instruction and use it to the benefit of their own students with severe handicaps.

Chapter 1

Assessment and Target Selection

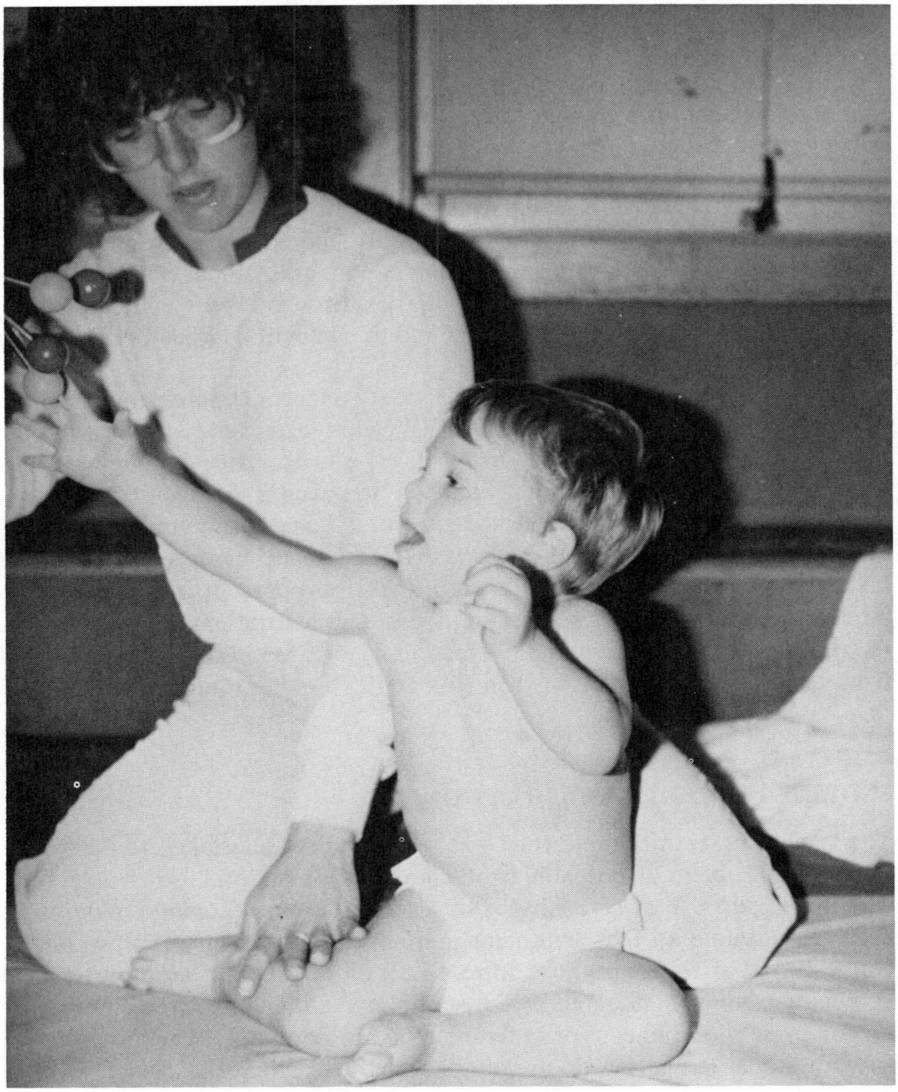

The first and possibly most important steps in teaching are determining the students' needs, what content to teach, and what strategies will be useful to convey that content. These steps are accomplished through *assessment*. The importance of assessment in special education cannot be overemphasized. Unless a teacher knows exactly what a student needs to learn and can pinpoint how that student can learn successfully, the goal of individualized education will not be reached. In special education, assessment is a process that begins early in a student's life and continues throughout the educational experience. During this time the student and the student's family participate in many assessment processes.

There are four major purposes for assessment: (1) screening to determine whether there is a problem, (2) diagnosis to determine exactly what the problem is and what may be causing it, (3) educational planning to determine what to teach the student and how to teach it, and (4) educational monitoring to determine whether the student is being taught according to the educational plan and whether progress is being made. Different assessment instruments are appropriate for each of these purposes. It is important that a teacher know when to use certain assessment instruments as well as how to use the information obtained. This knowledge helps safeguard the child from misuse of assessment instruments and assessment information.

Assessment for Screening Purposes

The type of assessment referred to as *screening* is undertaken to determine whether a problem or potential problem exists. It is a process of detection. The major purpose of screening is to discover a handicapping condition as early as possible so that treatment and education can begin immediately. Some types of screening are done on all children. For example, visual screening often is conducted by the school nurse on all children entering elementary school. Other types of screening are done only when a parent or a professional (usually a doctor) thinks that a problem may exist. Groups trying to locate developmentally delayed children during the preschool years (e.g., Count Your Kid In) usually use this type of assessment.

Although a screening instrument may pinpoint the presence of a problem, it is not designed to identify why such a problem exists or to determine the parameters of the problem. In other words, a screening instrument does not give a diagnosis. Dr. William Frankenburg (1983), the developer of one of the most widely used developmental screening tests, likens a screening instrument to a metal detector in an airport. Just as many persons will pass through a metal detector without triggering a signal, a screening instrument is designed to test a large group of people many of whom will not be shown to have a problem. Furthermore, just as the signal on a metal detector does not necessarily mean that a person is a hijacker, a poor score on a screening instrument does not mean that a child has any particular handicap. Both results simply indicate that further testing of the individual is in order. A child may be tested using a developmental screening instrument and may be shown to be behind age peers in language and motor development. The information gained from the screening instrument will not indicate whether this delay is due to the child being left in the crib for the majority of the day, to severe or moderate retardation, to autism, or to an organic cause such as hearing loss or previously unobserved seizure activity. All that is learned from screening is whether the child should be referred for diagnostic testing.

The screening component of assessment usually is skipped if it is obvious that the child has a problem. For example, if a child has severe hypotonia (poor muscle tone), has periods when he turns blue and seems to stop breathing, and has a head that is significantly smaller than normal, then a screening test is not needed to determine that this child should go through further tests to diagnose the problem. For this reason, many students with severe, multiple handicaps have never gone through screening. For such children the assessment process begins with diagnostic testing.

Characteristics of Good Screening Instruments

Because screening is not meant to yield a diagnosis and because it is used with a large number of individuals, a good screening instrument generally takes very little time to administer. Most screening tests can be given in less than an hour, and some take only 10 to 20 minutes. In screening large groups of children, lengthy tests make it difficult to identify children in need of help.

On the other hand, the brevity of the screening test also means that the information obtained is not very useful to an educator. The tests generally contain only a few items, and the "steps" between items are necessarily large. For example, on the Denver Developmental Screening Test (Frankenburg, Dodds, and Fandal, 1975), three sequential items in the language domain are (1) "Says Mama or Dada nonspecifically," (2) "Says Mama or Dada specifically," and (3) "Says three words other than Mama and Dada." Obviously, a teacher of severely handicapped students might have to go through a large number of steps to move a child from step 1 to step 2 or from step 2 to step 3.

A second characteristic of a good screening test is validity. A valid instrument has three characteristics. It identifies children who are shown to have problems after diagnostic testing, it does not miss children who have problems, and it does not identify children as having problems who do not. No test is perfectly valid, but some are more valid than others. Generally, a good screening test is designed so that errors are in the direction of over-identification. Just as metal detectors often signal when a person is simply carrying a large number of coins or keys, screening tests may identify children as having a problem that further testing will reveal to be nonexistent. Errors in the direction of oversensitivity are more protective of the child's rights than errors that would result in children with problems being missed.

A third criterion for screening instruments is that they be simple. This means that examiners should not need years of training or a professional degree to administer the instrument.

Also, the test should have clearly stated criteria for passing or failing each item. Instructions for administering the items should not be overly long or detailed, although they must be long enough to ensure that the items are presented the same way to every child. Most of all, the summary sheet should be easy to interpret and to explain to a parent or another professional.

Parameters of Screening Instruments

Almost all screening instruments are norm-referenced. This means that the child's performance is compared with the performance of other children of the same age, i.e., a normative sample. Norm-referenced measurements allow a determination of whether the child is developing the same skills seen in the majority of children who form the normative sample. Since children's skills at particular ages may differ because of such variables as geographic locale, ethnic origin, and the presence of handicapping conditions, it is important for a person who routinely administers screening assessments to be aware of the composition of the normative sample. The more closely characteristics of the normative sample resemble the characteristics of the population being screened, the more confidence the tester can have in the results.

The format of screening instruments varies. Some are based on direct testing or observation of the child whereas others rely on interviews with the parents or with a person who knows the child well. Still others employ a combination approach in which the parents are interviewed and then the child is tested directly on any skills about which the parents seem unsure. Unless the child is fearful or feels stress as a result of being in a new situation, direct testing and observation probably give the most valid results. Allowing the parents to watch or participate and give feedback as to whether the child's performance seems representative is another technique that helps ensure that the examiner will get a true picture of the child's skills and capabilities.

The Teacher's Role in Screening

Unless the teacher is part of a multidisciplinary screening team, it is unlikely that there will be a need to know how to administer or interpret the various screening instruments. This is particularly true for teachers of children with severe handicaps since, as was pointed out earlier, many of these children do not go through a formal screening process. It is, however, important for a teacher to know the names of various screening instruments in order to be sure that these instruments are not used inappropriately with students who demonstrate severe handicaps. In particular, a teacher should ascertain that a screening instrument has not been used in place of diagnosis, i.e., that a child is not placed in a particular class solely on the basis of performance on a screening instrument. The teacher also most recognize that it is inappropriate to use a screening instrument as a way of evaluating student change in educational programs. Screening tests are simply not sensitive enough to be used as comprehensive assessment instruments or used to evaluate the efficacy of particular educational interventions.

Representative Screening Instruments

There are three very popular instruments used to screen for developmental problems:

1. Denver Developmental Screening Test (DDST) (Frankenburg, Dodds, and Fandal, 1975)
2. Brazelton Neonatal Behavioral Assessment Scale (Brazelton, 1973)
3. Developmental Profile II (Alpern, Boll, and Schearer, 1980)

Other screening instruments that have been used by many professionals include the following:

1. Rockford Infant Development Scales (RIDES) (Project Rhise, 1976)
2. Comprehensive Identification Process (CIP) (Zehrbach, 1975)
3. Goodman Lock Box (Goodman, 1981)
4. Pre-school Screening Instrument (Cohen, 1979)

Diagnostic Testing

Once a child is identified as being at risk or as having delays in development, the child usually is referred for diagnostic testing. As the name implies, diagnostic testing is undertaken to define the problem.

Diagnostic testing may focus on physical capabilities such as hearing, vision, or mobility, or it may focus on a child's mental ability. Ability levels can be measured by intelligence tests, achievement tests, personality tests, and tests of adaptive functioning. Diagnostic testing usually is conducted by the school psychologist or by therapeutic personnel such as physicians, physical therapists, occupational therapists, speech clinicians, and audiologists.

Three Components

Diagnosis usually has three components: (1) ascertaining the problem, (2) determining the severity of the problem, and (3) referring the child to educational and therapeutic specialists who have the expertise to remediate the problem.

To illustrate the diagnostic assessment process, let us look at a hypothetical case. John, a 3-year old boy, has been referred for diagnostic testing because he shows considerable delay in language and motor areas on the Developmental Profile II and because his parents characterize him as being hard to handle. Testing by the physician and a physical therapist indicates that the delay in motor functioning is probably due to mild cerebral palsy (diagnosis). The therapist notes that the cerebral palsy is minimal in the lower limbs but is of moderate severity in the upper extremities and facial muscles (determination of severity level). The physician and therapist decide that this child should receive occupational therapy at least twice a week (referral to specialist for remediation). The therapist also notes that the physical involvement of the facial muscles will result in language delay but feels that the child needs to be assessed by a speech clinician. Diagnostic testing by the speech clinician shows that the child does not use any words and that his vocalizations are few and do not show any temporal pattern. Thus, the conclusion is that the child has profound language delay (diagnosis and severity) and that speech therapy may be appropriate.

However, the clinician needs more information before an adequate referral can be made. First, an audiologic evaluation to determine whether the child hears within normal limits is recommended. Second, a psychologist should examine the child to see whether the child has a problem such as retardation or autism. The audiologic examination in this case shows that the child's hearing is within normal limits (diagnosis) and that no specialized services are needed in this area currently. The psychological assessment shows that the child has severe deficits in intellectual and adaptive functioning (diagnosis and severity), and the psychologist recommends that the child be placed in a preschool classroom with a teacher trained to serve students with severe, multiple handicaps (referral for remediation). On the basis of this diagnosis and referral, the speech clinician recommends that speech therapy should be made available through the school on a consultant basis at this time (referral for remediation).

Several things become clear when this example is examined. First, it is apparent that diagnostic evaluation usually involves a number of specialists, particularly when the child has multiple problems. It is also clear that the recommendations for remediation that are made by one specialist may be modified when diagnostic information from other specialties is obtained. Thus, it is crucial that the people doing diagnostic assessment meet and discuss recommendations. It is equally critical that someone be assigned the task of coordinating all the diagnoses and recommendations and making sure that the child is receiving the services that have been prescribed. Often the teacher serves as the coordinator of services; in other cases the parent or an administrator takes this role.

The Controversy over Diagnostic Testing

Diagnostic testing is a very controversial area. Many professionals doubt that the process is valid enough to justify the time and expense. For example, Dreger, Lewis, Rich, Miller, Reid, Overlade, Taffel, and Fleming (1964, p. 1) state that, "looked at realistically what this [diagnostic testing] means is that after the elaborate procedures used in most clinics are completed, the child is placed in a category, which says exactly what we knew about him in the first place, that he has a problem." This issue may be particularly germane to students with severe handicaps who have obvious sensory, motor, behavioral, or intellectual dysfunction. Investigators also have noted that as many as 30 percent of parents of handicapped children report that their children have had three or more different labels over several years (Gorham, Des Jardins, Page, Pettis, and Schreiber, 1975). This implies that the tests may not be particularly useful in discriminating among problems.

Another issue that leads to controversy is that diagnosis of the problem usually results in a label being applied to the child. Being given a label such as "mentally retarded" has repeatedly been shown to result in problems, especially in cases of mild disability. Some of the objections to labeling are that: (1) labels often take on negative connotations that affect how others interact with the labeled person, (2) the label may result from a test that is culturally biased, (3) labels encourage people to think of a group of people as being exactly alike and thus to treat them without regard to their individuality, and (4) the label may be seen as predictive and take on a life of its own (no one tries to help the student get a job because "he's retarded and why should we frustrate him").

Thus, it is not surprising that many people distrust diagnostic testing and labeling. However, it should be pointed out that the labeling issue may be somewhat less significant for persons who are identified as having severe handicaps. Most persons who are labeled as severely retarded or multiply handicapped have physical anomalies or behavioral deficits that are extremely visible. Hence, labeling such persons as severely mentally retarded and placing them into special programs may not stigmatize them additionally. In fact, it may at times allow people in the community to be more tolerant of the deviations in their behavior. Of course, the educator must always be alert for possible misuse of labeling with all populations.

A third area of controversy has evolved because diagnostic testing usually results in recommendations for placement and therapy. Placement is an extremely important aspect of the educational process. If a child is misdiagnosed, it is probable that the services that are prescribed and provided also will be inappropriate. Inappropriate placements or theraputic procedures have the potential for serious damage.

Because the people who helped write Public Law 94-142 recognized that diagnostic assessment is the keystone of an appropriate education for all students but that it carries certain dangers, they made sure the law contained certain regulations pertaining to diagnostic assessment. These regulations cover seven basic points:

1. Tests and other evaluation materials must be validated for the specific purpose for which they are used and must be administered by trained personnel.
2. Tests and other evaluation materials must include assessment of specific areas of educational need; a single intelligence quotient is not sufficient.
3. Tests and other evaluation materials must be selected and administered to ensure that what is measured is aptitude rather than simply impaired sensory, motor, or speaking skills.
4. Interpretations of evaluation data must draw upon a variety of sources including aptitude and achievement tests, teacher recommendations, social or cultural background, physical condition, and adaptive behavior.
5. Evaluators must have procedures to assure that information from all such sources will be documented and considered.
6. The placement decision resulting from the evaluation must be made by a group of people knowledgeable about the specific child and the evaluation data.
7. The parents may request an independent educational evaluation at public expense if they have reason to believe that the test results are not valid. (Public Law 94-142, *Federal Register*).

Public Law 94-142 also guarantees the right to have the child assessed in all areas related to the suspected disability (even if services are not available to remediate the disability) and to have the child reevaluated at least every 3 years.

Criteria for Diagnostic Assessment Instruments

Diagnostic instruments may be either norm-referenced or criterion-referenced. It is probably best if placement decisions are made on the basis of information from both kinds of instruments. As noted earlier, norm-referenced assessments compare a child's performance with that of other children of the same age, ethnic group, and geographic distribution. Thus, norm-referenced tests are concerned with interindividual differences. Criterion-referenced tests, on the other hand, focus on differences in skill attainment within the same child, stressing the degree to which a child has mastered certain skills. Because a criterion-referenced test can indicate the level at which a child currently functions and the level of functioning that the student needs to reach (i.e., the criterion level), diagnostic tests of this type are usually more helpful for educational programming than norm-referenced tests.

Diagnostic tests usually are standardized. A standardized test is highly structured and includes a detailed description of the manner in which stimuli should be presented, the amount of time the child will have to respond, and the way each item will be scored. Teachers of children who are severely handicapped sometimes are distressed because strict standardization procedures can cause their students to obtain very low scores that do not seem to reflect their actual capabilities. For example, a child with severe motor disabilities may score low on items requiring that a motor response be made in a short period of time. The teacher may feel that the examiner "just doesn't understand these kids" if the examiner does not accommodate the student's special needs during testing.

Such a perception is unfair. If interpretations about a student are to be made from a standardized instrument, particularly one that is norm-referenced, it is imperative that the examiner administer the instrument in exactly the manner prescribed. It is not appropriate for the examiner to change the language (or communication mode), the timing, or the way cues are presented if the purpose of the assessment is to compare a student's performance with that of others. Such changes would invalidate the instrument. It is, however, possible and often valuable for the examiner to test the child twice. In the first testing, the standardized procedure should be followed in order to establish the student's performance in accordance with the norm or criterion. In the second testing, the examiner can be more flexible in the presentation of cues and timing. The two-test method gives the examiner a more accurate picture of the student's actual educational and therapeutic needs. If the differences between the two testings are quite marked, the examiner should try to find a more appropriate instrument for the student. It must be recognized, however, that few instruments can accommodate the many disabilities seen in this population and that the examiner may be using the best instrument available.

Naturally, a good diagnostic instrument should be valid (it should actually measure what it purports to measure) and reliable (if the student is retested using the same instrument within a short period of time, the same score should be obtained). Validity and reliability are characteristics of any good assessment regardless of its purpose.

Types of Diagnostic Assessment Instruments

Two types of assessment instruments are used for educational diagnosis and placement of children with severe handicaps: intelligence tests and adaptive behavior tests. Occasionally tests of neurologic functioning also are used for the purpose of educational diagnosis. Most professionals consider it critical that both intelligence measures and measures of adaptive functioning be taken before a student is diagnosed as mentally retarded. Similarly, both personality measures and measures of adaptive functioning must be considered before a student is diagnosed as emotionally disturbed. Using more than one type of measure helps ensure that an individual will not be labeled incorrectly. The inclusion of an adaptive behavior measure is of particular importance in evaluating students from backgrounds that are not similar to that of the white middle-class community.

Intelligence Tests. Intelligence tests must be given by certified psychologists, psychiatrists, or psychometrists who have had special training in their administration. It is inappropriate for a classroom teacher, a parent, or a school nurse to give such tests. Most intelligence tests rely heavily on receptive language skills, intact neurologic functioning, and absence of sensory deficits. Many severely and profoundly handicapped students can do none of the items on the more traditional tests of intelligence that are designed for their age peers. For this reason, severely handicapped children often are rated using infant intelligence scales, and severely handicapped adolescents and adults often are assessed using infant or child intelligence scales. This substantially limits the usefulness of information obtained from such instruments, as far as the educator is concerned.

Some of the instruments used to diagnose the intelligence level of students with severe handicaps include the following:

1. Bayley Scales of Infant Development (Bayley, 1969)
2. Cattell Infant Intelligence Scale (Cattell, 1940)
3. Extended Merrill-Palmer Scale (Ball, Merrifield, and Stott, 1978)
4. Haptic Intelligence Scale (Shurager and Shurager, 1964)
5. Kaufmann Assessment Battery for Children (Kaufman and Kaufman, 1983)
6. Stanford-Binet Intelligence Scale (Terman and Merrill, 1973)
7. Wechsler Preschool and Primary Scale of Intelligence (WPPSI) (Wechsler, 1967)

These scales are all norm-referenced, but most did not include severely handicapped or physically handicapped children in the normative sample. The Bayley scale included premature infants in its sample, but none of these children were severely handicapped. Special norms have been developed for deaf children on the Wechsler Intelligence Scale for Children—Revised (Wechsler, 1974), but these are not available on the Wechsler Preschool and Primary Scale of Intelligence. The Haptic Intelligence Test is designed especially for blind and partially sighted individuals and was normed on that population. All these scales appear to be reliable (though no data are reported for the 1973 version of the Stanford-Binet) and to be fairly valid predictors of future performance if the student does not fall off the bottom of the scale. The first two are probably the more appropriate instruments for students who have limited verbal and motor skills, but even they should be regarded as highly questionable unless the results are verified by tests of adaptive functioning.

Tests of Adaptive Behavior. Adaptive behavior has been defined as "the effectiveness or degree with which individuals meet the standards of personal independence and social responsibility expected for age and cultural group" (Grossman, 1983, p. 1).

Although most experts agree that tests of adaptive behavior should be administered before any child is labeled mentally retarded, there are serious problems with these tests. Tests of adaptive behavior, though considered diagnostic, do not actually indicate much more about the severity of the student's problem or its cause than screening instruments. However, they do define more clearly exactly what the problems are. Most tests of adaptive functioning also have been standardized inadequately, and the validity and reliability of these tests have been questioned by many psychometricians. Because of these problems, no child should be labeled or placed in a special class solely on the basis of the results of a test of adaptive functioning.

On the other hand, tests of adaptive behavior appear to be much more valuable to the educator than intelligence tests. The items on these tests are more likely to focus on behaviors that are critical to a student's adjustment in society than the items included in intelligence tests. Tests of adaptive behavior also tend to consist of more items than screening tests, thus giving the teacher more information about precisely which skills the child needs to learn. Tests of adaptive functioning are also much more likely to be criterion-referenced, giving the teacher an idea of how much training the student will need to acquire a particular skill.

Tests of adaptive functioning generally are not standardized and thus do not take specialized training to administer, and the results seem integrally tied to education; thus, teachers often administer these instruments. In fact, it is often difficult to decide whether a particular test of adaptive functioning is a diagnostic test or a tool for educational decision making. In this chapter adaptive behavior instruments that are not accompanied by instructional programs or instructional suggestions are regarded as diagnostic instruments. But most of these instruments can be used both for diagnosis and for deciding what to teach.

Some tests of adaptive functioning that have been used primarily for diagnostic purposes are listed here in alphabetical order:

1. AAMD Adaptive Behavior Scale: Public School Version (Lambert, Windmiller, Cole, and Figueroa, 1975)
2. Balthazar Scales of Adaptive Behavior for the Profoundly and Severely Mentally Retarded (Balthazar, 1973)

3. Cain-Levine Social Competency Scale (Cain, Levine, and Elzey, 1963)
4. Children's Adaptive Behavior Scale (CABS) (Kicklighter and Richmond, 1983) and the Children's Adaptive Behavior Report (Kicklighter and Richmond, 1982)
5. Child Behavior Rating Scale (Cassel, 1962)
6. TARC Assessment Inventory for Severely Handicapped Children (Sailor and Mix, 1976)
7. Vineland Social Maturity Scale (Doll, 1965)
8. Wisconsin Behavior Rating Scale—R (Song and Jones, 1979)

Each of these tests has some good features. The quickest instruments to give are the Vineland and the Cain-Levine since they rely only on interviews with parents or other persons familiar with an individual's level of behavior. Profiles of a student's performance in several areas rather than a single score are an integral part of the TARC, the Cain-Levine, the AAMD, and the Wisconsin. A particularly useful feature of the Children's Adaptive Behavior Scale and the Children's Adaptive Behavior Report is that when both instruments are used, the evaluator has parental reports and direct observation of the child on the same items. This helps ensure a more valid picture of the child's level of functioning. The TARC and the Wisconsin were normed on severely handicapped students, so they are particularly useful in determining how a particular child's skills compare with those of other children also designated severely handicapped. Because it includes alternative items for deaf and blind students, the Wisconsin Behavior Rating Scale is especially useful when a test is needed for a student who appears to have severe hearing or visual dysfunction. The AAMD allows a measure of a student's maladaptive behavior as well as adaptive behavior; this is quite useful with many children with severe handicaps. The Child Behavior Rating Scale is a personality and behavior test and also rates the degree of maladaptive behavior. This latter measure should be useful in helping identify children who may be seriously emotionally disturbed.

Some other tests of adaptive functioning that have been used for both diagnostic and program planning include the following:

1. The Basic Life Skills Screening Inventory (Becker, Schur, Paoletti, and Martin-Petty, 1982)
2. Behavior Rating Instrument for Atypical Children (BRIAC) (Ruttenberg, Kalish, Wenar, and Wolf, 1977)
3. Brigance Diagnostic Inventory of Early Development (Brigance, 1982)
4. The Callier-Azusa Scale (Stillman, 1978)
5. The Camelot Behavioral Checklist (Foster, 1974)
6. Competitive Employment (Shalock, 1978)
7. Developmental Pinpoints (Cohen, Gross, and Haring, 1976)
8. Developmental Record (Hutton and Talkington, 1974)
9. A Manual for the Assessment of a Deaf-Blind Multiply Handicapped Child (Collins and Rudolph, 1975)

10. Marshalltown Behavior Developmental Profile (Donahue, Montgomery, Keiser, Roecker, Smith, and Walden, 1978)
11. Pennsylvania Training Model: Assessment Guide (Somerton-Fair and Turner, 1975)
12. Priority Needs Assessment Scale (Burton, Balsamo, Carrington, Garozzo, Ierardi, Kailukaitis, Klaire, and Probert, 1978)
13. Project MEMPHIS Instruments for Individual Program Planning and Evaluation: Comprehensive Developmental Scale (Quick, Little, and Campbell, 1974)
14. UPAS: Uniform Performance Assessment System (White, Edgar, and Haring, 1982)
15. Vocational Adaptation Rating Scales (Malgady, Barcher, Davis, and Towner, 1980)

The Basic Life Skills Screening Inventory, the Vocational Adaptation Rating Scales, Competitive Employment, and the Camelot are particularly useful for identifying behaviors that are very functional for older students. Unfortunately, without substantial modification, these instruments are not appropriate for very low functioning or severely physically impaired students. Nonetheless, they are useful program guides for many adolescents with severe handicaps.

The Pennsylvania, Callier-Azusa, and Manual for the Assessment of a Deaf-Blind Multiply Handicapped Child are very useful with students who have severe motor or sensory impairments. These instruments, however, are extremely long and very time-consuming if every item is tested directly.

Other Diagnostic Procedures

In response to data indicating that diagnostic assessments and information from multidisciplinary team members do not consistently result in a coherent block of information that can be used quickly and reliably for therapeutic intervention, Bricker and Campbell (1980, pp. 12–13) proposed an alternative diagnostic system. Such a system would not result in a label for the tested child but instead would spell out the type and degree of needed therapeutic services. In the Index of Qualification for Specialized Services (Figure 1.1), Bricker and Campbell outlined nineteen dimensions on which a child should be tested.

Unfortunately, these authors did not describe clearly how each of these dimensions should be tested. If it could be refined and standardized, this approach to multidisciplinary assessment would have a great deal of merit and would generate much more relevant information for the educator than current practices. As it stands, these dimensions can be used by the diagnostic coordinator to give some therapeutically relevant structure to current multidisciplinary input. In other words, the coordinator could quickly summarize the information given by each member of the team according to each of the nineteen dimensions.

Figure 1.1 Nineteen dimensions on which a child should be tested.

1. *Surviving and thriving.* This initial dimension is rated by the physician and attempts to summarize the health of the individual in terms of disease processes, medication status, growth, and nutrition.
2. *Tonicity.* This measures the degree of tension in the body musculature providing the basis for all movement. Deviations in tone, ranging from hypotonicity to hypertonicity, are on this dimension and are derived from physical or occupational therapy evaluations.
3. *Visual acuity.* Scale values on this dimension are derived from opthalmologic examination and relate to abnormalities in the visual structures as well as overall measures of visual acuity.
4. *Auditory ability.* Abnormalities in the aural structures and disease processes are rated on this dimension by the ear-nose-throat specialist. Auditory acuity and the presence of conductive sensorineural and mixed hearing losses identified through audiologic examination also are represented on this dimension.
5. *Motor quantity.* The amount of movement that is possible in relation to both automatic and goal-directed (voluntary) movements is rated on this dimension by the physical or occupational therapist. Deviations in the amount of movement, ranging from excessive movement to absence of movement, are represented.
6. *Motor quality.* Movement occurs in patterns made up of various components that are sequenced to produce functional automatic and goal-directed movement. Physical or occupational therapy evaluations provide the basis for rating the quality of the patterns produced both automatically and voluntarily.
7. *Oral-motor/feeding.* Tone and movement quantity and quality are rated by the occupational or speech-language therapist as these dimensions relate to the muscles of the head, neck, anu mouth. Problems with food or liquid intake are represented as deviations.
8. *Oral-motor/vocalization.* The range of nonspeech and speech vocalization may be limited by problems with tone, movement quantity, and quality in the oral structures. The speech-language therapist rates deviations ranging from absence of vocalization to excessive (stereotypic) vocalizations.
9. *Mobility.* The extent to which an individual moves from location to location in the environment is related not only to the neuromotor dimensions but also to motivational conditions. This dimension rates the degree of mobility present regardless of the specific form the mobility takes.
10. *Manipulation.* The competence of the hand in interacting with objects can range from basic contact with an object to very complex assemblies. Both motor skill and motivational conditions influence the manipulative function. Deviations ranging from lack of grasp through the very complex manipulation schemes present in stereotypic behavior are rated by the occupational therapist or special educator.
11. *Consequence preference.* The extent to which a hierarchy of potentially reinforcing events can be defined empirically for an individual is rated by the psychologist or special educator. The range of reaction reflected is from limited (or lack of) preference for any objects, foods, or activities through fixation on a single class of reinforcing events.

Other diagnostic assessments that might be conducted to determine why a child seems to be developing abnormally include physical examinations, speech examinations, determination of nutritional status (if the child seems unusually small or large for age), and information about the home situation. All these elements can be useful in devising educational and treatment plans if the information and implications are presented in a way that can be used by classroom and therapeutic personnel.

It is important to realize that the people who assess these physical and sensory deficits do not have a large number of tools that are appropriate for

12. *Primary circular reactions.* A reinforcer can be operationally defined as a consequence that increases the rate of behavior for which that consequence is provided. Piaget has described this condition as a temporary increase in behavior that produces interesting consequences. The extent to which the interesting consequences derived from the preceding dimension can be used to increase behavior is rated by the psychologist or special educator.

13. *Secondary circular reactions.* When a particular set of events operates repeatedly as the basis for a particular response, the child is said to be secondary circular reactive (Piagetian), or under the control of antecedent conditions.

14. *Social responsiveness.* The degree of interest the handicapped person shows toward parents, care givers, and other individuals is rated by the special educator on a range from limited or absence of social responsiveness to high interest in a variety of persons.

15. *Compliance.* The willingness of an individual to respond to instruction, such as following directions, making appropriate responses to environmental cues, or allowing physical guidance, is rated by the special educator.

16. *Memory.* There is no reference to this process in the majority of writings about education and training of severely handicapped persons. However, many students who have learned a task need to be retaught after several days without practice. The maintenance of behavior over time is rated by the psychologist or special educator.

17. *Production of intentional chains.* When single components or behavior are linked in order to produce a desired outcome, an inference can be made that the behavior is intentional. The degree of intentionality demonstrated through participation in classroom or programming activities is rated by the educator or psychologist.

18. *Motor imitation.* The degree of imitation a student demonstrates is critical both to the selection of intervention strategies and to rapid learning of new skills. Competence in imitation of motor actions allows skills to be taught through demonstration without extensive shaping through physical guidance. The student's competence in imitation of motor actions on the basis of demonstration only is rated.

19. *Verbal imitation.* This dimension is an extension of the motor imitative dimension in that the student's skill at responding *to* verbalizations from a model is rated by the educator or speech-language specialist.

Source: Adapted from W. A. Bricker and P. H. Campbell, Interdisciplinary assessment and programming for multihandicapped students, in *Methods of Instruction for Severely Handicapped Learners*, ed. W. Sailor, B. Wilcox, and L. Brown (Baltimore: Paul H. Brookes, 1980), pp. 12–13. Reprinted with permission of Paul H. Brookes, © 1980.

students with severe handicaps. Most ophthalmologists and audiologists, for instance, have not been trained to test children who are nonverbal, have compliance problems, or have severe motor handicaps. Thus, the educator or diagnostic coordinator must take extra time to be sure that the information from these professionals is accurate and helpful from an educational standpoint. One way to get relevant information from such consultants is to use a form similar to the one in Figure 1.2. These are questions that might be outlined by the teacher before a student's visit to an ophthalmologist.

The items on the list were devised to answer the teacher's educational concerns. It has been our experience that many diagnostic personnel will not take the time to fill out the form if it is mailed to them. It seems to work better if the person who accompanies the student to the specialist brings the list and asks the questions verbally. Most specialists and diagnostic personnel are happy to answer such questions, but the educator must be careful not to make the list too long.

Figure 1.2 Example of a form used to obtain information from an ophthalmologist.

REQUEST FOR INFORMATION

Based on your assessment of ______________________________ (child's name)

vision on ____________________ (date), please tell us the following:

1. Does this child have vision problem(s)?

    ________ Yes ________ Probably ________ No ________ Cannot tell

2. Is the vision in one eye better than the other?

    ________ Better in right eye ________ Better in left eye ________ Both eyes equal

3. Will glasses help this child?

    ________ Yes ________ No ________ Maybe
    Describe when glasses are to be worn:

4. Will eye exercises help this child?

    ________ Yes ________ No ________ Maybe
    Describe exercises:

5. Will medications or surgery help this child?

    ________ Yes ________ No ________ Maybe
    Describe options:

6. Is visual information getting to the brain?

    ________ Yes ________ No ________ Cannot tell

7. At what distance do you think this child sees best?

    ________ 0 to 6 inches (from eyes) ________ 12 to 18 inches ________ Cannot tell
    ________ 2 to 4 feet ________ 20 feet ________ Sees well at all distances

8. Which of the following do you feel this child can see?

    ________ Light and shadow ________ Large objects (larger than 6 inches)
    ________ Small objects ________ Colors

9. Under what lighting conditions would this child see best?

    ________ Dim lighting ________ Bright light (incandescent)
    ________ Bright light (fluorescent) ________ Bright light (daylight)
    ________ Does not matter

10. Does this child see best when objects are

_________ At eye level _________ Above eye level _________ Below eye level

_________ Centered _________ To child's left _________ To child's right

_________ Does not matter

11. This child is currently taking ____

____
(list medications)

Can these affect vision? _____Yes _____ No _____ Do not know
Symptoms to watch for:

12. Do you think this child has any abnormal blind spots?

_________ Yes, in right eye _________ Yes, in left eye _________ No

13. Does this child show any problems in tear production or blinking?

_________Yes _________No

14. If child has problems in question 13, what should be done? ______________________

____

Assessment for Educational Decision Making

Fifteen to 20 years ago, when the emphasis in the field was on caretaking rather than education, the assessment process stopped after diagnostic assessment. Today a different attitude prevails. Assessment conducted to determine exactly which skills should be taught is now considered the heart of the process. If it were possible to conduct only one type of assessment process, most experts would choose an educational assessment.

Determining What to Teach

Two approaches to assessing what to teach have been developed. The first approach and the one that has been used most extensively involves comparing the student's current behavioral repertoire with the repertoire of a normally developing child. This approach is called *developmental assessment*. The other approach, which is becoming increasingly popular, involves examining the future home and school environments in which the student will have to function and comparing the student's current skills with the skills that will be needed in the future. This approach is called *environmental assessment*. With either approach, the educator is trying to answer the questions: What skills does the student currently possess? and What skills does he or she most need to be taught for optimum functioning?

Criteria for Educational Decision-Making Assessments. Whether a teacher decides to use instruments that exemplify the developmental approach or the environmental approach, it is important to remember that educational assessment is undertaken primarily to determine which skills the student needs to be taught at this point in time. Some guidelines to ensure that an instrument will be useful in planning a student's educational program include the following:

1. An instrument that has clear definitions of the tested and observed behaviors results in a more valid assessment.
2. An instrument that clearly specifies how to score each item results in more reliable assessment.
3. An instrument that allows scoring of partial independence is generally more useful for educational planning than one that scores items as either "present" or "absent." It is important, however, that the scoring system not be extremely complex, especially if it is important to complete the assessment in a short period of time or if it will be necessary to have teaching assistants help in the assessment process.
4. An instrument that specifies materials and cues is generally more reliable and will allow an evaluation of educational progress. Such an instrument, however, may be unduly restrictive if the materials specified are not age-appropriate and functional. Similarly, specification of materials and cues may result in scores that do not adequately represent the needs and abilities of those students who have severe motor or sensory impairments.
5. An instrument that has alternative items for students with motor or sensory disabilities can be used with a wider range of students. For example, assessments that allow a student to use an alternative communication system such as signing or a communication board are more likely to meet the wide range of needs seen in this population than those which focus only on verbal skills.
6. An instrument that has a fairly complete task analysis of skills will give the educator a better picture of exactly what needs to be taught than an instrument that assesses more global skills. For example, it is easy to plan exactly what to teach if you know that a student can hold and scribble with a pencil but cannot mark within a 3-inch square. It is less clear what should be taught if the assessment indicates only that the student does not use a pencil correctly. However, the finer the task analyses on an assessment, the longer it will take to administer. Sometimes an educator might prefer to use a more global educational assessment, choosing skills that seem particularly relevant and using the baseline period of training (see Chapter 4) to determine the entry level for teaching.
7. Instruments that assess several domains (e.g., language, gross motor, leisure) give a broader picture of the student's skills and allow the development of a cohesive curriculum. On the other hand, those designed to

test only one domain usually result in a more thorough assessment of that domain and are more valuable for developing specific instructional programs.

8. Instruments that assess functional behaviors such as dressing, eating, food preparation, mobility, and vocational tasks generally are more useful with older students than those which assess skills such as use of scissors, stacking rings, pegs, or names of animals.

Representative Developmental Instruments. Virtually all commercially available educational assessments are developmental assessments. They are designed to compare the student's current repertoire with the normal developmental repertoire. In the next few years, it is likely that environmental and ecological assessments will also begin to be available commercially. Following is a list of commercially available developmental instruments that have been used effectively for educational decision making. These instruments all are accompanied by some type of curriculum guide (task analyses, teaching instructions, teaching suggestions, prescription cards, or data sheets).

1. Basic Skills Screening Test (Schalock, Ross, and Ross, 1976)
2. Behavioral Characteristics Progression (BCP) (Special Education Information Management System, 1973)
3. C.A.D.R.E. (Cambridge Assessment Development Rating and Evaluation) (Welch, O'Brien, and Ayers, 1974)
4. Career Adaptive Behavior Inventory and Developmental Activities (Lombardi, 1980)
5. Community Living Skills (Schalock and Gadwood, 1980)
6. Infant Stimulation Training Skills (Roman, 1978)
7. Koontz Child Development Program: Training Activities for the First 48 Months (Koontz, 1974)
8. Learning Accomplishment Profile (LAP) (Sanford, 1974) and Learning Accomplishment Profile for Infants (Early LAP) (Griffin and Sanford, 1981)
9. Los Lunas Curricular System (Everington, 1982)
10. Portage Guide to Early Education, Revised (Shearer, Billingsley, Frohman, Hilliard, Johnson, and Shearer, 1976)
11. Prescriptive Behavioral Checklist for the Severely and Profoundly Retarded, volumes 1, 2, and 3 (Popovich, 1977, 1981a, 1981b)
12. RADEA Program (Dallas County Mental Health/Mental Retardation Center, 1972)
13. Sensorimotor Cognitive Assessment and Curriculum for the Multihandicapped Child (Fieber, 1977)
14. Sensorimotor Integration for Developmentally Disabled Children (Montgomery and Richter, 1977)
15. Skills Achievement Profile (Young, 1974)
16. Social Skills for Severely Retarded Adults (McClennen, Hoekstra, and Bryan, 1980)

Environmental Assessments. As mentioned earlier, there are few commercially available environmental inventories. Those that are available have focused primarily on the vocational environment. The primary difference between such instruments and developmental instruments is that environmental inventories assess the skills needed to perform successfully in a particular environment rather than the skills it is assumed all nonhandicapped people achieve developmentally. A good example of a commercially available environmental inventory is the Prevocational Assessment and Curriculum Guide (PACG) (Mithaug, Mar, and Stewart, 1978). This instrument is nonstandardized but has been shown to be reliable and valid. It was designed for use with moderately, severely, and profoundly retarded students ranging in age from 10 to 60 years. The instrument consists of forty-six items that address attendance and endurance, independence, production, learning, behavior, communication, social, and self-help skills. The scoring profile appears quite useful in assessing how closely the assessed student meets the expectations of most supervisors in sheltered workshops. The curriculum component consists of task analyses and objectives for each item. This is one of the few assessments available that is age-appropriate for older students with severe handicaps.

Although there are few commercially available environmental inventories, the process of doing an environmental assessment has been supported by research (Brown, Branston-McClean, Baumgart, Vincent, Falvey, and Schroeder, 1979). Generally, an environmental inventory includes the following steps:

1. Making a list of current and potential environments in which a student must function
2. Visiting these environments and listing the subenvironments within each one
3. Through observation and structured interview, listing specific activities that occur routinely in each subenvironment
4. Analyzing the activities to determine what skills are required; trying also to identify functional alternatives or prosthetics that would allow the student to function if the typical manifestation of the skill could not be taught (e.g., wheelchair or mobility for nonambulatory students)
5. Task-analyzing the required skills into smaller behavioral units
6. Assessing the student using the task analyses to determine the current level of functioning
7. Teaching the skills in which the student is deficient, preferably in the appropriate environment

For example, a teacher may decide that students need to learn how to use a large shopping mall that is relatively near the school and students' homes (step 1). The teacher then visits the shopping mall and determines that it includes the following subenvironments: parking lot, corridor and entrance areas, clothing stores, eating establishments, variety stores, movie theater, record stores, jewelry stores, bookstores, department stores, and specialty stores (e.g., fireplace equipment and boutiques). The teacher shows the list to several colleagues who often use the mall and talks to parents about their use of the mall.

It is determined quickly that the rest room and the escalator and elevator were forgotten in the list of subenvironments and that these may be vital areas for a student. Because the teacher does not have enough time to do an exhaustive survey of all the subenvironments, the parents are asked which environments are used most frequently (e.g., Do you ever take your child to any of these places? or Which of these places in the mall do you use most often?). It is learned that many parents feel the most important subenvironments are the parking area, the corridor and entrance, the restrooms, the escalator and elevator, and the eating establishments (step 2).

The teacher then begins to catalog activities that occur in each of these areas. For example, in the parking lot subenvironment, the student needs to know how to get in and out of the car, how to look for moving cars, how to look for cars that are backing out of parking spaces, how to step onto and off of curbs, and how to locate the family car or the bus (step 3). Each of these tasks then is analyzed further to specify what skills are needed. Getting out of the car consists of unfastening the seat belt, rolling up the window, opening the door from the inside, getting out of the car (wheelchair transfer will be needed for some students), locking the door, closing the door, and walking close to the car until the back bumper is reached. The teacher practices getting out of the car several times and watches others do it to be sure no vital skills have been forgotten (step 4).

Then each of these skills is task-analyzed further. For example, the skill of unfastening the seat belt is divided into pushing the seat belt button to unhook the belt, lifting the belt across the body, turning the body slightly, letting go of the belt, and checking to be sure the belt is fully retracted (step 5). The students then are assessed to determine how many components of each of the necessary skills they already know (step 6). The parents then are consulted once more to be sure that they approve of the skills that will be taught. Some parents ask the teachers not to teach their children how to unfasten the seat belt because they do not want to take the chance that the child will unfasten the seat belt while the car is in motion. Since this seems to be an important consideration, the teacher agrees not to teach the skill unless there is also time to teach the student the discrimination between the times the seat belt can be unfastened and the times when it cannot.

It should be clear from this example that doing an environmental inventory is time-consuming. This is probably why more teachers do not use this approach. However, it probably would not be too burdensome for a teacher to inventory two or three subenvironments every semester. If the subenvironments were chosen carefully, the assessment information would result in a more age-appropriate and functional educational program for the student than one that depended strictly on developmental assessments. This is particularly true for students over 12 years of age. The task of environmental assessment also can be simplified by sharing completed inventories with colleagues. In addition, educators should continue to demand functional environmental assessment instruments from commercial publishers.

Determining Learning Styles

Another critical component of educational assessment is determining how to teach skills to the student. This involves assessing the student to determine learning style and sensorimotor deficits. Much time is spent deciding what should be taught, but almost no time is spent determining the most effective and efficient ways to teach an individual student. As a result the content is individualized, but the teaching methodology is not. Teaching methods are chosen instead on the basis of the educator's preferences and experience. For an education program to meet the needs of its students, it is critical that both methodology and content by designed specifically for each student.

Learning style refers to the way in which a student learns best. Each individual develops certain preferences and methods of taking in and storing knowledge. Some people learn most effectively when information is given orally; others learn better when the information is written or demonstrated. Some people like to work in noisy environments with lots of other people around; some cannot work effectively in such environments. Some people work very hard for money; others work hard in order to become famous. Some people love to work outdoors; others hate it. All people have some kinds of work they really enjoy and some they cannot stand. People with handicaps are no different. They also have specific likes and dislikes that can affect how well they learn. The more aware a teacher is of a student's learning style, the more likely it is that the teacher will devise appropriate instructional strategies and materials to make the student's learning optimally effective and efficient. The requirement that a student's strengths be listed on an individualized education plan (IEP) is more than an empty exercise designed to soften the fact that most teaching is designed to remediate deficits. It constitutes an attempt to remind educators that students have skills and preferences that if used appropriately can enhance the educational process.

Laycock (1980) delineated six aspects of learning style that seem to have direct implications for educators choosing instructional techniques and materials: attentional control, modality preference, level of processing, reflection-impulsivity, grouping preferences, and reinforcement preferences.*

*V. K. Laycock, Assessment and evaluation in the classroom in *Implementing Learning in the Least Restrictive Environment: Handicapped Children in the Mainstream*, ed. M. I. W. Schefani, R. M. Anderson, and S. J. Odle (Baltimore: University Park Press, 1980). Terms and definitions reprinted with permission of PRO-ED, Inc., Austin, Texas.

Attentional Control. This term refers to a student's ability to focus on a particular task without being distracted by other things that happen in the environment. Several related variables that may be assessed are duration of attention span, length of time the student can work without teacher attention, distractibility, and presence of bizarre behavior. These behaviors will determine to a great extent the way time and space will be allocated in a classroom. For example, a student who is very wiggly and active and who seems to pay less and less attention to a task the more often it is presented should not be scheduled to work on the same repetitive task for a 30-minute period. Similarly, a student who is easily distracted from a task by other students or by outdoor events may need to be instructed in a portion of the classroom that is separated by dividers (a cubicle) to minimize distractions during certain sessions. A student who stops working unless given direct instruction may learn more if taught in a small group rather than a large one. Students whose bizarre behavior increases in the presence of noise, movement, or confusion may learn more efficiently in a cubicle. Other students whose bizarre behavior seems to occur primarily when they are unoccupied generally need a highly structured schedule to maximize learning. Still other students whose bizarre behavior seems to be related to self-stimulation may need to have tasks scheduled that incorporate the same type of stimulation that is obtained through the bizarre behavior. For example, a student who spends a great deal of time body rocking may be very receptive to learning the use of a teeter-totter, hammock, or swing.

If a student demonstrates problems in attentional control, a teacher may not always want to alter the teaching environment in the ways we have discussed. Instead, the teacher may wish to work on attentional skills in the context of the regular classroom environment. In either case, knowing what attentional skills are currently in the student's repertoire allows the teacher to decide how best to schedule a student's time and how to divide the classroom physically for optimal learning.

Modality Preference. This term refers primarily to the types of instruction that seem to result in the most rapid learning for a particular student. It also can refer to the types of tasks a student learns most easily.

As will be seen in later chapters, there are several ways to teach students to do a task. For example, the teacher can choose to use a time-delay prompting system, a prompt sequence system, or an errorless learning procedure. Each of these systems is effective with some students. The challenge is to discover which ones are most effective with each student. This can be done most effectively through assessment.

The most useful assessment of modality preference is a formal observation made while the student learns several tasks that are taught using different prompting systems. Obviously, this is a time-consuming process. It would be necessary to teach at least three different tasks with each of the prompting systems; otherwise, the results might simply be due to the type of task, the teacher, or some other variable. Thus, an assessment of modality preference may take several months. Although this sounds unmanageable, it actually is not. The assessment should be seen as part of the daily educational process. The educator must decide to teach a student different tasks using different methods. Then the teacher and the teaching assistants must discuss periodically how well the student is learning with each method. This discussion should include both the data that are being collected on the student's progress and the educators' subjective feelings about the teaching methods. Generally, after a month or so a pattern can be seen and the less effective methods can be replaced with those which have been shown to be more useful.

A less effective way to assess a student's modality preference is to interview the student's previous teachers. Sometimes this method, especially when combined with a review of old programs and data, can provide very useful information about how well the student responds to different types of prompting systems. However, do not be surprised if a previous teacher used only one technique with all students and cannot tell you whether the student will respond to others. Only in the past few years has the issue of learning style been emphasized in regard to students with severe handicaps.

Formal observation during classroom teaching sessions, teacher interviews, and data review are also effective methods of assessing the types of tasks a student prefers. A quicker method, however, may be to set up several tasks a student has been taught in previous years and allow the student to choose the one he or she wants to do. A data sheet illustrating this type of process is shown in Figure 1.3. This student was allowed to choose among tying a shoe, pushing a racecar, throwing a softball, kicking a soccer ball, pushing a lawn mower, watering plants, identifying objects, and singing along with favorite songs. The assessment showed that the student seemed to prefer pushing a lawn mower, kicking a soccer ball, and watering plants. The teacher chose tasks the student already knew how to do, so it was not necessary to teach these tasks. Then an attempt was made to figure out what the student liked about the tasks. A decision was made that the student preferred large motor activities and tasks that allowed him to be out of doors; therefore, it was decided that some of his new tasks would incorporate one or both of these elements.

The most difficult part of assessing what tasks a student prefers is determining which elements of the tasks are preferred. Unless the student is verbal and can tell you this information, the decisions will have to be made on the basis of best guesses. It may be useful to assess tasks initially from the standpoint of the response required. In other words, it may be informative to know that the student seems to prefer using fine motor, gross motor, or communication skills to make a response.

Another useful way to look at skills is to look at where they are performed. Does the student regularly do better on tasks that are performed at

Figure 1.3 Example of an assessment used to determine types of activities a student likes.

ACTIVITIES PREFERENCE INVENTORY

Student John Jones

Activities assessed: (1) Tie shoes (2) Water plants
(3) Use lawn mower (4) Play soccer (5) Play softball
(6) Sing (7) Use race car (8) ______

Date and time	Choice 1	Choice 2	Choice 3
8/1 8:30	___ Tie shoes	X Lawn mower	___ Softball
12:15	___ Water plants	X Soccer	___ Sing
8/2 12:30	X Sing	___ Softball	___ Race car
2:00	___ Identify object	___ Tie shoes	X Water plants
8/3 8:30	___ Race car	___ Soccer	X Lawn mower
12:30	X Water plants	___ Identify object	___ Race car
2:00	___ Sing	X Soccer	___ Softball
etc.			

desks, outdoor tasks, or tasks such as food preparation and bed making that permit movement? Yet another method is to divide tasks by domains. Does the student appear to dislike self-help skills but enjoy most leisure skills? If so, new leisure tasks probably will be learned more quickly than new self-help tasks.

Obviously, it is not always preferable or desirable for a student to be taught only the favored skills. But a good teacher will make every effort to be sure that a student has the opportunity to do preferred tasks several times a day.

Level of Processing. This term refers to how quickly a student can learn a task and to the way a student solves problems. One aspect of level of processing that may need to be addressed is how finely a task must be divided in order for a student to learn. Students who exhibit lower levels of processing generally need to have a task analyzed more extensively than those who exhibit higher levels. For example, one student may be able to learn to play a hand-held electronic game such as SIMON when the teacher uses a task analysis that has the following four steps:

1. Turn game on.
2. Push start button.
3. Push colored section that blinks.
4. Turn game off after buzz.

Another student may be able to learn to play the same game only when the teacher uses a task analysis that has the following eight steps:

1. Locate the on/off button.
2. Push the on/off button to the right.
3. Locate the start button.
4. Push the start button down.
5. Look at the game.
6. Push the colored section that blinks.
7. Locate the on/off button after a buzz.
8. Push the on/off button to the left.

Another aspect of level of processing involves the types of cues and prompts that are effective with a particular student. If a student has a very small receptive vocabulary, complex verbal cues probably will not be a particularly successful way to teach that student. If a student does not imitate any gross motor movements, demonstrating a fine motor skill (e.g., tying a shoe) is probably a waste of the teacher's time as well as the student's.

Educational time is at a premium, and it is imperative that educational techniques be chosen appropriately. Again, this does not mean that the student should never be challenged. For example, a teacher may argue that a student will never learn to imitate if the teacher uses only physical assistance cues. This is certainly true, and it is perfectly appropriate for a teacher to teach a student how to use the skill of imitation. However, simply exposing a student to opportunities to imitate (e.g., giving demonstration prompts) does not necessarily teach the student how to imitate. If demonstration cues or prompts are used with a student who does not know how to imitate, careful attention must be paid to how the imitative portion of the training will be conducted. Simply using cues and prompts on a rote basis without attention being paid to whether the student can utilize such cues and prompts is not teaching; it is superstitious behavior that wastes everyone's time.

Another aspect of level of processing is manifested in the pattern seen when a student is learning a new task. Some learners may require several sessions before learning the first part of the task, followed by rapid learning of the remainder of the task. Others seem to learn some portions of a task very quickly but then take many sessions before any further improvement is noted. Some of these learning patterns may be the result of the way tasks are taught, but sometimes the patterns seem to be integral to the student.

The final aspect of level of processing is how quickly or slowly the student likes to receive information. Students characterized as having high levels of processing generally learn efficiently when information is presented in a fairly rapid manner. Such students seem to be able to absorb information quickly and use it immediately. These students seem to learn efficiently under the massed-trial instructional format in which the student is given several opportunities to do the same skill within a short period of time. Other students who have less efficient processing levels need a slower-paced presentation format. These students seem to need to let the information sink in before they can use it. These students seem to learn more efficiently under a distributed-trial instructional format in which the student practices once or twice on a task and then does some other task(s) before trying the original task again.

Assessments of level of processing can be done as an ongoing procedure in the classroom in the manner described for modality preferences or can be conducted more formally. Two commercially available assessments, the Trainee Performance Work Sample (Irvin, Gersten, Taylor, Heiry, Close, and Bellamy, 1982) and the Autism Screening Instrument for Educational Planning (Krug, Arick, and Almond, 1980), have sections designed to assess some aspects of level of processing. Naturally, discussions with previous teachers and the parents also will give some insight into a student's level of processing new information.

Impulsivity and Reflectivity. *Impulsivity and reflectivity* refers to the speed with which a student makes a response. A student who makes a response quickly and appears not to be concerned with the correctness of the response can be characterized as impulsive. A student who responds slowly but whose responses are usually correct can be characterized as reflective. It should be obvious that different teaching techniques and materials presentations are needed for these very different styles of learning. The teacher of an impulsive student, for example, may need to maintain control of the materials to ensure that the student has time to think about the answer or response before allowing the student actually to respond. The teacher of the reflective student may wish to speed the process by setting time limits. Some students do not respond at all unless the teacher gives them some sort of extra assistance. Such students have been labeled prompt-dependent. The teacher of such students needs to be aware of this problem before designing educational programs, or the problem may inadvertently become worse.

Assessment of impulsivity and reflectivity generally can be conducted by teaching the student two or three simple tasks for a week and observing the speed and correctness of the responses. A sample assessment form for this aspect of learning style is shown in Figure 1.4.

Figure 1.4 Form for measuring impulsivity and reflectivity in a severely handicapped student.

IMPULSIVITY/REFLECTIVITY INVENTORY

TASKS

(1) Monday: Present ten trials of "Put the penny in the slot." Cue is a demonstration. Give no feedback on errors. On last five trials, praise correct responses.

(2) Tuesday: Present ten trials of "Buttoning 1-inch button." Cue is a demonstration. Give no feedback on correctness. On last five trials if student errs, say, "Do it this way," and physically assist child.

(3) Wednesday: Present ten trials of "Put the car under the table." Cue is verbal. Give no feedback on correctness. On last five trials if student errs, say, "Do it this way," and demonstrate correct response.

(4) Thursday: Present ten trials of "Find the (object)." Cue is verbal. Give no feedback on errors. On last five trials, praise correct responses.

(5) Friday: Present ten trials of "Stand on one foot" alternated with "Touch your toes." Cue is demonstration. Give no feedback on errors. On last five trials, praise correct responses.

	Mon	Tue	Wed	Thur	Fri
Child performed quickly on trials with feedback					
Child performed quickly on trials without feedback					
Child took a long time on trials with feedback					
Child took a long time on trials without feedback					
Child refused to perform on trials with feedback					
Child refused to perform on trials without feedback					
Child got angry on trials with feedback					
Child got angry on trials without feedback					
Child got worse on trials with feedback					
Child improved on trials with feedback					
Number of correct trials					

Grouping Preferences. This term refers to the types of groups in which students seem to learn most effectively. Generally, three grouping arrangements are used in classrooms for students with severe handicaps. The first is the one-to-one arrangement. This format allows one teacher to teach one student. The student has the teacher's undivided attention, and the pace of instruction is generally rapid. The second common grouping is the small group. This generally consists of two or three students being taught by one teacher. This grouping allows the students to be exposed to more instruction, although there is often less individual attention. The small group format allows a student to rest and observe part of the time, and so the pace for any one student is generally slower than in one-to-one. The third grouping, which is less common in classrooms for students with severe handicaps, is the large group. In this format five to eight students work with one teacher; this generally requires that the students be able to sit without disturbing their neighbors for fairly substantial periods of time while the teacher instructs the whole group or works with each student in turn. The large group is most like the format used in classrooms for less handicapped and nonhandicapped students.

Students respond differently to different formats. Some students seem to learn best in the one-to-one format, in which all the attention is focused on them. Other students can tolerate short periods without attention and seem to welcome the chance to rest or observe others during the teaching session. These students often do better learning in small group situations than in one-to-one groups. Finally, many students can learn well in a large group situation, but there are others whose behavior and performance deteriorate markedly.

Assessment of a student's grouping preferences can be done fairly quickly using a form similar to the one shown in Figure 1.5. The assessment procedure exposes the student to both small group and large group formats. A number of positive and negative behaviors are tabulated in each of these formats. Completion of the form can give a teacher an idea of the grouping arrangements that are most effective with each student. The teaching staff, however, probably will wish to discuss and reassess the efficacy of the grouping arrangements on a regular basis during the school year. This is because a student may learn best in a small group but may not be doing well in a particular small group because of task difficulty, poor student-teacher interaction, or problems with one of the other students in the group.

Reinforcement Preferences. Motivation is often a problem in classrooms for students with severe handicaps. Much of the early literature in the field discussed methods of enhancing motivation through the use of reinforcement. The effectiveness of reinforcement techniques, however, is based on the premise that the teacher has been able to identify several things that are reinforcing (or motivating) to each student. With some students it is very easy to identify things that can function as reinforcers, but with others it is very difficult. Nonetheless, it is extremely important to discover at least one powerful reinforcer for every student. Having a reinforcer on hand will make it much easier to teach tasks that are deemed crucial for the student's development but are not preferred by the student. Assessment of reinforcement preferences generally is done formally and then supplemented by observation and interviews with parents and former teachers (see Chapter 2).

Figure 1.5 Assessment used to determine grouping preferences.

GROUPING INVENTORY

Student: ______________________________

(1) Monday and Tuesday: In a group of two students, present ten trials each of ______________ to student 1 and ______________ to student 2. Alternate trials between students. Cue is stimulus presentation and verbal. Give physical assistance if student errs. Reinforce correct performance in both students.

(2) Wednesday and Thursday: In a one-to-one situation, present ten trials of one of the activities used on Monday/Tuesday. Cue, prompts, and reinforcement are the same as before.

(3) Friday: In a group of four or five students, have every student do five to ten trials of an activity. Two activities should be used to prevent boredom. Randomize calling on the different students. Cue is stimulus presentation and verbal. Prompts and reinforcement should be the same as before.

	Mon	Tue	Wed	Thur	Fri
Overall, student seemed interested					
Overall, student seemed bored					
Child watched others perform					
Child smiled at others					
Child touched others					
Child ignored others					
Child took materials from others					
Child engaged in high-rate stereotypy					
Child engaged in aggression or tantrum					
Performance improved during session					
Performance stayed stable during session					
Performance got worse during session					
Number of correct trials					

Representative Learning Style Instruments. There are very few commercially available assessment instruments that are keyed specifically to any of the components of learning style. Following is a list of instruments that include at least one component of a learning style assessment.

1. Autism Screening Instrument for Educational Planning (ASIEP) (Krug, Arick, and Almond, 1980). This instrument has a subtest that allows an assessment of patterns of learning in a student. It is suitable for most children diagnosed as severely handicapped as well as those suspected of being autistic. This instrument is an excellent test of adaptive behavior.
2. Trainee Performance Sample–Revised (Irvin et al., 1982). This instrument measures an individual's ability to learn a new task rather than measuring what the student already knows. It systematically varies three types of instruction, four types of task attributes, and the number of ob-

jects involved in a task. Because of the content, this assessment is most useful with students of junior high age or older, but it could be used with younger students. It has been validated extensively in field tests. This assessment instrument can be used to determine what vocational tasks to teach and how to teach them. Thus, it is a time-saving assessment.

3. Social Skills for Severely Retarded Adults (McClennen, Hoekstra, and Bryan, 1980). This assessment contains a section designed to assess reinforcement preferences. This is an excellent instrument for students of any age with severe handicaps. It provides for assessment of adaptive behavior in the area of social skills and includes a curriculum for remediation of deficits in this domain.
4. Managing Behavior 7: Teaching a Child to Imitate (Striefel, 1974). Although not designed as an assessment instrument, this manual provides a very clear explanation of exactly how to test for reinforcer preferences. Data sheets for reinforcer testing are included.
5. Carey Infant Temperament Questionnaire (Carey, 1972). This scale assesses student temperament, which is another component of learning style. This test was validated on nonhandicapped infants, and so results on older handicapped children may not be valid. Nonetheless, the scale may provide some interesting insights into how to handle a student most effectively. It also may prove valuable with students diagnosed as profoundly retarded. The scale consists of seventy items that are to be answered by the parent(s); the items relate to sleep, feeding, elimination patterns, and play behaviors. The stated purpose of this scale is to help parents determine alternatives in handling, caring for, and interacting with the child. The author emphasizes that the instrument is most useful when it is used to provide an opportunity for parent-professional interchange. It is quick and easy to administer and may be very useful in establishing parent-teacher interactions centered on how to teach the student effectively.

Recognizing Sensorimotor Deficits

As noted earlier, decisions about how to teach a student will be based in part on information about the student's sensorimotor deficits as well as information about learning style. For example, it obviously would be inappropriate to try to use only a verbal prompt with a student who is totally deaf. It also would not be particularly fruitful to use visual demonstration prompts with students who have severe visual impairments. The more information that can be gained about designing educational programs to compensate for a student's sensory and motor deficits, the more effective the programs will be. Often this information can be gained from specialists and consultants. Forms similar to the request for information shown in Figure 1.2 will be very useful in helping the teacher design instruction for students with sensorimotor handicaps as well as choose appropriate goals.

Sensory Assessments. On occasion, however, the teacher will not have access to a consultant or the consultant will not have time to assess the individual until late in the school year. This seems more likely to happen in the area of vision and hearing assessment than in the area of motor assessment, perhaps because most audiologists and school nurses are not trained to manage populations that are more difficult to test. It also may reflect the fact that until 5 years ago there were few sensory assessments available to test students with multiple handicaps. Therefore, it appears that a teacher of severely handicapped students should be familiar with some of the many assessment instruments that are now available for testing vision and hearing in children with very severe handicaps. Many of these instruments can be administered by the teacher, but it may be more helpful in the long run if the teacher and the school nurse or audiologist work together to use the instrument. In this way the school nurse or audiologist will become familiar with the assessment instrument(s) and learn how to work with this population. As other professionals become more proficient in the use of the newer tools, the teacher may wish to turn over the assessment of these functions to them.

Obviously, simply knowing that deficits are present is not enough. Unless the teacher knows how to use this information to improve instruction, there is little point in spending time on the assessment. Teachers of students with multiple handicaps must search the literature of other disciplines (such as deaf education) constantly and talk to other teachers and consultants to determine how to present information in a way the student can use most effectively.

It is also important to recognize that sensory and motor deficits, like the aspects of learning style, can be targets for remediation as well as problems for which the teacher must compensate. The best educational programs use assessment information both ways.

Representative Instruments. Following is a list of vision and hearing assessments that have been used successfully by teachers, nurses, vision specialists, and hearing specialists.

1. Assessment of Auditory Functioning of Deaf-Blind/Multihandicapped Children (Kukla and Connally, 1979)
2. Auditory Assessment and Programming for Handicapped and Deaf-Blind Students (Goetz, Utley, Gee, Baldwin, and Sailor, 1982)
3. Auditory Assessment of the Difficult-to-Test (Fulton and Lloyd, 1975)
4. Comprehensive Intervention with Hearing-Impaired Infants and Preschool Children (Hasenstab and Horner, 1982)
5. Functional Vision Inventory for the Multiply and Severely Handicapped (Langley, 1980)
6. Low-functioning Vision Assessment Kit (Rock, Litchfield, Jans, Schulz, Ulrich, Pray, and Vedovatti, 1974)

7. Vision Assessment and Program Manual for Severely Handicapped and Deaf-Blind Students (Utley et al., 1982)
8. Parsons' Visual Acuity Kit (Spellman and Cress, 1980)
9. Functional Vision Inventory (Peabody Model Vision Project, 1980)
10. A Vision Guide for Teachers of Deaf-Blind Children (Efron and DuBoff, 1975)
11. Visual Functioning Assessment Tool (VFAT) (Costello, Pinkney, and Scheffers, 1981)

Each of these instruments has been used successfully with many students diagnosed as severely or multiply handicapped, autistic, deaf-blind, and profoundly retarded. None of these tests are designed to substitute for a complete audiologic or visual examination but are designed to function as screening instruments that indicate whether a problem is present. If these instruments indicate a problem in vision or hearing, the student should be referred to a physician for diagnostic examination and possible prescription of glasses or hearing devices. Often it will be helpful to send the results of the visual or hearing screening with the child to the specialist along with any specific questions concerning the manner in which materials or cues should be presented to best compensate for the problems.

The Assessment Process

The information in this chapter thus far has been concerned with deciding what type of assessment would be appropriate and the criteria for choosing particular instruments to use with students in a classroom. But choosing an appropriate instrument is only half the battle. The teacher also must know how to conduct an assessment, interpret the results, present the information to others, and develop a coherent educational program based on the student's performance on various assessments. Only when all these skills have been learned can the teacher truly say that assessment is an integral part of the educational practice. Once the assessment instruments are chosen, the assessment process appears to encompass four phases: (1) discussing the assessment process with the parents and obtaining permission to do assessment, (2) preassessment preparation, (3) conducting the assessment, and (4) interpreting the assessment information and making educational decisions.

Discussion of Assessment with Parents

The completion of screening or diagnostic assessment requires that parental permission be obtained before the assessment is undertaken. P.L. 94-142 specifies that no child may be given an assessment that may result in special education placement unless the parents are notified ahead of time and voluntarily give consent. The parents also may withdraw consent at any time. The parents are further entitled to an explanation of all evaluation results (whether used for placement or not) and an explanation of any actions taken on the basis of those results. If the parents do not agree with the results of a screening or diagnostic evaluation, P.L. 94-142 gives them the right to request that an evaluation be conducted by someone not associated with the school and that those results be considered in deciding on the best placement or choice of curriculum for the child.

Even though parental permission to conduct assessments for the purpose of determining what to teach and how to teach is not mandated by law, it is good educational practice to contact the parents before doing these assessments. It is important to let the parents know what information is being sought through the assessment and how it will be used. This will give them an opportunity to express any concerns they may have and will set the stage for later discussions concerning the child's educational program.

Preassessment Preparation

Before an assessment can be conducted, several preliminary steps must be taken. If the teacher has not reviewed the student's medical history and previous educational records, it should be done at this time. Some teachers prefer to do this after the assessment is completed in order not to form biases before testing. Others find that knowing something about the student helps them tailor the assessment situation to the student's needs. A second preliminary step is scheduling the assessment. With screening and diagnostic instruments, such scheduling may involve calling the parents or other teachers. With educational assessments, scheduling is done to ensure that all students in the classroom are tested as quickly as is feasible.

Figure 1.6 shows an assessment schedule for a classroom with six students, one teacher, and two teaching assistants. Note how this teacher gave each teaching assistant only one or two portions of the formal assessment (the Los Lunas) to do and had them assess all the students on these portions. This method allows quicker training of the teaching assistants than trying to train them to do an entire assessment. It also is more likely to produce consistent presentation and scoring across students. Note also how the teacher alternated assessments of what the student needs to learn with assessments of how the student learns. This practice should reduce student fatigue and boredom. Also note that the staff members were almost always assigned two students at a time. Assessment was completed by doing an item with student 1, then an item with student 2, etc., until all items were completed with every student. The person doing group assessment, however, must take special care to make sure that the same item is not presented to each student in turn; otherwise, opportunities for imitation of other students' performance may invalidate the results.

Figure 1.6 Schedule for assessment in a classroom serving six students with severe handicaps.

	José	Ross	John	Amy	Rosie	Jenny	Mon/Tue duties	Wed/Thur duties
8:30–9:00	T	T	T_1	T_1	T_2	T_2	T = Hearing assessment T_1 = Dressing (Los Lunas) T_2 = Social (Los Lunas)	T = Vision assessment T_1 = Impulsivity T_2 = Language (Los Lunas)
9:00–9:30	T_2	T_2	T	T	T_1	T_1	Same as above	Same as above
9:30–10:00	T_1	T_1	T_2	T_2	T	T	Same as above	Same as above
10:00–10:30	P.E. in gym for all students						T_1 and T_2 = break	T_1 and T_2 = break
10:30–11:00	T	T	T	T_1	T	T_2	T = Large group assessment T_1 = 1:1 assessment T_2 = 1:1 assessment	Same as Mon/Tue
11:00–12:00	T	T	T_1	T_1	T_2	T_2	All do feeding assessment	All do feeding assessment
12:00–12:30	OT	OT	T_1	T_1	T_2	T_2	OT = Reflex (Los Lunas) T_1 = Activity preference T_2 = Grooming	OT = Fine motor (Los Lunas) T_1 = Activity preference T_2 = Grooming
12:30–1:00	T	T	OT	OT	T_1	T_1	OT = Reflex T_1 = Activity preference T = Grooming	OT = Fine motor T_1 = Activity preference T = Grooming
1:00–1:30	T	T	T_2	T_2	OT	OT	OT = Reflex T = Activity preference T_2 = Grooming	OT = Fine motor T = Activity preference T_2 = Grooming
1:30–2:00	Music/art for all students						Help as needed	Discuss toileting assessment on all students

T = Sue (teacher) T_1 = Joe (T.A.) T_2 = Marylou (T.A.) OT = Ralph (O.T.)

After scheduling is completed, the teacher must read the assessment manual, locate the needed materials, and train the teaching assistants to do their portions of the assessment. Hopefully this training should occur just before the fall session actually beings.

The teacher also needs to decide where in the classroom each person will conduct the assessment as well as obtain and place the proper materials, dividers, assessment forms, tables, chairs, stopwatches, etc., in those areas. It is particularly frustrating to be completing a group assessment and suddenly discover that needed materials are in use by someone else or that the noise level of another staff member's activity interferes with testing.

After all preliminary details are taken care of, the teacher and assistants can move on to the next phase of assessment: conducting the test itself.

Conducting the Assessment

Conducting the actual assessment is fairly straightforward if the teacher has read the manual and trained the teaching assistants. Many teachers feel it is more beneficial to demonstrate the assessment techniques to the teaching assistants and then practice assessing each other than simply to have the assistants read the manual. The method of training needed probably will vary with the amount of experience the teaching assistant has had with assessment.

More supervised practice may be necessary when using a nonstandardized test than when using a standardized one because standardized tests have very clear instructions regarding how to present and score each item. These instructions usually are given item by item either on the scoring profile or in the manual and can be referred to in the course of assessment. Nonstandardized tests have no guidelines for presentation or scoring, and so the teacher will need to show the teaching assistants how the test items should be presented and scored.

Special attention should be given to problem situations that may occur during testing, such as the child who has a seizure, the child who needs to go to the bathroom, the child who throws materials, or the child who has a physical disability that prevents a response on certain items. Deciding ahead of time how such situations will be handled, whether trials will be presented again, and how to score questionable items will save time and make the assessment process much smoother.

Interpreting the Results and Making Decisions

When the assessment is finished, the results must be interpreted and decisions must be made. The first step in interpreting the results is to summarize the information. Most assessment tools include some type of summary system. Some common types of summarization are IQ scores, social quotients, subtest scores, and profiles. These allow the person conducting the assessment to determine overall performance levels or determine the consistency of a student's performance across several domains. These scores can be used as a general guideline when listing a student's strengths and weaknesses on an IEP.

More informal measures, such as those used to determine learning style, probably will not have a summary score. In such cases, the teacher must look over the results of the assessment and write some sort of summary statement such as "This student seems to learn slightly faster in a small group than in a large group or in one-to-one instruction."

Next, recommendations for remediation must be made. In the case of screening instruments, the person in charge of interpretation will make written recommendations regarding the necessity for further testing. With diagnostic testing, the person in charge will make written recommendations for placement or special services. When using educational assessments, the teacher will want to determine which of the items missed during the assessment process should be chosen for possible remediation. Generally, students with severe handicaps "fail" more items on an assessment than can be targeted for remediation in a single school year. The teacher's job is to pick from that array of needs the skills that are the most age-appropriate and functional for the student to learn at this point in time. There are few formal guidelines to help the teacher make these decisions. Therefore, such decisions usually are based on the teacher's preferences (what the teacher likes to teach and feels comfortable teaching) as well as parental preferences with regard to priority teaching targets. Some school administrators also recommend that each student be taught skills in several different domains in order to present a "balanced" program.

Figure 1.7 shows a form that can be used to make the decision-making process more systematic (Johnson, 1981, n. 2, derived from Dardig and Heward, 1981). This form was designed to help teachers select more functional goals for students with severe handicaps.

To use this form, the teacher lists several possible skills across the top of the page in the boxes labeled "Skills/Goals." There is space for ten possible objectives, so most teachers use two or three of these forms for each student. Once the possible objectives are listed, the teacher rates each objective using the eighteen-point criteria listed in the left-hand column. A four-point system is used to rate each aspect of the possible objective. For example, if the teacher were to evaluate the skill of "putting together a three-piece puzzle," a rating of 2 might be given to question 1 (Can the student use the skill in the immediate environment?), a rating of 1 on question 2, a rating of 1 on question 3, etc. When all the possible objectives have been evaluated on these eighteen criteria, the totals are then compared, and those eight to ten objectives which are rated highest would be chosen as probable educational targets.

Once eight to ten educational targets have been selected, the teacher should present them to the parents and ask for input. The parents may want other or additional skills targeted, and some negotiation may be needed. Nonetheless, use of this form or some similar instrument will help systematize the decision-making process and may prove helpful in discussions of why some objectives are chosen and others are not.

Once educational targets have been selected and approved by the parents, the teacher is ready to decide how to teach these skills to the student.

Figure 1.7 Determining goals for instruction.

INDIVIDUAL SKILL AND GOALS PRIORITY RATING SHEET

Student: Elijah W. Evaluator: John P. Date: 9/10/84

SCORING KEY

0. No or never
1. Rarely
2. Maybe or sometimes
3. Usually
4. Yes or always

NA Not applicable

Skills and Goals	Puzzle-piece	Tie shoe
1. Can student use skill in immediate environment?	2	2
2. How often will skill be encountered by student in environment?	1	2
3. Can skill be worked on across several environments and situations?	1	0
4. Can skill be taught naturally using realistic materials in realistic settings?	4	4
5. Does skill produce immediate consequences for the student?	2	2
6. Does skill build on existing strengths or skills?	4	2
7. Does skill facilitate development in other domains?	0	0
8. Does student have prerequisites for the skill?	4	4
9. Does this skill remediate an identified problem?	2	2
10. Does skill help student to compensate for sensory or motor deprivation?	0	0
11. Is skill a prerequisite for later learning?	0	0
12. Will student be more independent as a result of learning this skill?	0	4
13. Will this skill facilitate movement to a less restrictive environment or educational placement?	0	4
14. Will this skill improve quality of life, choice, power, independence?	1	3
15. Is this skill necessary for medical or physical reasons?	0	0
16. Is this skill critical for social acceptance?	0	0
17. Is this skill fun for the student?	4	2
18. Is this skill age-appropriate?	2	4
Total: (72) high to (0) low priority	21	35

Source: Originally appeared in J. C. Dardig and W. L. Heward, A systematic procedure for prioritizing IEP goals, in *Directive Teacher*, 1981, 3: 6–7, © The Directive Teacher 1981. The version that appears here was adapted by Linda Cook Johnson, Winfield State Hospital and Training Center, Winfield, Kansas. Used by permission of Linda Johnson and The Directive Teacher.

Summary

The assessment process is an important endeavor in developing effective educational programs for students with severe handicaps. The different aspects of the assessment process were described in this chapter. Screening is a first, gross step in detecting whether a student manifests developmental delays. Diagnostic testing is a more comprehensive procedure that may categorize or label an individual as well as determine whether that person is in need of special education services. The teacher may play a part in screening and diagnosis. Usually diagnosticians from many disciplines contribute to the assessment process. Teachers should be familiar with the different screening and assessment instruments as well as the multidisciplinary assessment process.

A fundamental criticism of assessment is that it provides little new information and tells educators little about what and how to teach. Criteria for determining what to teach and information on the often overlooked matter of learning style are closely linked to assessment. Assessment findings can be used to develop instructional strategies that deal with the learning style variables of attentional control, modality preference, level of processing, etc. Finally, a four-part sequence for implementing the assessment process was examined.

Chapter 2

Instructional Design for Skill Acquisition

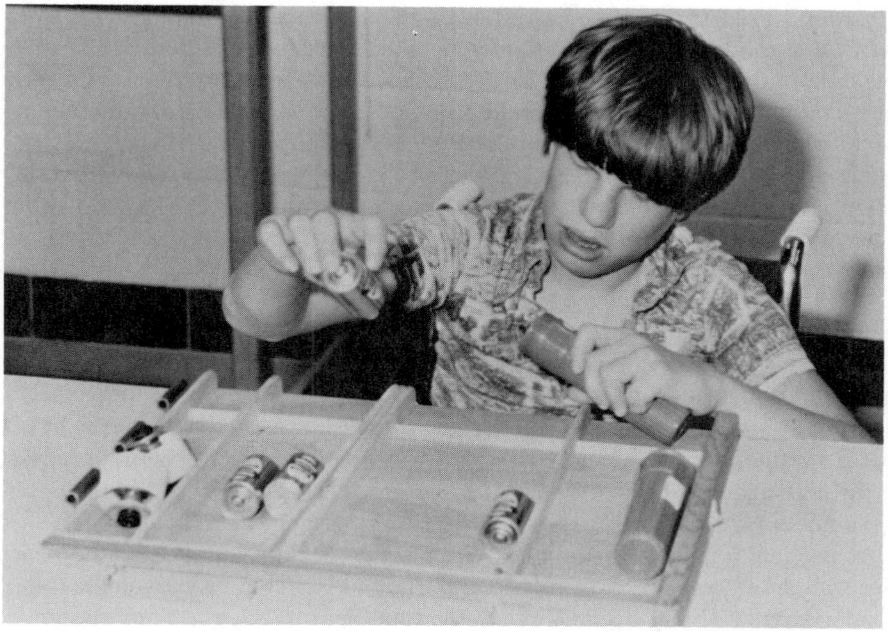

Chapter 1 presented methods for assessing and selecting goals for students with severe handicaps. This chapter helps the instructor determine how to teach the goals that have been selected. The focus is on teaching individual goals to individual students. Chapter 3 will provide details on conducting individualized instruction in natural contexts, and Chapter 7 will discuss organizing one's class into time schedules and grouping students for instruction. Here the focus is on how to get a student to learn particular tasks such as tying shoes, stating a request, or lifting his or her head for longer periods of time.

We feel that the decision about how to teach a student a certain task should be viewed as a problem-solving process. A certain amount of information is presented to the teacher, such as past records and current assessments. An instructional program must be developed from this information and the brainstorming of the teacher and other staff members, often with input from the parents as well. The brainstorming or problem-solving process must pull together an instructional program that will work. In this chapter we shall walk through this process by presenting hypothetical students who have particular instructional needs. We provide background information and describe how to teach the student. By studying specific case examples, the reader should obtain a good understanding of how to design instructional programs.

An Instructional Model for Teaching Students with Severe Handicaps

Ann is a profoundly retarded 6-year-old with limited control of her body who has been diagnosed as spastic diaplegic with severe to profound cognitive delay. Most of the time she sits in a wheelchair with her head flexed forward so that the direction of her eye gaze is toward her lap. She is capable of raising her head to gaze at people or objects around her, and she has been observed to hold her head erect for extended periods of time; in fact, there are several recorded instances when Ann watched an activity of some kind with her head erect for up to 4 minutes. Assessment information indicates that she now raises her head to look at the world around her only 10 percent of the time and for periods of up to 30 seconds on the average. Ann's IEP team felt that it was important for her to spend more time holding her head upright because this would:

1. Stimulate perceptual learning by enabling Ann to observe the many events happening around her in her school, home, and community
2. Enable her to attend to instructional tasks that could be presented to her, e.g., distinguish functional objects on a communication board; in this sense, the "head-up" response serves as a prerequisite to many types of learning tasks
3. Permit her to participate in social interactions by observing other people in her immediate environment

Because Ann apparently has the muscle control and strength to change her behavior significantly, the IEP objective set for Ann is to increase the amount of time she spends holding her head erect from 10 percent to 50 percent of the time, and for at least 1 minute per instance. Thus, a behavioral objective states the behavior and the numerical criterion at which it must be performed.

The teacher must design an instructional program to increase the percentage and duration of head-up behavior for Ann. Before developing a method to accomplish this objective, let us say a few things about the ways we might proceed in this endeavor. Undoubtedly, a teacher could devise dozens of programs in order to get Ann to attain this instructional objective. The approach we shall suggest is not necessarily the one that will work best in all situations. Our approach is derived from a theory of learning called *operant conditioning* (Skinner, 1938). Operant conditioning employs a functional analysis of behavior by investigating the events that precede the behavior (its antecedents) and the events that follow the behavior (its consequences). An operant view presents the simplest and most effective way to analyze and promote learning for students with severe handicaps.

Operant conditioning does not present a pat formula for remediating learning problems. In fact, the approach requires extensive and expert decision making on the part of the teacher. In addition to conducting a functional analysis of the individual behavior, the teacher must know about the child's current skill repertoire (what the child can do) and environmental needs (what must be learned). Once the teacher has organized this information and conducted the functional analysis, an operant conditioning approach requires an experimental perspective. Based on existing information, the teacher must hypothesize whether a particular instructional program will result in the desired change in the student's behavior.

Once it is implemented, the instructional program becomes the experiment. After a number of sessions, the effectiveness of the procedure is evaluated in terms of how well the student has performed. If the student has mastered the instructional objective, a new and more advanced objective is set to further the student's development. If the student has not reached the objective within a reasonable amount of time, the teaching procedure must be reviewed. A new procedure probably will be designed and tested in the same manner as the first procedure; through ongoing program modification, it is hoped that the student will master the instructional objective.

Thus, an operant teaching approach involves continuous development and testing of instructional procedures. Fortunately, not every learning activity requires a new experiment. Earlier educators in the field have developed curricula that work. Therefore, the teacher can refer to these previously written programs just as a regular education teacher uses a textbook at a particular grade level. Yet because of the idiosyncratic learning characteristics of students with severe handicaps, it will be necessary to modify already existing programs and in many cases write completely new programs. Let us return to Ann and take the initial steps in writing an instructional program.

Discrete-Trial Learning

Even within the operant conditioning approach there are numerous ways in which one can proceed to devise instructional programs. An approach called *discrete-trial learning* is probably the simplest way to organize an instructional session. We might decide that for 20 minutes every day Ann will practice lifting her head. The discrete-trial format involves separation of the session into a series of training trials. Each trial provides Ann with the opportunity to raise her head. Her performance on each trial will be scored pass or fail according to whether she successfully raises her head. Thus, the learning session simultaneously serves as an instructional period and a continuous assessment of pupil performance.

The procedures described in this chapter are appropriate for use in a single trial or in a sequence of single trials, which generally is referred to as massed-trial instruction. Massed-trial procedures work best for certain kinds of instructional needs but are not appropriate in many cases. Chapter 3 elaborates on single-trial versus massed-trial approaches to instruction. In Ann's case, the massed-trial instructional format is used.

Defining a Response. The first step in constructing a discrete-trial learning session is to formulate a clear definition of the student's response or behavior. In Ann's case a correct head-up response might entail:

1. Moving the head up within 5 seconds of a request to do so
2. Moving the head into position so that the child is able to look straight ahead rather than down at the floor

Figure 2.1 The discrete trial paradigm.

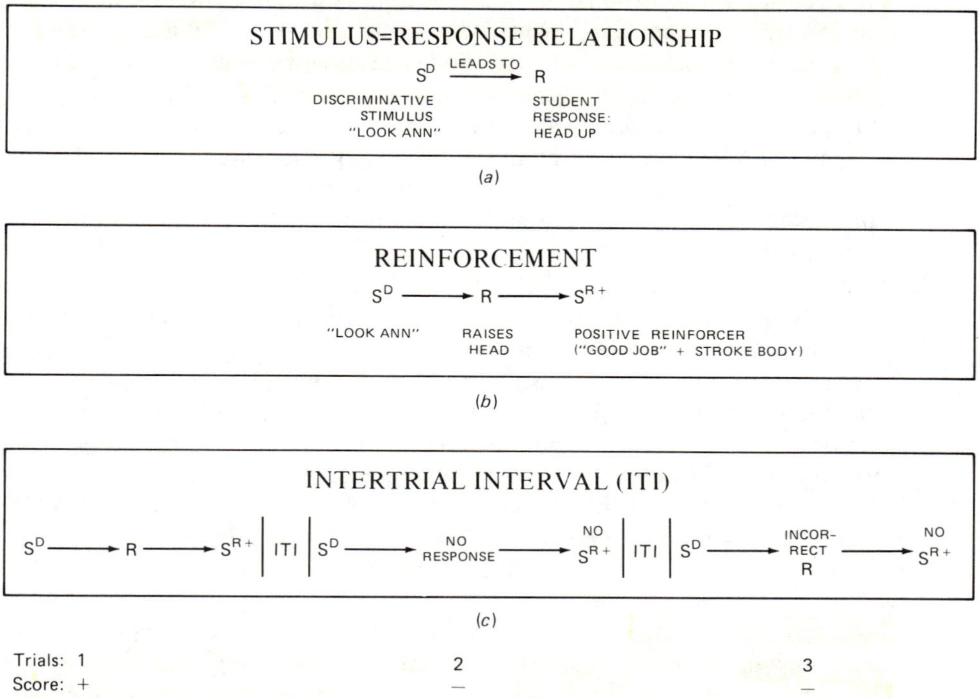

3. Maintaining the head-up position for a minimum of 30 seconds

These three descriptions define the criteria for the response. They are similar to the response criteria that define a behavioral objective, and they must be clear and observable. The standard for determining whether the response is clearly defined is to have two observers watch the student perform the behavior. If the observers can agree on the presence or absence of the behavior at least 80 percent of the time, it can be concluded that the response or response class is defined adequately. In Ann's case, for example, the teacher and the occupational therapist together can observe her and be certain that they agree on these criteria for a "successful" response.

Defining a Stimulus. After the response is defined, the next step is to describe the event that precedes the response. This event is called the stimulus or antecedent event (technically the discriminative stimulus, or S^D). In contrast to the response, which is a student-produced behavior, the stimulus is an event that either the teacher delivers or is part of the natural environment. The stimulus-response notation is seen in Figure 2.1*a*. In operant terms, the stimulus sets the occasion for the response to occur. From a teaching perspective, the choice of a stimulus that the teacher uses in instruction is extremely important. The event must be one that is likely to set the occasion for a response to occur not only during instruction but also in the natural environment after instruction has ended. A hallmark of operant conditioning is that the antecedent and consequent events chosen are those which are likely to result in a minimum number of errors. In Ann's case, it is important to select an event that is most likely to get her to raise her head. If Ann had a hearing impairment, an obviously poor choice of an S^D would be the verbal statement "Look, Ann." An S^D would have to be selected from another sensory modality, e.g., a touch on her chin and a point upward. But Ann's hearing is adequate, and she has been responsive in the past to simple verbal commands. Thus, the selection of "Look, Ann" as the S^D would represent a good choice. It is also important to remember that the S^D appears in conjunction with other stimuli. The setting where learning takes place presents stimuli such as the location in which the student is sitting or standing, sounds from other persons or radios, the sight of people, a dark room, an outdoor park, etc. All these background stimuli may facilitate or deter the production of the response by the student. However, it is important for the teacher to realize that the intended S^D may not always be the one to which the student learns to respond. In some cases the student may not even notice the S^D. This issue will be covered in more detail later in this chapter.

Presenting a Reinforcer. The next step a teacher must make when formulating a discrete-trial session is to identify a reinforcing event that follows a correct response by the student. The presentation of a contingent reinforcing event is the central property of operant conditioning. A behavior that is followed contingently by a positive event will increase the rate of appearance of the behavior. Thus, in Ann's case, if we wish to increase the amount of head raising, we must guarantee that whenever she raises her head there will be an immediate presentation of a positive reinforcer.

The establishment of this response-reinforcer relationship has proved to be a powerful means of teaching persons with severe handicaps. When selecting a reinforcer, we must be sure that it does in fact motivate the student to increase performance. The teacher knows that Ann enjoys verbal praise and strokes on her arms and shoulders and has established the reinforcing properties of these "rewards" through their use in previous programs. Both verbal praise and strokes, when provided immediately after Ann has displayed a behavior desired by the teacher, have been associated with subsequent increases in performance.

It is important to remember that a behavior is determined by its consequence. If the consequence increases that behavior, it is a reward and is indeed reinforcing for the student. If, however, the intended reward does not change the behavior or actually results in a decrease in performance, the consequence provided by the teacher clearly does not constitute a reinforcing event. In Ann's case, her teacher knows that she has great difficulty chewing and swallowing food. In fact, Ann does not seem to enjoy eating and dislikes most foods. Thus, providing edibles on a contingent basis is not a good choice for a positive reinforcer in Ann's program.

Other criteria teachers should use when they identify reinforcers for students are: Do the reinforcers normally appear in the child's natural environment? Is the reinforcer appropriate for the child's age? Ann is 6 years old, and so verbal praise and physical touches seem natural and appropriate for interactions between her and her teacher. But if Ann were a teenager, the use of physical touch as a reinforcer would be avoided if a more age-appropriate consequence could be found.

With the selection of verbal praise and body rubs as the positive reinforcers, we have completed our description of the rudiments of a discrete-trial learning session. Figure 2.1*b* displays the operant notation for the stimulus-response-reinforcer paradigm. Note that S^{R+} is the symbol for a positive reinforcer, i.e., a stimulus event (S) with positive (+) reinforcing (R) value.

Intertrial Interval. When the S^D, R, and S^{R+} events are completed, the trial is over. At this point a time period called the *intertrial interval* (ITI) follows. The ITI is the period between trials that allows the student to take a short break from work and allows the teacher to record data and prepare materials for the next trial. The ITI also can be crucial to ensure that attention will be switched from the reinforcement just delivered on the previous trial to a state of readiness to attend to the next S^D. ITIs generally last from 5 to 20 seconds. When the ITI is over, the teacher presents the S^D for the next trial. Figure 2.1*c* presents a sequence of trials with S^D, R, and S^{R+} trials separated by ITIs. In trial 1, Ann raised her head correctly and was positively reinforced. On trial 2, Ann gave no response to the S^D; she kept her head down, staring at her lap. Therefore, she was given no reinforcement.

In order to determine when no response occurs, a latency period must be defined. The *latency period* is the time permitted between the presentation of an S^D and the appearance of a response. Latency periods vary in length, usually from 1 to 20 seconds. If a student is slow in responding, longer latencies should be used. In Ann's case, the teacher determined that 5 seconds is sufficient time for her to respond (this is a typical response latency time period). Thus, for Ann's program, after the verbal S^D is delivered, the teacher counts to 5 seconds (generally a covert count rather than using a stopwatch) silently, and if Ann has not responded by the end of that time period, the trial is terminated by the teacher looking away from Ann and recording a minus on the recording sheet.

After the 10-second ITI, the S^D for trial 3 was presented. Here Ann produced a head-up response within the 5-second latency period but did not meet the criterion of holding her head up for at least 30 seconds. Since the response failed to reach criterion, it was scored as a minus trial, and no reinforcement was delivered. A review of this three-trial sequence shows that Ann received a score of 1, meaning that she had one correct response along with two incorrect responses. Often the teacher wants to know more about the nature of the incorrect responses than the fact that Ann did not perform correctly. Data recording systems that provide this information are described in Chapter 4.

Consistency. We have described the format for presenting discrete trials. A note must be made regarding the importance of being consistent when conducting trials. The logic behind presenting S^D's and S^{R+}'s in such a structured format is that the student begins to perceive a certain order in the environment and simultaneously starts to respond to the environment in a regulated fashion. As a result of their severe cognitive limitations, severely handicapped learners may experience difficulty in the initial processing of naturally occurring stimuli and consequences to regulate their own behavior. A series of discrete trials contrasts markedly with the "information overload" often presented by the natural environment. Discrete trials thus can be used to control the environment for the learner by displaying only the most relevant cues and consequences.

Nonhandicapped children acquire information through more natural and less structured means, for example:

1. Watching their peers: learning through observation or peer imitation
2. Receiving an explanation through a conversation with or lecture from the teacher or parents
3. Reading a book or manual on how to complete a task; e.g., pitching a tent or playing Space Invaders on a video game

Thus, "normal" children may learn important skills and activities in a few tries (trials), through advanced ways of processing information (observing, listening, or reading), and in less controlled circumstances. Persons with severe handicaps do not learn easily in nonstructured situations, and they rarely acquire new skills in a few trials or from observing the behavior of their peers in nonstructured situations. The learning of difficult tasks, such as the first spoken word, may involve hundreds of trials. Furthermore, students with severe handicaps are easily distracted and may not discriminate relevant cues. They often are not able to focus on the S^D in the presence of multiple stimuli. This is why in some instances instruction is carried out with one teacher and one student in an area set off from the rest of the room. In these conditions, the effect of competing stimuli can be minimized. The discrete-trial format further ensures that the important stimulus, the S^D, will become salient and that all other stimuli will be minimized or removed. This prevents an irrelevant stimulus from interfering with learning by distracting the learner's attention.

The teacher must be careful that an idiosyncratic S^D or S^{R+} does not control the learner's behavior (Schreibman, Kogel, and Craig, 1977). For example, the teacher may lean very close to Ann in order to deliver the next verbal cue ("Look, Ann"). While doing so, she may touch Ann's knee after she says, "Look, Ann." Ann may learn to respond to the knee touch rather than the verbal cue as the relevant S^D; this, of course, would be an "irrelevant" stimulus. Since the irrelevant stimulus of the knee touch is not likely to occur outside of the discrete trial session or be a useful S^D in the natural environment, much learning would be lost. Ann's response would be nonfunctional in any other situation. For these reasons, it is important that the teacher present the antecedent and consequent events in a clear and consistent fashion. Inconsistent presentation will mask the S^D's and S^{R+}'s, confuse the student, and lead to few increments in learning.

Although the discrete-trial format is simple, we have found that teachers may make errors in certain aspects of cue and reinforcer delivery. The following list (Falvey, Brown, Lyon, Baumgart, and Schroeder, 1980; Koegel, Glahn, and Nieminen, 1978; and Koegel, Russo, and Rincover, 1977) enumerates the key aspects of delivering the S^D and S^{R+} in the correct manner:

1. The S^D must be *identical* from trial to trial. The use of "Give ball" on one trial and "Hand me the ball" on another would violate this rule. Placing a flash card 6 inches in front of a person's eyes on one trial and placing a card 12 inches from the person and on the table in another trial also would be an error. Saying the S^D loudly on some trials and softly on others constitutes an inconsistency.
2. The S^D must be presented in an uninterrupted fashion. There should be a quiet pause before and after presentation of the S^D. A common error occurs when the teacher continues to talk to the student in the middle of S^D presentation; e.g., "Come on, Bill, let's do well, now hand me the ball." The S^D, "Hand me the ball," is embedded within extraneous verbiage, which probably changes from trial to trial and can serve only to interfere with the accurate perception of the S^D. Thus, the S^D must have a clear onset and a clear termination.
3. The S^{R+} must be delivered contingently. The most powerful tool of operant conditioning is that students learn that their behavior produces certain desired outcomes. The reinforcing property of the outcome, e.g., a smile or a touch, plus the feeling of controlling one's environment should motivate the student to continue performing that behavior. If the teacher does not reinforce correct responses consistently, the student cannot learn the response-reinforcer contingency. The major step in ensuring the contingent presentation of S^{R+} is to define the response clearly. If the teacher can distinguish correct from incorrect responses, there is less likelihood of reinforcing an incorrect response.
4. The positive reinforcer must be presented immediately after the correct response. The longer the delay in reinforcer delivery, the less likely that an association will be made between the two events, thus decreasing the

chance of learning. If the teacher inadvertantly delivers reinforcement late, e.g., several seconds after a correct response, the student may not realize there is reinforcement for the previous behavior. Thus, the association between R and S^{R+} can best be facilitated by ensuring that S^{R+} occurs immediately after the response. A common error occurs when the teacher first records the student's response and then delivers the S^{R+}.

5. The positive reinforcer must be delivered consistently from trial to trial. Just as with presentation of the S^D, consistency is important. A common error occurs when verbal praise, e.g., "Good job," is being used as the positive reinforcer. On one trial, the teacher gives an enthusiastic "Good job" and on the next trial mutters "Good" in a soft voice. The reinforcer must motivate the student to perform. If enthusiastic verbal praise is a motivator for the student, it is not likely that meek verbal statements will serve as an incentive. Another typical error is for the teacher to forget to deliver one of the events in the S^{R+}. For example, if the S^{R+} for a correct response is verbal praise plus rubbing of the student's shoulders and neck, it would be an error to give only verbal praise and not the physical contact.
6. After each complete trial, the teacher must *wait* for the specified ITI before delivering the S^D for the next trial. Particularly if the student has just responded correctly and received a preferred reinforcer, there should be a period to enjoy the reward. Some children become quite excited over their performance or when they receive a reinforcer and are simply not in a position to attend to the next S^D until the necessary ITI has passed. Teachers often deliver the next cue while a child is still consuming an edible or immediately after they have provided social praise. These practices make it almost impossible for the student to attend to and discriminate the next relevant S^D.
7. The instructional cue should be tailored to the natural cue that eventually should control the behavior. For example, if a traffic light (natural cue) is to control street-crossing behavior, an instructional cue should be selected with this cue in mind. Thus, pictures of traffic lights may be used to teach and simulate street crossing in the classroom. Eventually, though, street crossing must be taught in the presence of the natural cues (see Chapter 3 and Falvey et al., 1980).

Selecting Positive Reinforcers. Like all human beings, individuals with severe handicaps tend to learn new things only when they are motivated to learn. With nonhandicapped persons, though, it is easy to find positive reinforcers that can serve as motivators, e.g., money, praise, food, a good grade, or an intrinsic interest in the subject. Yet nonhandicapped persons often have idiosyncratic preferences for positive reinforcers, and this is also the case for severely handicapped learners. Some students like food but are indifferent to praise. Some students become upset if they are physically handled, whereas others dislike food as a reinforcer but thrive on praise and hugs. The point is that each student's reinforcer preferences must be determined on an individual basis. Teachers who use the same rewards for all their students are likely to obtain negligible gains in pupil learning, because these same rewards will not act as reinforcers to all the students.

Reinforcer preferences can be determined in two ways. If successful learning has occurred in the past through the use of a particular reinforcer, it may be inferred that the S^{R+} functions in an effective manner. If past records are inconclusive or if uncertainty remains concerning effective reinforcers, the teacher can administer a *reinforcer preference test*. Although the test is simple and takes little time, its benefits are potentially large. First, the teacher selects a number of possible reinforcers that are based on interviews with parents or past teachers, observations of the student's behavior, intuition, and reinforcers that have worked for the teacher with similar students in the past.

Suppose the preferred activity for a child named Johnny is to spend periods of free time voluntarily manipulating various objects. Also, Johnny does not like to be touched, and resists eating most foods. Social reinforcers such as touches and hugs are not pleasing to him. It may be unwise to use food as a reinforcer during instruction. Eating is already a problem, and Johnny's nutritional intake is so low that his health could be jeopardized should he be satiated with the foods he now eats. (*Satiation* is used to describe a loss of interest in a reinforcer that previously was highly motivating to the learner.) Both common sense and clinical experience show that using one reinforcer a great deal will decrease its effect on the child's behavior. Eventually, the child appears to become quite neutral to the reward and may even learn to avoid it. Thus, it would be particularly important not to risk further eating problems by using food as a reinforcer with a child such as Johnny, who already exhibits finicky eating behavior.

Since Johnny does display a preference for certain activities, the teacher may gather several objects the child plays with and present them to him to determine which one would be the most effective reinforcer. The teacher conducts a series of trials (perhaps 20) to see which items the student selects for play. A trial would begin with an S^D of "Pick something to play with." The objects are arranged in an array in front of the student within his reach. After the S^D, the student may have a 10-second latency period to pick an object and 60 seconds to play with the material. When the student selects one object, he or she should not be allowed to play with another object on that trial. The teacher carefully observes the child's behavior with the object selected on each trial and then writes down a description of what the child does, how long he or she plays with the object, etc.

The testing procedure should be repeated for three sessions on separate days. With five objects, if an object is picked at least 8 times in 20 trials in each of the three sessions, it can be considered a preferred reinforcer and can be used for a variety of teaching purposes. The test can be repeated with different materials if no one object shows a preferred quality. In addition, the test should also be administered at different times of the year whenever there is a drop in pupil learning, in order to examine whether the loss may be due to the absence of an effective reinforcer.

One limitation of the test is that it does not permit the testing of actions delivered by the teacher, e.g., hugs or praise. To test whether these events are reinforcing, actual learning sessions have to be conducted and evaluated to see whether performance has increased. It is also possible to infer reinforcer preference by looking at the reactions of the student to the event. Smiling, facial brightening, and an increase in certain types of general activity are indicators that the event is positively reinforcing. Figure 2.2 presents a student interest inventory designed to identify preferred leisure activities that may be utilized as reinforcers on a contingent basis. This form is completed by someone who knows the student well (e.g., the teacher or the parent) while watching the student interact with the materials. The behavior samples can be collected on videotape and observed at another time when it is convenient for a care giver to complete the rating.

Prompt Strategies

The final step in defining a discrete-trial session is to describe the prompts that are used. In some discrete-trial tasks no prompts are used. The absence of prompts during training may be described as trial and error training, a system that assumes that the student will learn the behavior from the reinforcement received on correct trials and the absence of positive feedback received on incorrect trials. This process of *differential reinforcement* is the key to learning in operant conditioning. Thus, when Cindi touches the picture of her mother after the S^D "Point to Mom," she receives the S^{R+} of a hug and praise. If Cindi points to the picture of her mother after the S^Δ "Point to Cindi," no S^{R+} is given. When Cindi starts to point to the picture of her mother consistently in the presence of the S^D, her behavior is said to be coming under *stimulus control*; that is, Cindi is learning to discriminate the stimulus that will lead to reinforcement from those stimuli which do not lead to reinforcement (termed S^Δ, or S delta). Thus, Cindi is reinforced for touching the picture of her mother after the S^D "Point to Mom," but she is not reinforced if she touches this picture after an S^Δ such as "Point to Cindi."

In many cases trial and error learning is sufficient to produce learning. For some students with severe handicaps, though, the S^D in trial and error learning is not effective in producing stimulus control. When the pupil cannot yet produce the response, trial and error learning is even less likely to result in acquisition. The pupil may never exhibit the behavior, in which case there will never be delivery of reinforcement in the presence of the S^D; hence, there will be no opportunity to learn the discrimination.

In Ann's case, she failed to raise her head consistently after the instruction "Look, Ann," even with the presentation of differential positive reinforcement. When learning does not proceed at an acceptable rate, a number

Figure 2.2 Inventory to identify preferred leisure activities and potential reinforcers.

STUDENT INTEREST INVENTORY

Student Maile Kahana

Instructions: For each activity, answer each of the questions below by placing the number of the description which best matches the child's behavior in the appropriate box for that activity.	Activity	TV Game	Simon	Bowling	Music Stick	Pinball
	Date	4/10/80	4/10/80	4/10/80	4/10/80	4/10/80
	Rater	Amy	Amy	Amy	Amy	Amy
A. For this child's usual level of interest in play materials, he or she is 1. Not as interested as usual 2. About as interested as usual 3. More interested than usual		3	3	2	3	3
B. For this child's usual level of physical interaction with materials (pushing control buttons, turning knobs, putting things together, etc.), he or she is 1. Not as busy as usual 2. About as busy as usual 3. Busier than usual		2	3	2	3	3
C. For this child's usual "affective" behaviors (smiling, signs of enjoyment, etc.), he or she seems to be 1. Enjoying this less than usual 2. Showing about the same amount of enjoyment as usual 3. Enjoying this more than usual		3	3	2	3	3
D. For this child's usual level of "looking" or "visual regard" of an activity, object or person, he or she is 1. Not looking as much as usual 2. Looking as much as usual 3. Looking more often or longer than usual		3	3	2	3	3
E. Compared to this child's usual behavior during a short period of time with minimal supervision, he or she is 1. Engaging in more negative behavior than usual 2. Engaging in about the same amount of negative behavior as usual 3. Engaging in less negative (or off-task) behavior than usual		2	3	2	3	3
Activity interest scores: Total the numbers written in each column.		13	15	10	15	15

Source: Adapted from B. B. Wuerch and L. M. Voeltz, *Longitudinal Leisure Skills for Severely Handicapped Learners: The Ho'onanea Curriculum Component* (Baltimore: Paul H. Brookes, © 1982), p. 182. Reprinted with permission of Paul H. Brookes.

of things can be examined in order to remediate the problem. First, it is wise to see whether the S^D's and S^{R+}'s are being delivered in a consistent fashion. Second, a reinforcer test can be given to reestablish that the S^{R+} is in fact serving as a motivating consequence. If there are no problems with consistency or reinforcement, the teacher should consider using a prompting procedure.

Figure 2.3 A prompt sequence.

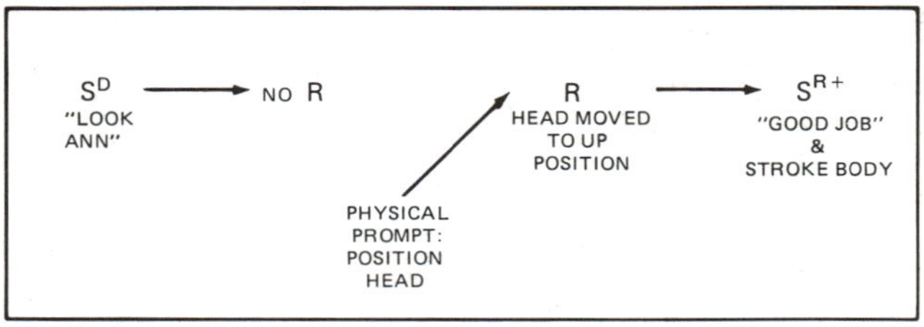

A *prompt* is an additional stimulus—extra help—given to set the occasion for a behavior after the S^D has failed to produce the response. Prompts are designed so that they focus the student's attention on the expected response, or the teacher actually may help the student physically in performing the response. For example, Figure 2.3 shows a sequence in which

1. The S^D "Look, Ann" was delivered
2. No response occurred within 5 seconds
3. The teacher gave the physical prompt of manually positioning Ann's head to a partially upright position
4. Ann continued moving her head on her own after the prompt ceased until it was all the way up
5. The S^{R+} was given to Ann for her prompted correct response

In this case, the physical prompt worked in getting Ann to initiate raising her head. A prompting stimulus was used when the original S^D failed to induce the response. Prompts are usually more powerful or controlling as stimuli than the designated S^D. For Ann, the verbal S^D of "Look, Ann" that was used to set the occasion for the behavior was not effective. Then, Ann was partially guided through the behavior with the physical prompt. The S^D event required Ann to initiate the behavior after only hearing a verbal request and apparently was not sufficient to control her correct response. The prompt that provided physical assistance in instigating the response was more powerful, and Ann finished the correct behavior on her own.

The logic behind prompting is to transfer stimulus control over a series of trials from a more powerful stimulus to a weaker, more natural stimulus. By prompting Ann on her error trials, the intent is that she will come under stimulus control of the verbal S^D. The successful transfer of stimulus control from a prompt to an S^D cannot be assumed to occur automatically. One of the major learning problems of students with severe handicaps is the tendency to depend on more powerful prompts. For example, Ann responded only after she received a physical prompt, and it is possible that she may never respond to the verbal cue alone but may always wait for the teacher to give her more help.

Thus, it is important to select prompts judiciously and to plan ahead for fading those prompts systematically. The prompt should serve as a facilitator to respond to the S^D rather than inhibiting transfer of stimulus control to the S^D. One way to prevent the student from becoming dependent on the prompt is to reinforce only those responses which appear after the S^D. This means that the teacher will not reinforce prompted responses at all. In this way, differential reinforcement should take place so that the student understands that prompted trials are not reinforced whereas correct trials are. If an effective reinforcer is being used, the student should increase the rate of correct nonprompted responses in order to obtain reinforcement. When a prompted response is reinforced, though, the student may learn that it is easier to wait for the prompted assistance and still receive the reinforcer. This pattern of "laziness" is not uncommon but can be avoided by not reinforcing prompted responses.

In the initial acquisition phase of learning, a correct response may never occur or may occur only rarely unless the prompt is provided. Thus, the child may never receive reinforcement following a correct response, and if the S^{R+} is an important motivator, a crucial component of learning will be entirely absent from instruction. Thus, the teacher should reinforce early prompted correct responses so that the child has an opportunity to realize which behaviors are expected. Gradually, the teacher should thin (eliminate) the reinforcement of prompted trials and introduce more stringent performance criteria; i.e., voluntary or nonprompted responses, to obtain the S^{R+}.

There is another strategy for reinforcing prompted trials that avoids the necessity of deciding whether to reinforce. When a student is not highly reinforced by verbal praise, there can be reinforcement by an effective S^{R+} (e.g., touching) plus verbal praise on correct trials. On prompted trials that are completed correctly, only praise is given. The praise gives informational feedback that the response has been completed correctly (on prompted or unprompted trials). Praise is not given when the student fails to complete the response correctly after the prompt is given, e.g., "does not move" the head up to the criterion position. The student should learn to distinguish complete responses from error responses. Furthermore, positive reinforcement in the form of touching is used only to motivate correct unprompted trials. Figure 2.4 presents an example of using verbal feedback and other positive reinforcers in this manner.

We also should consider the types of prompts that can be used to set the occasion for behaviors that do not occur in the presence of the S^D alone. Generally, four types of prompting stimuli are used to encourage learning in students with severe handicaps. They will be described in order from less intrusive to more intrusive stimuli.

Verbal Prompts. Verbal prompts require the teacher to make a statement after the latency is completed and no correct response has occurred. A verbal prompt may simply be a repetition of the S^D, e.g., "Head up." In this

Figure 2.4 The use of verbal feedback in conjunction with prompts and positive reinforcement.

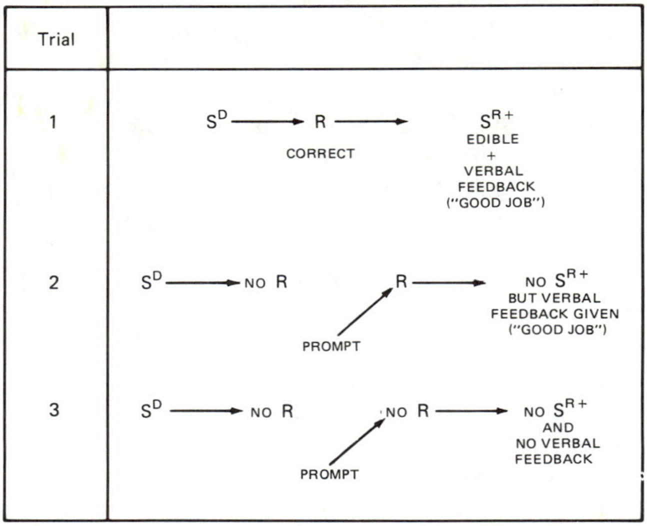

case, the student may not be responsive after hearing the phrase only once; if it is repeated a second time, there is a better chance of obtaining the correct behavior. This is most likely to occur when the behavior is in the student's repertoire and is appearing at a fairly high frequency, e.g., 7 out of 10 trials. By repeating the S^D, one avoids having to use a more intrusive stimulus. Thus, the student is required to function at a higher cognitive level.

A second kind of verbal prompt can be an expansion on the S^D. For example, instead of "Head up, Ann," the prompt could be "Pay attention, Ann, let's get your head up high!" The elaborated phrase may be more successful than the abbreviated S^D statement. Elaborated verbal prompts also may serve an explicative function. That is, the phrase may describe or explain how to complete the behavior. For example, the student can be given the S^D to "Get a carton of milk" in a grocery store. If the student does not respond correctly, the verbal prompt could be given to "Get a carton of milk. It's in the aisle where the butter is." This prompt provides additional information that assists the student in completing the behavior.

Figure 2.5 shows examples of the use of verbal prompts. Verbal prompts can be used only if the student can process verbal information. Processing and using linguistic symbols constitutes an impressive cognitive ability in which many students with severe handicaps are extremely limited. However, because verbal cues (prompts) are often natural stimuli to which students will be expected to respond, it may be important to pair such verbal cues (e.g., "free time") with more effective nonverbal cues (e.g., a point or a physical assist) throughout the instruction. Eventually, a goal could be to

Figure 2.5 Examples of verbal, modeling, and physical prompts.

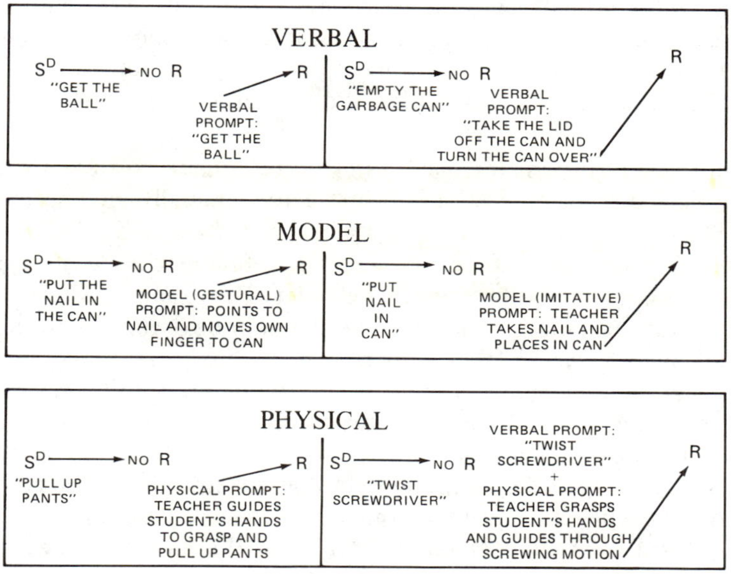

transfer stimulus control to the verbal stimulus from more powerful (and less natural) kinds of assistance.

Observational Prompts. The use of observational prompts assumes that the student can learn from observing another person's behavior. Observational learning ability may or may not be present in a particular student with handicaps. If a student is visually impaired or intellectually unable to imitate gestures or other modeled stimuli, this form of prompt is not recommended. An observational prompt consists of the teacher providing visual cues for the student to watch after the latency period has passed without a correct independent response. The observational prompt may be a simple gesture or a complete demonstration of the target behavior.

For example, suppose a student is doing a three-choice vocational task of sorting nuts, bolts, and washers. A pile of these objects is mixed in a bin, and the student is given the verbal S^D "Sort." There are three bins, each of which contains either all nuts, all bolts, or all washers. The student is expected to sort the objects from the mixed bin into the separate bins. When the student makes an error, e.g., puts a nut into the washer bin, a modeling prompt is given. With a *gestural* prompt, the teacher can point to the nut bin where the nut was to have been placed. The prompt will be effective if the student then corrects the mistake and places the nut in the nut bin. An *imitative model* prompt would be used if the teacher took the nut out of the washer bin and placed it into the nut bin. The student would then repeat this behavior. Thus, gestural prompts rely on "hints" such as pointing, with the assumption that the student can emit the behavior. An imitative prompt models the entire behavior and is therefore more intrusive. It should be used only when a gestural prompt will not suffice in producing the student's behavior. Figure 2.5 describes more examples of observational prompts.

Physical Prompts. The most intrusive kind of assistance is a physical prompt. A physical prompt consists of an instructor manually guiding the student through the behavior after the latency period has elapsed without a correct response. Physical prompts, or *primes*, require the teacher to put the student partially or completely through the behavior. For example, suppose a student has the task of putting a quarter into the coin box when boarding a bus. If a teacher gives the S^D "Put a quarter in the box" and no correct behavior is forthcoming, a physical prompt may be used. A full physical prompt (sometimes called a total physical assist) would have the teacher take the student's hand, move it into his or her pocket for a quarter, move the hand toward the slot in the coin box, and help the student release the coin into the box. A partial physical prompt (sometimes called a partial physical assist) would provide manual assistance for part of the movement, e.g., helping the student grasp the coin in the pocket and assisting the hand in moving 6 inches toward the coin box and then giving no further help. The student then has to complete the movement of reaching to the coin box and dropping the coin in the slot. Partial physical prompts are preferred because they require the student to complete part of the movement unassisted.

Over trials, the amount of assistance should be progressively removed, or *faded*, so that the students complete more and more of the behavior on their own. Complete physical prompts should be avoided if possible. Whenever they are used, movement to partial prompts should be written into the program. Since total physical prompts do not require that the students do any of the behavior on their own, they increase the chances that the students will become dependent on the physical prompt; i.e., no transfer of stimulus control will be made to the S^D. If the teacher has observed that the student completed part of the behavioral movement in the past—e.g., dropping the coin in the coin box—a full physical prompt should not be used. If the behavior is not in the student's repertoire, however, a full prompt may be necessary. Over trials, quickly fade the degree of the prompt to less and less assistance. Figure 2.5 describes other examples of the use of physical prompts.

Sequencing Prompts. A final consideration concerning prompts is sequencing more than one prompt on a given trial. A teacher may decide that more than one prompt or chance to perform should be given after an error is made on a trial, and then a sequence of prompts may be constructed to achieve this purpose. For example, suppose a 4-year-old student is being taught to ride a tricycle. On each trial, the student was expected to ride the tricycle 30 feet. During an assessment, the student rode the criterion distance 2 out of 10 trials. During assessment trials, the S^D "Ride bike" was given at the beginning of each trial, but no prompts or reinforcement were provided. During instructional trials, it was decided to reinforce correct responses with gleeful verbal praise such as "Good, you are riding!" Since the student was responsive to verbal stimuli, a verbal prompt of "Come on, let's ride that bike" was given after a 5-second latency expired without a correct response. It also had been observed that the student at times had difficulty beginning the pedalling to reach the 30-foot mark. Therefore, a physical prompt was provided after 5 seconds had elapsed after the verbal prompt without eliciting a complete response. The physical prompt consisted of the teacher holding the handlebars and pushing the bike from behind for 25 feet. The teacher then released the handlebars, and the student was expected to continue pedalling for 5 feet. Thus a prompt sequence had been arranged of S^D—verbal prompt—physical prompt. A reinforcement system was designed so that the student received verbal reinforcement for correct responses after the S^D, the verbal prompt, or the physical prompt. No S^{R+} was given when a correct response did not occur after the physical prompt.

The example just described sequenced a verbal and physical prompt together. It is possible to generate many possible sequences of prompts such as the following:

Verbal—model—physical
Model—physical
Verbal—model

It is possible to repeat the same prompt, e.g., verbal—verbal—physical. Two prompts also may be combined into one event. For example, in the tricycle example, after the S^D the teacher might combine both verbal and physical prompts by saying, "Let's really ride the bike," and at the same time physically guiding by the handlebars and pushing the tricycle for 5 feet. Notationally, the sequence would be S^D—verbal + physical. Figure 2.6 gives a number of other examples of prompt sequences and combinations.

The main consideration is to select and sequence prompts that work, i.e., produce or occasion the desired behavior. There are no hard and fast rules to determine which prompt will be effective because effectiveness must be determined for each individual learner, just as reinforcers are an individual matter. The teacher must experiment with prompts for each student. When a given prompt has proved successful in eliciting behaviors for a particular student, the teacher should continue using it. Prompts are a means of transferring stimulus control to the S^D. If the use of a prompt or sequence of prompts fails to obtain a transfer of stimulus control to the relevant stimulus cue, alternative prompting or reinforcement patterns should be explored.

Figure 2.6 Examples of prompt sequences.

Delivery Order	Examples							
First prompt	V	V	M	V + M	V	V + P	V	V
Second prompt	M	M	P		V + M		V + P	V + M
Third prompt		P						V + P

V = Verbal prompt M = Model prompt P = Physical prompt

Time Delay of Prompts. Time delay procedures also may be used as a strategy to fade prompts gradually. In time delay, increasingly greater increments of time are allowed to pass after the delivery of the S^D and before the delivery of the prompt. Time delay procedures work best with one type of prompt rather than a prompt sequence. The prompt may be delivered in a similar manner throughout the instructional sequence; i.e., it is the time interval that varies rather than movement from a more intrusive to a less intrusive prompt. At the beginning of instruction, a no-delay or 0-second "time delay" is employed—the teacher gives the prompt *immediately* after the S^D. The student is given no opportunity to respond without assistance at first, thus ensuring that no errors will occur. This also provides the student with a series of fully prompted trials that permit the learning of the correct behavior. The teacher provides reinforcement after completion of each prompted correct response.

After a number of trials under the no-delay condition, the teacher may move to the next level of time delay, gradually increasing the time increments before the presentation of the prompt. This allows the student more time to initiate the response independently. Delay levels may consist of 0, 2, 4, 6, or 8 seconds, increasing from 0 seconds to 8 seconds, 2 seconds at a time, or any other combination that seems to work well for the student. It is important to minimize errors and not move to the next delay level until the teacher has some indication that incorrect responses will be kept to a minimum.

After selecting delay levels, the teacher should decide whether to follow one of two procedures for movement from level to level. The teacher may (1) specify a sequence in which one, three, five, ten, etc., trials will always be conducted at each delay level, that is, run one trial at 0 seconds, three trials at 3 seconds, etc., or (2) run a whole session of trials at 0 seconds, followed the next day by a session at 3 seconds, then a session at 5 seconds, etc.

Since time delay procedures always begin with a zero delay and move very gradually to increased time intervals before the prompt is delivered, they effectively prevent large numbers of errors from occurring. The use of prompting procedures without a time delay procedure requires that the teacher wait for a specified latency period (e.g., 5 seconds) after delivery of the S^D to give the pupil time to respond. During this wait period, the student may respond with many errors or some trials may result in no response. By combining a prompting procedure with the use of time delay, the teacher can prevent errors from occurring and at the same time ensure that the correct behavior is being demonstrated consistently during the initial period of instruction. Time delay procedures seem to be a logical strategy to use whenever the student is expected to acquire a new response or demonstrate an existing response at a higher rate.

Operant Fading, Thinning, and Chaining

An understanding of S^D's, R's, S^{R+}'s, and ITIs should enable teachers to run discrete trials with their students. In this section, we describe a number of other behavior analytic techniques that use operant conditioning principles. These techniques can be used to assist students when they are having difficulty learning a task. The procedures change the manner in which stimuli, responses, or reinforcers are presented.

Fading of Stimuli. The problem of bringing a student under stimulus control is the main objective in operant conditioning. When there is an absence of stimulus control and the student is making numerous errors, an operant analysis of behavior suggests that there are problems with antecedent and reinforcing events. Besides checking on consistency of delivery, reinforcement value, and prompts, the teacher can use the technique of *fading* to establish better stimulus control (Sidman and Stoddard, 1966). In fading, alterations are made in the S^D over trials. For example, suppose a student is being taught to set a table with plates, forks, and knives. After running a number of assessment trials, the teacher knows that the student can lay out each utensil in the appropriate area on the table but never places the utensils in the correct position. On the assessment trials, the S^D consisted of one plate, glass, fork, knife, and spoon placed in a bunch in the area of the table where they were to be set along with the verbal request "Set the table." The student had the fine motor ability and experience to handle the utensils with no difficulty. The problem appeared to be in placing the utensils in the correct position.

The records from the previous school year show that place setting was taught to the student but that little progress was made. In the previous teaching procedure, an effective S^{R+} was used and a pointing prompt was given after every error response. The pointing prompt required the student to reposition the utensil. Since attempts to fade the pointing prompt failed,

Figure 2.7 The fading of additional stimulus information.

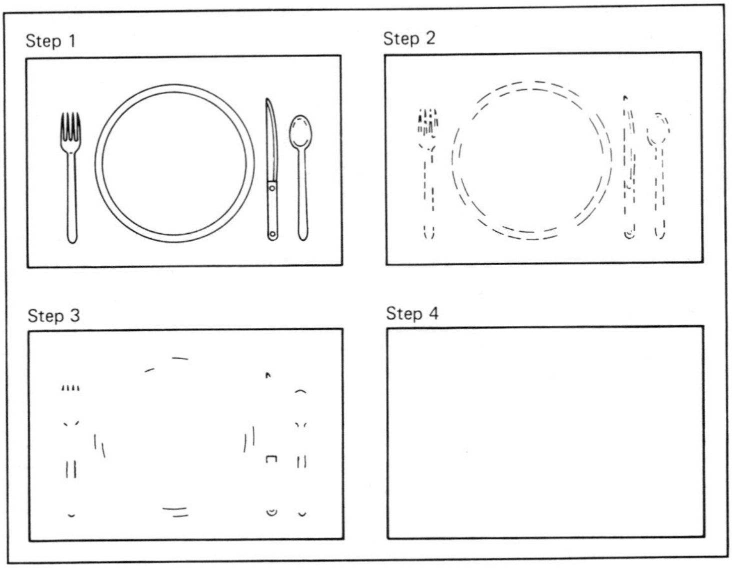

another procedure was attempted. The new prompt and fading procedure consisted of using a place mat that had the shapes of the utensils drawn in the correct position. Thus, additional stimulus information—the markings—was added to the original S^D (see Figure 2.7). The information was added to facilitate the production of the response. With the markings present, the student correctly set the utensils four out of five times.

The problem then became one of transferring stimulus control from the S^D markers to the verbal S^D alone. The use of stimulus fading solved this problem. At the next session the same markings were used, and the student made five out of five correct responses. Because of this fine performance, part of the markings were deleted in the subsequent session. Figure 2.7 shows the deletion or fading of the markings. In this session, the student again succeeded in five out of five correct trials. Thus, at the next session more of the marker stimulus was faded, and the student remained at five out of five correct responses (Figure 2.7). At the following session, the marking was completely eliminated so that the S^D of the materials and the verbal instruction appeared alone. The student performed a perfect five out of five correct trials. The student was brought to criterion (five out of five) performance with the original S^D by means of the fading procedure. Effective fading procedures often result in learning without errors; thus, stimulus fading often is referred to as *errorless learning*. Although fading is an effective technique, it does take extra time and effort to construct the materials, and it requires the student to go through a number of extra fading trials. For this reason, it is usually

Figure 2.8 Fading a within-stimulus cue to teach a letter discrimination task: "Point to F."

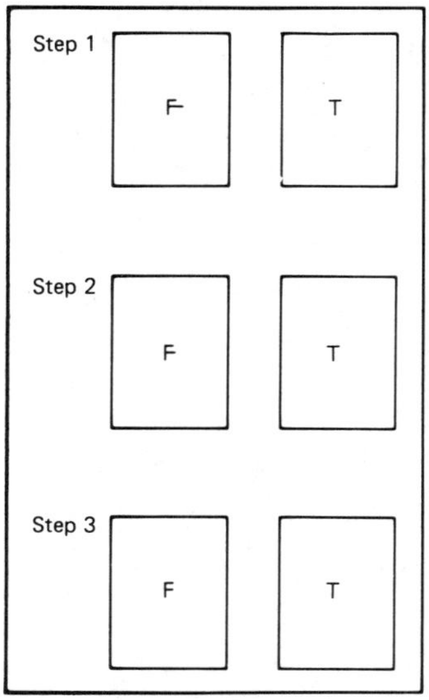

better to use fading only after the teacher has tried a nonfading of S^D procedure and the student has not responded correctly.

Fading procedures can be used in a number of different ways. In the example just given, the form of a figure was changed gradually over trials. In fact, since the "extra help" was an exaggerated outline of the utensils themselves, some behavior analysts would refer to this as a *within-stimulus* prompt (Schreibman, 1975). Other dimensions of distinctive features can be exaggerated and then faded to provide within-stimulus prompts. A within-stimulus prompt changes some dimension of the given S^D. An *extra-stimulus* prompt changes some dimension unrelated to the S^D. For example, a student may have to select a picture of a glass of milk by pointing to it. Initially, the correct picture of a glass of milk is placed quite close to the student, while the incorrect "distractor" picture (e.g., a picture of a dog) is on the table but out of reach. Gradually, the extra-stimulus prompt of proximity is faded by moving the two pictures closer and closer together. Eventually the student will be able to select the correct picture even though both pictures are placed at exactly the same distance from the student. Figure 2.8 shows how a within-stimulus S^D can be highlighted and then faded gradually for an alphabet letter recognition task.

Fading, or errorless learning, is a powerful and proven procedure that often is used in classes for students with severe handicaps. The teacher should construct a reasonable set of fading steps. The student should reach criterion (perfect) performance at each step before being moved on to the faded stimulus configuration. In the utensil example, there were five trials per session, and perfect performance moved the student from session to session. If a session has many trials, e.g., the student can be moved on within a session. For example, a run of five correct trials within a session can move the student to the next faded stimulus within the session. Also, it is possible that learning will not proceed errorlessly. A particular step may not lead to immediate learning. In that case, it is necessary to break the fading step into smaller steps. For example, in Figure 2.7 a teacher could have omitted step 3 and had the student go from step 2 to step 4. If errors had occurred at step 4, the teacher could have made a change by inserting intermediate step 3 in the hope that the student would learn step 3 and then step 4 with few or no errors.

Thinning of Reinforcement. In our descriptions of discrete trial learning we have stated that every correct response is reinforced immediately with an S^{R+}. When a student is learning a new skill, it is important to use this *continuous reinforcement* (CRF) schedule. The CRF schedule enables the student to associate the making of a particular response with the delivery of a specific reinforcer. The absence of the $R \leftarrow S^{R+}$ association would cause a lower rate of response since it would not be clear to the student that responding leads to reinforcement. Therefore, CRF is recommended for new learning or the acquisition phase of learning. Once a student has reached a learning criterion for a new skill the teacher can conclude that the behavior has been acquired. At this point other phases of learning begin that relate to performing the skill under more natural circumstances.

One factor that relates to the natural appearance of the skill is the *schedule of reinforcement*. A CRF schedule is one type of schedule of reinforcement. In notational terms, it indicates that one response leads to reinforcement:

$$1\ R \leftarrow S^{R+}$$

CRF schedules are used in structured learning situations for the acquisition of new and difficult skills. A CRF schedule rarely appears in natural settings such as the home, the workplace, or regular education classes. Rather, natural reinforcement is typically intermittent and unpredictable. For example, parents of children may praise the child for good behavior on the average of once a day or once a week. The day-to-day reinforcement may vary considerably from five praise statements one day to none the next day to two the following day, etc. Just as in the work world an employee may get paid (reinforced) once per week or month and receive praise from a boss once a year, in the real world the schedule of reinforcement is very inconsistent and sparse. For students with severe handicaps the issue becomes how to move them from good, stable behavior in a structured learning situation with CRF to a more natural, varied reinforcement schedule. This issue can become critical when we examine the next and ultimate environments

Figure 2.9 Fixed ratio schedules.

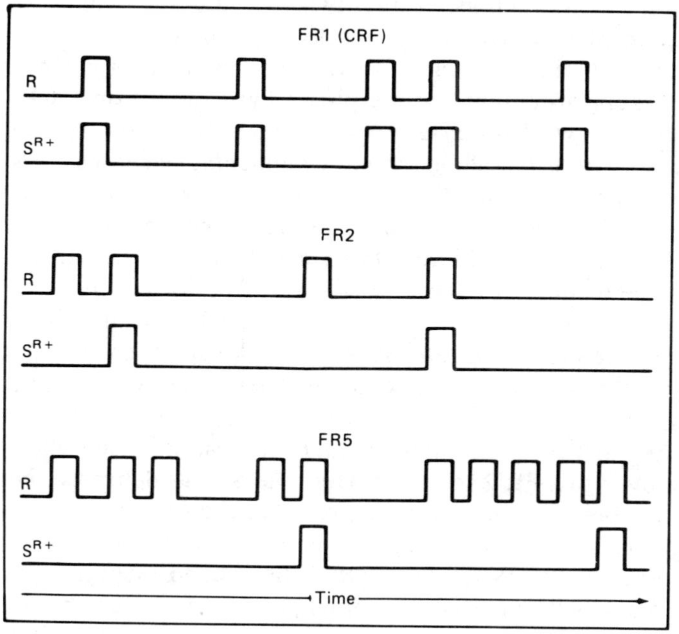

planned for severely handicapped persons, e.g., a group home, a work situation, etc.

The operant procedure that moves a person to a more natural schedule is called reinforcement *thinning*. Basically, the thinning process moves the person from dependence on CRF to perform the response to a schedule in which more than one response is needed to obtain the same reinforcement. There are different ways to accomplish this objective. The most important thinning procedure for students with severe handicaps involves ratio schedules. The simplest ratio schedules are fixed ratios. The *fixed ratio* designates the number of responses that the student must emit to obtain reinforcement. A fixed ratio (FR) 2 schedule states that the student must emit two successive responses to obtain reinforcement. For example, in Figure 2.9 the upward blips indicate the occurrence of a response. Horizontal movement across the page indicates the passage of time. A pattern can be seen in which every "run" of two R's leads to immediate S^{R+}. Other schedules could be FR 4, FR 50, FR 100, etc. One can see that an FR 1 schedule is equivalent to CRF, i.e., 1 R◄— S^{R+}.

Let us look at how FR schedules can be used in the thinning process. Suppose there is a 20-year-old student named Jerry who attends a secondary program for students with severe handicaps. Jerry functions at the severely mentally retarded level. He has no physical disabilities but has been characterized as autistic because of his self-stimulation and assaultive behavior to peers. During vocational training time in the class, Jerry has learned a number of functional skills such as sorting, twisting, and assembling. He learns new tasks quite rapidly. He always works in a one-to-one (staff to student ratio) learning situation. During these sessions, the teacher sits next to him and delivers reinforcement (praise plus a handshake) on a CRF schedule. Although Jerry works well under these conditions, the teacher notices that whenever Jerry is left alone for a few moments, he ceases working. This behavior pattern undoubtedly will be dysfunctional for any future vocational placement, since no work setting can offer constant one-to-one attention. The problem is how to thin out the presence of the teacher as a reinforcing event while maintaining Jerry's high rate of performance.

A thinning program was established by which the teacher would stand 5 feet from Jerry and give the S^D "Sort" (or assemble, take apart, etc.). When Jerry correctly completed one sorting task, the teacher would walk over to him, verbally praise him, and shake his hand. A 30-minute session of about 15 trials was run with this CRF procedure. In the next session on the following day Jerry was moved to a FR 2 schedule. Here the S^D was delivered, but after he completed the behavior, no S^{R+} was given. For the second response no S^D was given (though it could have been) as the teacher remained in a position 5 feet away from Jerry. When he emitted the second response, the teacher approached him with enthusiastic praise and pats. After about 5 seconds of reinforcement, the teacher returned to the distal position and announced the S^D. The 2 $R \longleftarrow S^{R+}$ cycle then was repeated. Since Jerry's rate of about fifteen correct responses was maintained in the session, the teacher decided to move him to a thinner schedule the next day. If his rate of responding had dropped with the new FR 2 schedule, he would not have been advanced to a thinner schedule but would have remained on the same schedule of sessions until he established the higher rate of response, and then he would be moved to a thinner schedule. In session 3 he was under FR 4. Here the S^D was dropped completely so that he would just have materials presented at the beginning of the session and be expected to work. From FR 4 the schedule was changed to FR 6, then FR 10, and finally FR 15. Figure 2.10 shows the development of this thinning procedure. Thus, when Jerry reached FR 15 successfully, he was being reinforced only once during the session. He had changed from being very dependent on adult attention to being relatively independent of it. At FR 15 the teacher started moving about the room to help other students while Jerry was working on his own.

There can be problems with FR schedules. As is the case with FR 1, in which the learner is reinforced after every response, the student may discriminate the schedule rapidly, e.g., may understand that reinforcement occurs after every third correct response. This may lead to incomplete or "sloppy" behavior on the first and second trials and appropriate behavior on the third trial, when reinforcement is anticipated. However, careful programming of responses and reinforcers should overcome this problem.

Figure 2.10 Thinning a fixed ratio schedule.

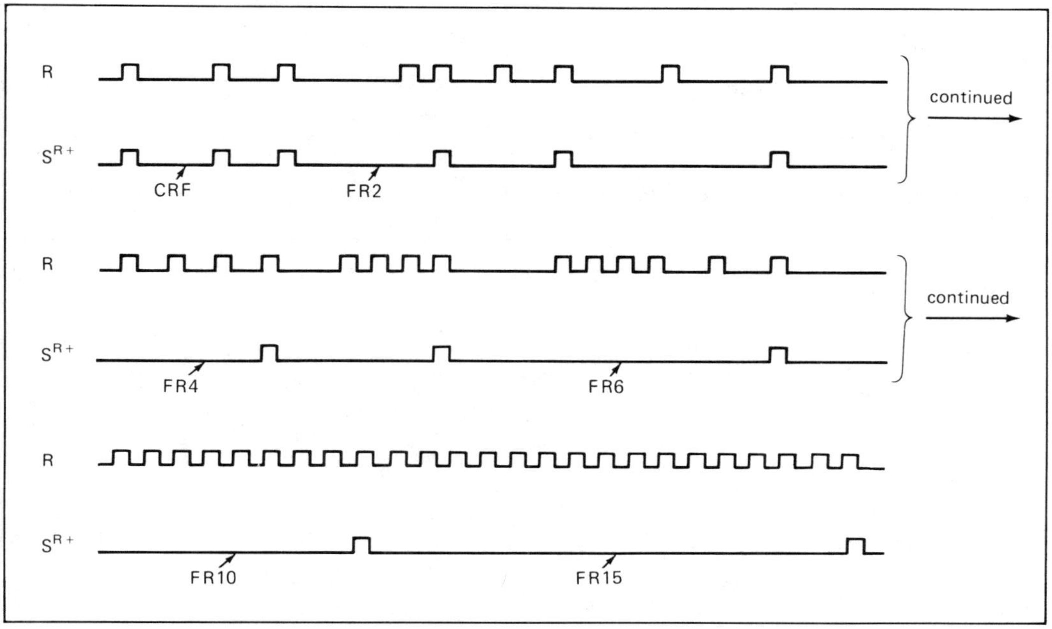

An alternative to FR schedules that is more resistant to failure is *variable schedules*. Variable ratio (VR) schedules work on the same principle as FR schedules except for the number of responses needed for reinforcement changes in each ''run'' or block of responses. An average number of responses is reinforced over a series of blocks of responses. For instance, in Figure 2.11 a VR 3 schedule shows that in the first run two responses led to reinforcement and that in the second run, four responses led to S^{R+}. In the third block, three responses were needed. Over these three runs, the average number of responses leading to S^{R+} was three; thus, the schedule was VR 3. In Figure 2.11 we see that subsequent runs of responses and S^{R+}'s followed this VR 3 pattern. In VR schedules, one can designate the range of responses that may appear in separate runs. For example, in the VR 3 schedule in Figure 2.11, responses ranged between one and five.

VR schedules are appealing because they approximate many natural schedules of reinforcement that also do not follow a fixed pattern. The student never knows when reinforcement will be delivered since there is an expectation of possible reinforcement on every trial. This expectation tends to enhance motivation in a consistent response-to-response fashion. Therefore, when programming for functioning in the natural environment, it is a good idea to have the student eventually operating under a variable schedule. A useful strategy for obtaining this aim proceeds as follows:

Figure 2.11 The schema and schedule for an intermittent reinforcement schedule.

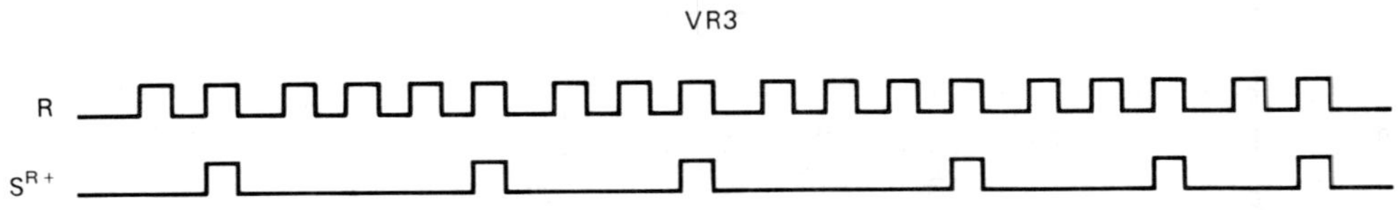

RECORDING SHEET

Trials

	1	2	3	4	5	6	7	8	9	10	11	12	13	14	15	16	17
Performance	+	+	−	+	−	+	+	+	+	−	+	+	−	+	+	+	−
VR3 Schedule	✓	✓	✓	✓	✓	✓	✓	✓	✓	✓	✓	✓	✓				
Reinforcement given on trial:		S^{R+} 2				S^{R+} 8			S^{R+} 11				S^{R+} 16				

1. Start the student on CRF until acquisition or a high rate of responding has been reached.
2. Move the student gradually through intermittent FR schedules, e.g., FR 2→ FR 4→ FR 6→ FR 8. Thin the schedule gradually and do not move the student on to a thinner schedule until stable, correct responding has been established at the richer schedule of reinforcement.
3. Switch the student to a VR schedule. When FR 8 has been established, for example, the student can be switched to VR 8. From there it is possible to thin the schedule further to VR 10, VR 15, VR 20, etc.
4. When the student is responding on an FR or VR schedule of 10 or above in a stable manner, this signifies a point at which the behavior can be maintained successfully by natural reinforcers. The contingent instructional reinforcers can be dropped if natural reinforcers are present.

With very thin reinforcement schedules, the student often develops the habit of responding or develops an intrinsic liking of the task so that rich, artificial reinforcement schedules no longer are needed. At that point, the student may be rewarded only at the end of the session, day, or week. This more flexible way of rewarding student performance corresponds more closely to the ways of reinforcing pupil performance used in regular education.

Moving the student from CRF through the intermittent schedules to no systematic schedule is beneficial not only for the student but also for the teacher. The recordkeeping for intermittent schedules can be tedious. To carry out intermittent schedules, one must plan before the session the pattern in which responses will lead to S^{R+}. In Figure 2.11 the recording sheet shows how trials were blocked beforehand so that the teacher knew when to deliver S^{R+}. Without this preset pattern, it would be confusing for the teacher to run intermittent schedules. Even with the preset pattern, the teacher still must check each trial to see whether a given response should be reinforced. In CRF, though, it is simpler because the teacher knows that all correct responses will be reinforced.

Another type of reinforcement schedule deals with *time intervals* rather than response ratios. The classic operant schedules are fixed interval and variable interval. Their pattern of reinforcement parallels fixed ratio and variable ratio schedules. Interval schedules require the teacher to keep track of the passage of time with a watch. Monitoring time while recording data and managing a group of students with severe handicaps can be demanding and sometimes overwhelming. For this reason, fixed and variable interval schedules rarely are used in classes for students with severe handicaps and will not be described here.

One interval schedule that is manageable and useful with groups of severely handicapped students is a *time-sample* schedule. This schedule permits reinforcement at fixed periods of time if the student emits the correct behavior at that point in time. The time-sample schedule is helpful in teaching a group of students who may have difficulty working on the task to which they have been assigned.

For example, suppose a teacher wishes to increase on-task behavior in a student who spends a great deal of time looking off into space, body rocking, and engaging in other forms of self-stimulation. The teacher defines on-task behavior as including sitting in the chair, looking at the assigned work materials, and manipulating them appropriately. The teacher sets a kitchen timer to a given time interval, e.g., 5 minutes. When the alarm goes off, the teacher looks at the target student to see whether on-task or off-task behavior is present. If the student's behavior fits the on-task definition, the teacher delivers a preferred reinforcer. If the pupil is off-task, the teacher may ignore the pupil and deliver no reinforcer. After each interval, the teacher resets the timer and continues teaching until the timer goes off again.

In Ann's case, reinforcement for head-up behavior can be implemented throughout the day with such a time-sample program. The teacher may set the timer for specified time intervals and reinforce Ann whenever she happens to have her head up when the timer goes off. The advantage to time-sampling schedules is that the teacher need not monitor behavior continuously or even for a set amount of time. The teacher observes the student's behavior only at the designated time. Time-sampling procedures also can be used to improve the behavior of a number of students simultaneously. For example, when the timer goes off, the teacher may reinforce all those students who are on-task and ignore those who are not. If the off-task students are capable of observing how their peers are differentially reinforced, there should be an increase in on-task behavior over time for all the students. Potential disadvantages of the procedure are that if the off-task behaviors are being exhibited at a high rate so that reinforcement is unlikely, intermittent checking on students' performance will not bring them under behavioral control.

Shaping of Responses. To this point we have discussed ways to increase the rate of a desirable behavior through changing various stimulus events, i.e., discriminating, reinforcing, and prompting stimuli. In our discussion and examples, it was assumed that the student already could emit the behavior, e.g., raising the head, but that the behavior had to be brought under better control by a discriminative stimulus and had to be produced at a higher rate. In some cases, though, a student cannot display the behavior in a complete fashion. It then becomes the goal of the teacher to enable the student to demonstrate the complete behavior. The operant techniques of *response shaping* and *response chaining* provide means to construct new behaviors. Let us introduce these procedures with a case example.

A 4-year-old student named Adam has been diagnosed as severely mentally retarded with associated physical disabilities. He observes people around him and recently has developed an interest in watching television, particularly when one of his parents is with him. His physical disability consists of paralysis of both legs. Adam has very limited movement of the hands and arms. His teacher did an assessment of hand and arm movement and found that after the S^D "Touch the (milk, hand, toy)," he would move his hands between 0 and 1 inch. An evaluation by a physical therapist similarly indicated that he has limited range of motion with the hands and arms, but the therapist felt that with repeated practice he could increase his range of motion substantially. The teacher, therapist, and parents worked together to develop a program to maximize the opportunities for Adam to practice functional hand and arm motions. A home program was developed so that Adam ultimately could participate in the leisure act of turning on the television in the home to watch it alone or with his parents.

The program used the procedure of response shaping. Adam sat in a chair next to his mother or father. A remote control switch that would turn on the television was placed 1 inch from Adam's hand on a table. The table contained toys and other objects that he enjoyed looking at or touching. The other materials were cleared away, and Adam's parent would give him the S^D "Turn on the TV." A response-shaping procedure was implemented in which Adam would be reinforced with verbal praise and the T.V. going on if he moved his hand 1 inch and placed it on the switch. When Adam failed to move his hand 1 inch within a 10-second latency, his mother would say,

Figure 2.12 A changing criterion program to shape hand movements.

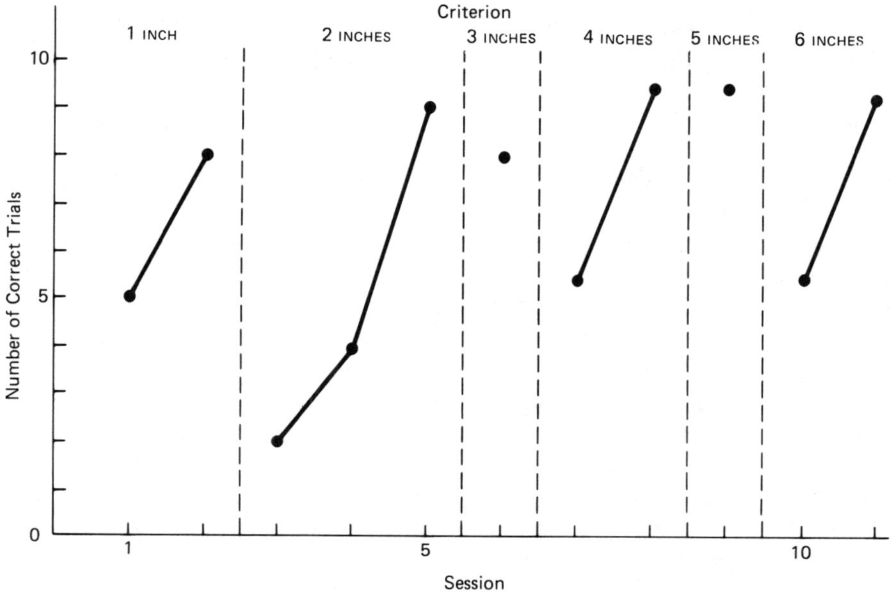

"No, you didn't get the TV on," and end the trial. Since the 1-inch hand movement was a behavior Adam emitted on a fairly consistent basis, a prompting procedure was not used. A discrete-trial format was used with a 10-second ITI, the S^{R+} of watching TV for 30 seconds, and his parent recording trial-by-trial (pass or fail) data for the 10 trials. A *changing criterion* was set for the response shaping so that whenever Adam produced five consecutive correct trials, the distance he was required to move his hand for the S^{R+} was increased by 1 inch.

Figure 2.12 shows Adam's progress. In the first session, he made five correct responses, but not in a consecutive fashion. In the second session, he made eight correct responses and had a five-correct trial run, and so the criterion was increased to 2 inches. With this setting his hand was placed 2 inches from the switch. Adam did not reach this criterion the next three sessions. Once the 2-inch criterion was reached, he rapidly progressed through the other criteria so that he reached the terminal objective 6-inch criterion within eleven sessions. When this occurred, Adam was capable of moving his hand 6 inches in a consistent fashion in order to turn on the television. At that point the training sessions were terminated, but his parents made sure that he practiced the new skill a couple of times a day. The practice was done more naturally so that no S^D was given, and when Adam touched the switch, the television would stay on indefinitely. Fortunately, Adam frequently hit the switch and appeared to enjoy both watching television and having control over this piece of equipment.

This example shows how shaping can change an incomplete behavior into a correct response. Initially, a part of a complete behavior was reinforced differentially. Over trials, the criterion for reinforcement was changed gradually so that the response successively approximated the terminal behavior. Shaping can be used for a variety of behaviors, such as reaching and pedalling.

Chaining and Task Analysis. A second type of procedure called *chaining* can be used to establish responses. Chaining attempts to sequence together a number of responses so that they are displayed in an ordered sequence. The aim of chaining is not to teach a new behavior, as is the case in shaping, but rather to get the student to emit a sequence of familiar behaviors in a coordinated fashion. The process of breaking a task into its component parts or a series of responses for training is called *task analysis*. Task analysis has been applied in a multitude of areas for teaching skills to students with severe handicaps, e.g., grooming or vocational. Task analysis, in a sense, is used in response shaping. In shaping, instead of breaking a task into separate responses, one response is broken into its separate components. In Adam's example, this involved the number of inches required for the hand movement. Task analysis usually is associated with chaining, since a number of independent responses must be linked together. Let us look at how task analysis and chaining can be used to teach a response sequence by returning to the example of Adam.

Three months have passed since the television switch training was completed. Adam has been successful in turning on the television independently. He is moving his hand easily and purposefully to turn the switch a couple of times a day. His parents, teacher, and therapist are happy with his progress but have agreed that Adam can be advanced further to extend his motor and leisure skills in a more functional direction; he can be taught to turn on the television from more than just a sitting position. Since Adam can ambulate in his wheelchair throughout the house, a response chain could be taught by which Adam would be given the S^D "Turn on the TV" when he was in his wheelchair at some place in the house. The chain would consist of two responses. R_1 would require Adam to ambulate from wherever he was in the house to the table where the switch is located. R_2 would have Adam reach and turn on the switch from his walker. Thus, two responses that Adam could do independently were being linked together in a coordinated chain. His parents conducted daily sessions consisting of five trials of practice. Progress was swift and Adam reached his instructional objective of completing five out of five correct trials for two consecutive sessions. After reaching criterion, he was encouraged to practice the two-step chain on his own in order to maintain this skill.

The previous example of response chaining represents the simplest type of chain since there are only two responses. Most chains consist of many more responses, e.g., R_1——R_2——R_3——R_4——R_5. In performing a task analysis of a skill, there is no fixed number of responses into which the skill may be broken. A rule of thumb is that the more limited the cognitive abilities of the student and the more challenging the task, the more responses the skill should be broken into. For example, the task of digging dirt with a shovel (as part of gardening skills) may be taught in three steps to a nonhandicapped student: Grasp shovel, dig shovel into earth, throw dirt onto a designated pile. For a student with learning problems, the task may have to be broken into many more steps: Look at shovel, touch handle, grasp handle, touch bar, grasp bar, move shovel toward earth, dig into earth, etc.

The importance of task analysis for students with severe handicaps is that such a careful breakdown of the skill often is needed for any substantive learning to take place. In contrast, nonhandicapped students often can learn skills in a few trials without a task analysis or a careful presentation of S^D's and S^{R+}'s. Therefore, natural and often sloppy instruction will result in task acquisition by nonhandicapped students. For example, nonhandicapped children usually learn how to brush their teeth and many other personal management skills merely through observing someone else a few times and then practicing. Such natural ways of learning are usually insufficient for students with severe handicaps. Unless the various components of systematic instruction such as task analysis are used, one can expect little or no learning of valued skills.

There are two major ways to teach response chains. *Serial chaining* involves the cumulative addition of responses to a chain over successive training trials. As Figure 2.13 shows, R_1 first is taught in isolation. Then R_2 is chained to R_1 so that the student emits them in a sequence. After R_1 and R_2 are emitted sequentially, a third response, R_3, is added to the chain so that R_1——R_2——R_3 are established. Figure 2.13 gives an example of the construction of a bolt-washer-nut chain through the serial method. The method of *concurrent chaining* teaches the total task from the first trial on. Figure 2.13 also shows how the same bolt-washer-nut task was taught concurrently; i.e., all trials required the student to emit R_1——R_2——R_3. Let us examine in more detail how each of these procedures is implemented.

To teach the bolt-washer-nut task through serial chaining, the student first receives a number of trials in which R_1—placing the bolt through the holes of two metal pieces—is practiced until the criterion of five successive correct trials is reached. An S^D is given at the beginning of each trial, e.g., "Assemble." When the trial is completed, an S^{R+} is given for correct responses. One or many prompts are given for error responses. Performance is recorded as plus or minus on each trial. At the next step of learning the same S^D is delivered, and the student is expected to emit R_1——R_2. The student must display both R_1 and R_2 in sequence for a plus to be recorded and an S^{R+} to be given. Errors on either response could be prompted. When criterion is reached on step 2 (R_1——R_2), trials begin on step 3 (R_1——R_2——R_3). The same S^D, prompting, recording, and S^{R+} procedures are used. For a trial to be scored as a plus, all three responses must be produced cor-

Figure 2.13 Constructing serial and concurrent chains.

Serial Chain		
	Description	Schema
Step 1	Place bolt through hole in metal piece (behavior A). (Run trials to criterion; go to step 2.)	A
Step 2	Place bolt through hole in metal piece (A), then place washer around bolt (B). (Run trials to criterion; go to step 3.)	A-B
Step 3	Place nut through hole (A), place washer around nut (B), then screw nut around bolt until secure against washer (C). (Run trials to criterion.)	A-B-C
	Concurrent Chain	Schema
Step 1	Place bolt through hole (A), place washer around nut (B), screw nut around bolt (C). (Run trials to criterion.)	A-B-C

Figure 2.14 A recording sheet for a concurrent chain.

Sessions and Trials												
Responses	11/1			11/2			11/3			11/4		
	1	2	3	1	2	3	1	2	3	1	2	3
A. Bolt	+	−	+	−	+	−	+	−	+	+	+	+
B Washer	−	+	−	−	−	−	+	−	−	−	−	−
C. Nut	+	−	+	+	−	−	+	+	−	+	+	+
Total	5			2			5			6		

rectly. One or more response errors will lead to scoring the whole trial with no S^{R+} given. The serial procedure progresses in this fashion by adding a response to the chain until the complete chain has been mastered.

The concurrent procedure is more straightforward in that from the first trial of the first session the student is expected to perform the complete chain, e.g., R_1——R_2——R_3. Thus, an S^D "Assemble" is given at the beginning of each trial. R_1 (bolt), R_2 (washer), and R_3 (nut) are performed in sequence. Errors on each response are prompted. A data sheet (see Figure 2.14) records a plus or minus for each response in each trial. Trials continue until a terminal criterion is reached, e.g., five consecutive trials with no response errors.

Serial and concurrent procedures are effective ways to teach students with severe handicaps a variety of skills. Each has advantages and disadvantages. A concurrent chain should be used if the teacher expects the student to learn the task in a relatively rapid manner. Conceivably, the student could emit perfect performance on one of the first trials of the step. Thus, if fairly rapid learning is expected, the concurrent method permits the student to move along at a more rapid pace without having to do the extra trials on intermediate steps. In contrast, the serial method requires that the student go through each of the chaining steps. For example, in a four behavior chain the student would have to do at least four trials (at least one trial per step). More likely, it would take a considerable number of trials for the student to reach criterion on each step of the task analysis.

Being able to predict rapid or slow learning with severely handicapped students is not easy. The teacher should consider the student's cognitive level, performance on past tasks, and familiarity with the responses in the chain. For example, if the student previously has spent time learning how to manipulate nuts, washers, and bolts (or turning on the television switch and ambulating in a wheelchair), the teacher can predict that it will be fairly easy to link the responses together through the concurrent method. If each response is new and unfamiliar to the student, the concurrent method may produce a stimulus overload by requiring the student to learn many new things at once. In this case the serial method may be preferred because it allows the student to learn each new response separately while integrating the response (e.g., R_3) with previously learned responses (R_1 and R_2).

There is another way to use the concurrent method with relatively difficult or unfamiliar responses. This procedure requires that the concurrent method be implemented for a number of trials. After the trials have been run, the teacher reviews whether certain responses in the chain are leading to particular difficulty in learning. For example, Figure 2.14 shows that R_1 and R_3 were learned quite rapidly but that R_2 was producing many errors. Through the *isolation training* method (compare Bellamy, Horner, and Inman, 1979), R_2 can be taught separately from the rest of the chain in a series of massed trials. That is, the teacher runs a number of trials in which the student only has to place the washer around the bolt. Many trials are run until criterion (e.g., five consecutive correct responses) is reached on R_2 alone. At this point the concurrent training is resumed with the expectation that the student now will have little trouble with R_2 and can learn the whole chain in a rapid fashion.

When learning single responses, discrete-trial learning of the S^D and S^{R+} events are defined and delivered easily. In multiple-response chains, the identification of S^D and S^{R+} events is more complex and may affect the learning process. For instance, in our bolt-washer-nut example, an S^D is given at the beginning of the chain and an S^{R+} may be given at the end of the chain (see Figure 2.15*a*). From an operant perspective, though, there must be discriminative stimulus events intervening before each response in

Figure 2.15 Multiple response chains.

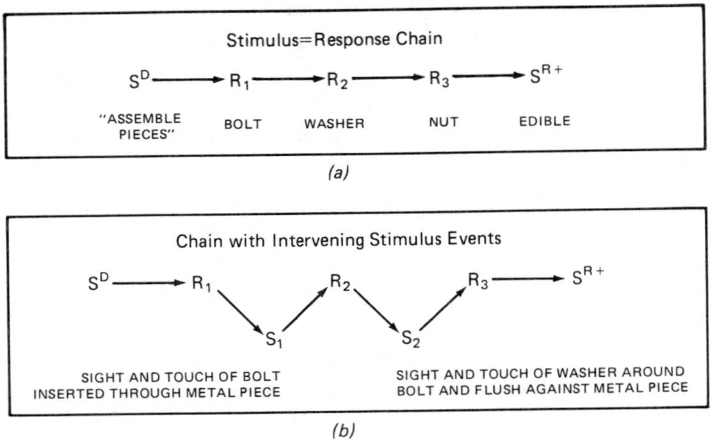

the chain (see Figure 2.15*b*). However, the teacher does not deliver these intervening S^D's. They are the changing configurations of materials that the student must perceive after each response in the chain is completed (see Figure 2.15*b*). Thus, S_1 is the configuration of the materials after the bolt is placed through the two metal pieces. This configuration S_1 serves as an S^D for the next response R_2 to occur. In a long chain, there are many intervening S——R associations that the student must make. Concurrent chaining places many demands on students because they must learn all the S——R connections simultaneously on each trial. In contrast, the serial method has the advantage of introducing only one new S——R connection at a time, and this should simplify learning. The isolation method attempts to remedy these multiple processing problems of concurrent chaining by taking the S——R connection with which the student is having difficulty and teaching it as a single S——R association.

In serial chaining, a series of responses are reinforced differentially as a single response unit; that is, only when the student performs all the responses in the chain correctly is reinforcement delivered. Differential reinforcement is all or none for the whole chain, with errors likely to appear on the most recently learned response in the chain. These properties of serial chaining make it easier for the student to learn which behaviors lead or do not lead to positive reinforcement.

Concurrent chaining is more complex. On a given trial a student may get pluses on R_1 and R_3 but not on R_2. Should reinforcement be given on this trial? A criterion could be imposed that only chains with all correct R's will be reinforced. This approach applies to the few trials being reinforced in early learning since there is bound to be at least one error on most trials. The absence of reinforcement on trials removes a major motivator for the student to learn. Another tactic is to reinforce every trial noncontingently, regardless of the number of error responses emitted. This approach also suffers from not following the principles of differential reinforcement; i.e., the student is rewarded irrespective of performance. A third tactic is to give S^{R+} after all or some R's in the chain. If S^{R+} is given by the teacher after every R, it may interfere with the learning of intervening S^D——R associations. The selective use of S^{R+} for high-error R's is a more appealing strategy. If the data show that R_1 has reached criterion, S^{R+} is given contingently only for R_2 and R_3. When R_3 reaches criterion, S^{R+} is given only for R_2. Reinforcement problems with concurrent chains are not immediately resolvable. When using concurrent chains, the teacher should do the following:

1. Select the concurrent approach only when the student is expected to learn the chain rapidly (if not, use a serial approach).
2. If there are many errors on a particular response, train that response in isolation through massed-trial instruction. During this phase, continue the concurrent chain instruction, including whatever prompts are needed on that particular response. When the response has been learned in isolation, reintroduce performance expectations within the concurrent chain for further training.
3. If the isolation method does not succeed, switch to a serial method of training.

Related Topics in Instructional Design

We have described the basic methods of instructional design for students with severe handicaps. A number of additional procedures are related to antecedent, response, and consequent events; a teacher should be familiar with these procedures and capable of using them.

Attending and Learning

One of the defining characteristics of students with severe handicaps is that they do not properly perceive the most noticeable stimuli in the environment. Loud sounds, bright visual displays, and extreme temperatures may induce no observable reactions from such students. These inconsistent attending behaviors may cause problems during instructional programming. According to various explanations of how humans learn, an initial attending period is essential so that a person can scan the information present and focus on the relevant stimulus. After the initial attending and stimulus discrimination phases, the person makes a decision concerning the action to be taken (Zeaman and House, 1963). Correct actions or responses are based on the success of the attending phase in terms of providing all of the relevant information, and incomplete attending will lead to response errors. Let us relate this issue to teaching students with severe handicaps by presenting an example.

Suppose a student is being trained to use a communication device. The student has little or no success in vocal or sign communication. Therefore, a card communication system has been established in which the student carries around a number of laminated picture cards on a key chain that represent different functional actions and objects. The student is just beginning to learn the first three cards: drink (a picture of a glass of milk), ball, and eat (a picture of a sandwich). These are all favored activities of the student. Eventually the student should be able to carry the cards and point to them in order to indicate what she would like to do, e.g., go to the bathroom or play with a friend. Initially the student is given a three-choice discrimination task in which the teacher gives the S^D "Point to ——— (drink, ball, or eat)," and the student must correctly identify (through pointing within a 5-second latency) the correct card. Correct responses lead to the S^{R+} of having 10 seconds of drinking, ball playing, or eating. The session consists of 20 repeated trials.

During the first three sessions the student performs at a chance level. The chance level will be 33 percent correct since guessing would give a correct answer one out of three times. The teacher notices that after the S^D is presented, the student does not seem to scan the three cards visually. Instead, the student immediately points to one card or looks around the room for a few seconds and then points to another card without ever scanning all the cards.

To change this behavior pattern and to improve discrimination performance, a *forced attending* procedure is introduced. The procedure involves providing a pre-S^D stimulus before giving the S^D "Point to." The initial stimulus consists of the teacher saying, "Look at the cards," and manually guiding the student's head to look at each card for a second. Immediately after the student has scanned the three cards, the teacher presents the S^D. In this case the procedure worked because the student started to make correct selections of the cards. As performance improves, the teacher fades out the manual guidance so that the student scans the cards on her own after hearing the command "Look at the cards." With further progress the pre-S^D command is dropped completely and the student is just given the "Point to" S^D.

At this time the student visually scans the cards after the S^D and before she points. Thus, the forced scanning procedure is another technique for transferring stimulus control to an S^D. It should be used when there are attending problems that can be remediated by providing a pre-S^D verbal and manual stimulus.

Response Adaptations

Severely handicapped learners may not be able to perform all behaviors independently even though they may be able to display most of the responses in a behavior chain. Because of their physical limitations (e.g., sensory and motor impairments), they also may require the substitution of an alternative response form or the use of a prosthetic device for a more "normalized" behavior that the teacher may teach a nonhandicapped child. *Partial participation* (Baumgart, Brown, Pumpian, Nisbet, Ford, Sweet, Ranieri, Hansen, and Schroeder, 1980) refers to a situation in which the handicapped learner may perform some of the steps in a certain activity, while someone else performs those steps which are temporarily too difficult or which the learner may never be able to master. *Alternative response forms* imply that the handicapped learner does perform the step independently but uses another strategy or an extra tool to accomplish the behavior.

Whenever possible, such adaptations should be modified or even abandoned when use of a more normalized response form is possible at a later time. Thus, increased control over the movements associated with a particular task may lead to decreased dependence on a prosthetic device such as a special bowl or spoon for eating. As the learner matures and acquires new skills over a period of months and years, a particular step that was initially too difficult may later become a behavior the student can learn. Although the adaptations discussed in this section are essential to initial success with a new skill, they should be re-evaluated continuously to determine whether the learner's need for such adaptations and extra help may no longer be necessary.

Prosthetic Devices. A variety of prosthetic devices have been designed to allow students with severe handicapping conditions to perform behaviors they would not be able to accomplish otherwise. These prosthetic devices can be regarded as tools to extend the learner's abilities and permit access to activities and environments in the same way that nonhandicapped persons depend on tools such as pencil and paper to aid memory, ladders to reach objects on a shelf or in a tree, or automobiles to cover long distances. Examples of prosthetic devices for severly handicapped learners include

1. A specially curved spoon for self-feeding (needed for a learner with limited motor coordination)
2. A cup with a semicircle cut out of one side (needed for drinking by a student who is initially learning to drink from a cup and who "panics" when vision is blocked)
3. A wheelchair or walker (needed by students whose motor impairments prevent them from ambulating without support)
4. A picture-communication board (needed by a severely handicapped learner who is profoundly deaf or has severe cerebral palsy in which there is no coordination of the motor movements associated with speech)
5. A wedge, gurney, tilt table, or prone stander (needed by students who lack sufficient strength and muscle tone to support themselves independently in a sitting or standing position or a partially upright position while engaging in other activities)

These are only a few examples of prosthetic devices that may be used by teachers working with severely handicapped learners. Each device or tool modifies the response expected of the student to some extent but allows for the expression of some form of the behavior that is needed to perform a task or function. Prosthetic devices imply that the student is dependent on the tool itself, but when there is access to that tool, the person is independent and can perform the skill.

The creative teacher not only will utilize commercially available prosthetic devices but also will be able to devise "homemade" prosthetics that permit students to engage in activities that normally would be inaccessible. Again, the use of a prosthetic device should not be viewed as a limitation on the handicapped person's functioning but rather as the use of an apparatus that can open new vistas for participating in the world at large.

Partial Participation. In some situations a severely handicapped learner may be able to perform many responses in an activity but not the complete response chain. For example, the student may be able to complete all the various steps associated with playing cards but he cannot keep score. Rather than waiting until the score can be kept (which may in fact never happen), the student can be taught the steps of playing cards and allow another person to keep score. Thus, the student can participate at least partially in playing cards. In some situations the severely handicapped learner may lack the skills or capabilities to perform most of the steps in a behavior chain but can do one or two behaviors in the sequence. Again, someone else, perhaps a sibling or a nonhandicapped peer, can provide the remaining steps of the activity.

Partial participation is no substitute for independence, of course, since the learner is unable to conduct the activity at all unless the other person also is present to assist with the missing steps. However, partial participation can become a strategy for arranging interactions between the handicapped individual and nonhandicapped persons, such as a leisure-time activity in which the nonhandicapped person plays with the handicapped individual by means of "turn taking." The nonhandicapped person can perform the difficult steps while the severely handicapped person can perform up to his or her capability.

Partial participation is not very different from the practices used by parents with very young children. For example, a child may know how to put on underwear, shirt, and pants in the morning when getting dressed for school, but the parent will finish up the dressing task by zipping the pants and buttoning the shirt. This analogy to the learning process for nonhandicapped children should remind teachers that although partial participation may be needed today to engage in an activity, the child eventually may develop to a point of full participation. Thus, whenever partial participation is used in a behavior chain, the teacher and care givers should reevaluate the

Figure 2.16 Forward and backward chains.

	Description
R_1	Grasp left side of coat.
R_2	Pull coat over left shoulder.
R_3	Pull coat off left arm.
R_4	Pull coat around back and right shoulder.
R_5	Pull coat off right arm.
	Forward
Step 1	R_1
Step 2	R_1—R_2
Step 3	R_1—R_2—R_3
Step 4	R_1—R_2—R_3—R_4
Step 5	R_1—R_2—R_3—R_4—R_5
	Backward
Step 1	R_5
Step 2	R_4—R_5
Step 3	R_3—R_4—R_5
Step 4	R_2—R_3—R_4—R_5
Step 5	R_1—R_2—R_3—R_4—R_5
	Prompted Backward Serial Chain
Step 1	Prompt: R_1—R_2—R_3—R_4 || Do—R_5
Step 2	Prompt: R_1—R_2—R_3 || Do—R_4—R_5
Step 3	Prompt: R_1—R_2 || Do—R_3—R_4—R_5
Step 4	Prompt: R_1 || Do—R_2—R_3—R_4—R_5
Step 5	DO: R_1—R_2—R_3—R_4—R_5

situation periodically to see whether the student now can learn a step that was too difficult at an earlier time.

Forward and Backward Chaining

In regard to teaching a response chain with the serial method, there are two ways the chain can be constructed. *Forward* serial chaining recommends that the first response in the chain is taught first, i.e., R_1 followed by R_1——R_2 being taught, then R_1——R_2——R_3, etc. Figure 2.16 shows an example of a "taking off coat" skill taught by forward chaining. The first step involves teaching grasping one side of the coat, R_1. The next step entails grasping the coat, R_1, and removing it from one shoulder, R_2. As the student reaches criterion on each of the successive steps, the chain is lengthened until the student masters the complete chain.

In *backward* serial chaining, the first step of instruction begins with training on the last step in the chain, e.g., R_5. As the student reaches criterion on the last response, the next step involves learning the next to last response and the last response, e.g., R_4——R_5. With subsequent learning, more responses are added to the chain until the complete chain is learned. Figure 2.16 shows a backward chaining scheme for the same "taking off coat" skill. This time the last response of pulling jacket over the right arm is taught first, and the teacher performs all the steps to that point for the student. The rest of the steps in this sequence are self-evident.

Earlier in this chapter we outlined procedures for concurrent chaining (sometimes called *total task* or total cycle instruction) in which all steps in the task analysis are taught concurrently, with the teacher providing only the necessary assistance on each step based on the student's performance during each trial. Concurrent chaining has the advantage of allowing the student to acquire whatever steps can be learned initially rather than requiring learning the steps in the chain in a predetermined order. In either serial chaining method the student must reach criterion performance on a particular step simply because it is the first, second, etc. (forward chaining), or last, second to last, etc. (backward chaining), step in the behavior chain. In contrast, concurrent chaining, or total task instruction, continues to provide help on "difficult" steps for a maximum amount of time (from the beginning of instruction until the student finally acquires all the steps) and also removes help on "easy" steps as soon as the student can demonstrate that behavior.

There is no simple criterion for whether the teacher should use total task or forward or backward chaining. For some tasks one type of chaining procedure will seem more appropriate than another, just as one type will be related to more success than another with particular students. We have pointed out the advantage of total task instruction, which is that the student can progress rapidly through easier tasks. The disadvantage of the total task approach is that on difficult tasks there is a high proportion of errors. Backward chaining has one main advantage over the other approaches. From the first trial of the first session, the student always obtains "closure," or completion of the task. In most cases, this also involves experiencing S^{R+} at the end of the chain, immediately after the student has performed one or more steps. This S^{R+} is most likely to be a powerful, functional, and naturally occurring reinforcing event. In the last example, the student always produces the functional effect of "getting the jacket off" with backward chaining. This closure effect may be more satisfying to the student and produce more rapid learning. Furthermore, as the student moves through the task, it becomes increasingly easier because there is a performance of steps that have been mastered in earlier instruction.

Forward chaining, in contrast, does not allow the student to get a sense of completion of the task, e.g., getting the jacket off, until the last step in the chaining process, when all the steps have been performed. For this reason backward chaining probably is used most often with students with severe handicaps. Yet on certain types of activities—particularly where natural reinforcers are available throughout the behavior chain, e.g., with many leisure activities—this very argument supports the use of the total task approach, in which the student can experience reinforcement at various points in the chain naturally rather than simply at the end of the task.

There is another procedure that appears to combine aspects of serial and concurrent chaining. In the *prompted serial* method the teacher physically prompts the student through the untaught responses of a chain and requires the student to emit the response under instruction. Figure 2.16 shows a backward prompted serial chain. At step 3, for example, the teacher physically prompts the student through the first two responses in the chain, and the student then must perform the last three responses. A forward prompted serial chain operates in the opposite manner. The student emits the first set of responses independently and is prompted through the last set.

It is not known whether prompted serial chains are superior or inferior to unprompted serial chains. Prompted serial chains do permit the student to experience the complete response chain on every trial. Even though the student is guided through some of the responses, he or she may learn the chain faster than would be the case if responses were never practiced (as in the unprompted method). Yet the prompted serial method approximates concurrent chains because the student emits responses in the chain on every trial. For this reason, the prompted approach may cause a stimulus overload just as it was hypothesized that concurrent chains do. Thus, it may be wise to avoid prompted serial chains with skills that are expected to give a particular student considerable difficulty.

Token Economies

An important reinforcement procedure that can be used with students with severe handicaps is a *token economy*. This is a reinforcement system that uses a material item to motivate behavior that originally had no reward or reinforcement value. The technical term that defines a token economy is *secondary reinforcement*. A secondary reinforcer gains motivational value through repeated conditioning trials. A *primary* reinforcer is intrinsically motivating to the individual; most secondary reinforcers are assumed to become motivating because they are associated with primary reinforcers. Two examples of primary reinforcers are food and sexual stimulation. An individual does not have to be taught to work for primary reinforcers but learns to value and work for secondary reinforcers.

Money is a classic example of a secondary reinforcer. At some point in a person's life, a coin or paper currency has no meaning or motivational value. Through a number of learning trials, the money becomes paired with a primary, backup reinforcer so that the person can exchange money for the primary reinforcer. After a number of trials, the money obtains secondary reinforcing value; i.e., the person will work or produce operant responses to obtain money for its own sake. In the case of money, an individual has thousands of trials in which the secondary reinforcement value of money is established through exchanging it for a variety of goods and services. Since a secondary reinforcer has no intrinsic or primary value, there always exists the possibility that it will lose its reinforcing value when it no longer can be exchanged for primary reinforcers. A notable example would be Confederate currency at the time of the demise of the southern Confederacy after the Civil War.

Secondary reinforcement and token economies have been used extensively by applied behavior analysts in schools and residential programs. The system works the following way. A person may gain points or tokens (small chips or bogus coins that have no intrinsic value) for certain good behaviors, e.g., grooming or schoolwork. The person also may lose points or tokens for emitting certain negative behaviors, e.g., hitting or stealing. At certain times, such as the end of the day or the end of the week, the person may exchange tokens for backup reinforcers such as candy, toys, or movie privileges.

Careful records must be kept of the specified good and bad behaviors. An ample supply of backup reinforcers valued by the individual also must be present in order to motivate the person to continue to emit good behaviors and avoid displaying bad behaviors. Often, token economies are applied for an entire group of students so that the backup reinforcers must be varied to allow for individual preferences. An effective token economy should not allow students to go into debt by continually losing more tokens than they earn. If this happens, the token economy system becomes punishing, with the student ceasing efforts to earn more tokens. Since the effectiveness of the system depends on eventual access to primary reinforcers, the students can be expected to emit good behaviors only so long as they eventually result in obtaining the backup reinforcers.

Token economies have been used infrequently for students with severe handicaps. Since a token or secondary reinforcer is a symbol that stands in the place of a primary event and since severely disabled persons may have limited ability to associate symbols with actual events, it has been inferred that they are not capable of working within token economy systems. In some cases this belief is warranted, but often the ability of severely disabled persons to work for secondary reinforcers has been underestimated. Almost every student with severe handicaps should be evaluated with respect to the ability to work for tokens. Secondary reinforcers have the motivational advantage of avoiding satiation; that is, a student is not likely to be satiated on earning tokens as quickly as is the case with receiving a primary reinforcer such as food. Also, when real or play money is used as a secondary reinforcer, the student can learn money identification and numerical skills.

There is a straightforward way to evaluate a student's ability to work for tokens. First, the teacher should select a task that the student can perform easily (e.g., grasping a shoe or hat). The teacher then conducts series of massed-trial sessions in which the student must identify these or other familiar objects. After every correct trial, the student is reinforced in the following manner:

1. For a number of trials, the student is handed a token, e.g., a poker chip, immediately after the correct response. The student then is made to give the poker chip right back to the teacher, who in turn immediately gives the student a primary reinforcer, e.g., a raisin.
2. If the student continues to perform at a high and accurate rate, a thinning procedure is put into effect. Here the student is given the token immediately after a correct response. On the first correct response the student keeps the token, and after an ITI the teacher goes on to present the S^D for the next trial. Thus, no primary reinforcer is given. On the second correct trial, the token is given immediately, the student then gives the teacher both tokens, and the teacher immediately gives the student a raisin. Thus, the schedule of reinforcement has changed from CRF to FR 2.
3. With continued high rate and correct responding, the schedule is thinned gradually until the student is reinforced only at the end of the session. The student hands in all the accumulated tokens at the end of the session to receive primary reinforcement. A card with circles drawn to the size of tokens may be used. The student can place the tokens over the circles until a given number of circles on the card are filled up. This shows the student that reinforcement has been earned.

Token economies have numerous advantages, and teachers should be encouraged to put their students on token economies whenever possible. One advantage is that the token system stimulates the student intellectually to work within a symbolic framework. Some students progress to counting the number of tokens they have accumulated, and this enhances their mathematical skills. A second advantage is that the student is weaned from artificial primary reinforcers such as food. Tokens are an artificial event, but they are more "normalized" in the sense that they are used widely in society by all people in various situations.

The student who is motivated by a token economy has moved along a continuum of reinforcers in which more natural ones can be used. For example, poker chips can be replaced by real money so that the student gets practice with currency and learns to associate it with natural backup reinforcers. In addition, the teacher can decrease the use of artificial backup reinforcers such as edibles and increase the use of more age-appropriate primary reinforcers such as listening to records or playing a video game. A reinforcement area of the classroom can be established so that when students complete their work by earning a sufficient number of tokens, they may go to the reinforcement area to play with toys or records or sit quietly. Token economies thus can promote more independent functioning by having students monitor their own progress on the token card and move themselves to the reinforcement area. A third advantage is that tokens are easier for the teacher to manage. Foods and other idiosyncratic reinforcers do not have to be handled continuously if a token economy is in effect. Token chips are easy to store, are portable (i.e., can be taken along on instructional sessions conducted in the community), and can be delivered to students in a simple fashion. Thus, a common reinforcement medium exists across students that can be used by different staff members in different settings. This ease of handling and portability is bound to promote more consistency in programming across staff and is likely to encourage better generalization of behaviors by students across persons and settings.

Designing Instructional Programs

There is a great deal of technical information with which a teacher of students with severe handicaps must be familiar. The operant stimulus-response framework and its related techniques provide a powerful set of methods for designing instructional programs, yet familiarity with these operant procedures alone will not ensure effective programs. There is a big step between the knowledge of and the application of a set of principles. It is therefore important to practice these instructional procedures with students with severe handicaps. Just reading and knowing these operant procedures does not guarantee that students will learn in a rapid and efficient manner.

Although operant techniques are grounded in scientific research, there is an intuitive aspect to designing effective instructional programs. Teaching is similar to other professions in the sense that only through years of experience does one gain insights into which approach will work and which will not. For any single instructional objective there may be at least five or ten different possible programs. One or two of those programs may be equally effective in reaching the objective; many of the other programs, though, would produce little or no learning in the student. Through experience as a program designer, you will be able to predict which program will be most successful. It also will be most helpful if you share your experiences—and your instructional "problems"—with other members of the educational team.

The importance of experience in designing programs should not prevent you from writing effective programs now. Just as the systematic operant approach to teaching emphasizes repeated practice by your students, you will benefit by writing and implementing as many programs as possible. There are certain things you can do to acquire the intuitive aspects of programming as well as the necessary technical information.

First, become as familiar as possible with your students. Learn their idiosyncracies, preferences, and behavior patterns. No matter how limited in functioning your students may be, never assume that they do not have idiosyncratic, personal behaviors and preferences. Part of this information will be forthcoming from your assessment of the student; much will be derived from the informal observations you make from being around the student on a day-to-day basis. Watch the students during noninstructional, or "down," time. Note their reactions to different people, activities, and situations. Observe their response to different types of S^D's, prompts, reinforcers, and changes in routines and programs. All this information can give you clues as to which types of instructional programs will work best.

Talk to other people who have significant contact with the student. Often they have tried a procedure that they can recommend or make sure you avoid. Such advice will save much time that you might have spent evaluating different programs. Accurate recommendations also may help the student avoid working on programs that were unsuccessful and frustrating and may direct the student to activities that are fun and induce learning. When talking to other people such as parents or teachers, describe the program you plan to use. The other person may see flaws in the program that are not apparent to you, or the other person may support your ideas and give you needed assurance when you begin a program. Chapters 8 and 9 provide more specific suggestions regarding team coordination and interactions with caregivers that can be critical to the success of your programs.

Whenever you are unsure about a program you intend to implement with a particular student, it is helpful to discuss your concerns with a person whose opinion you respect. This may be a master teacher, a former professor, or a school administrator. Because you will be using a data-based model, the success of the program ultimately will be validated by the student's performance.

In addition to using operant techniques and collected data, be sure to use the resources that are around you. Be a perceptive observer of your students. Be familiar with the tasks and situations in which instruction takes place. Talk to others who can assist you in instructional design. Designing effective instructional programs is not simply a matter of assembling the ingredients in a menu. There is much experimentation and problem solving involved in the process.

Designing an instructional program is not the end of the process. It is then necessary to translate that idea into written form. Accurate documentation of a program allows you and other staff members to carry out the program in a reliable fashion. Documenting programs also allows you and your colleagues to build a "library" of successful programs. In this way, it will not be necessary to reinvent the wheel or write a new program for every instructional objective.

The essential characteristics of a program document are that it is comprehensive and clear. It should include all the information needed for another person to follow the description and implement the program. Another teacher, e.g., a substitute teacher, who is unfamiliar with the student or the task should be able to read the document and implement the program successfully. Another related characteristic is brevity. When the necessary information is presented in a concise format, it is likely to be understood and implemented by aides, parents, substitutes, and others. A number of examples of ways to document instructional programs will be presented in Chapter 4.

When the program document has been written, it is useful to watch a person carry out the program. When a program fails to teach a student, it may be the case that the instructor is not carrying out the procedures correctly. Two or more staff members may then meet to observe the delivery of the program and rectify the problem.

Summary

For students with severe handicaps to learn new skills and behaviors, a powerful instructional technology must be designed and delivered. The principles of operant conditioning offer such an instructional technology. The chapter described a discrete-trial format for teaching severely handicapped students. This approach carefully identifies the reinforcers, prompts, behaviors, and discriminative stimuli in a learning situation. It is important to reinforce correct responses contingently in order to motivate students. When students err, it is possible to prompt them to emit the correct behavior. For more complex behaviors, the process of task analysis enables the student to learn chains of responses by breaking an activity into its component parts. Other learning difficulties can be overcome with techniques such as stimulus fading, prosthesis, and partial participation. When a student has learned a new skill, it is important to transfer stimulus control from artificial to natural stimuli. The use of token economies and thinning of reinforcement can facilitate this process. Finally, the ability to design successful instructional programs requires a combination of knowing operant principles, being familiar with the students and learning tasks, and having extensive practice in implementing programs. Other ways to facilitate effective programming are to communicate with colleagues and to document the instructional programs clearly.

Chapter 3

Making the Curriculum Natural and Functional

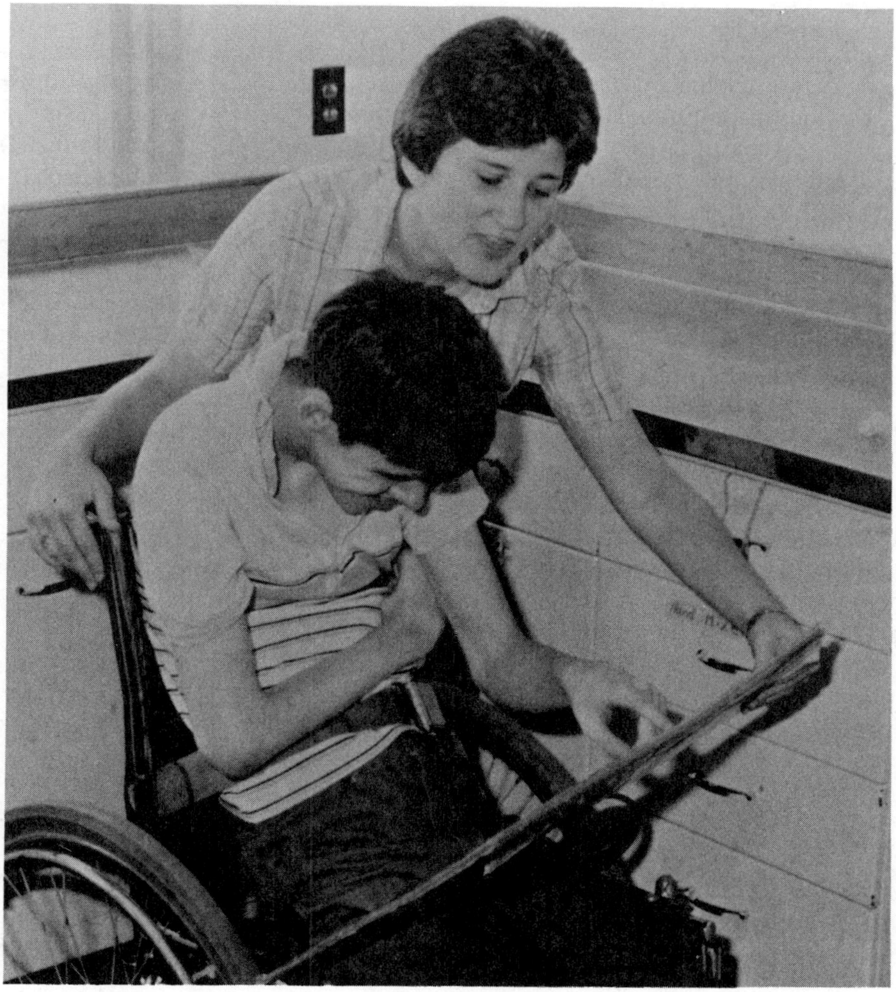

So far this book has dealt with how to determine which instructional programs are needed by a student and which procedures are most useful for teaching an individual skill. Now the emphasis will shift to the issue of melding separate instructional programs into a cohesive curriculum. Although there are several approaches to structuring a curriculum, this chapter will focus on the methods used to develop the *functional curriculum model*. This model has been the basis for many curricula developed for students with severe mental retardation and students with autism. Examples include the Individualized Curriculum Sequencing Model (Holvoet, Mulligan, Schussler, Lacy, and Guess, 1982), the Process-Oriented Curriculum (McLean, Snyder-McLean, Jacobs, and Rowland, 1981), Project Pride (Neel, Billingsley, McCarty, Symonds, Lambert, Lewis-Smith, and Hanashiro, 1983), and Model Education Services for Autistic Children and Youth (Egel and Neef, 1983).

Bases for Developing a Curriculum

The functional curriculum model has emerged in response to some of the special problems presented by students with severe handicaps.

Students' Lack of Stimulus Generalization

One of the special problems often seen in this population is an apparent inability to perform a skill in environments that differ in some way from the environment in which the skill was learned. This apparent inability to perform a skill when the materials, the setting, or the person asking the student to do the skill are different is referred to as a lack of stimulus generalization. Because this lack is seen in so many students with severe handicaps, the functional curriculum is organized to help teach the student a generalized skill. This is done by ensuring that the student is taught the same skill by different people, in different settings, with a variety of materials.

Figure 3.1 Different trial arrangements over time for massed, spaced, and distributed trial training. Time is indicated by the arrow.

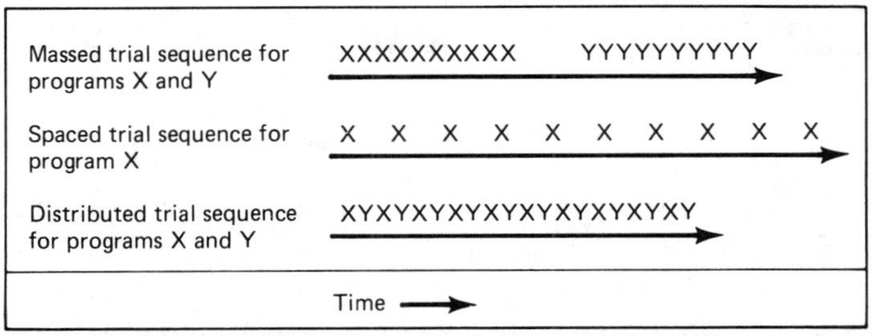

Source: Adapted from J. Holvoet, D. Guess, M. Mulligan, and F. Brown, The individualized curriculum sequencing model (II): a teaching strategy for severely handicapped students, *Journal of the Association for the Severely Handicapped* 5 (1980): 337–51. Reproduced with permission of *Journal of the Association for the Severely Handicapped.*

Students' Inability to Learn Quickly

Another problem seen in most students with severe handicaps is that skills are not learned quickly. Repeated practice on a skill is always necessary. Although this may seem obvious, since being mentally retarded means that the student has difficulty learning skills quickly, remediation strategies for slow acquisition rates have not been incorporated into most curricula.

In most traditional curricula, repeated practice is done in a drill and practice format. In other words, the student practices making the same response over and over in a limited amount of time while the teacher gives feedback on the correct form of the response. Although this is certainly a sensible way to approach teaching a student who needs repeated practice, research findings indicate that the timing of practice sessions also influences the speed of learning. In particular, it has been shown that individuals who have an opportunity to rest between practice trials learn much more quickly than individuals who are asked to practice the skill over and over with no rest between trials (Ebbinghaus, 1885; Hovland, 1939, 1940a, 1940b; Kimble, 1949a, 1949b; Kimble and Bilodeau, 1949; Underwood, Kapelak, and Malmi, 1976).

The technique of allowing rests between practice trials is called *spaced practice*, and the technique of practicing without any rests is called *massed practice*. It also has been demonstrated that allowing an individual to do a different task instead of resting between practice trials results in faster learning than results when massed practice is used (Baumeister and Berry, 1976; Dent and Johnson, 1964; Hovland, 1939, 1940b; Madsen, 1963). Allowing a person to do another task between practice trials is called *distributed practice*. These three methods of conducting practice sessions are illustrated in Figure 3.1.

Research has shown that the benefits of spaced and distributed practice are particularly marked in mentally retarded persons (Baumeister and Berry, 1976; Dent and Johnson, 1964; Madsen, 1963; Mulligan, Lacy, and Guess, 1982). Thus, the functional curriculum approach incorporates spaced and distributed trials in addition to the massed-trial format of most other curriculum models.

Students' Inability to Know When and Where to Use Skills

A third problem often encountered in persons with severe handicaps is that they may learn a skill but not know when or where to use it. Until the late 1970s, most students with severe handicaps were taught skills in quasi-laboratory settings within the classroom. Students were taught one at a time; the needed materials were placed in front of the student, and the student was taught to do a skill in the absence of context. Blocks of time were allotted to each instructional program; thus, skills such as communication were taught during the "communication" session, and mobility skills were taught during the "mobility" session. It generally was assumed that the students would be able to figure out when to use the skill once it had been learned.

Unfortunately, the students learned that they were to do the skill at a certain time when they were given certain materials instead of learning the appropriate times and places to use the skill. For example, a student might be taught to say, "Want water," during the ten o'clock session after the teacher said, "What want?" But that same student never said, "Want water," at any other time of day or in any other setting. The student had not learned a critical portion of the skill, that of saying, "Want water," when thirsty or in settings where water was not already poured into a glass (e.g., the kitchen, the bathroom, or a garden hose).

It is understood that the teacher may not know when a student is thirsty, but scheduling such training at times when the student is quite likely to be thirsty, such as after eating salty foods or after doing strenuous exercise, seems more likely to teach the timing of the skill. If this is not possible, teaching the student to ask for water in settings where water is regularly available is a compromise that may result in a more useful skill. Because teaching the student when and where to do a skill is important, the functional curriculum model emphasizes that the cues used should be as natural as possible, that scheduling of skill practice is vitally important, and that the skills must be taught in as realistic a context as possible.

Eight Components of the Functional Curriculum

The functional curriculum model incorporates eight components designed to meet these special needs. The first component deals with content, and the other seven describe processes by which instruction can be made more effective and time-efficient. The eight components of the functional curriculum approach are as follows:

1. Select functional materials and activities.
2. Teach in functional settings using natural cues whenever possible.
3. Use varied materials and allow students to choose materials whenever feasible.
4. Incorporate communication programs into natural, functional routines.
5. Incorporate motor programs into natural, functional routines.
6. Sequence skills in a logical and normative manner.
7. Incorporate deceleration programs into skill sequences.
8. Teach in groups as well as in one-to-one settings.

Selecting Functional Skills

In the functional curriculum model, the first step is to select instructional goals and objectives that will be functional, or useful, for a particular student. These skills will form the backbone of the IEP for that student.

It is important to understand the theoretical orientation underlying the model. Teachers who espouse the functional curriculum model believe that a student can be taught to do any skill if the teacher can devise a good instructional program. Obviously, there are some commonsense limits to this belief when dealing with students who have severe physical disabilities that may require skill adaptations or prosthetics, but otherwise the belief holds for all students and all skills. This theoretical orientation is in contrast to another curriculum approach called the *developmental* curriculum. In such a curriculum, students are considered able to learn a skill only if they are "ready" or have the prerequisite skills.

In both the developmental and the functional models, a teacher selects the skills to teach through an assessment process, but the type of assessment differs. In the developmental model, as we saw in Chapter 1, the teacher assesses a student by comparing the student's behavior with the normal developmental sequence (the sequence in which nonhandicapped students learn to perform skills) in the domains of gross motor, fine motor, language, self-help, socialization, and cognition. Then the teacher selects the next "step(s)" in the developmental sequence as the logical skills to teach. In the functional curriculum model, the skills to be taught are derived from assessments of the environment(s) in which the student must function. The skills taught are those which nonhandicapped students of the same chronological age use within each of the designated environments; these skills are called functional skills. Brown, Nietupski, and Hamre-Nietupski (1976) proposed that functional skills should meet the following criteria:

1. The skill should be chronologically age-appropriate.
2. The materials and activities needed to perform the skills should be present in the environment(s) in which the student currently lives or participates.
3. The skill should make the student more independent.

4. The skill should prepare the student to function in community environments.

The contrast between the skills taught using the developmental approach and those taught using the functional approach is most marked when the students are adolescents or young adults.

Environmental Inventories. Selecting functional skills can be accomplished several ways. Obviously, the simplest way is to use an environmental inventory to determine what skills are needed, assess the student on those skills, and then teach the skills the student does not have. If the student has many deficits, the teacher can decide which skills are the most functional by evaluating them according to criteria similar to those described in Figure 1.7.

Educational Assessment Scales. Another way to select functional skills is to assess the student using educational assessment scales that emphasize skills used by persons of different ages in a wide range of environments. Examples of such skills are mobility, eating, dressing, using the toilet, entertaining oneself, shopping, housekeeping, grooming, talking with others, and playing with others. Using these skills as a basis ensures that the students will learn functional skills but can lead to a very restricted program. As Marc Gold (1980, p. 7) points out, skills such as these are "zero-order" skills.

> Zero-order skills are those tasks or skills which attract negative attention if absent, such as dressing or bathing. Because society assumes everyone will do these tasks, their presence is usually unnoticed but their absence is conspicuous. As the term implies, when a person cannot perform a zero-order task, her value as perceived by others is diminished; on the other hand, if she can perform that task, her value is not enhanced. In other words, the ability to perform zero-order tasks leaves one at zero. To get a plus reading on society's "Who are you?" scale, a person must also have competence.

Gold goes on to point out that competence constitutes having a needed skill that not everyone has. Note that the skill must be needed; in other words, competency skills also must be functional. If this approach is used, the teacher must ensure that both functional zero-order skills and competencies are taught.

Functional Objectives. A third way to select skills is to use an educational assessment scale but translate the items into more functional objectives. Translation is often necessary because many of the assessments used with the severely handicapped population have been derived from developmental theory. It is obvious that many of the skills listed on such assessments (e.g., putting rings on a cone-shaped stacker) are not necessarily going to increase the student's ability to live independently in a community or a semisheltered setting.

There are three steps involved in the translation of objectives. The first involves determining whether the skill is used by nonhandicapped peers or adults in a number of environments and then deciding how often the skill is used in each of these environments. This step serves as an evaluation of how critical or useful the skill will be to the student. For example, an assessment may list walking on a line as an objective. This skill is not used in the home, at school, or at work. In fact, it is very rare for adults, teenagers, or children to use this skill at all. Thus, walking on a line is not a very critical skill, but this does not mean it should not be taught. The teacher still must implement the second and third steps in the translation process. The second step involves determining what underlying skills if any are being tested. For example, walking on a line tests the underlying skills of dynamic balance and eye-foot coordination. The third step involves determining whether the *underlying* skills are critical skills. This is done by asking when and where the identified underlying skill is used by nonhandicapped persons. For example, an adolescent or young adult may need dynamic balance and eye-foot coordination to walk along a narrow footpath without straying, go through a grocery checkout counter, walk through a narrow doorway, or walk among various obstacles in the home or classroom. Any or all of these tasks can be chosen as objectives and would accomplish the same thing as teaching the student to walk on a line.

Sometimes translating the objective "loses" some of the skill. For example, it is apparent that a student needs less eye-foot coordination and balance to go through a checkout counter than to walk on a line. The question, however, is whether the environment really requires the high degree of dynamic balance and eye-foot coordination used in walking a line. If the student lives or works in an environment, such as a circus, where such a high degree of balance is needed, it may be worth the teaching time. But if most people in the environment use a lesser degree of the skill (even though they could walk a line if necessary), teaching can be made functional and more efficient by dealing only with the functional uses of the skill.

Functional Materials. A fourth way to develop functional skills is similar to translation of the skills from an assessment. In this case the skills are not changed, but the materials are made more functional and age-appropriate. Changes in materials from those specified in the assessment usually are not needed with preschool and younger grade school students. Changes are often important, however, for preteens, teenagers, and young adults.

The combination of age-appropriate materials and useful skills will allow most students to engage either partially or totally in activities that are enjoyed by nonhandicapped peers of the same age. For example, fine motor skills in a 9-year-old may be assessed using busy boxes, wooden puzzles, and stacking rings, but the same child can be taught to open the door, turn on the lights, turn on the radio or television, adjust the venetian blinds, use the paper towel dispenser, hold onto soap, push a doorbell, use a toilet paper dispenser, tear paper out of a tablet, put coins in a vending machine, or use a three-ring binder instead. It appears that the latter skills would be useful and would make the child more able to function in nonsheltered environments. Selecting functional materials to teach a skill can be accomplished by asking two questions about every skill that you plan to teach: (1) What materials and activities used by nonhandicapped persons of the same age could be used to teach this skill? and (2) What materials and activities are available to teach the skill in the places (subenvironments) where the student currently goes or may be able to go in the future?

Assembling a list of materials and activities that involve basic skills is a good idea. Making such a list will save work in the long run, since the list can be used to determine functional skills for other students. The list is also helpful in later phases of developing a functional curriculum.

Teach in Functional Settings Using Natural Cues

It has been pointed out that students with severe handicaps have a difficult time generalizing to environments that differ from the environment(s) where they have learned to perform a skill. One way to approach this problem is to make the teaching environment as similar as possible to the environment where the student is expected to perform the skill. This is done best by teaching in natural settings and using cues that are similar to those used by nonhandicapped persons. The staff members of the IMPACT project (Neel et al., 1983) suggest that most skills can be taught in one of three contexts: the school environment, a school environment that has simulated home or community activities, and the community. Some skills, such as getting out materials, locomotion, communication, eating, using the toilet, and grooming, can be taught easily in the natural school context. Other skills, such as cooking, making a bed, dressing, eating family style, doing laundry, and setting the table, may not occur in the natural school context, but a realistic context can be created or simulated within the school setting. Still other skills, such as shopping, using public transportation, bowling, and eating at restaurants, require a community context for the most effective teaching.

Analysis of Settings and Cues. The most appropriate context generally can be determined by an analysis of the setting and cues to be used. This analysis involves five questions.

1. Is the skill being taught in the place(s) where the student will be expected to perform the skill independently? If not, can the natural environment be used or a more similar environment be devised?
2. Are the materials kept in a location that is similar to their location in nonschool environments?
3. Is the student learning where the materials needed to do this skill usually are kept?
4. Are the cues used to teach the skill similar to the cues that will be avail-

able in nonschool environments? If not, can the cues be changed without sacrificing the quality of teaching?

5. Is the time at which the task is being taught similar to the times when the student will need to do the task? If not, is there any way to teach the student when to perform the task?

Some skills intrinsically demand functional settings and cues. For example, most teachers who teach students to wash dishes use a sink with running water, some type of sponge or dishcloth, and a commercial dish soap. Most teachers also teach dish washing using dirty dishes, and many teach it after a cooking lesson or after the student has eaten. Thus, this skill is taught in a functional manner for the majority of students. But some students would profit more if they were taught in other settings. Some students should be taught to use a dishwasher, if this is the primary mode of dish washing in the home. Other students should be taught to wish or rinse dishes in a plastic dishpan because that is the way their families wash dishes. Still other students should learn how to wash large quantities of very dirty pots and pans since these students will be working as dishwashers at local restaurants. The point is that an analysis of the settings in which the student will be asked to function is always appropriate, even when it seems that the skill is being taught in the most functional way possible.

Setting and cue analysis are especially important for skills that can be taught at a classroom table or desk. For example, it is not uncommon for a teacher to place a shoe on a student's desk and say, "Tie the shoe." A teacher who teaches this highly functional skill this way often is disappointed when the student goes around with untied shoes. A teacher who is thinking functionally, however, will realize that most people do not tie shoes that are just lying around. Instead, shoes that need to be tied are on a person's feet. Thus, it would be better to have the student learn to tie a shoe that is on the foot. The teacher who is committed to functional teaching also will try to determine the best position for shoe tying by looking at how nonhandicapped people tie their shoes. Most do not leave their feet flat on the ground but instead put the foot on the opposite knee so that they do not have to bend over so far. This position may not be possible because of the student's other disabilities, but at least the teacher should think about teaching the student a functional way to tie shoes. The teacher who thinks functionally probably will not provide the shoes every time but will teach the student how to look around the floor of the environment in order to locate the shoes. This student also will be taught to tie the shoes after putting them on, when changing them, and when they come untied during the day. In this way the teacher can be fairly sure that the time spent teaching the student will result in a skill the student can use at the appropriate time and place.

Importance of Verbal Cues. Verbal cues also need to be as appropriate as possible without sacrificing teaching precision. Short verbal cues such as

"Bite cookie" may be necessary to establish stimulus control, but the teacher must be aware that such cues may not be available from persons other than the teacher and parents. The teacher can elect to fade in a more natural verbal cue or fade out the verbal cue altogether. The procedure by which a cue is made more natural is less important than the fact that the teacher is aware of differences between cues used in the classroom and those used in the natural environment.

Sometimes it is easier to change a verbal cue entirely rather than take the time to fade to a more natural cue. For example, many teachers when doing object discrimination ask the student to point to the shoe. This type of cue has evolved in response to a concern that teachers should give cues that specify the desired response clearly. It is considered easier for both the teacher and student to determine whether the behavior is correct if a precise cue such as "Point to shoe" is given instead of a more general cue such as "Find the shoe." Nonetheless, in real life the student probably never will be asked to point to his shoe. It is probable, however, that the student will be told to find his shoes, get his shoes, or bring his shoes to an adult. Thus, using the cue "Get the shoe" may be more functional.

There is no general rule to follow here. Sometimes a teacher will opt to use the more precise cue in order to ensure that the student is learning the correct response; at other times a more functional cue will be preferable. The important thing is to think about the cues that are given and choose one that will result in optimal learning.

Similarly, it is recognized that not all skills can be taught in natural settings. Sometimes time and budget constraints make it necessary to teach skills in simulated or classroom settings. Nonetheless, careful consideration of where skills ultimately must be performed usually results in more functional teaching. Incorporating instructional programs into ongoing routines also will help ensure that the skills are taught in the functional settings.

Using Varied Materials

The developers of the functional curriculum approach encourage the use of a variety of materials in teaching a skill. It is anticipated that using a variety of materials will help alleviate three problems that often are encountered in students with severe handicaps. First, it is felt that using a variety of materials will help the student learn to generalize. In other words, the student may learn to perform the skill with several relevant materials rather than associating it with one particular stimulus. Second, using a variety of materials may help relieve the boredom and subsequent lack of motivation that often occurs when the student is asked to practice with the same object day after day. Third, it has been documented that many students with autism and some students with severe mental retardation show a phenomenon known as *stimulus overselectivity* (Koegel and Wilheim, 1973; Lovaas, Schreibman,

Koegel, and Kehm, 1971; Schreibman, 1975). Stimulus overselectivity refers to the difficulty some students have in responding to multiple cues, for example, a visual cue and a verbal cue presented simultaneously. When such students are given stimuli with multiple attributes such as color, texture, and shape, they apparently focus on only one attribute. Thus, a student with overselectivity who is trying to learn the concept of "glove" may focus only on the color and ignore the shape. For example, this student may call all white objects "glove" if a white glove was the only item used to teach the concept. Careful presentation of several gloves that differ in color, texture, and shape may help such a student learn to use more than one cue to discriminate among objects.

Object-Specific and Generic Materials. Most skills that are taught to students with severe handicaps are of two general kinds. The first kind may be called *object-specific*. Object-specific skills require a certain object in order to be performed. Examples are combing hair, brushing teeth, tying shoes, putting paper in a three-ring binder, going to the toilet, and labeling objects. The other group of skills are called *generic skills*. These can be performed with a wide variety of objects. Examples are grasping an item, putting an item away, looking at an item, packaging, stacking, matching, imitating, and sorting.

When teaching an object-specific skill, several examples of the same object should be used. For example, if a student is learning to identify and use a comb, at least three different types of comb should be provided during training. These combs can differ in size (small versus large), color (white versus black or yellow), and type (rat-tail versus pocket). The teacher may use one comb for trial 1, a different comb for trial 2, and yet another comb for trial 3. This will allow the student to focus on the concept of "comb" rather than the irrelevant details of a single stimulus item. For some students, however, varying the stimulus items on every trial may be so confusing that it will take them a long time to learn the concept. Such students may learn more effectively if initial trials are conducted with only a single object and the other objects are introduced slowly in later sessions, using carefully programmed errorless procedures.

The choice of how to introduce the varied stimuli must be made on an individual basis, but it is important to realize that using varied stimuli is an important facet of teaching. Also, teaching still should occur in a functional setting. In this example, the student would encounter the comb in a bedroom, a bathroom, or a purse, and the student probably should be shown how to use the item after identifying it. This combination of varying the materials, demonstrating the function of an object, and demonstrating where the item normally is found should enable the student to use the skill spontaneously when the need arises.

If generic skills are to be taught, several different types of objects should be used. For example, if a student is being taught to stack objects, the teacher may use books, boxed games, papers, plates, cups, or linens to teach the skill. The teacher also may teach the student to stack things on tables and on shelves. This type of teaching should help the student learn that different things are stacked, thus making the student more adaptable when she or he is asked to stack something that has never been taught.

Again, deciding how many varied items to teach and how to introduce them is a decision that should be based on the needs of the individual student. As a guideline, Holvoet et al. (1982) report that most adolescent students with severe mental retardation can tolerate three or four different materials when learning a generic skill, and some are able to learn when as many as ten varied materials are presented in a single session. These authors also point out, however, that students who have a hard time learning new skills probably should be taught using fewer objects than students who seem to grasp new skills quickly.

Of course, good teaching procedures are extremely important no matter how many materials are used. Varying the materials will confuse the student unless the teacher employs clear cues and consistent correction procedures.

Sometimes it is quite difficult to vary materials, particularly when working with students who have very severe physical handicaps. Such students often require such extensive modifications of the materials that variation is difficult to achieve. In such cases, the teacher should enlist the help of therapists and parents to determine innovative modifications. Occasionally no variations are possible, but even in this case all is not lost. At least the student has learned to do the skill with one object and is better off than he or she would be if the skill had not been taught. Nonetheless, variation of materials is a technique that can greatly extend the usefulness of most teaching.

Students' Choice of Materials. A natural extension of the use of varied materials is to allow the students to make choices about their educational programming. Research has shown that both nonhandicapped and handicapped students who are given opportunities to choose materials, reinforcers, or tasks learn more quickly than students who are given the same stimuli but are not allowed to make any choices (Alexander, 1974; Berk, 1976; Felixbrod and O'Leary, 1973; Holvoet, Brewer, Mulligan, Guess, and Helmstetter, 1983; Perlmutter and Monty, 1977).

Allowing students to make choices has not been part of the traditional curricula for persons with severe handicaps. In part this is because teachers have felt that they need to maintain control over the cues, materials, and reinforcers to be sure that the student learns what they are trying to teach. After all, what would happen if Sally decided she did not want to learn to stand up? But when varied materials are used, the student can be allowed some choices without sacrificing the teaching. For example, before beginning a program designed to teach buttoning, the student may be allowed to choose which of two shirts she or he wants to button. A student learning to fold objects can be allowed to choose two or three items from an array of five.

It is possible and even probable that many students will not know how to make such choices initially. This means that they need to be taught how to choose. Most students, however, seem to quickly learn ways to indicate what they want to do. As pointed out earlier, encouraging the student to make choices may improve the speed of learning. In addition, the students get to practice the very important adaptive skill of making choices.

Incorporating Communication Programs into the Daily Routine

Communication with others is one of the most basic and important skills an individual can acquire. Most students with severe handicaps, however, show a serious lack of communication skills. Although many will acquire a fairly good receptive vocabulary (be able to understand what others tell them), most will have difficulty learning to produce even a few words, manual signs, or symbols. Perhaps more distressing is the fact that most severely handicapped students who do learn to produce words, manual signs, or symbols rarely use them spontaneously. This may be due in part to teaching techniques that relegate communication training to a single period or session each day.

Although the session method may be extremely useful and efficient in teaching the student how to communicate, it is not at all well suited to teaching the student the whys of communication. Nietupski, Schuetz, and Ockwood (1980, p. 14) point out that nonhandicapped children "learn to communicate through parent-child interactions in which real conversation, real requests for attention and assistance, real question-asking and answering are carried out. Children learn to communicate in a social context in order to make changes in their environment." Thus, if the student is to learn that communication is a valuable tool for gaining attention or making changes in the environment, the student must be urged to communicate throughout the day. This concept is not new; it has been pointed out by teachers and speech therapists for years. It is a goal that is widely preached but rarely practiced.

The Gap between Theory and Practice. Why is there such a gap between what teachers know should be happening and the reality seen in most classrooms for severely handicapped students? Holvoet et al. (1982) have identified several obstacles to implementing communication programs throughout the school day:

1. The words being learned by the student are not useful in any other classroom or school setting.

2. The staff members are so engrossed in teaching other programs that they simply do not think about having the student use communication skills.
3. The staff members do not know what words the student knows or is learning.
4. The staff members do not know how to get the student to produce the words he or she knows or is learning (i.e., do not know the cues and prompts).
5. The staff members do not know how strict to be when a student does produce a word (does the word have to be said perfectly or are there acceptable approximations).
6. The staff members do not know how to correct wrong responses.
7. The staff members do not know how to use the student's communication system (e.g., do not know how to manually sign although the student is being taught to do so).

A Functional Communication System. These obstacles are serious enough and common enough that it is probable that the simple suggestion of incorporating communication throughout the school day will be insufficient. For this reason, the developers of the functional curriculum model created a system that would alleviate some of these obstacles.This system has three goals:

1. Making sure the student is learning words, signs, or symbols that are useful in other classroom and school activities
2. Making sure all classroom staff (and possibly other facility staff and peers) know what communication programs are being taught
3. Making communication an integral part of every instructional program

In order to accomplish these goals, teachers using a functional curriculum model often use an activity grid to determine when and where communication instruction should occur. An example of such a grid can be seen in Figure 3.2. Activities and instructional programs that occur regularly are listed on the left-hand side of the grid and communication goals (objectives) are listed across the top of the page. The teacher decides how each communication objective can be combined with the activities and instructional programs. For example, in Figure 3.2 the teacher has determined that the student could imitate the word "hi" in at least four activities (getting off and on the bus, morning group with two other students, recess, and lunch). This is shown on the grid by the teacher writing in the names of the persons the student is to greet in each activity. If the greeting skill was not to be taught during an activity, an X was marked in that box. In Figure 3.2 it can be seen that since this student was being met at the bus by a staff member each morning, the teacher decided that the student could say "hi" (in imitation) to that staff member. The teacher also decided that there was time for the staff member and the student to detour by the office and have the student say "hi" to the school secretary.

Figure 3.2 Example of a grid outlining how John's communication objectives could be taught in the context of regular activities.

Activity or Objective	Imitate "Hi"	Imitate "Thanks"	Identify Cup, Toy, Shoe, Toilet
Getting off bus	1. Staff member(s) 2. School secretary	X	X
Putting coat, boots, etc., in locker	X	After being helped with coat	X
Prevocational group (Sam, Jenny, John)	1. Sam 2. Jenny	After supervisor gives materials	X
Toileting and grooming	X	X	Identify toilet and shoe
Recess	Two students from another class	X	Identify shoe and toy
Preacademic group (Jason, Emily, John)	X	To peers after being given reinforcers	X
Occupational therapy	X	X	X
Lunch	Lunchroom supervisor or cook	After being given food	Identify cup
Toileting and grooming	X	X	Identify toilet and shoe
One-to-one: independent living skills	X	X	Identify cup during dishwashing or setting table
Get on bus	Bus driver	X	X

When the student arrived in the classroom, the first activity was a group prevocational task. The teacher decided that the student should be required to say "hi" to the other two students in the group. The student then would not be required to say "hi" again until recess, when the teacher determined that the student should be taught to say "hi" to two students from other classes who shared the same recess period. Finally, the student would be required to say "hi" to the lunchroom supervisor or cook during the lunch period. At the end of the day, the student would be escorted to the bus and would be taught to say "hi" to the bus driver.

It is assumed, of course, that the same instructional program will be used in every activity to teach the student to imitate "hi." Since different staff members will be conducting different activities (meeting the bus, conducting the group program, etc.), it follows that every staff member will have to learn how to teach the "hi" program. In this manner the problems of not knowing what to teach, how to teach, how strict to be, and how to deal with incorrect responses should be alleviated. Incorporating communication instruction into usual routines thus has the advantage of teaching the student to perform the skill in several environments with several people. If skillfully taught, the student also may learn that greetings are given when you enter a new environment or see someone new.

Incorporating communication skills into daily activities that occur at different times of the day also ensures that distributed practice will occur. It has been pointed out that distributed practice results in faster learning than the more traditional massed practice generally used when communication is taught in a session format. Furthermore, incorporating the instruction into daily routines allows other people to become aware of what the student is learning. It is possible that over time the school secretary, nonhandicapped peers at recess, the lunchroom supervisor, and the bus driver may take over the job of eliciting a "hi" from the student spontaneously. This probably would not happen if these people had not been exposed to classroom staff working with the student on this skill.

The grid in Figure 3.2 also illustrates how the teacher incorporated two other communication objectives. There is no rule governing how many communication objectives a student should have. This must be determined by the student's overall needs, the desires of both the teacher and the parents, and the teaching time available.

Sometimes a problem can arise because a speech therapist, parent, or teacher feels that a student needs more intensive instruction and repetitive practice than can be obtained by integrating the communication training into natural routines. For example, if a therapist is working on articulation of certain consonants, there may be a need for the therapist to do most of the teaching because the majority of the staff members have not been trained to hear the subtle differences in articulation patterns. Since the therapist probably will have a very limited amount of time to spend with the student, there will continue to be a speech session.

Such a situation can be handled a number of ways. The therapist may be asked if the session could be arranged so that the student had to practice the targeted sound in a variety of environments or with a variety of objects. Another approach is to continue to incorporate the communication objective into the regular routine and schedule an additional speech session with the therapist. This is somewhat expensive in terms of time but is often a good alternative. However, this approach should never be used without the knowledge and consent of the therapist. If the classroom staff and the therapist do not maintain a consistent approach, the student may get confused and make very little progress.

A third way to handle the problem is to schedule speech sessions with the therapist until the student has learned a skill to the therapist's satisfaction and then begin incorporating the skill into the daily routine. Obviously, this alternative is the least desirable. It will lengthen the time the student must spend learning the skill, or, as often happens, it will take the student so long to learn the skill that teaching when and where to use it will be overlooked.

The question of how many activities a communication objective should be incorporated into also has no definitive answer. Obviously, the student should have several opportunities each day to practice the skill. Sometimes these opportunities occur so often within the context of the regularly scheduled activities that the teacher can decide that it is more convenient to teach the skill in some activities and not in others. For example, the teacher in Figure 3.2 could have added the "hi" program to every activity. Instead, only four activities were chosen because these activities represent times when there is a distinct change in the environment, and the teacher felt this would help the student learn when to perform the skill.

It often happens, however, that the communication objective can be incorporated into only a few activities. The teacher must decide whether these few activities offer sufficient opportunities for practice. If they do not, the teacher can make alterations in the daily routine or schedule a short supplementary communication session. Column 2 (imitate "thanks") in Figure 3.2 shows that the teacher had peers give the child tangible reinforcers during the preacademic group activity to ensure enough daily practice on this communication skill.

If a communication objective cannot be incorporated into any regularly scheduled activities, the teacher should reexamine the skill carefully to see whether it is truly useful. Sometimes it will be obvious that the time would be better spent teaching some other objective. But if the skill seems functional, it may be necessary to make some changes in the usual activities to acommodate the instruction. Examples of this type of accommodation can be seen in Figure 3.2, column 3. Putting socks on was added to the grooming session, and the student was encouraged to identify the shoes as they were taken off and put on. The student also was required to change the shoes (from school shoes to tennis shoes) before and after recess and physical education. In this way, the teacher ensured that the student had several opportunities to practice the communication skill.

In summary, advocates of the functional curriculum model feel that communication instruction should be incorporated into as many routine classroom activities and instructional programs as possible. One method of accomplishing this is to use an activity grid format to schedule communication instruction.

Incorporating Motor Programs into the Daily Routine

Most students with severe handicaps show some degree of motor delay. This delay simply may be associated with mental retardation, or it may be due to additional motor or sensory impairments such as cerebral palsy or blindness. Thus, training in motor skills is usually an integral part of the educational program for this population.

Motor Programs. Motor skill training usually is divided into four subareas: tone normalization, gross motor skills, fine motor skills, and perceptual-motor skills.

Educational activities in the area of tone normalization generally are concerned with inhibiting abnormal reflexes, relaxation activities, and development of primitive balance skills (termed *righting* or *equilibrium* skills). These goals generally are attained through proper positioning and exercises designed to facilitate or inhibit certain types of motor movement. Such activities are especially important for students whose motor delay seems to be related primarily to cerebral palsy.

Educational programs designed to teach gross motor skills generally focus on motor skills involving large muscles or groups of muscles that typically are acquired by a child during infancy. Skills such as head control, rolling over, reaching, sitting, weight bearing, kneeling, standing, and walking are examples of gross motor skills. General physical fitness activities also may be included under the subcategory of gross motor skills.

Programs designed to teach fine motor skills focus on complex and coordinated movements that generally are controlled by small muscles. These programs are particularly concerned with hand and finger movement and the oral musculature. Skills such as pincer grasp, pointing with the index finger, tongue lateralization, swallowing, and chewing are examples of fine motor skills.

Perceptual-motor educational programs generally are concerned with ocular (eye) movements, eye-hand coordination, and refinement of tactile (touch), auditory (hearing), and vestibular (where the body is in space) senses.

The importance of motor skill training cannot be overemphasized. A lack of motor skills severely curtails exploration of and interaction with the environment, thus closing many traditional avenues of learning to the student. In addition, the immense amount of effort required to move or attain objects coupled with repeated attempts that fail may cause the student to give up and become apathetic and unmotivated. This can cause further retardation of the student's development, since the student no longer will respond actively to instructional efforts.

Massed Practice. As with communication training, the traditional method used to train fine and gross motor skills has been massed practice in a session format. Often an occupational or physical therapist was responsible for conducting the motor skills training, and the training occurred in a therapy area outside the classroom. It was assumed that therapy sessions would result in substantial improvement of motor functioning that would be demonstrated spontaneously by the student in all other environments. Even when motor training was conducted in the classroom, it generally was done in a massed-trial format at a particular time of day. This resulted in a scenario similar to the following. A student was placed in a walker. The teacher then moved 10 feet away and told the student, "Come here." The student struggled over to the teacher, a process often requiring several minutes. The teacher then rewarded the student with a hug, an edible, or verbal praise. The teacher then moved the student and walker back to the starting point. Then the student was asked to do the whole thing again. This went on until the student had completed ten walking trials or until time had expired. The walker then was put away, and the student was carried to the next instructional area.

Similarly, perceptual-motor skills were conducted by classroom staff in a massed-trial format. A student working on visual tracking, for example, would be presented with a stimulus such as a penlight and a cue to "Look." If the student looked, the teacher removed the penlight and gave the student some type of unrelated reinforcer. The teacher then repeated the process until 10 to 20 trials had been conducted.

This traditional massed-trial approach to motor training was successful with some students. Many students, however, seemed to learn the skill in the motor sessions but never demonstrated the skills spontaneously at any other time. Still other students did not seem to progress at all. For students who failed to learn or generalize, it appeared that the assumptions underlying motor training sessions needed to be examined more closely. It was pointed out (Guess, Horner, Utley, Holvoet, Maxon, Tucker, and Warren, 1978) that the traditional session method had several drawbacks. The most obvious drawback is fatigue. Using muscles in new ways is extremely fatiguing and can result in muscle stiffness and soreness. Any person who has just begun a new exercise program can attest to that. Asking a student to perform a motor pattern such as using a walker, sitting up, or reaching repeatedly can result in fatigue. Most of the students did not complain since they were nonverbal (any whining or moaning that did go on was usually ignored), but examination of the data indicated that a fatigue factor might have been at work. It was not uncommon for a student to show very good performance on the first few trials and then show increasingly poorer performance as the session progressed.

Another drawback seen primarily in perceptual-motor programs is habituation. When a stimulus is presented over and over within a relatively short period of time and the student is asked to visually fixate, orient, or track the stimulus, there is generally a decrease in performance over time. In fact, if enough trials are presented, the student will stop performing altogether. This decrease in responding is interpreted as being the result of decreased cortical awareness of the stimulus; in other words, the brain ceases to respond to the stimulus. This process of ceasing to respond to a stimulus after repeated presentations, where it can be demonstrated that fatigue is not a factor, is referred to as *habituation* (Switzky, Woolsey-Hill, and Quoss, 1979). Although the process of habituation can be viewed positively as the student's way of showing stimulus discrimination and memory, it can interfere with perceptual-motor training when the session model is used.

There are two ways to avoid the phenomenon of habituation. One is to use a variety of stimuli, and the second is to use a distributed-practice schedule instead of a massed-practice schedule during perceptual-motor training. Habituation is seen in virtually all senses but has been documented most extensively for the auditory and visual senses.

The third drawback is that the student does not learn the why of movement. The lack of spontaneous use of the movement in other settings can be interpreted as an indication either that the student does not realize when or where to do the skills or that the student is unmotivated because the skill requires too much effort compared with the benefits of doing the skill. Such problems may be eliminated if the student is taught in a more functional manner. In our example of the student who was being taught to use a walker, what was really being taught? A careful analysis would show that the student was not being taught that using the walker was a way to get to some other place where something interesting was happening. Instead, the student was being taught that she is supposed to walk when the teacher says, "Come here." Even more distressing is the fact that the student may be learning that when she finally gets to the adult who has called her, the adult does not want her there at all; instead, he wants her back where she started! Is it any wonder the student becomes confused or frustrated and does not bother to do the skill on her own?

How would you feel if your teacher told you to write a ten-page essay on motor skills, and you spent a lot of effort on it. Then, when you turned it in, the teacher told you, "That's really nice," and asked you to do another one? After your teacher had done this once or twice, you would be very frustrated and would probably stop putting so much effort into the papers. You certainly would not be thinking how nice it was to have the opportunity to learn even more about motor skills. If your teacher continued this behavior—even though he supposedly was reinforcing you with nice comments about your paper—you would probably never, *ever*, want to write a paper again. Even if another teacher asked you to write a paper, you would probably not want to do it.

Because traditional methods of motor training may be perceived as punishing rather than opportunities to learn, it is very important to develop alternative approaches to motor skill training.

The fourth drawback is that isolated training, whether done in another

Figure 3.3 Example of a grid outlining how Felicia's motor objectives could be taught in the context of regularly occurring activities.

Activity or Objective	Reaching	Controlled Release	Visual Scanning
Arrival	X	X	Two lockers (her own and someone else's)
Housekeeping	Broom and dustpan	Put broom away in closet	(any two) broom, dustpan, wastebasket
Leisure (home)	Magazines, books, records, games	Place item gently on shelf with similar items	(any two) magazines, books, records, games
Self-help and grooming	Towel and clothing	X	Soap and towel
Food preparation	Food items on counter or refrigerator	Put toast in toaster	X
Mealtime (family style)	Food being passed; also passing food	Put glass on table gently (three times)	Any 2 foods
Self-help and grooming	Towel and clothing	X	Soap and towel
Prevocational	X		X
Leisure (work)	Magazines, soda pop	X	X
Departure	X	X	Two lockers

room by a therapist or in the classroom by one staff member, leads to the student not being required to exhibit the skill in other settings with other people. Staff members often are afraid that they will mess up the program or hurt the student. This makes it even more difficult for the student to learn when to do the behavior.

Distributed Practice. What is needed is an approach that utilizes distributed practice, different environments, different staff members, and natural scheduling. This can be achieved by incorporating motor programming into the daily classroom routine through the use of a grid format in the same way described earlier for communication programs. Figure 3.3 shows a grid in which a gross motor skill, a fine motor skill, and a perceptual-motor skill were incorporated into a secondary classroom routine.

In this example, the routine includes arriving at school, doing housekeeping chores in a bedroom or bathroom area; engaging in leisure activities that can be done at home; preparing simple foods; setting the table, eating, and cleaning up after a meal; grooming activities such as toothbrushing, hair care, face and hand washing, and deodorant use; self-help activities such as dressing skills; working in a prevocational setting; engaging in leisure activities that can be found in the workplace; and leaving school.

Listed in the grid are some items that require the use of the target skill. These items generally are available in the listed activities. For example, the student can practice reaching for the broom and dustpan in the housekeeping area. The environment naturally would need to be arranged so that these items are kept slightly below or slightly above the student's usual reaching range. During food preparation, the student can reach for the items kept in the cabinets and in the refrigerator. During leisure activities, the magazines, books, and records can be placed on shelves that would require the student to reach farther than usual. If the student is unable to grasp, the teacher should help the student grasp the item after the student has reached for it satisfactorily. This will help the student learn that people reach for things in order to obtain them. The teacher also may teach grasping to the student, but sometimes it is simpler to concentrate on one motor skill at a time.

It is important to note that when a teacher is trying to incorporate both motor and communication programs into the classroom routine, all the student's programs can be placed on the same grid. A separate grid is not needed for each skill domain. The domains have been separated in this chapter for clarity and to illustrate the concept with different routines. Additionally, domains other than motor skills and communication skills can be incorporated into the classroom routine. Many teachers like to incorporate instruction in the domains of socialization and auditory training in addition to communication and motor instruction. Again, this is done simply by adding these skills to the activity grid and determining when the activity can be scheduled. A grid that incorporates communication, motor, and socialization programs is shown in Figure 3.4. This grid will be used to illustrate the next steps in functional curriculum organization.

Sequencing Skills in a Logical and Normative Manner

Once all the skills that are to be integrated into the normal classroom routine have been put into the grid format, the next step is to put these skills into a logical and normative sequence. To do this, examine the skills listed across the grid for each activity. For example, in Figure 3.4 three skills are listed for the activity of getting on and off the bus: wheeling to and from the classroom, imitating "hi" and "bye," and looking from staff person to staff person. Then determine a logical sequence for teaching these skills. The student in this example could:

Figure 3.4 Example of one student's activity grid that incorporates communication, motor, and socialization objectives.

Activity or Objective	Wheelchair Mobility	Imitate Words	Scanning	Interaction with Peers	Supported Standing
Getting on and off bus	Wheel to and from classroom	Imitate "hi" and "bye"	Scan staff, peers	X	X
Morning group with Sue and John	Wheel to and from group	Imitate "hi" and "bye"	Scan peers, toys used	Pass toy to peer, take from peer	X
Using the toilet	Wheel to and from toilet	Imitate "finished"	Scan toilet, chair, toilet paper	X	Stand at toilet holding bar across back (male)
Grooming	Wheel to and from sink	X	Scan materials	X	Stand at sink
Snack time	Wheel to and from snack time	Imitate name of food, utensils used	Scan materials	Make snack while cooperating with peer	X
Toothbrushing (total cycle)	Wheel to and from sink	Imitate "finished"	Scan materials	X	Stand at sink
Physical education	Wheel to and from gym	Imitate "hi" and "bye" to peers	X	Group games	X
Recess	Wheel to and from playground	X	X	Group games	X
Eating	Wheel to and from dining area	Imitate "finished"	Scan food, service, peers, etc.	Pass food to peer, take from peer	X
Reinforcing	X	X	Scanning array of S^{R+} choices	Ask peer for S^{R+}, give peer S^{R+}	X

1. Get off the bus
2. Wheel to the classroom
3. Scan two or more staff members in response to a cue such as "Look at Joe and Mary"
4. Imitate saying "hi" to Joe
5. Imitate saying "hi" to Mary

This is a fairly natural sequence, although the placement of the scanning trial seems a bit contrived. If it seems too awkward, the teacher may wish to eliminate it entirely. However, it may be necessary to put up with a slightly contrived sequence in order to get enough trials on a particular skill.

This student's morning group activity could follow a different sequence, for example. He could

1. Wheel to the group
2. Imitate "hi" to Sue
3. Imitate "hi" to John
4. Look at two toys (scanning)
5. Take one toy
6. Pass the other toy to a peer
7. Activate toy
8. Look at two peers to determine who is going to give him a toy (scanning)
9. Take a toy from the peer
10. Imitate "thank you" to peer
11. Activate toy
12. Wheel to next activity

This is a very natural sequence, and the taking and giving of toys can be repeated several times during the session.

Continue making logical sequences until a sequence has been devised for each routine activity. If the student has no behavior problems that require remediation, these sequences can be transferred directly to data sheets. Each activity should have a separate data sheet. Such data sheets will provide visual reminders to the staff of when and where to teach each skill as well as provide a place to record the student's performance. A data sheet is shown in Figure 3.5. If, however, the student needs instructional programming to decrease inappropriate behavior, the next step should be implemented before making any data sheets.

Incorporating Behavioral Programs into the Daily Routine

Most classrooms for students with severe handicaps include one or two students who show disruptive or inappropriate behaviors. Some disruptive behaviors that are fairly common in members of this population are repetitive movements or sounds (stereotyped behavior), self-injury, vomiting, eating of inedible substances (pica), aggression, spitting, tearing up materials, playing with feces, screaming, and running away. Techniques to deal with these behaviors are outlined in Chapter 5.

Basic Components. Behavioral techniques have two critical components: (1) rewarding the student when he or she is being good and (2) ignoring, interrupting, or punishing the undesirable behavior. Both components must be present for maximal control of the problem. Although these ideas seem very simple, two problems may occur. First, it appears that catching kids being "good" is much more difficult than catching them being "bad." This is the

Figure 3.5 Example of a data sheet for a skill sequence. This sequence was derived from the morning group activity portion of the grid illustrated in Figure 3.3.

Student: Joshua

Activity: Morning group

date	11/19									
Wheel to group (4 feet)	+									
Imitate "hi" to Sue	+									
Imitate "hi" to John	+									
Look at toy 1	I									
Look at toy 2	D									
Take one toy	V									
Imitate "ball" or "record"	+									
Pass other toy to peer	D									
Activate own toy	P									
Imitate "play"	+									
Look at John	I									
Look at Sue	D									
Take offered toy	I									
Imitate "thank you"	+									
Imitate "ball or record"	–									
Activate toy	P									
Imitate "play"	–									
Look at toy 1	D									
Look at toy 2	D									
Take one toy	V									
Imitate "ball or record"	–									
Pass other toy to peer	D									
Activate own toy	P									
Imitate "play"	+									
etc.										

case because good behavior, such as not spitting, is taken for granted, whereas bad behavior attracts people's attention. An effective curriculum will take this tendency into account and provide opportunities for the student to demonstrate "good" behavior and cues to the teacher that ensure the student will be rewarded for that behavior.

A second problem is being sure that the program is carried out consistently across the school day. Most teachers know that consequating the behavior for only 10 to 20 minutes a day is rarely effective. Deceleration programs, more than any other programs, must be in effect across the entire day if they are to be effective. This is not an easy task, however, and so many teachers compromise. They give up on implementing the program, implement it for only a short time each day and hope that it will generalize, or simply implement punishment when necessary without ensuring that the student is also rewarded for not doing the behavior. Each of these compromises usually results in a frustrated student, a frustrated teacher, and a negative classroom atmosphere. A successful curriculum must use a methodology that incorporates rewards for desirable behavior and consequences for undesirable behavior across staff and classroom activities.

Behavior Checks. The functional curriculum approach encourages scheduling behavior checks into each of the skill sequences devised in the previous step. A *behavior check* is a reminder to look at the student to see if he or she is engaging in desirable or undesirable behavior. These reminders are written on the data sheet as part of the skill sequence. Determination must be made as to how frequently the behavior needs to be checked. Generally, the higher the rate of the problem behavior, the more often behavior checks must be scheduled.

First and most important, behavior checks should be scheduled in such a way as to maximize the chances that the student will be caught being *good*. For example, in teaching a student who frequently puts his hands in his mouth, behavior checks can be scheduled right after the student is asked to hold or reach for objects. This type of scheduling probably will be more likely to allow the teacher to reward the student than would be the case if the behavior checks were scheduled when the student's hands were empty. It should be pointed out that this technique biases data collection by making the behavior appear to be less frequent than it actually is. If this causes concern, the teacher also can record a rate or frequency count in which every instance of the behavior is counted.

A second thing to consider when scheduling behavior checks is the natural flow of the skill sequences. The teacher should try to schedule behavior checks in places where they do not interrupt at critical points in the sequence. For example, assume that a student has the following sequence. He has to:

Figure 3.6 Example of a skill sequence that includes behavior checks.

Approximately 3 minutes	*behavior check*: hands not in mouth come to side, sit look at object reach for object pincer grasp of object (Help student activate object)
Approximately 2 minutes	*behavior check*: hands not in mouth look at object reach for object pincer grasp of object (Help student activate object)
Approximately 3 minutes	*behavior check*: hands not in mouth look at rollator reach for rollator pull to stand with rollator
Approximately 3 minutes	*behavior check*: hands not in mouth look at target area walk 4 feet to target area *behavior check*: hands not in mouth

1. Look at an object
2. Grasp the object
3. Bring the object in front of the face
4. Vocalize

In this case it would disrupt the natural flow of events to place a behavior check between looking at the object and grasping it. Remember that one reason for developing skill sequences is to help the student learn how behaviors go together. Since it is desirable for the student to learn to look at an object and then pick it up, it is important not to interrupt at that point with a behavior check. Figure 3.6 illustrates the placement of behavior checks within two skill sequences.

Teaching in Groups

A very important aspect of the functional curriculum approach is group instruction. *Group instruction* refers to the provision of structured, data-based activities with two or more students within the same session. Instruction can be given to all members of the group simultaneously or sequentially. Most teachers of students with severe handicaps who teach in groups use the sequential format because it is slightly easier to give individualized prompts when each student is instructed in turn. Group instruction is very important for several reasons, including (1) increasing control of motivational variables, (2) providing opportunities to respond to and learn from peers, and (3) providing opportunities to learn certain skills, such as conversation, that require the presence of other persons (Brown, Holvoet, Guess, and Mulligan, 1980).

Control of Motivational Variables. In a one-to-one teaching situation, a teacher who is faced with a student who refuses to respond to a prompt can either wait until a response is given or try to coax the student. Either method can be very reinforcing to some students. In a group, however, a teacher can go on to another student instead of waiting or coaxing, thus removing any reinforcement for refusing to respond. In addition, if the other student is learning the same skill, the student who refused can see both the desired response and the reinforcers gained from participating. Thus, it is likely that refusal will be extinguished without sacrificing opportunities to learn. Similarly, if a student engages in an inappropriate behavior during a one-to-one instructional session, it is more difficult for the teacher to use extinction techniques than it would be during a group session.

Materials, cues, and consequences presented to other students can be highly motivating. It seems to be part of human nature to want what the other person has. In our experience, it may be difficult to get a child to perform a skill such as reaching by offering the child an object. If instead the object is offered to a neighboring child, it is not uncommon to see the first child straining to reach it or to grab it from the neighbor. This behavior can be used to advantage with a student who seems to become easily bored with programs but is very interested in people.

Opportunity to Respond to and Learn from Peers. Studies by Bandura and Walters (1963) and Kazdin and colleagues (Kazdin, 1973; Kazdin, Silverman, and Sittler, 1975) show that both nonhandicapped and mildly handicapped children are very much aware of responses made by other children. Furthermore, children make changes in their responses on the basis of what they see happening to other children. If a peer is punished for stealing, the children watching are less likely to steal in the same situation. If a peer is reinforced for being aggressive, children who observe this are likely to become more aggressive. Thus, it would seem useful to harness this motivation and behavior change technology. Use of the group format is a logical way to begin.

Sometimes, however, severely handicapped students seem to ignore or not even be aware of their peers. Obviously, such students are losing opportunities to learn from their peers. Unfortunately, one-to-one training methods perpetuate this problem. In a one-to-one instructional setting, the adult is always in control of the materials, cues, and reinforcers. Therefore, the student never has the opportunity to learn that other children also have the power to control the environment. Since children are not seen as powerful (i.e., they do not control valued materials or reinforcers), the student may just tune them out.

A group instructional setting gives students the opportunity to interact with one another (though the teacher may need to facilitate these interactions). The students can present materials and reinforcers to each other and thus be perceived as persons worthy of each other's attention. A study by Ruggles and LeBlanc (1979) showed that toddlers learn much more efficiently (faster) when they are taught in groups that are organized in ways that encourage the students to attend to one another's responses or in which the students are in charge of giving cues or consequences. Similar findings have been noted with severely handicapped students (Brown and Holvoet, 1982; Rea, Holvoet, and Schussler, 1983).

Groups do not always have to consist only of handicapped students or be led by adults. The potential for integrating nonhandicapped students into instructional groups designed for handicapped learners constitutes another strong reason for including group instruction in the classroom. Researchers have shown that nonhandicapped students can fulfill several different types of instructional roles successfully if they are adequately trained and supervised and given feedback (Egel, Richman, and Koegel, 1981; Kohl, Moses, and Stettner-Eaton, 1983; Stainback, Stainback, and Hatcher, 1983). For example, a nonhandicapped student can serve as a model and demonstrate the responses that the teacher is trying to elicit from the handicapped student(s). This allows the teacher to ensure that a correct model will be given (since theoretically the nonhandicapped peer already will know how to do the skill correctly) and to demonstrate that reinforcement follows correct performance. The peer model role also makes use of the fact that some children pay more attention to the behaviors of other children than to those of adults.

Nonhandicapped students also can be used in group settings to dispense reinforcers. This can be done very formally by having the teacher give the cue and the peer give the reinforcement if the handicapped student responds correctly. It also can be done less formally by having the nonhandicapped peer reinforce those students in the group who are not being instructed directly by the teacher. The peer in this case can reinforce social behaviors such as looking at the teacher, holding the head upright, not drooling, not engaging in stereotyped or aggressive behavior, and staying seated in the group. The nonhandicapped student also can serve as a peer tutor and take over the teacher's role of presenting materials, presenting cues and prompts, and deciding when to provide reinforcment. This role should be entrusted only to students who have been trained adequately by the classroom teacher. Furthermore, it is very important to supervise and give feedback to peer tutors directly on a weekly basis.

Using nonhandicapped peers in both instructional and noninstructional roles (i.e., special friend programs that encourage interaction in leisure settings) is beneficial not only to students with handicaps but also to nonhandicapped students. Through such contact, understanding and tolerance begin to replace irrational fears and prejudices. The nonhandicapped students learn appropriate ways to interact with persons who differ in some way from themselves and, if properly guided by the classroom teacher, begin to think in terms of what disabled people can do rather than focusing only on the disability.

Opportunity to Learn Group Skills. Working and living in community settings demands that students have skills in interacting with other people. For example, students need to learn to tolerate people who are sitting or standing close to them, to take turns, to cooperate, to compete, to attend to what others are doing, to answer questions, to take and give materials, and to interact socially. It obviously would be difficult to teach such skills in a one-to-one format.

Brown et al. (1980) suggest that there are three major reasons for grouping in community environments: (1) work, particularly in an assembly line, (2) many leisure activities, and (3) conversation. They propose that these skills should be taught in appropriate sized groups. They stress that particular attention must be paid to the area of communication. It is essential that students be taught to communicate with one another as well as with staff members.

It is not recommended that all classroom instruction be done in a group format. Many students need the intensive attention that is available only in a one-to-one teaching situation. It is hoped, however, that a teacher will endeavor to provide every student in the classroom with a mixture of group and one-to-one programming.

Organizing a Functional Group. Brown et al. (1980) have designed a group instruction model that emphasizes the interaction of students participating in the group and the organization of curriculum content for heterogeneous and homogeneous groupings of students. The remainder of this chapter is based on that model. One efficient way to organize a group is to determine which students need to learn the same skill. A session then can be scheduled, and students who need to learn the skill can be placed together in the group. In this way, the students get to practice the skill themselves and also have the opportunity to watch others practice it. An example of such a group can be seen in Figure 3.7.

This group illustrates several students practicing obtaining juice. Note that the organization of this group is fairly artificial. In an actual setting, juice pouring might be done in a group, but one person generally would obtain and pour everyone's juice. In this group, however, the juice is returned to the refrigerator each time so that every member of the group has the op-

Figure 3.7 Example of a group in which all members are learning the same skills. Student 1 practices first, then student 2, then student 3. If time allows, each student is given another turn.

FOOD PREPARATION

Student 1

1. Say "juice"
2. Go to refrigerator
3. Find juice
4. Carry to table
   (Teacher pours, then puts juice away)

Student 2

1. Say "juice"
2. Go to refrigerator
3. Find juice
4. Carry to table
   (Teacher pours, then puts juice away)

Student 3

1. Say "juice"
2. Go to refrigerator
3. Find juice
4. Carry to table
   (Teacher pours, then puts juice away)

Figure 3.8 Example of a group in which all members are learning the same skills. Student 2 can begin as soon as student 1 moves away from the cabinet rather than having to wait until the entire sequence is completed. This sequence is slightly less artificial than the one shown in Figure 3.7.

SETTING TABLE

Student 1	Student 2	Student 3
1. Get plate		
2. Get silver	1. Get plate	
3. Carry to table	2. Get silver	1. Get plate
4. Set place correctly	3. Carry to table	2. Get silver
	4. Set place correctly	3. Carry to table
		4. Set place correctly

portunity to practice the skill. This is not necessarily a bad technique, but a teacher must recognize that it is artificial.

Figure 3.8 illustrates a group in which all three members are being taught to set the table. This group is slightly less artificial than the previous one, since it is possible that a student may be responsible for setting only her own place. At least, items do not have to be removed from the setting and reintroduced by each student in order to practice. In addition, this group could be taught simultaneously or alternately depending on the amount of prompting needed. Nonetheless, this group instruction is also somewhat artificial.

Figure 3.9 describes a group in which all three members are being taught a simple board game. This is an example of very functional and natural group instruction. Most board games depend on each member going through the same motions (rolling the dice and moving the marker) in turn. Thus, the skills learned in this game can be transferred directly to nonschool environments. Admittedly, it is not always possible to devise such functional group instruction, but the teacher must strive for this ideal constantly.

Unfortunately, in a classroom for severely handicapped students, it is rarely possible to organize a group in which all the students are taught the same skill. Generally, the students have such diverse needs and abilities that grouping them to teach a particular skill is impossible. One way to avoid this problem is to organize groups around a domain (or theme) rather than a particular skill. The teacher should try to pick a domain, such as prevocational activities, that includes skills that normally are practiced in a group setting. This will improve generalization of the learned skills. By picking a domain instead of a single skill, the teacher maintains a clear organization for the group but broadens its scope.

Figure 3.10 illustrates a group structured around the prevocational domain. With this structure, the teacher can individualize programs so that each student has the opportunity to learn skills that are at his or her ability level. This is generally the most practical method of grouping in a classroom with a diverse population.This type of group instruction does not give the students an opportunity to watch other students doing the same task, but it may give them the opportunity to learn portions of a variety of tasks. Again, the degree of artificiality of group instruction can vary. In the example shown in Figure 3.10, there was no cohesiveness imposed on the group. Each student did the skill in turn, and the skills were not related in any way. This same group might have been made more natural and cohesive if the teacher had organized it slightly differently. A more functional organization is shown in Figure 3.11.

All the examples of group training presented thus far have been typical of what is called an *intrasequential* group. In the intrasequential group, each student has a short skill sequence, but there is no systematic attempt to have the students interact. Even in groups that show a fairly natural alternation from student to student (Figures 3.9 and 3.11), the students are not re-

Figure 3.9 Example of a group in which all members have the same skill sequence. The alternation among students is natural, as is the skill sequence.

BOARD GAME ACTIVITY

Student 1

1. Roll dice
2. Move marker to designated spot

Student 2

1. Roll dice
2. Move marker to designated spot

Student 3

1. Roll dice
2. Move marker to designated spot

Figure 3.10 Example of an intrasequential group in which each member has a different skill seqence but all sequences are related to the prevocational domain.

PREVOCATIONAL GROUP I

Student 1

1. Say "work"
2. Choose correct screwdriver
3. Insert screw
4. Use screwdriver

Student 2

1. Find bolt or screw
2. Put on template

Student 3

1. Get box
2. Get faucet
3. Put faucet in box
4. Put box aside

Figure 3.11 Example of an intersequential group in which each member is learning a different skill sequence but all sequences are related by domain and materials. Interaction among the group members is structured.

PREVOCATIONAL GROUP II

Student 2

1. Find bolt or screw
2. Put on template

(T. gives template to Student 1)

Student 1

1. Choose correct screwdriver
2. Insert screw into faucet
3. Use screwdriver

(T. gives completed faucet to Student 3)

Student 3

1. Get box
2. Put faucet in box
3. Put box aside

Figure 3.12 Example of an intersequential group designed to improve socialization and communication between peers.

COMMUNICATION AND LEISURE GROUP

Student 1	Student 2
1. Communication board ("I want ______")	
	2. Object discrimination (finds desired object)
3. Communication board (uses verb "give me" or "open it" or "wind it")	
	4. Receptive language (follows one part command given by Student 1)
5. Communication board ("Thank you")	
	6. Expressive language ("Welcome")

quired to interact. The materials are given to each student in turn by the teacher, and the students are not required to look at one another's work or to judge it. Each student's skill cluster is managed by the teacher and involves only the student to whom it is presented.

An alternative format—*intersequential* group instruction—is often possible. The intersequential format requires some sort of *interaction* among group members. In an intersequential group, one skill in each student's sequence specifies an interaction with another student. This interaction could be providing a cue, materials, or a reinforcer to another student. For example, in the leisure group shown in Figure 3.9, the students could pass the dice to the next player. This would be a natural interaction in this context. In the table setting group illustrated in Figure 3.8, each student could check another student's place setting and reinforce that student for a correct performance. In the prevocational example shown in Figure 3.11, a student could pass the materials on to the next student as in a regular assembly line. Another example of an intersequential group is shown in Figure 3.12. The possibilities for interaction are many. The teacher simply needs to determine whether an intersequential or intrasequential group best meets the needs of the students.

When organizing group instruction, it is important to keep each student's skill cluster short (probably no more than two to three skills). The teacher must remember the correct cues, prompts, and reinforcers for each skill. Thus, if the teacher is working with three students, each of whom is working on three different skills, the teacher must be on top of nine programs during the session. Short clusters also help keep students who are waiting for a turn from getting bored or getting into mischief.

Also remember that it is not always necessary or best to alternate among the students. Simultaneous group instruction is sometimes a good alternative if the students require similar levels of prompting or if some of the students are imitative. Although the first few sessions of a simultaneous group are likely to be chaotic, teaching several students the same skill simultaneously can be very efficient and will do away with behavior problems that occur when students are not engaged directly in instruction. If there is one student who seems to need more attention than others, another possibility is to give that student more turns. Also remember to use behavior checks to maintain good waiting behaviors (e.g., hands to self, sitting in seat, no stereotyped behavior).

In Figure 3.13, student 1 tends to have behavior problems. As can be seen, the teacher focuses on this student more often than on the other two students in the group. When using this method, it is important to be sure that *all* students are receiving adequate amounts of reinforcement and attention. Even if a student has not previously shown any problems waiting for a turn, it may be wise to reinforce good waiting occasionally to be sure that the student does not decide to begin acting up in order to gain the attention given to students who misbehave.

Figure 3.13 An intrasequential group that has behavior checks built into student 1's sequence. All skills sequences are related to the domain of mealtime and fine motor skills.

SNACK SEQUENCE

Student 1	Student 2	Student 3
1. Behavior check		
	2. Say "hi" to student 1	
	3. Say "hi" to student 2	
	4. Say "hi" to student 3	
5. Behavior check		
6. Take cookie from teacher		
7. Take bite		
	8. Open jar	
	9. Take candy	
10. Behavior check		
		11. Unwrap candy
		12. Hand to mouth
13. Behavior check		
14. Take cookie from teacher		
15. Take bite		

In summary, group programming is an essential part of the functional curriculum approach. Group programming allows the students to be exposed to many skills that can be learned in no other setting and provides the students with natural opportunities to interact. It can be used even in classrooms where the population has a diversity of abilities and needs.

Summary

The initial advances in teaching students with severe handicaps followed the principles of operant conditioning. Instruction often was carried out under artificial circumstances including laboratory settings, massed trials, and one-to-one instruction. Recent developments have shown that skills can be better generalized and the student better motivated when instruction is carried out in more natural and functional circumstances. The functional curriculum model recommends ways to select functional skills and teach them with natural cues and materials. The model emphasizes the relatedness and meaningfulness of a behavior to other behaviors and to the environmental context. The chapter suggests ways in which functional skills can be taught in groups, in the daily routine, and in communication, motor, and behavior programs.

Chapter 4

Measurement

Dolores Jenkin

So far, we have focused on selecting appropriate goals and developing teaching procedures that enable students with severe handicaps to acquire, maintain, become proficient in, and generalize their newly taught skills. The next step is to institute a measurement system that will monitor pupil progress accurately as a function of instruction. A working assumption in describing instructional procedures is that the power of teaching techniques must be increased proportionately to the severity of the handicap of the student (Gold, 1975). Students with severe handicaps need more carefully specified instructional programs in order to induce meaningful amounts of learning. Similarly, a more precise measurement system is needed for students who exhibit severe handicaps. With nonhandicapped students, it may be sufficient to give grades on a quarterly basis and give tests once a week or even once a month. With students who have severe handicaps, these intervals between measurement of pupil progress would be too long to evaluate instruction properly.

The Importance of Measurement

Because instructional time is so precious and because learned behavior often deteriorates rapidly, the teacher must know on an almost daily basis exactly how well the student is progressing. At the end of each week, the teacher should judge whether the student is progressing sufficiently on each targeted skill. The main pieces of evidence that influence this judgment are the student's performance on written objectives as measured by data recorded throughout the week. Without carefully recorded data, the teacher will not be in a position to make an accurate judgment as to whether the student is progressing, regressing, or maintaining the same level of performance. The behaviors being taught are often minuscule acts that represent small bits of a task analysis, e.g., a glance at a light or a quarter rotation on a bicycle pedal. Without a precise measurement system, there is no way to tell whether the student is learning these bits of behavior.

Figure 4.1 The learning of a bolt-washer-nut assembly task.

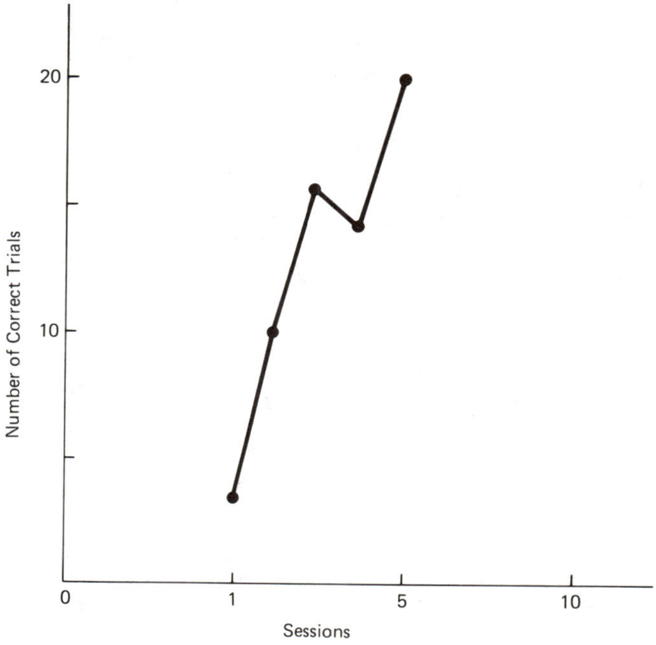

The main reason for collecting daily, formative data is to assist the teacher in ascertaining whether a teaching technique is working and whether there need to be changes in the instructional procedures. Because of the serious learning problems of students with severe handicaps, there is no guarantee that the program you design will work. The programs are likely to require persistent fine-tuning to make them maximally effective. For success in the fine-tuning process, accurate data must be fed back to the teacher constantly to indicate the extent of pupil progress.

Let us give a few examples that illustrate the importance of a formative measurement system. Consider a student who is learning to assemble a nut, bolt, and washer in a vocational training session. She is given 20 trials per session. Figure 4.1 shows the progress made over five sessions. Clearly, the task was learned rapidly to the 100 percent correct criterion in session 5. The short-term objective on the student's IEP stated that the skill would be learned in 1 month. The student's actual learning rate was much faster than the one predicted by the IEP team that set the objective. If daily data had not been kept, the teacher might not have been aware of this rapid progress but instead might have continued to run sessions on a task that already had been mastered. This would have wasted valuable instructional sessions in which the student could have been learning the next objective on the IEP.

Figure 4.2 Failure to master an instructional task.

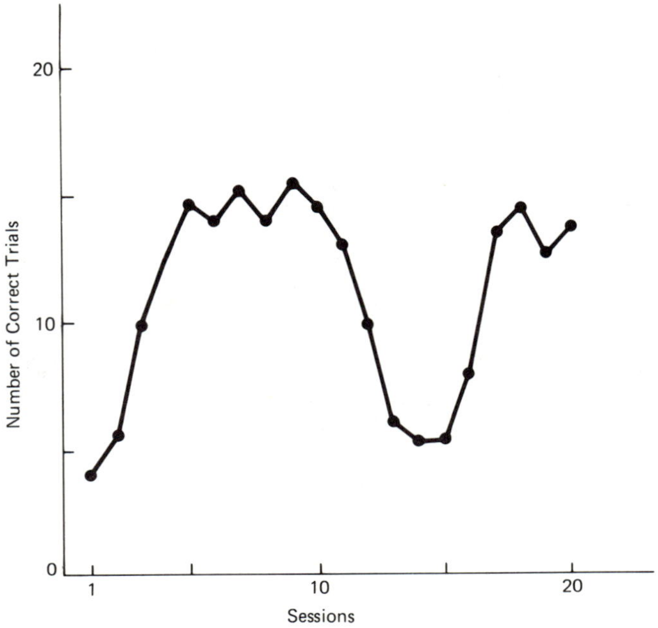

The more likely result of failing to collect formative data is shown in Figure 4.2. Here a student is unsuccessful in mastering a task. There are initial increases in performance. A second phase shows a plateau in performance (sessions 6 through 10). This is followed by a regression in performance (sessions 11 through 15). Finally, there is an increase but a failure to reach criterion. If the teacher had failed to collect data, there would have been much ambiguity concerning how the student was progressing. The occasional increases in performance might have led the teacher to believe that the student was mastering the task. Daily data collection would have allowed the teacher to review progress after the first week (session 5) and again after the second week (session 10). After the first week review, the accelerated graph would tell the teacher that learning was occurring and that the teacher should continue with the same intervention. Review of the graph after the second week would indicate no substantial progress and would lead the teacher to conclude that a change in teaching procedures was needed. The failure to collect data would not permit the teacher to be aware of the absence of pupil learning and the need for changes in instruction.

In summary, there are a number of reasons why frequent and repeated data must be collected on the performance of students with severe handicaps. These students make small gains in learning over time that are discernible only with reliable and repeated measurement. The collection of accurate data indicates to the teacher when the student has learned a task and can move on to the next skill or objective. Formative data also tell the teacher when learning is not taking place so that there is a need to alter the teaching techniques. In addition to collecting data on the pupil's performance during instruction, it is important for the teacher to monitor the instruction itself, particularly when several different individuals participate in teaching the students each program. A program may not be working because it does not meet the student's instructional needs and learning style. Another reason for failure may be that the written program is not being implemented as it should.

Developing a Recording System

There are numerous ways in which a teacher may proceed in establishing a system to record pupil progress. As with instructional procedures, there is no simple or set way to proceed. The teacher must be aware of the different recording systems available and select them according to the characteristics of the task, the student, and the learning situation. We shall describe the different recording techniques and provide rules of thumb for their selection and use.

Trial-by-Trial System

Trial-by-trial recording is a straightforward measurement system that blends directly into the discrete-trial teaching format. In Chapter 2 we examined the various ways in which prompts and reinforcers can be used in discrete-trial teaching. In Chapter 3 we expanded the use of those strategies to distributed trials and functional curricular sequences. A *training session* is defined as a given number of learning trials. The accumulated number of correct trials for a particular response—whether in massed, spaced, or distributed trials—is an indication of the student's performance for that session.

Recording Performance. Figure 4.3 shows a recording sheet for a series of discrete-trial sessions. The teacher records a plus or minus after each individual trial, and the pluses are summed at the bottom of each session column for a score. Figure 4.4 shows how the data have been transferred from the recording sheet to a graph. The ordinate, or *Y* axis, represents student performance, in this case the number of correct trials. In trial-by-trial measurement the performance score can be converted to percent correct. For example, in Figure 4.4, session 1, five out of ten correct would be plotted as 50 percent. When there are the same number of trials across sessions—as is often the case in discrete-trial instruction—it is optional to convert the score to percentages. The form of the graph will be the same whether it is plotted

Figure 4.3 Recording sheet for a discrete-trial session.

	Session						
Trials	9/20	9/21	9/22	9/23	9/24	9/27	9/28
1	+	−	+	−	+	−	+
2	−	+	+	+	+	−	+
3	−	−	+	+	+	+	+
4	−	+	+	+	−	+	+
5	+	+	−	−	−	+	+
6	+	−	−	+	−	−	+
7	−	−	+	+	+	+	−
8	−	−	+	+	+	+	+
9	+	+	−	−	−	+	+
10	+	+	−	+	+	−	−
Total	5	5	6	7	6	6	8

Figure 4.4 Plotting repeated measure data on *xy* coordinates.

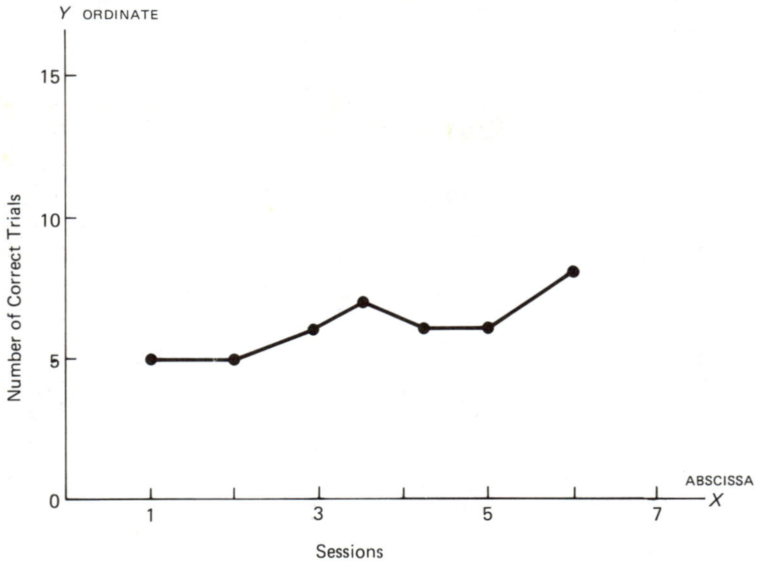

in percentages or the actual number (frequency) of correct trials. When the number of trials varies from session to session, it is mandatory to convert the raw score into percentages. For example, a score of eight correct on sessions containing ten, twelve, or twenty trials would represent percent correct performances of 80, 67, and 90 percent, respectively. These rather different performance levels must be represented by percentage scores rather than raw frequency scores.

Returning to Figure 4.4, the abscissa, or *X* axis, represents consecutive learning sessions. In general, formative measurement graphs present the passage of time on the abscissa. The repeated measurement of performance on the abscissa can be expressed in units of sessions, calendar days, or other units of time such as minutes or weeks. The ordinate indicator of performance can be displayed with a variety of measurement units that are described in this chapter, e.g., correct trials, duration, or rate. Become familiar with the performance by time format of repeated measure graphs. You should be able to pick up a graph and within seconds interpret the learning progress of a student correctly. This is the main reason for graphing data; the graph quickly summarizes past performance in a way that memory, words, or numbers cannot.

Recording Devices. The most frequently used recording medium for trial-by-trial recording is paper and pencil. A recording sheet is placed on a desk or clipboard, and entries are made after each trial. When it is inconvenient to carry around a recording sheet, there are a number of alternatives for recording. A strip of adhesive tape may be pressed onto an article of the teacher's clothing, such as the thigh part of the trousers. Responses then are scored in a row of pluses and minuses along the tape with a pencil or pen. At the end of the session, the tape is removed and the session score can be plotted on a graph. It is also possible to use a wristwatch golf counter or a hand-held calculator to record pluses after each correct trial. At the end of the session, the accumulated number of correct trials will appear in the window of the device. A disadvantage of window devices is that they do not provide a trial-by-trial tally of performance or let the instructor keep track of which trial is taking place. For these reasons, golf counters and calculators are better suited for measuring rate than for measuring trial data.

Multiple-Response Measurement

So far we have mentioned trial-by-trial recording in which one behavior is measured on each trial. It is also possible to have more than one response recorded per trial. For example, a skill behavior and a problem behavior both can be measured on each trial. The skill behavior is recorded plus or minus in the fashion described above. In addition, if a problem behavior (e.g., hand

Figure 4.5 Recording sheet for the simultaneous measurement of a skill and a problem behavior.

Sessions

Trials	10/1		10/2		10/3		10/4		10/5	
	S	P	S	P	S	P	S	P	S	P
1	+	+	+	+						
2	–	+	–	–						
3	–	+	–	+						
4	–	+	–	+						
5	–	+	–	–						
6	–	–	–	–						
7	–	–	–	+						
8	–	+	–	+						
9	–	+	–	+						
10	–	+	–	+						
Total	1	8	1	7						

S = Skill behavior
P = Problem behavior

biting) appears between the delivery of the S^D and the presentation of the reinforcer, a plus is scored in the problem behavior box for that trial. Figure 4.5 shows a recording sheet in which each trial in each session has two entry boxes, one for the skill behavior and one for the problem behavior. At the end of the session, the totals for each of these behaviors are plotted on a graph. Figure 4.6 shows how the curves for the two behaviors can be plotted on the same graph. This graph displays the desired result of having the two curves cross, which shows that the problem behavior decreases as the skill behavior is acquired.

This data collection format is especially relevant when the teacher expects a problem behavior to change as a function of learning a new skill. This format also can be useful if a teacher suspects that certain behaviors become worse when the student is experiencing failure. For example, data may show that on trials in which errors occur a student emits self-abusive behavior, whereas on correct trials self-abusive behavior does not appear. The teacher can use this information to reduce the level of difficulty of the task presented to the student and thus decrease the amount of self-abuse.

Concurrent Chains. Another kind of multiple-response measure can be used when concurrent chains are taught. On each trial, a chain of behavior is

Figure 4.6 Plotting a skill and problem behavior on a repeated measures graph.

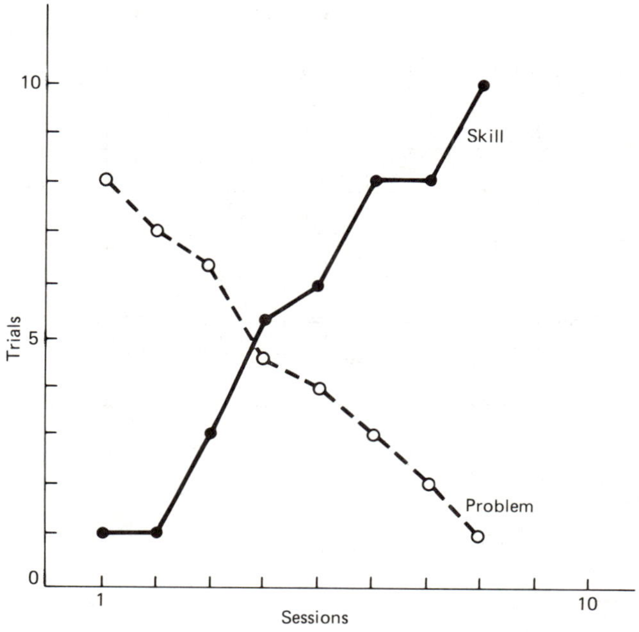

emitted. Figure 4.7 shows a recording sheet for a concurrent chain. Each trial in the session has a column of five boxes representing the five behaviors of the chain R_1——R_2——R_3——R_4——R_5. At the end of each trial, the teacher makes plus or minus entries in each box. At the end of the session, the total number of pluses across trials is summed to give a session score. In this case, there were five trials and five responses per trial. Therefore, the session score could range between 0 (no correct responses throughout the session) to 25 (5×5, no errors in the session). Figure 4.8 displays the graph of these data. The total scores for each session are plotted successively on the ordinate.

The recording sheets for concurrent chains permit an analysis of what responses in the chain are causing the most difficulty. One can sum the pluses and minuses across the rows of each behavior and note which behaviors are producing numerous errors. For example, in Figure 4.7, response 3 is rarely correct, but the other four behaviors seem to be showing steady improvement across sessions. The difficulty in response 3 tells the teacher that some modifications in instruction may be needed to teach this behavior, such as task-analyzing the step into two or more smaller steps.

Functional Skills Sequences. Charting skill sequences also requires a multiple-response data recording system. Several responses will appear in

Figure 4.7 Recording sheet for a concurrent chain.

Sessions and Trials																
Responses	11/3					11/4					11/5					Total
	1	2	3	4	5	1	2	3	4	5	1	2	3	4	5	
1. LOOK	+	+	−	+	+	+	+	+	−	+	+	+	+	+	+	13
2. REACH	−	−	+	+	+	−	+	+	+	−	+	+	+	+	−	10
3. GRASP	−	−	+	−	−	−	−	−	+	−	+	−	−	−	−	3
4. PLACE	+	+	−	+	+	−	−	+	+	+	+	+	+	+	−	11
5. DROP	−	−	+	+	+	+	+	+	−	+	−	−	−	+	+	9
Total trials	2	2	3	4	4	2	3	4	3	3	4	3	3	4	2	
Sessions	15					15					16					46

Figure 4.8 Graph of concurrent chain data.

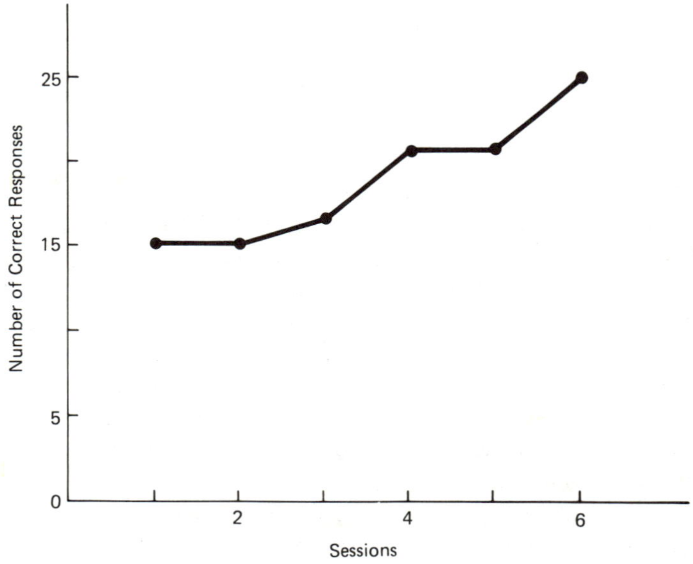

one skill sequence, some only once, and others perhaps more than once. Figure 4.9 shows a recording sheet for the skill sequence introduced to reflect several of Ann's IEP objectives. The data sheet has a recording procedure to indicate Ann's response on each step. The teacher begins at the top of the list of responses on the left, giving the cue "Look, Ann" to begin a sequence focusing on both motor behavior and language objectives. If Ann successfully raises her head into an upright position, the teacher marks a

Figure 4.9 Recording sheet for one of Ann's skill clusters using a modified self-graphing procedure.

Responses	Date and Teacher's Initials							
	9/10 RR	9/11 LV	9/11 RG	9/12 RG	9/13 LV	9/14 RG	9/14 LV	9/15 RG
Head up	10	10	10	10	10	10	10	10
Look at picture to left	9	9	9	9	9	9	9	9
Look at picture to right	8	8	8	8	8	8	8	8
Point to "drink"	7	7	7	7	7	7	7	7
Look at picture to left	6	6	6	6	6	6	6	6
Look at picture to right	5	5	5	5	5	5	5	5
Point to "Mommy"	4	4	4	4	4	4	4	4
Look at picture to left	3	3	3	3	3	3	3	3
Look at picture to right	2	2	2	2	2	2	2	2
Point to "drink"	1	1	1	1	1	1	1	1
	0	0	0	0	0	0	0	0

slash through the number next to that response (in this case, a 10). The teacher then proceeds to deliver the instructional cue to Ann to "Show me drink": Ann is supposed to scan both of the two picture choices, which would be varied for position on each of the three trials for drink versus Mommy. On this first opportunity to respond, the teacher would note whether Ann scanned both right and left and whether she pointed correctly to the drink. The next trial would involve the same scanning behaviors and then pointing to the picture of Ann's mother, followed by a final trial in which Ann is to point to the drink again. When the teacher is finished with the "session" for this particular skill sequence, one would know which behaviors Ann performed correctly (these would be marked with a slash across the number on each row) and which she did not (no slash would be marked). To use the data sheet as a graph of the number of steps in the skill sequence performed correctly, the teacher can total the numbers in the column for each "session" that have a slash through them and circle this number.

We have entered several days of performance data for Ann, showing that she initially did not point correctly to the drink and did not scan the picture to the left. After several days, her scanning behavior improved markedly so that she could look at both pictures before she made a choice. Also, her performance on the entire skill sequence improved considerably, with the last 3 days of data showing eight out of ten steps performed correctly. However, she still was not correctly identifying "drink." The teacher probably should

Figure 4.10 Recording sheets for an intersequential group following different programs, same theme format (playing with Lego® blocks).

Trainer ______________________ Person charting ______________________

Ann	Date	Step	Trials					Summary	Date	Step	Trials					Summary	Comments
Head up	1/12	1	+	+	PA	+	+	4/5	1/13	2	PA	+	/	+	+	3/5	
Reach for Lego®		1	−	PA	PA	V	−	0/5		1	PA	PA	+	+	+	3/5	Not reaching far enough but much better
Grasp Lego®		3	+	PA	+	PA	PA	2/5		4	PA	+	V	+	+	3/5	"
Release Lego® in Kim's hand		2	+	+	+	+	+	5/5		3	−	PA	+	+	+	3/5	Ann seems to enjoy giving Kim the Lego piece.

Kim	Date	Step	Trials					Summary	Date	Step	Trials					Summary	Comments
Look at Lego®	1/12	1	+	+	+	+	+	5/5	1/13	2	−	PA	+	−	V	1/5	Progress OK, stay at step 2
Ask Ann for Lego®		1	−	V	V	+	−	1/5		1	V	+	+	/	+	3/5	
Take Lego®		3	+	+	−	+	+	4/5		3	V	+	−	V	+	2/5	Needs occasional verbal to not move hand
Put Lego® on baseboard		4	+	+	−	+	+	4/5		4	−	+	−	−	+	2/5	*Failure on previous step seems to lead to refusal to put on board.

Scoring key: + = correct PA = physical prompt / = partially correct
− = incorrect V = verbal prompt

structure some additional practice with this task either by designing other skill sequences with "drink" or by doing isolated mass-trial practice with the picture of a drink.

Multiple-Student Measurements. Figure 4.10 shows a sample data sheet for recording the performance of two students, Ann and Kim, who are learning to engage in mutual play with Lego blocks. The teacher is using an intersequential group instruction format, as described in Chapter 3. Note that each student has separate target objectives (Ann has four steps to perform, and Kim also has four different steps to do) and that the behavior of one student functions as a stimulus (or consequence) to the behavior of the other student.

With this more complex type of data recording format and instructional situation, the teacher probably will not be able to collect data during instruction. Thus, the data sheet assumes that a second person will observe the group and collect data on the pupil's behavior. Since this will require considerable staff time, the teacher can schedule data collection on a probe basis rather than continuously. Initially, the teacher may want to have a paraprofessional monitor the group instructional session every other time it is scheduled. Later these probes can be conducted less frequently, perhaps once a week. Since intersequential groups are designed so that the behavior of one student affects the behavior of another, it is crucial that the flow of activity not be interrupted, as might happen if the teacher were to stop after each step to record an individual response. Collecting data on a probe basis should give an accurate representation of a student's pattern of learning. The probe data sessions should be collected more frequently in the initial stages of instruction or when the error rate on a task increases.

Because of the complexity of multiple-response measurement, some type of paper and pencil sheet is needed. A clipboard with an 8 1/2 by 11 inch surface area to attach the data sheet may be used. It is also possible to use hand-held 5 by 8 inch cards listing the behaviors in the chain and a scoring grid across trials and sessions in the same way that a larger sheet would. The smaller cards are more portable and less visible and can be handled easily in community settings.

Recording Prompts

So far we have described the score on each trial as being either a plus or a minus. The student performed the behavior either correctly or incorrectly. In a discrete-trial format in which no prompts are provided, this recording procedure is straightforward. You may have noticed, however, that on Figure 4.10 the teacher went beyond recording merely whether the behavior was correct. In many cases, the teacher will want more information about the student's performance, particularly since the behavior is seldom completely correct (plus) or completely wrong (minus). Valuable pupil performance information would be lost if the recording system did not allow the teacher to record small changes in behavior.

For example, data for 2 weeks of trial-by-trial performance could look like the following (note that the letter R is used in such a program to signify Thursday):

	Week 1					Week 2				
Tom's %	M	T	W	R	F	M	T	W	R	F
Correct Responses:	0	0	10	30	10	10	20	20	20	20

For this program, Tom was expected to sign "water" whenever he was asked, "What do you want to drink?" The teacher might conclude from this summary that Tom's program is not working. Suppose, however, that on

Wednesday, Thursday, and Friday of the first week, the responses that were scored with a minus were trials on which Tom signed "cookie" instead of "water."

At the beginning of the second week, Tom's incorrect responses changed. Instead of signing "cookie" for water, he signed "more." Finally, on Wednesday of week 2, almost all his incorrect responses were not the signs for "cookie" and "more" but were unacceptable approximations of the sign for "water." Because the teacher's recording system scores only plus or minus, Tom's interesting changes in behavior across the 2 weeks would be lost. Furthermore, the teacher might conclude that he was not learning even though by the end of week 2 learning was developing.

Thus, in addition to scoring correct and incorrect responses, the teacher usually wants to include scoring symbols for other behavior variations, such as partial corrects or prompted responses (see Figure 4.10). In addition, a "comments" column by the date of each session allows the teacher to record any notes that may be important regarding the pupil's incorrect responses, behavior during prompting, etc.

On tasks in which prompts are delivered on error trials, there are two ways to record pupil performance. The first and simpler way is to continue to record only pluses and minuses. Pluses are recorded for correct trials and minuses for any trial that requires a prompt. A more in-depth recording procedure would be to designate the type of prompt given on the recording sheet. For example, on Figure 4.11 the recording sheet contains VP for verbally prompted trials, PPA for partial physical assistance, TPA for total physical assistance, and / for partial corrects. At the bottom of the trial column a space for comments allows the teacher to enter even more information regarding the child's behavior.

Recording this information enables the teacher to understand how the child's behavior is actually changing, such as whether there is movement from more intense (TPA) to milder (PPA or VP) prompts. The teacher also may discover that one type of prompt is being used more often than may be necessary or that there has been a failure to try out less intrusive prompts after a string of correct responses.

It is also possible to designate each prompt or plus score with a number. This system assumes that there is a hierarchy of prompts with more or less assistance provided. Such a system might score as follows: correct performance = 4, verbal prompt = 3, model prompt = 2, and physical prompt = 1. The recording sheet grid would be filled with these numbers rather than with pluses, VPs, TPAs, etc. At the end of the session, a score can be tabulated by adding up all the numbers. For example, a ten-trial session could have a range of possible scores from 10 (10 trials × 1, all physical prompts) to 40 (10 trials × 4, all correct responses). The ordinate on the graph would reflect this numerical range of 10 to 40. Besides looking at the total session

Figure 4.11 Recording sheet with entries for type of prompt.

Student ____________________

Program objective ______________

S^D __________ Response(s) ____________

Recording key: + = correct
— = incorrect
/ = partially correct
PPA = Partial physical assist
TPA = Total physical assist
VP = Verbal prompt

Session Date									
2/5	2/6	2/7	2/8	2/9	2/12	2/13	2/14	2/15	2/16
10 —	10 —	10	10 —	10	10	10	10 +	10 +	10 /
9 TPA	9 —	9	9 +	9	9	9	9 /	9 +	9 /
8 —	8 TPA	8	8 TPA	8	8	8	8 VP	8 —	8 +
7 TPA	7 TPA	7	7 TPA	7	7	7	7 /	7 /	7 +
6 —	6 —	6	6 +	6	6	6	6 +	6 /	6 /
5 —	5 TPA	5	5 +	5	5	5	5 /	5 VP	5 /
4 TPA	4 —	4	4 TPA	4	4	4	4 VP	4 VP	4 VP
3 TPA	3 TPA	3	(3) TPA	3	3	3	3 /	3 /	3 VP
2 TPA	2 —	2	2 —	2	2	(2)	(2) PPA	(2) /	(2) /
1 —	1 TPA	(1)	1 TPA	(1)	(1)	1	1 /	1 /	1 VP
(0)	(0)	0	0	0	0	0	0	0	0
Comments									
Signed "cookie"			Signed "more"		Incorrect sign "water"				

score, the teacher can scan the recording sheet to see whether there has been progress from more intense to less intense prompts.

Designating prompts with letters or numbers is certainly a more precise recording procedure than simply using pluses and minuses, but in some cases the plus and minus system will suffice. If the behavior to be learned has been broken down into a response that the student should be able to learn in a reasonable number of sessions (say, five to ten), acquisition should be rapid enough so that the shift from minus to plus scores provides an adequate information base. But if the student is a slow learner and the task is particularly difficult so that several weeks of instruction may be needed or if the student has a past history of needing many prompts before mastery occurs, it is advisable to use the letter or numerical scoring system for recording prompts.

Finally, it is possible to combine features of trial-by-trial data collection, prompt recording strategies, and graphing of correct responses on one data sheet. Figure 4.11 displays the results of instruction with Tom's sign for "water." This format is extremely convenient to use since the teacher does not need to construct a separate graph to plot the data after instruction. Rather, a recording sheet and a graphing sheet are combined.

Rate Data

Discrete-trial learning is probably the most precise measurement system when a student is acquiring a new behavior. Once the student acquires the behavior, the issues of production, generalization, and maintenance become important (White and Haring, 1976). *Production* refers to the number of items completed. *Generalization* entails the transfer of a learned behavior to another setting, person, material, or cue. *Maintenance* is the correct performance of a learned behavior after time has elapsed (days or months) since its initial acquisition. For these types of learning we want to make sure that the student produces the behavior at a substantial rate in the appropriate settings. Since we do not have to monitor the prompts and reinforcers used for each response, we are often interested in the number of responses appearing in a given amount of time. This is precisely the definition of *rate*. *Frequency* simply denotes the total number of responses appearing and does not tell how rapidly the responses occurred. Rate indicates the number of responses emitted in a specified unit of time. Since we often are interested in the number of responses per session, day, or hour, rate is a commonly used measure in programs for students with severe handicaps.

Suppose a 16-year-old student named Alice had been working on an IEP objective to assemble ball-point pens. As is usually the case when a new task is first being learned, during the acquisition phase there was no concern with the speed or rate of assembly of the pens. A discrete-trial format was used in which she learned the concurrent chain of the pen assembly. When she reached the criterion of 100 percent correct assembly for fifteen trials on three consecutive sessions, she attained the acquisition objective. At this point, her formative data indicated she was assembling about fifteen pens in a 30-minute session. That is, Alice had a rate of 0.5 pens per minute, or 30 pens per hour. A long-term goal for Alice was to work in competitive employment at a factory in the community not far from where she lives. In that factory, new employees were expected to be able to assemble pens at the rate of sixty per hour, or one per minute. It was decided by the IEP team that a reasonable and functional goal for Alice would be to approximate that rate of pen assembly. Therefore, a production IEP objective was set so that Alice would assemble sixty pens correctly in an hour for three consecutive sessions.

A measurement system was needed to monitor Alice's production rate

Figure 4.12 Recording sheet and graph for rate data.

	Session					
	1	2	3	4	5	6
Rate per minute	1.0	2.0	5.0	3.0	.5	4.0

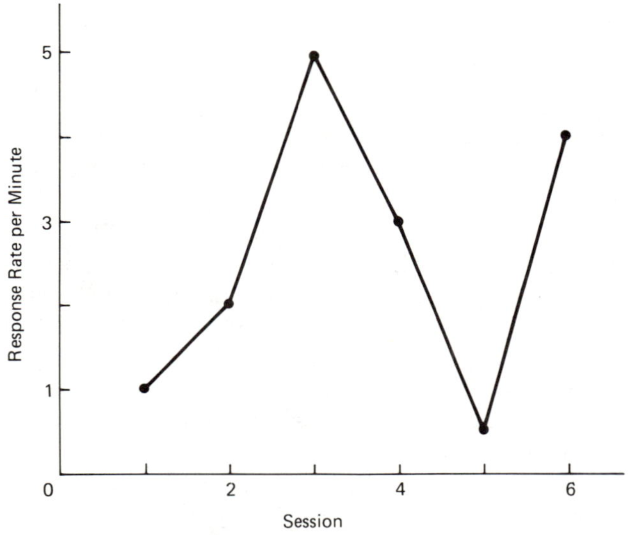

accurately. A simple recording sheet was established on which each day the teacher would enter the rate of correctly assembled pens in that session. Figure 4.12 shows this recording sheet, on which the numerical rate is entered for each session.

Another common use of rate data is to measure problem behavior. The rate of occurrence of a problem behavior can be keyed to a particular learning session. It is likely to be keyed to a school day, and so an IEP objective might indicate that the student is to reduce the rate of striking others from five per day to one per day (for 30 consecutive days). In the case of problem behavior, a rate lower than the targeted one would of course be desirable. In this case, the teacher can set up a recording sheet on which the instances of striking behavior can be tallied throughout the day. Figure 4.13 displays such a sheet. Each day has a large box where check marks for each response can be entered. At the end of the day, the check marks are summed, entered on the recording sheet, and plotted on a graph. The metric on the graph would be the number of responses per day.

The recording of rate data may take other variations. In discrete-trial data collection the teacher is always with the student, and recordings are made at the end of each trial. The session is teacher-paced, since the teacher con-

Figure 4.13 Sheet for recording continuous rate data throughout the day.

	Day				
	3/1	3/2	3/3	3/4	3/5
Tally	✓✓✓ ✓✓✓	✓✓	✓✓✓✓ ✓✓✓✓ ✓✓✓	✓✓✓ ✓✓	✓✓✓ ✓✓✓✓ ✓
Responses	6	2	11	5	8

trols when the S^D is given and how long the intertrial interval will last. Recording is less demanding since the teacher can slow the pace of instruction to make sure that all behaviors are recorded accurately.

In some instances, though, recording becomes more demanding. For example, if a student has a high-rate problem behavior, the constant recording may tax the teacher and detract from the instructional stimuli delivered to other students. In the case of a student getting out of the seat once per minute, there are several ways to approach the issue of recording a high-rate behavior. The teacher can have a tally sheet like the one in Figure 4.13 on a clipboard and enter recordings each time the behavior occurs. A proliferation of clipboards for all students may be engendered, though, and the tally sheet thus may not be the most viable recording device. The teacher instead can use adhesive tape on the arm or leg to tally each response. Wristwatch golf counters are also quite useful in recording rate data. Their compactness, ease of operation, and portability make them appealing for recording high-rate behavior across different settings. A teacher also may reserve a portion of the chalkboard for recording and then transfer the tally to recording sheets at the end of the day.

In the case of low-rate behaviors (one per hour or one per day), the demands of recording are appreciably lessened and any of these recording devices should suffice. For higher-rate behaviors, it is sufficient to collect *probe* data once or twice each day as long as the time period is consistent (e.g., from 8:30 to 9:00 A.M. daily) and reflects a time when the behavior is likely to appear.

Recording Intervals

There is another way to conceptualize the appearance of behavior in a given time. Rather than counting the number of occurrences per unit of time (rate), a recording is made of whether the behavior appeared at all during a given interval. Thus, a school day from 9 A.M. to 3 P.M. can be broken down into twelve half-hour intervals. Whenever the targeted behavior, e.g., soiling underwear, occurs, the teacher makes a single check in the box for that half-

Figure 4.14 Recording sheet for the interval recording of toileting accidents.

	Day							
Time	4/1	4/2	4/3	4/4	4/5	4/6	4/7	4/8
9:00	✓		✓		✓		✓	✓
9:30		✓		✓		✓		
10:00								
10:30								
11:00								
11:30								
12:00								
12:30	✓	✓		✓	✓		✓	✓
1:00								
1:30			✓					
2:00						✓		
2:30	✓							
Total	3	2	2	2	2	2	2	2

hour interval (see Figure 4.14). The recording should be made at the time of the occurrence of the behavior. If the teacher can reliably remember whether the behavior occurred or if there is a residue from the behavior, e.g., soiled underwear, the recording can be made at the end of the interval. At the end of the day the occurrence intervals are summed to produce a daily score. This score can be plotted on a graph in terms of number of intervals per day. Interval recording sheets are also informative because they may indicate a pattern for the time of day when the behavior is appearing. For example, in Figure 4.14 the student tends to have toilet accidents between 9 and 10 A.M. and between 12:30 and 1:00 P.M. This information can help the teacher establish intensive programs at times when the behavior is most likely to occur.

Interval recording can be used most easily by teachers when there are rather long intervals, e.g., 15 minutes or more. When the intervals are brief, e.g., 20 seconds, it becomes quite difficult to teach one or more students, pay attention to a stopwatch, and make the recordings every 20 seconds. Small interval recording is done primarily in the context of research in which separate observers spend all their time recording behavior.

Time Sampling

In our discussion of rate and interval data, the demands of recording and teaching a number of challenging students with high-rate behaviors were mentioned. In some cases it is too difficult to record all the targeted behaviors throughout the school day. Rather than carrying out no data collection, there are alternatives that permit the collection of systematic data. We already have mentioned probes, in which the teacher monitors a student's behavior for a sample of all of the sessions. Another compromise alternative is time sampling, which allows the teacher to make recordings at brief designated times throughout the day. For example, the teacher may want an indicator of the proportion of time that students spend working on tasks. A time-sample system can be set up so that every 15 minutes the teacher looks around the room and records a plus for each student working on tasks. The teacher and students continue their work for the next 15 minutes with no observations or recordings made. When the next 15 minutes elapse, the teacher takes another fast look around the room and records pluses and minuses for each student. A recording sheet is generated that contains twenty-four boxes for each day (6 hours × 4 times per hour). The pluses are tabulated for each day and then are plotted on a graph across days.

The length of the "look" and "no-look" intervals can vary during time sampling. For example, in the previous case there was a 15-minute no-look interval and a 1-second look interval. It is possible to have shorter no-look intervals and longer look intervals, e.g., 30 minutes of no-look, 1 minute of look. Whatever length the intervals are, make sure that you understand the difference between interval recording and time sampling. In interval recording the observer constantly looks at behavior throughout the school day or session. At the end of the interval, a recording is made based on whether the behavior occurred at any time during the interval. As soon as the recording occurs, the next observational interval begins, and this procedure repeats itself. Thus, the observer is looking continually at pupil behavior. In time sampling there is no observation for an extended period of time (the no-look interval). Then, for a relatively short time period (the look interval) the observer looks at the students and records whether the behavior occurred during the look interval.

Time sampling, like other measurement systems, can be keyed to a reinforcement schedule. For example, if a skill behavior is observed during the look interval, the student can be reinforced. Similarly, if a negative behavior appears in the look interval, the behavior can be consequated (see Chapter 5). Interval recording also can cue a teacher to reinforce behavior at the end of each interval. With rate data, the student can be reinforced after a given amount of time if a designated level of correct responding has been maintained.

Time-sample data recording must be distinguished from other systems, though, because it amounts to throwing away much of the data. With time sampling, an assumption is made that the behavior occurring in the look interval is representative of the behavior that appears in the no-look interval. This may or may not be the case.

Thus, there is a risk of making inferences about a student's behaviors on the basis of an incomplete data base. These potential risks are counterbalanced by the practical advantages of freeing the teacher from the demands of constant recording. In selecting any measurement system, always weigh the advantages against the disadvantages. Time sampling, as the name implies, provides only a sample or portion of pupil behavior. Yet almost all of the measurement and assessment that one can conduct provides only a sample of behavior. One always is left to make inferences about student skills and abilities from these samples. Therefore, select a measurement system that is both comprehensive and practical for implementation in your class.

Duration of Responses

The final measurement unit to be discussed is duration. *Duration* refers to the amount of time it takes to complete a behavior from the beginning of its appearance until it is completed. If the defined behavior is the phrase "How are you doing today?" the duration is the time from the statement of "how" to the completion of "today." This is a good example of a behavior in which a teacher may be working on a duration objective. A number of handicapped students have language delays that can lead to the slow articulation of a phrase like "How are you doing today?" The teacher may set up an instructional program in which the goal is to reduce the duration of saying this phrase from 10 seconds to 5 seconds. Duration objectives also are common in production and vocational activities in which a given amount of work, e.g., vacuuming a room, must be completed in a fixed amount of time. In this context, duration overlaps somewhat with the notion of rate, which refers to the number of units completed in a given (standard) amount of time; duration is the amount of time it takes to complete a specific behavior.

For example, a child may be able to dress herself correctly, but if it takes more than 10 to 15 minutes to do so, this skill will not benefit busy parents who must get several children off to school in the morning. They probably will have to continue dressing the child on most occasions because they do not have time to wait for the child to finish dressing. Similarly, being accurate in playing a video game like Pac Man will not enable a teenager to play a coin-operated game longer than 10 seconds unless the player also acts quickly when a monster is about to consume the Pac Man.

In school contexts, duration usually is recorded with a stopwatch. A student is given a task, and the stopwatch is run from the beginning to the completion of the task. The number of seconds or minutes taken to complete the task constitutes the score. If one response is timed, the duration time will be the score for the session. The session score then can be plotted on a repeated measures graph with the number of seconds on the ordinate and the sessions on the abscissa. If more than one response is emitted in a session, the duration times for every response are summed to give a total duration score for the session. Furthermore, the total duration score can be divided by the number of responses to give a mean duration score per session.

Duration also may be used in a classroom setting in which there is a very high rate behavior. Suppose a student is scratching his hand in a self-abusive manner. When the person scratches, the rate of scratching is about 70 responses per minute. The rate proves to be so rapid that a teacher cannot obtain reliable recordings. A solution to this problem is to switch from a rate measure to a duration measure. As soon as scratching begins, the teacher turns on the stopwatch; when scratching ceases, the stopwatch is turned off though not returned to zero. The watch is turned on and off repeatedly (allowing the time to accumulate) pending the appearance of the behavior. With high-rate behavior that appears in "bursts," the measurement of the total duration is an easier and more accurate way of recording than counting the single occurrences of each response for a rate index. Some very serious behaviors may occur at a low enough rate that it will be easy to count them, but duration may be a more meaningful measure. For example, a student may bite her hand. Once the body part is in the mouth, contact with the teeth may continue for many seconds or even minutes. Counting the numbers of times the hand is put in the mouth is not likely to be as sensitive a measure as timing the duration of the behavior. In fact, in some situations the amount of tissue damage may be most closely related to how long the behavior continues, i.e., duration.

Finally, the difference between duration and latency should be stated. Duration is the time between the onset and termination of a behavior, whereas *latency* refers to the time between the delivery of an S^D and the onset of the response; it is the time it takes the person to start responding. An example would be a teacher who tells a student who is sitting in a chair in the school cafeteria to go and get lunch. The latency would be the time from when the teacher gives the instruction to the time when the student gets out of the chair to get food. The duration would be the time it takes for the student to get out of the chair, go through the cafeteria line, and return to the chair. Students with severe handicaps sometimes have difficulties with response latencies and duration, and this must be addressed in their instructional programs.

Determining Reliability

We have stated that the main reasons for collecting repeated measurement data are to get an indication of how well a student is performing and to help make decisions about changing the instructional procedure. Inferences made from the collected data are based on the assumption that the recorded observations are accurate, but this assumption cannot be made without an empirical test. Data must be collected to test the accuracy and reliability of the measurements.

This section will describe ways in which teachers can calculate the reliability of their data as an indication of accuracy. In a program for students with severe handicaps, many factors can interfere with the collection of accurate data. There are often auditory and visual distractors, such as noise and pupils moving about the classroom, that can interfere with the observer's attention while taking recordings. Also, a teacher may be taking multiple recordings of data on different students at the same time. Undoubtedly, a teacher has many things in mind while executing an educational program that may detract from perceiving and recording accurate data. In addition, there is considerable evidence that people interject their biases in recording (Rosenthal, 1966). For example, teachers like to see their programs work for a number of reasons. Program success shows that the students are benefiting and reinforces the teacher for doing a good job. This ego investment in successful programs can lead teachers to bias their observations so that skill behaviors tend to improve and problem behaviors seem to decrease in frequency.

Observer Agreement Check

The main way reliability is demonstrated in the social sciences is to have two individuals observe the same behavior at the same time. A mathematical calculation then is made of the proportion of instances in which the observers agree on the appearance of the behavior; this is called an observer agreement check. If the observers agree over 80 percent of the time, the reliability of the data has attained an acceptable level. Interobserver agreement above 90 percent indicates excellent reliability.

Figure 4.15 shows a graph of the number of correct trials per session in a shoe-tying program. The teacher, observer 1, recorded that the student demonstrated two correct trials in each of three baseline sessions. A second observer recorded four correct trials in each of the three baseline sessions. For five sessions of training, the teacher recorded an average of six correct trials that increased across sessions. The reliability observer, though, continued to record four correct trials in all sessions. How does one interpret these findings? If we look at the teacher's data, we conclude that the student is making substantial progress from baseline and that we should continue this program. In contrast, if we look at the reliability observer's data, we see no change in performance between baseline and training and conclude that the program is ineffective. Two observers watched the same learning sessions and recorded notably different results. The differences in recording led to completely different instructional decisions.

Define Behavior to Be Recorded. How can we avoid unreliable data? The main way to ensure reliable observation is to have clearly stated definitions

Figure 4.15 Graph of interobserver agreement during baseline and instructional conditions.

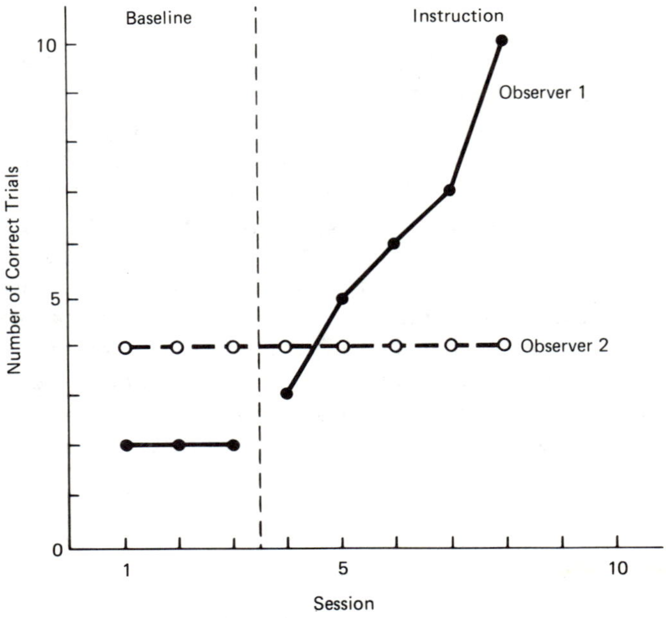

of the behavior that is to be recorded. When observers are not clear about what behavior is to be recorded, there are likely to be disagreements. As in writing instructional objectives, the data to be recorded must be defined in terms of observable behaviors. Examples of good and poorly defined behaviors are shown in Figure 4.16. Behaviors should be defined in terms of a clear onset and termination; for example, a single hand-biting response may be defined as the point at which the mouth and teeth make contact until the time when contact is broken.

When a behavior has been defined carefully and both observers verbally agree that they understand it, it is good practice to have them briefly role-play the occurrence or nonoccurrence of the behavior. Instances that are borderline or that could be scored either way should be role-played and discussed so that there is clear agreement concerning their measurement. When role playing has been completed satisfactorily, it is possible to collect the reliability data.

In conducting scientific research, it is important to carry out numerous agreement or reliability checks throughout the study. For classroom purposes it is sufficient to collect one successful agreement check before the intervention is implemented and one shortly after the intervention is associated with a behavior change. The first check should occur in the first or second session of data collection. Have another person—the reliability observer—

Figure 4.16 Examples of poorly versus well-defined behaviors.

WELL-DEFINED BEHAVIORS
Coat buttoning: The student correctly inserted the buttons through the button holes on the winter coat.
Envelope stuffing: The student placed a folded letter in an envelope.
Face cleaning: The student wiped his or her face with a washcloth so that there was no dirt remaining on the face.
Arm scratching: The student took the fingernails of one hand and rubbed them across the other arm in one motion.
Hair pulling: The student took his or her hand to grasp and pull a peer's hair; when hands were released from the hair, one response was scored.
POORLY DEFINED BEHAVIORS
Sorting: The student learned how to sort the nails in the bin.
Toileting: The student became toilet-trained.
Reading: The student understood the "stop" sign.
Problem behavior: The student threw a "temper tantrum."

sit or stand near the student. The second observer can be the paraprofessional, the occupational therapist, a student teacher, or a volunteer. Both observers should be as unobtrusive as possible throughout the session, i.e., should try not to speak and should move as little as possible. The observers should not be able to see what the other person is recording. Throughout the session both adults should record the behavior(s) of the student(s) independently in the metric being used, e.g., rate or duration.

At the end of the session, the observers should examine each other's recordings and calculate the percentage agreement for the session. If agreement is below 80 percent, the observers should discuss why they disagreed in so many instances. They may role-play the behavior further to isolate their point of disagreement. The idea is for the problem to be resolved through discussion and role playing. If it cannot, the definition of the behavior or response class may have to be changed so that it can be measured more accurately. After these changes have been made, another session should be conducted with both observers recording. Agreement again should be calculated. It is hoped that agreement then will reach an acceptable level. Until agreement has been established, the collected data should not be used for instructional or assessment purposes.

After agreement is established on the first check, one more check should be made after the intervention has been in place long enough to produce some change in behavior. Data are particularly vulnerable to bias when a change is desirable and is expected to occur. If there has been an unsuccessful check, it is good practice to conduct two consecutive agreement checks that reach the 80 percent level.

Total Agreement. The easiest reliability calculation is the total agreement, which is based on interobserver agreement on the total session score. It can be calculated for all measurement units, i.e., rate, interval, trial-by-trial, duration, and time sampling. One merely takes the total session score for each observer and applies a simple formula. Let us apply the total agreement formula to some rate data. Suppose observer 1 (01) tallies a rate of forty-five responses during a session. Observer 02 scores a total of fifty responses for the session. The total agreement formula is

$$\frac{\text{Smaller score}}{\text{Larger score}} \times 100 = \text{percentage interobserver agreement}$$

One takes the smaller of the two observed scores, in this case forty-five, and divides it by the larger score, fifty. The quotient is multiplied by 100 to produce the percentage of interobserver agreement. In this case:

$$\frac{45}{50} \times 100 = 90 \text{ percent}$$

In this example, the observed behaviors were rate data, i.e., responses per session. If duration data were being observed, the formula would be the smaller divided by the larger number of seconds. The same formula would be applied of dividing the smaller by the larger number of total intervals, trials, etc. Of course, when there is no larger number, e.g., 01 = 35, 02 = 35, the reliability coefficient is 100 percent.

Partition Agreement. A more precise way of calculating reliability is to examine how observers agree during different parts of the session. Partition reliability can be calculated only with measurement units that divide the session into subparts, i.e., trial-by-trial, interval, or time-sample. Rate and duration data only produce tallies for the total session. Let us examine an example with discrete-trial data. The recording sheet shows ten trials that have been scored by two independent observers. The recording sheet would look identical if we had scored ten intervals or ten time-sample look intervals. The calculations are done in exactly the same manner for these three measurement units, as Figure 4.17 explains.

The scoring sheet shows that there was not complete agreement between observers on all trials. Let us first calculate the total agreement and then compare it with the partition agreement. The total agreement would be $(5/7) \times 100 = 71$ percent. Thus, there is 71 percent agreement on the total score. To calculate the partition agreement, one must look at the agreement

Figure 4.17 Agreements (A) and disagreements (D) between observers for partition and occurrence reliability (* = both observers agree the behavior did not occur).

	1	2	3	4	5	6	7	8	9	10	Total
01	+	−	+	+	−	+	−	+	+	+	7
02	+	−	−	+	−	−	+	+	+	−	5
	A	A*	D	A	A*	D	D	A	A	D	

between observers within each trial. On the recording sheet, a D or an A is written under each trial score, indicating whether the observers agreed (A) or disagreed (D) on that trial. It can be seen that there was agreement on the first trial (both recorded the behavior as appearing), agreement on the second trial (both recorded it not appearing), disagreement on the third trial (01 = +, 02 = −), etc. The formula for calculating the partition agreement is

$$\frac{\text{Total number of agreements}}{\text{Total number of agreements + disagreements}} \times 100 = \text{partition agreement}$$

In this case there were six agreements and four disagreements:

$$\frac{6}{6 + 4} \times 100 = 60 \text{ percent}$$

Thus, the agreement percentage calculated by the partition method was notably lower than the total agreement. If there is a difference between these two methods in terms of actual calculations, the partition method usually will produce a lower score since it is a more conservative indicator. It is also a more accurate indicator because it compares observations on a trial-by-trial or interval-by-interval basis, that is, at the exact time when both observers should agree that they either did or did not see the behavior. Its superior accuracy can be seen in Figure 4.18.

Figure 4.18 Agreements and disagreements between observers for partition and occurrence reliability.

	1	2	3	4	5	6	Total
01	+	+	+	−	−	−	3
02	−	−	−	+	+	+	3
	D	D	D	D	D	D	

Here the total agreement method would indicate perfect 100 percent agreement between observers. In actuality the observers never agreed on the appearance of a behavior within a given trial. This absence of agreement is reflected in the 0 percent partition agreement result. This example points out an advantage of measurement units that break down a session into parts. It allows one to examine when a behavior occurred during a session, and it further permits more exact calculations of reliability based on this information.

Occurrence Agreement. There is one other kind of agreement calculation that is even more conservative in nature. Occurrence agreement, like partition agreement, is calculated in measurement units that divide sessions into trials and intervals. The difference in the two approaches is that occurrence agreement tabulates only trials in which at least one observer recorded the behavior as appearing. It is felt that there is an interest only in instances in which the behavior occurs, not in its nonoccurrence. The occurrence agreement discards all trials in which both observers state that the behavior did not appear. Including these intervals of nonoccurrence in the calculation can inflate the actual reliability of the observations artifically.

Let us return to the previous recording sheet in which there were six agreements and four disagreements (Figure 4.17). Under the row of A's and D's one can see that trial 2 and trial 5 contain asterisks. These are the two trials in which both observers stated that the behavior did not appear. In calculating occurrence agreement, these two trials would be discarded. The formula for occurrence agreement is identical to that for partition agreement: (number of agreement)/(number of agreements + disagreements) × 100. In this case:

$$\frac{4}{8} \times 100 = 50 \text{ percent}$$

This figure is considerably lower than the partition agreement (60 percent) and the total agreement (71 percent). Both partition agreement and occurence agreement are valid ways of calculating interobserver agreement. When there are many cases of both observers giving nonoccurrence scores, the two percentages can differ considerably. Select one procedure versus the other on the basis of how often the behavior occurs. If many of the observations reflect nonoccurrence of the behavior, use the occurrence agreement method. Otherwise, the partition method is fully acceptable.

Graphing and Taking Reliability Data

It is helpful to report the percentage of agreement on the graph of the student's data. This can be done in two ways. In Figure 4.19 the percentage of interobserver agreement appears on the abscissa beneath the session number when it was taken. Thus, session 1 has a score of 86 percent. It is also

Figure 4.19 The plotting of reliability observations and coefficients.

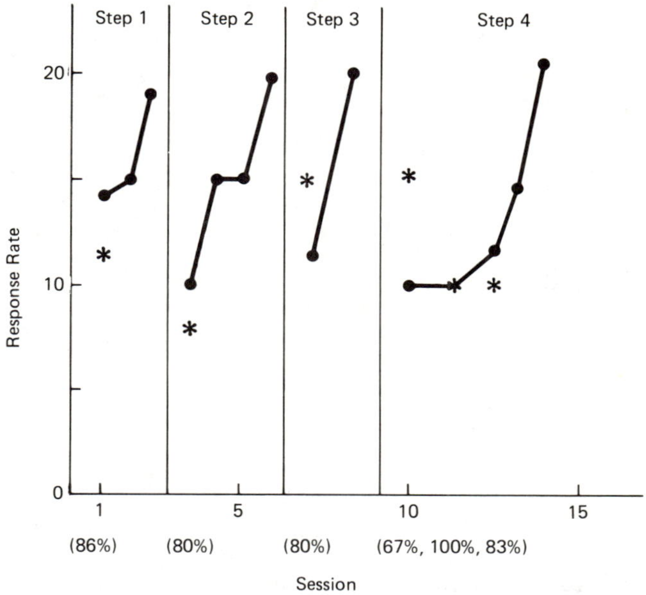

useful to plot the actual score recorded by the reliability observer. Above session 1, an asterisk indicates that the reliability observer scored a rate of twelve responses per session. The teacher's score in session 1 falls on the curve and is fourteen. Thus, whenever agreement is calculated, the percentage score should appear below the session number, and the total score should appear as an asterisk point on the graph.

Finally, for teaching purposes two successful agreement checks will suffice. When an acceptable level of agreement is not obtained on the initial check, two additional consecutive sessions with above 80 percent agreement are needed. There is also the possibility of serial chains in which the behavior observed changes from step to step in the task analysis. Thus, it is necessary to calculate an agreement percentage each time a new behavioral chain is introduced. Therefore, in Figure 4.19 there are six agreement checks; a check is made in each step of the program. One can see that the check was done in the first session of each step.

Interpreting the Data

We have stated repeatedly that the two main reasons for collecting formative data are to give an accurate picture of student performance and to indicate whether changes are needed in instructional procedures. The major way to accomplish these objectives is by inspecting the graphed data visu-

Figure 4.20 Curves with upward, downward, and horizontal trends.

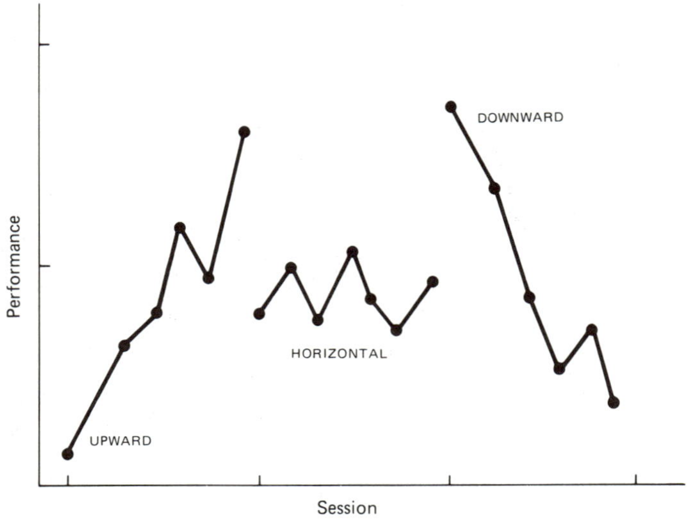

ally. The trend of the curve can be upward, downward, or horizontal. With skill data, an upward, accelerating trend indicates an improvement in performance, a decelerating curve indicates a deterioration in learning, and a horizontal trend indicates that there is no change in learning. For a graph of problem behavior, the opposite relationships hold: Upward trends indicate a worsening in the problem behavior, a horizontal trend shows no improvement in the rate of appearance of the behavior, and a deceleration in the curve indicates that the behavior is improving. Data trends that show worsening or no change in behavior over 5 to 10 days tell the teacher that there is a need for a change in the instructional program. Steady improvements in behavior indicate that the student is on the way to reaching criterion performance and that there is no need to make substantial changes in the program.

First Judgments

Judgments about the upward, downward, or horizontal trend usually can be made in a straightforward manner through visual inspection of the data. Figure 4.20 depicts three curves that show these trends, but it is possible that the direction of the plotted points will not be self-evident. In Figure 4.21 the curve on the left has upward and downward trends in the earlier and later sessions, respectively. How would we characterize these data in terms of a clear trend? The second curve in Figure 4.21 is also somewhat ambiguous. There appears to be a gradual upward trend, but there is so much scatter, or variation, around this trend that it is difficult to make an indisputable judgment. The curves in Figure 4.20 do not show this variation and therefore are

Figure 4.21 Curves with ambiguous trends.

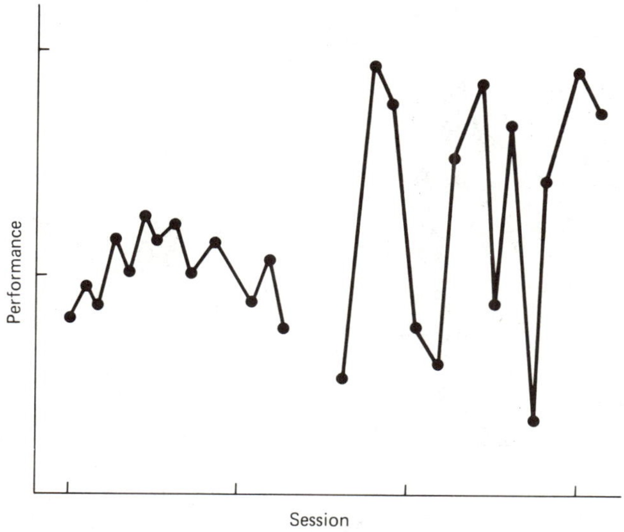

much easier to interpret. When graphs are not so easily interpretable, there is a need for a more precise indicator of their real trend. Fortunately, a number of devices can give a clear characterization of the trend of a data set.

The Quarter-Intersect Trend Line

A mathematical procedure called a regression line gives a precise marking of where the data are headed. A *regression line* is a line that intersects the data and summarizes the true trend or direction of the data. Figure 4.22 shows a trend line that characterizes a set of accelerating data. Although a regression line is mathematically precise, it requires extensive statistical calculations that do not permit its use by classroom teachers. Fortunately, there is a simple way to project a trend line onto repeated measures data that can be used by teachers. The *quarter-intersect* trend line (White and Liberty, 1976) is a procedure that requires a couple of steps that can be completed in a few seconds. The trend line produced by the quarter-intersect method is almost identical to that generated by the mathematical regression line. Let us list the steps necessary to plot the quarter-intersect trend line. At first the procedure may seem tedious, but once it is mastered, it can be completed quickly and efficiently.

It is best to carry out all the steps with a pencil so that they can be erased from the graph later. The resulting trend line can be left in pencil or marked over in pen. However, do not let the trend line detract from the visual salience of the plotted data points. The first step in the quarter-intersect method is to split the number of data points being analyzed in half. Figure 4.23 shows

Figure 4.22 An accelerating regression line.

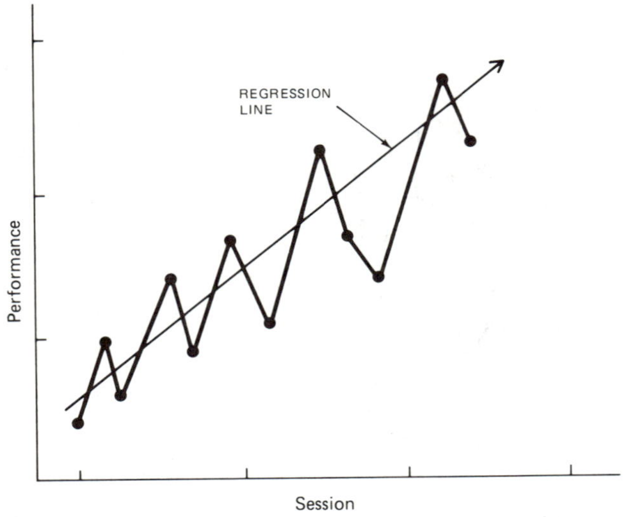

how a vertical line has been drawn between the points in sessions 5 and 6. In data sets that have an odd number of points, the vertical line runs through the middle session point, e.g., session 6 on a graph with thirteen points. When there is an even number of points, the vertical line falls between the two middle points, e.g., between sessions 5 and 6 in Figure 4.23. The data have been split into their initial and latter halves.

Now a vertical line must be drawn for the middle session days in the initial and latter half data subsets. The middle session line is determined in the same way as was done in the first step. For data subsets with an odd number of points, a vertical line is drawn through the middle session points. Figure 4.23 shows how vertical lines were drawn through sessions 3 and 8 in the first and second data subsets, respectively. If the data subsets contain an even number of points, the vertical lines are drawn between the two middle points. The third step is to draw horizontal lines in each of the subsets that divide the points into the higher and lower halves. Figure 4.23 shows how session 2 was the middle level point in the first subset; that is, there were two points above it (sessions 4 and 5) and two points below it (sessions 1 and 3). A horizontal line thus was drawn through the data point for session 2. The same procedure was followed in the second subset, with session 9 being the middle level point. The example in Figure 4.23 contains an odd number of points, and so the horizontal line was drawn through the middle level point. When there are an even number of points in the subset, the horizontal line is drawn between the two middle level points.

The fourth step is to plot a point where the vertical and horizontal lines intersect in each subset (see Figure 4.23). The fifth and final step is to connect a line between the points plotted in each subset. This line is the trend

Figure 4.23 Plotting a quarter-intersect trend line.

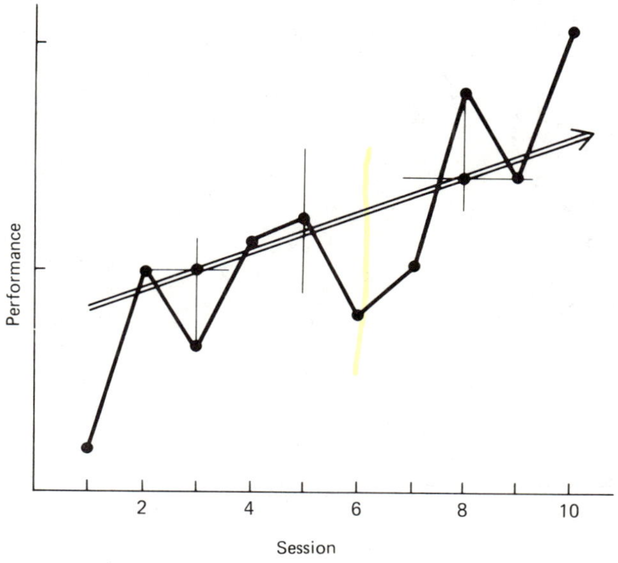

line. The line can be extended beyond the two connecting points, and an arrow may be added to accentuate the direction of the data (see Figure 4.23).

The quarter-intersect trend line should be drawn on a regular basis, e.g., once every five to ten sessions. This will provide an indication of where the data are headed over the most recent sessions, with instructional changes being made when necessary.

The Aim Star Procedure

Another way to tell whether a student's data are progressing adequately is to use the *aim star* procedure (White and Liberty, 1976). This method requires the instructor to set a goal for when the objective should be met. Assume that it is predicted that a student will reach a particular objective in twenty sessions. An aim star then is plotted at the criterion level of the goal at the twentieth session. Figure 4.24 shows an aim star plotted at the point where the twentieth session and 100 percent on the ordinate intersect. A line then can be drawn between the aim star and the data point from the first session (on baseline sessions). This aim star line indicates the rate of progression the student needs to reach the objective by the projected session. The actual data points for the student should stay on or above the aim star line. A rule of thumb is that when three consecutive points fall below the aim star line, there should be a change in the instructional program. The aim star line, like the quarter-intersect trend line, is a valid measurement because it keeps the teacher continually aware of whether the student is progressing in a satisfactory manner.

Figure 4.24 Plotting the aim star and the aim star line.

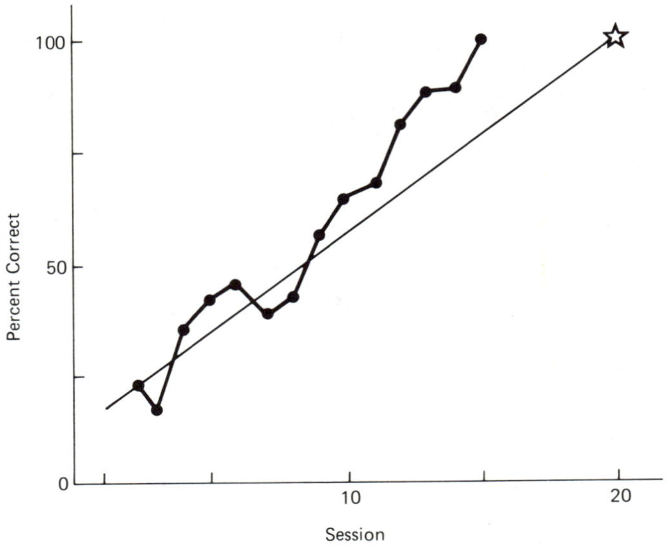

Other Aspects of Graphing

There are a few other aspects of graphing that must be mentioned here. One procedure deals with marking the criterion level of performance on the graph. Figure 4.25 shows a graph on which a horizontal line has been drawn across the 80 percent mark on the ordinate. The student had to reach the 80 percent mark for two consecutive sessions. The horizontal line makes it clear when the student has reached criterion level. The criterion line is optional. Do not clutter the graph with too many lines and other marks that may detract from the visual presentation of the data. But if the criterion line is needed and does not serve as a distractor, by all means use it.

Another optional graphing procedure is to combine a recording sheet and a graph on the same form. Figure 4.11 shows a form on which there are successive columns of numbers sequenced from 1 to 10. Each column represents a ten-trial session. As the session proceeds, the teacher scores the student's performance according to the key, which includes information on accuracy as well as levels of prompting. That is, each number represents a trial that is marked with a plus for correct performance and one of the other notations for incorrect performances. At the end of the session, the pluses are summed, and the corresponding number on the same numerical column is circled. These circles are connected from session to session to form a curve. This combined form replaces the step of transferring data from a recording sheet to a graph.

Figure 4.25 The criterion line.

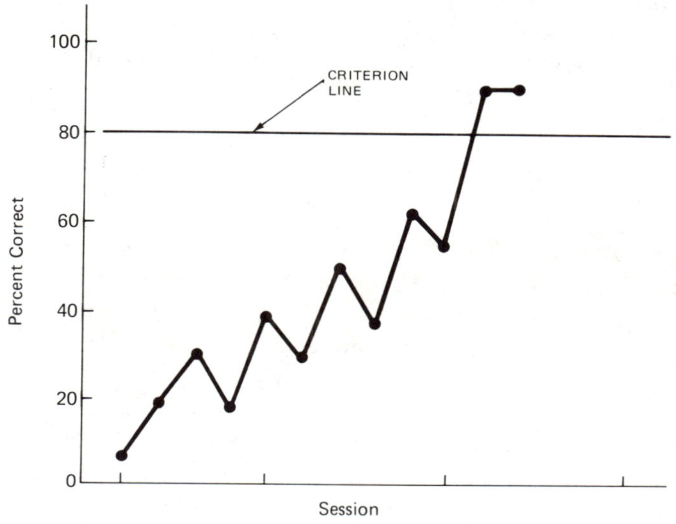

A potential problem with this form is that it becomes hard to discern because of its continued use in the class. To make the graph discernible, it is important to enter the recordings in pencil but to plot the points and connecting lines with a dark pen or magic marker. This will make the curve stand out.

On all graphs it is important to be neat and legible. The graph does not have to be of professional quality, but the linear coordinates and connecting lines should be straight. There should be no distracting marks or smudges. Upon inspection, the primary data should be immediately visible. Avoid placing too many curves on one graph. When necessary, plot another baseline (*xy* coordinate) to accommodate additional curves.

Organizing a Data Management System

We have described the various kinds of measurement techniques that can be used in programs for students with severe handicaps. With a considerable amount of practice, teachers can learn to measure student behavior effectively in a variety of settings. Besides the actual collection and graphing of data, though, another skill must be mastered in order to have a comprehensive measurement system in place. A teacher must organize a data management system that includes the data from individual programs in an organized fashion. The key to an effective data system is accessibility. The data must be compiled so that they are easily retrievable.

A potential threat to a data system is that the data will not be used by staff members to make programming decisions. Teachers can get into the habit of routinely collecting data and storing it away. The data sit in a file but rarely are accessed for instructional decision making. The way to avoid this problem is to have a well-organized measurement system that includes guidelines for how often data will be reviewed.

Basic Steps

When a session is run, a teacher should have three documents: a task analysis describing the program, a recording sheet, and a graph of the data. At minimum, the recording sheet (or tape, watch, etc.) must be present. The task analysis and graph can be stored somewhere else at the time of the session.

At the next level, these documents must be organized in a meaningful fashion. A clipboard or folder system can serve this purpose. Each student can have his or her own clipboard or folder. The clipboard contains copies of all the current programs (their task analysis, recording sheet, and graph). The clipboards are located at a designated place, e.g., hanging on a wall or in a desk. (Note, however, that identifiable individual student data should not be on public display since access to student records of any kind by noninstructional personnel can violate confidentiality.)

When a session is to be conducted, the teacher takes the clipboard to the session and "pulls" the relevant documents. It is important to return the clipboard to its storage location at the conclusion of the session; otherwise, the classroom can start to look sloppy with forms scattered about. Furthermore, when forms are scattered, it becomes difficult to locate them, and data can be lost. With all current programs filed on the clipboards, an easy and accessible system has been established.

When a program has been completed, the documentation should be moved to a permanent individual file. Each student should have a permanent file that is under lock and key and is located preferably in the classroom. The file should contain the student's IEP, assessment information, and old formative data. This information should be accessible, though it will not be referred to as often as the clipboard file. It is critical to pass on data from old programs to teachers from year to year. This information shows what has been tried and what has succeeded in a detailed fashion so that future teachers can make educational decisions in an effective manner.

Data Entries and Decisions

Initial entries on a recording sheet are made during a session. The data may be plotted onto a graph at the end of the session or at the end of the day. Some programs, particularly problem behavior programs, are conducted throughout the day. For these programs it is possible to carry the recording device (sheet or wristwatch counter) throughout the day. Another method is to post a recording sheet at an accessible location or use a space on the chalkboard and then walk over to make entries whenever the behavior occurs. Whichever method is used, the data should be recorded (if the chalkboard is used), graphed, and reviewed at the end of the day. The daily review should be brief.

One day a week should be set aside to review the program progress for every student. Every graph should be pulled and examined for the extent of progress during that week. The teacher should meet with other staff members for this review. A decision should be made for each graph as to whether there has been acceleration, deceleration, or no change in the curve. When appropriate, the quarter-intersect and aim star trend procedures should be used. Based on the trend in the data, decisions should be made concerning changes in the instructional programs. Prompts may be changed or reinforcers altered. If after various modification attempts the student is making no progress in acquiring an objective over a period of several weeks, a decision may be made to change the objective or drop it entirely. Such changes in IEP objectives must receive approval from a parent and an administrator. The changes can be made without a meeting (e.g., over the phone), and the changes can be entered as an addendum to the student's IEP. IEP modification procedures vary from district to district, so be sure to follow the guidelines for your district.

How Much Information Is Enough?

Suppose you have a class with eight students, and each student has five programs being conducted at a given time. This means that forty graphs are being plotted during the week. The forty graphs and their accompanying recording sheets and task analyses are affixed to each student's clipboard. It is easy to see that a rather large working data system will be accumulated. Keeping documents neat, organized, and accessible is critical to avoid having a chaotic clutter of papers.

Within this working data base the question can be raised as to how often it is necessary to record data on pupil performance. If we follow our previous example of eight students and five programs, it is possible that each program is run daily. This means that the teacher and her staff will make 200 recordings or data entries per week (8 students × 5 programs × 5 days). This number split among two or three staff members is not necessarily as large and unwieldy as it may seem, but a question may be raised with respect to the point at which the rigors of measurement begin to interfere with the quality of instruction.

A teacher may become overwhelmed with the amount of recording and graphing that is being done. Some teachers have few problems in managing large data bases, but others have difficulty coping with so many numbers and graphs. The pressures of being overwhelmed by data organization can contribute to teacher burnout. A teacher who is burning out from measurement and other pressures will be a less effective instructor of students with severe handicaps. It is thus important to design a data system that can be handled successfully by the teacher. If you are a new teacher or are starting a new program, begin modestly. Do not try to record everything that moves in the classroom. Make sure that the behaviors you are recording can be measured reliably and that you have good organizational control over the data system. As you get familiar and confident with your system, you can add more behaviors to be recorded and graphed. Gradually you will build up a large and impressive measurement file.

Aside from the difficulty of coping with large data systems, another factor should be considered when you are deciding how much data should be collected. In some situations and on some tasks the collection of data can interfere with the delivery of quality instruction. For example, if a teacher is running a group session with three fairly hyperactive students, it may be taxing just to deliver cues and reinforcers as well as manage the disruptive behaviors. Having the teacher record data during the session may detract from instructional and behavior management duties.

Many data may be collected on a probe basis or by another adult, for example, the paraprofessional. Another difficulty occurs when a teacher is working with a group of students who are producing items at a fairly high rate. There are no great behavioral or instructional demands placed on the teacher, yet the students are flying through multiple-step concurrent chains at such a fast pace that it is difficult to record all the behaviors being emitted. In these circumstances it may be necessary to modify the measurement system so that not every behavior in every session is recorded.

We shall give some guidelines for how one can make such adjustments to a measurement system while not sacrificing the quality of formative data needed to make effective instructional decisions. The first rule of thumb is to start from the position that all targeted behaviors in all sessions should be recorded. Thus, each behavior on the student's IEP for which sessions are being conducted must be recorded for every trial in the session. This is a total measurement approach for skill behaviors in sessions and for problem behaviors being monitored throughout the day. This total approach should be the starting point in the process of deciding what actually will be measured. The total measurement model can be compromised only when there are good, substantive reasons for why data should not be collected on all behaviors at all times. We now shall list these reasons.

The decision to curtail certain types of recording should be taken seriously. If the same instructional decision can be made with fewer collected data, by all means use the less demanding measurement procedure. At the same time, remember that data decisions are made by examining the trend in the plotted data. If fewer data points are plotted because fewer recordings have been made, the teacher will not be in a position to analyze the trends of the data and make instructional modifications. Some reasons for compromising the total measurement model include the following:

1. Behavior is being produced at too high a rate to be recorded reliably.
2. The student's behavior is too disruptive to manage and record at the same time.
3. The class is understaffed or there is absenteeism among staff members so that data cannot always be recorded.
4. The nature of the instructional program is such that recordings cannot be made continuously without an additional external observer.
5. You can identify a shorter time period than the entire day when the response occurs reliably, thus giving you a representative sample of the student's behavior.

For these and possibly other reasons it may be necessary to record or sample some behaviors but not record all targeted behaviors at all times. The sampling process can be done in one of two ways. First, you may record data only on certain probe days of the week. The days selected can be determined randomly for each program. Thus, in one week data may be collected on Tuesday and Friday and in the next week on Monday and Thursday. On the other days instructional sessions would be run, but data would not be collected formally. Collecting data 2 or 3 days per week can be an acceptable procedure. Remember that when you are not recording 50 percent of the time, you are essentially throwing away 50 percent of the information you could obtain about pupil performance. An absolute minimum for recording data would be one session per week on every program for each student. In most cases this amount of recording is unacceptable. Under extenuating circumstances and when the pupil's behavior is stable and predictable, one session per week, per program, per pupil may be permissible.

The second way to sample behavior is within the session. Rather than sampling across days, a behavioral sample is taken so that not all of the session is recorded. For example, suppose a twenty-trial session is run. No data are collected on any of the trials. At the end of the session (or the beginning or middle), five test trials are run. Data will be recorded on these five test or probe trials. Thus, twenty-five trials are run altogether, but data are collected only on five of them. The sampling of behavior within a session is a legitimate procedure. Try to run the test trials at a time during the session when the pupil's behavior is reflected accurately. That is, if the student does poorly toward the end of the session, you may run the trials at the beginning. Better yet, it is possible to intersperse test trials randomly throughout the session.

Summary

In this chapter we have described a number of measurement procedures that should equip the teacher of students with severe handicaps to run a comprehensive data-based program. All the techniques can be mastered with a reasonable amount of practice. Data can be recorded in trial-by-trial, rate, interval, duration,and time-sample formats. Select a measure that meets your educational needs. Also, conduct reliability sessions to ensure that your instruments have adequate interobserver agreement. Additionally, the raw data should be graphed and an indication of their trend determined. Then decisions should be made about the success or need for modification or intervention. Be familiar with all these techniques and implement them according to the characteristics of your students, settings, and tasks. Do not institute a measurement system that will overwhelm you and your staff. Be selective in the initial behaviors you measure and gradually expand your system in a more comprehensive fashion.

Chapter 5

Behavior Management

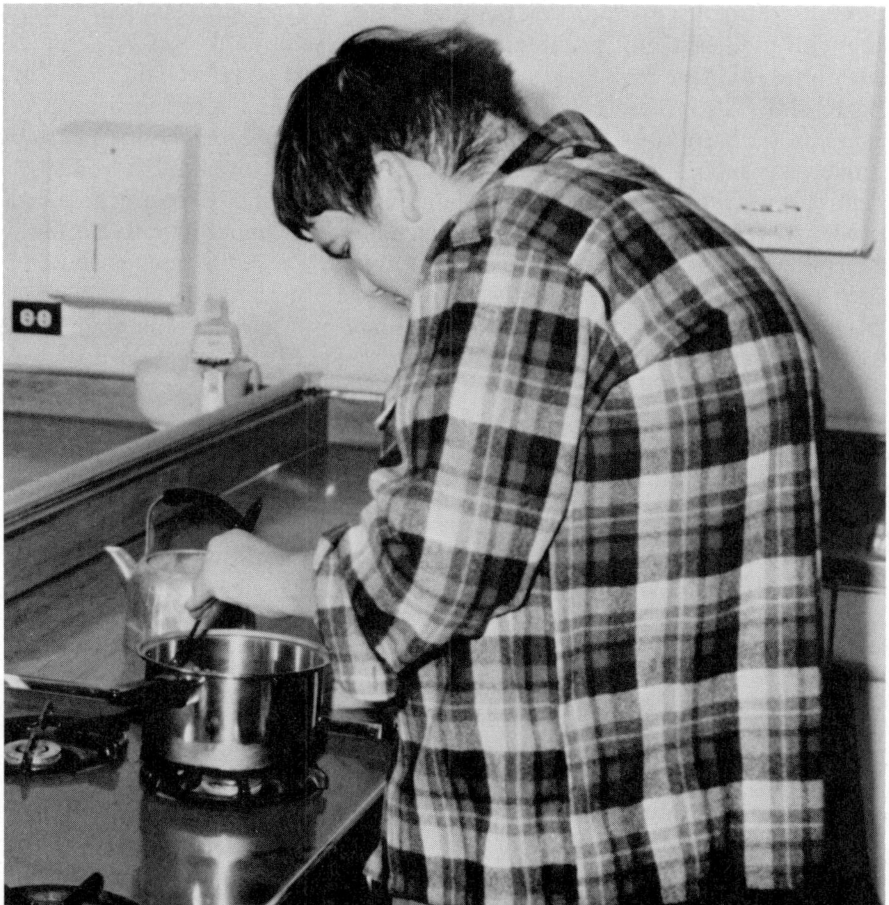

A major difficulty in educating many students with severe handicaps is coping with their behavior problems. Unfortunately, a number of students display maladaptive behaviors such as self-injury, self-stimulation, and aggression. Also, these behaviors often appear at a high if not incessant rate, and can be harmful to the student and to others. The behaviors inevitably stigmatize such students beyond their labeled difficulties of disability and retardation. Furthermore, the problem behaviors usually interfere with the student's learning of constructive skills. Thus, it is imperative that effective behavior management techniques be developed. These techniques should be incorporated within the student's instructional programs; they rarely should be invoked as separate behavior modification sessions. This chapter describes a set of behavior management procedures and suggests a plan for implementing them in an effective sequential order.

Distinguishing Characteristics of Persons with Severe Handicaps

In the past, one of the key distinguishing characteristics of persons with severe handicaps was the presence of problem behavior. Severely handicapping conditions tend to be associated with certain factors. With respect to intelligence test scores, individuals with severe handicaps have IQ scores below 55, or at least 3 standard deviations below the mean of 100. In terms of a theoretical model of cognition such as Jean Piaget's (1963), this population does not display the logical thinking depicted in the concrete operational stage of development; instead, they function no higher than the sensorimotor and preoperational stages of cognitive development. As a rule, for individuals to be considered severely handicapped, they have to display a substantial degree of intellectual impairment, with their serious cognitive deficits limiting their participation in the regular school environment. We thus exclude from the severely handicapped category an individual who has serious physical disabilities, e.g., cerebral palsy, but has relatively normal intelligence.

A second critical defining characteristic of the severely handicapped condition is the presence of serious deficits in adaptive behavior skills. *Adaptive behaviors* include a wide range of skills such as grooming, feeding, shopping, social interaction, leisure, and community mobility. These adaptive behaviors enable a person to function effectively in society. Largely because of the slow rate of learning by persons with severe handicaps many of these important adaptive behaviors never are acquired. More recently, though, as a result of more intense educational efforts in natural settings, persons with severe handicaps are acquiring more of these adaptive behaviors. Still, a key characteristic of this population is the failure to display a number of important adaptive behaviors without intensive training.

A third defining characteristic is the presence of a biomedical problem, for example, Down's syndrome, hydrocephalus, phenylketonuria, and cerebral palsy. There are over 200 chromosomal, metabolic, neurologic, and congenital disorders that can lead to mental retardation and severe handicaps (Grossman, 1977). Some biomedical disorders are slight and are not easily diagnosed; they may show up only as an abnormal brain wave pattern on an electroencephalogram. Although the majority of persons with severe handicaps display an observable biomedical anomaly, some severely handicapped individuals show no biological manifestations. Thus, unlike deficits in intellectual and adaptive behavior, a biomedical affliction is not a necessary or defining characteristic of a severely handicapping condition.

A similar description is appropriate in the case of problem or aberrant behaviors. In the past, another defining feature of severely handicapping conditions was the presence of problem behaviors. Although a large number of severely handicapped individuals do not display aberrant behaviors, the notion persists that persons with severe handicaps by definition display such behaviors. There is a high prevalence of mild to serious problem behaviors among the severely handicapped population, but as in the case of biomedical disorders, there is no defining relationship between aberrant behavior and possessing a severely handicapping condition.

The high incidence of aberrant behaviors can be linked to the types of environments in which persons with severe handicaps have been placed and to their poor learning abilities. Severely handicapped individuals often have been placed in large institutions or other custodial facilities in which little emphasis is given to education and treatment. The inmates, as they came to be thought of, were listless and inactive and often modeled their behavior after the deviant acts of other residents. The absence of instruction coupled with the slow learning rate of many individuals did not lead to the acquisition of functional skills. Thus, poor and understimulating residential environments set the occasion for disorderly behaviors to appear and be maintained. It is our belief that when intense educational environments are provided, persons with severe handicaps can acquire functional skills that tend to preclude the appearance of problem behaviors. The earlier education begins, the less likely that problem behaviors will manifest themselves.

Thus, our approach to treating aberrant behaviors is primarily a curricular one. The teaching of functional curriculum content in the natural environment enables the student to operate successfully on the environment. When a person cannot control the environment through acceptable means, that individual tends to resort to deviant response patterns in order to receive gratification or avoid harm. It is thus the duty of professionals to develop longitudinal skill sequences that enable the student to succeed in the environment while not displaying maladaptive actions.

Types of Problem Behaviors

Severely handicapped children and youth display some problem behaviors that are similar to those exhibited by nonhandicapped persons and other behaviors that are unique to this population.

Generic Problems

A behavior that is evident among both handicapped and nonhandicapped students is *aggressive* and *destructive* behavior. An aggressive act might be pulling another person's hair. Destruction of property could be a matter of throwing a glass at a wall so that it shatters. Aggressive acts also include slapping, pinching, biting, or kicking another person. Destructive acts include throwing items, spilling fluids, and harming plants or equipment. The end result of aggressive and destructive behavior is that damage is done to persons or things.

Another type of problem behavior common to both handicapped and nonhandicapped students is *off-task* behavior. Here, the student should be working on an academic or leisure task and instead is out of his or her seat, running around aimlessly, or not following the instructions of the teacher. Severely handicapped students often have short attention spans and are easily distracted. This often leads to wandering behavior or leaving a group or task to find another source of stimulation. The chances of off-task behavior are heightened if there is no potent reinforcer in the learning situation to consequate correct behavior. Essentially, off-task behavior is the absence of stimulus control in a situation; the instructions or materials in the setting are not leading to defined on-task behaviors such as stacking, speaking, writing, etc.

There are two kinds of problem behaviors that tend to appear only among severely handicapped students. The most common is *self-stimulatory* behavior. Self-stimulatory behavior involves the repetition of some action like waving a hand in front of the face. The repetitive act may last ten seconds, ten minutes, or more. The action serves no purpose—i.e., it accomplishes no apparent work or leisure goal. There are many types of self-stimulatory behaviors, including: rocking in a chair, rocking the whole body while standing, repeating meaningless sounds, waving an object, flicking fingers in front of one's eyes, etc. The term self-stimulation derives from the original notion that the repeated action was a form of self-gratification; that is, since the action produced no external reward, gratification was derived from the kinesthetic or vestibular feedback received from the body motion. Since no harm is incurred to the individual, self-stimulation differs from a fifth problem behavior: *self-injury*.

Self-injurious behavior produces tissue damage to the person in varying degrees of severity. Self-injurious acts include striking one's head with the hand, sucking the lips, gouging the ears or the eyes, banging the head against an object, and scratching the face or arm. Self-injury tends to be a repeated action that may last a few seconds or many minutes and persists from day to day. Self-injury is not like masochism or suicide among nonhandicapped persons since the latter are infrequent or one-time actions. Self-injury, like self-stimulation, is a recurrent behavior. It is particularly puzzling because there is no apparent reward system or gratification inherent in the act. In fact, the act is likely to produce pain in the individual. Self-injury, like other problem behaviors, may appear because it is under the control of social reinforcement or the avoidance of other noxious events. However, for many children there are no apparent controlling contingencies, and so the etiology of self-injury remains largely a mystery.

A Case Study: Tommy

Let us illustrate the case of a boy with severe handicaps who displays a number of problem behaviors. The case is presented to give a feel for the types of behavior problems that can appear in a severely handicapped individual. Unfortunately, some professionals used to characterize a person with severe handicaps by the types of behavior problems which were displayed, e.g., a self-abuser. In our view, the aberrant behavior should be depicted as one behavior within a whole cluster of behaviors that characterize the individual. The successful treatment of the aberrant behavior is likely to occur when attention is given to skill behaviors, personality characteristics, and family dynamics as well as the particular deviant acts.

Tommy was an 8-year-old boy whose primary diagnosis was severe mental retardation. He lived at home with his parents and a teenage sister. Tommy attended a primary class for students with severe handicaps that was located on an elementary public school campus. Tommy had been in the program for 3 years and had been making considerable progress in personal management skills such as using the toilet, dressing, feeding, and grooming. He had an expressive language of about 25 words (e.g., "eat" and "Mom") and a receptive language of about 200 words. He was ambulatory and had good use of his sensory faculties.

When working on an instructional task, he performed well; that is, he stayed on task for up to 25 minutes, learned new tasks at a fairly rapid rate, and rarely displayed aberrant behaviors. When instruction ceased, though, and Tommy was in free play, he would engage in a couple of problem behaviors. He would pick up inedible objects such as paper or sponges, chew them, and then swallow them. This unusual disorder of ingesting inedible objects is called *pica* and appears among some severely handicapped individuals. Tommy emitted pica about once per week.

The second problem behavior Tommy displayed was self-injury. He would take his open hand and slap it on his face or the upper portion of his head. The self-injury occurred on a daily basis at the rate of 10 instances per hour during free play. He would not strike his head continuously but would unleash a burst of five to ten responses, emit no self-injury for 5 minutes, and then emit another burst.

Both pica and head striking also were reported to occur at home. Since there was much less programmed time at home, the problem was even more serious there. Tommy's parents and teachers had tried to reduce the problem by praising him for not displaying aberrant behavior. They tried to ignore him when he was self-abusive, but they often had to hold his arm and comfort him when he emitted numerous head-striking responses.

Thus, Tommy is an example of one type of severely handicapped child who displays serious aberrant behaviors. The behaviors of pica and self-injury are unusual and not normally observed among nonhandicapped children. Also, these behaviors are serious in that they threaten the health of the individual. On a few occasions Tommy had to have his stomach pumped after ingesting dangerous materials.

Despite these problem behaviors, there were a number of positive developments in Tommy's life. He came from a nurturant, caring home and had a dedicated, energetic teacher at school. He had made a number of advances in his personal management and communication repertoires over the years. He was a "likable" boy whom peers and adults enjoyed being with. Thus, Tommy was a complex individual who had a number of assets but displayed serious behavior problems.

In analyzing a behavior problem, it is useful to look at the whole individual and examine positive skills and interpersonal developments as well as negative behaviors. This total analysis leads to a better understanding of the causes and potential treatment procedures that can lead to remediation of the disorder.

Targeting Behaviors for Treatment

Most students display a range of behaviors that include prosocial and antisocial acts. When considering the problem behavior, teachers must determine whether a particular behavior needs to be treated with a formal behavior modification program. The decision to treat a behavior with a formal program is an important one. Behavioral programs require considerable effort on the part of the professional staff, and such efforts may detract from the time and amount of instruction that can be given to other students. Behavioral programs also may involve the introduction of an artificial aspect to the student's program (e.g., giving tokens) that detracts from the natural educational setting. Also, behavior modification programs may stigmatize the student. Both peers and professionals are likely to be aware of the program and associate the student with the stigma of being behavior-disordered.

Analyzing Behavior. The process of analyzing a behavior problem should start by looking at the whole person: strengths and weaknesses, personality, and family and social world. From these holistic impressions it is possible to focus on the problem behavior and determine whether it warrants special programmatic treatment. Above all, the behavior should be perceived in the total context of the person's social world. The same behavior appearing at the same rate in one individual may warrant a behavior modification program, yet for another person no such program may be needed.

The main criterion for determining whether to treat a behavior problem is how much the behavior is *disturbing* or *dangerous* to the individual and those around her or him. Behaviors such as aggression and self-injury may bring serious physical harm to the student or others in the area. In the past, some severely handicapped individuals were so chronically aggressive toward themselves or others that they had to be restrained through mechanical (e.g., straitjacket) or chemical (e.g., tranquilizers) means on a continual basis. Dangerous behaviors require immediate behavioral remediation. Problem behaviors that disturb the environment can be aggressive or off-task acts that disrupt the quiet and organizational flow of the class. When professionals or parents must intercede constantly to calm or restrain a child, the student is likely to be placed in a more restrictive setting, for example, a state hospital. Placement in less restrictive, natural settings is done with the assumption of more independence with regard to the student's functioning. Natural settings usually do not include constant surveillance and management by staff members. Therefore, the behaviors most likely to receive treatment are those which may bring physical harm to a person or be so disruptive that they jeopardize a less restrictive residential or school placement for the child.

There is a second level of problem behaviors that must be considered for treatment. These actions may be aggressive, self-injurious, off-task, or self-stimulating, but they do not bring imminent danger or disruption to the environment. Rather, these second-level acts clearly interfere with learning by the student. The student may spend a considerable amount of time misbehaving, and this is incompatible with working or playing in a constructive manner. When the behaviors are selected for a formal behavior modification program, a judgment has been made that learning is being deterred significantly by the student's excessive display of deviant acts. Interference with learning may be manifested by much off-task behavior, poor attending, or slow rates of learning. In addition to producing learning difficulties, second-level behavior problems are likely to continue at an undesirable rate in the absence of formal treatment.

Third-level behavior problems can come from the same response classes (aggression, self-injury, etc.), but their impact on the individual and the surrounding environment is nominal. That is, no significant danger, disruption, or learning difficulty is produced by the problem behavior. Clearly, the aggressive or self-stimulatory behavior is undesirable, but the student may continue in his or her placement and function effectively. Third-level behavior problems are not likely to require a formal treatment program. Rather, emphasis is placed on reinforcing alternative responses that constitute a functional curriculum. Through differential reinforcement of responses that are part of the instructional curriculum, it is expected that the problem will decrease in frequency.

We have followed the model of Voeltz, Evans, Derer, and Hanashiro (1983) in outlining three levels of problem behaviors. In terms of priority of treatment, these authors suggest that level 1 behaviors are the most serious and therefore must be attended to first. Level 2 behaviors are of intermediate seriousness and usually will be targeted after level 1 behaviors have been remediated. Level 3 behaviors are the least intrusive and usually can be dealt with by normal classroom reinforcement procedures. Figure 5.1 shows a flowchart for the sequence of targeting problem behaviors. To some extent, the flowchart model assumes that only one behavior is treated at a time. In many cases one problem will be selected for treatment and one or more other behaviors will not be selected for treatment until the first one has been eliminated successfully. In some cases it may be necessary or logistically possible to treat more than one behavior at a time. Thus, two or more behavior management programs will be run simultaneously. If the problem behaviors appear at a low rate, it may be easy to run simultaneous programs. For higher-rate behaviors it may not be possible to run two or more behavior modification programs in addition to the skill-building programs and maintain a high level of program quality. In other situations more than one level 1 problem behavior may be present that threatens the security or placement of the student. In these cases it may be necessary to treat more than one behavior in a simultaneous fashion.

The Example of Tommy. Let us continue with the example of Tommy in order to demonstrate how problem behaviors may be targeted for treatment. Tommy had two problem behaviors: pica and head slapping. In applying the three-tier model for selection, it seems evident that pica is a level 1 behavior. Although the behavior occurred at a low rate (once per week), its con-

Figure 5.1 Targeting problem behaviors.

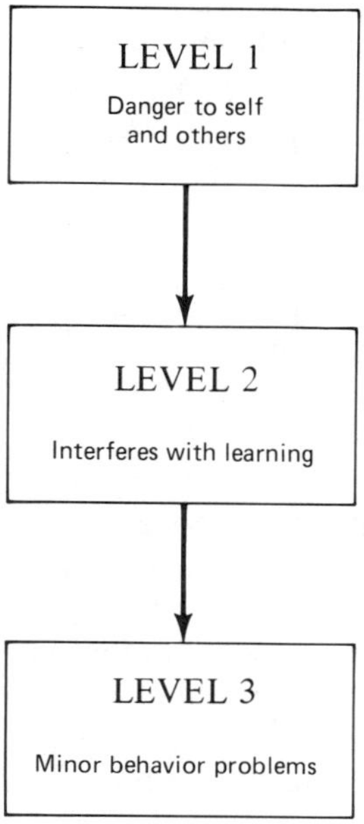

sequences were serious in terms of physical harm to the student since Tommy could have ingested toxic or other dangerous materials. Thus, it is important to immediately set up a treatment program for a level 1 behavior such as pica. It is not as easy to determine the level of seriousness of head slapping. Repeated slapping of the head can cause bodily harm. The slaps appeared to be light in force, and there was never bleeding or bruises, yet continued blows can lead to brain damage or other afflictions. Interestingly, if head slapping appears during instruction, it certainly may be considered a level 2 behavior because it will compete with the appearance of skill behaviors and thus interfere with learning. However, it was pointed out that Tommy's head slapping occurred only during free play and not during instruction. The behavior did have the other level 2 characteristic of not going away without formal treatment. Tommy had been in a systematic educational program for a number of years, and this problem behavior had not yet subsided. Therefore, though the behavior was not interfering with instruction, it was not likely to be remediated solely by the positive reinforcement of curricular responses in instructional sessions.

We probably could refer to Tommy's self-injury as a level 2 behavior. In this case it was not too important whether it was designated as level 1 or level 2. The teaching staff met and realized that they needed to implement behavior modification programs only during free play sessions. Since this amounted to relatively few minutes per day, staff members felt that two behavior modification programs could be implemented simultaneously (one for pica and one for head slapping) during the four free play sessions each day.

When the behavior modification programs were considered for extension to the home, though, it was realized that both behaviors could not be treated simultaneously. For one thing, most of the time Tommy spent at home was free play. His parents would have to be carrying out behavioral programs continuously for hours at a time. Second, although the parents were enthusiastic about running home programs, they were not skillful in behavioral technology. For these reasons the school staff and the parents decided that only the level 1 behavior would be treated at home first. It was planned that after pica had been treated successfully a home program for the level 2 behavior of self-injury would be instituted.

This example demonstrates how in some cases or situations multiple problem behaviors are targeted for simultaneous treatment. In these circumstances the designation of level may be less important since all or most of the student's behavior problems are being treated concurrently. Here, the level 1 and 2 behaviors were simultaneously treated at school. In other situations, one behavior at a time will receive treatment in a sequential manner. In these cases it is important to decide which behaviors are in need of the most immediate remediation. Again, in Tommy's case, in the home the level 1 behavior was dealt with first, to be followed by treatment of the level 2 behavior.

Strategies for Treatment

Much of the research literature written about persons with severe handicaps has been concerned with behavior modification techniques. This early preoccupation probably resulted from the fact that the highest-rate behaviors displayed by individuals with severe handicaps often were aberrant behaviors. For early investigators, the main issue in research and service was how to reduce these problem behaviors.

Our philosophy is that the main focus of educational programs should be on skill building. In general, the best way to prevent or ameliorate problem behaviors is to deal with the student in terms of longitudinal curriculum. As the student is reinforced for the acquisition of functional skills, the skill repertoire is expanded and competes with the appearance of deviant acts. When the student engages in few skilled behaviors, the response repertoire is dominated by aberrant behavior. Therefore, much problem behavior can be eliminated or prevented by the successful implementation of skill-building programs. Yet in the classroom you may find that even when effective skill-building programs are being utilized, some students with severe handicaps will continue to display a variety of problem behaviors. Thus, there is a need to develop treatment strategies that specifically will ameliorate behavior problems. Let us look at these behavior management strategies.

Assessment

Once a behavior has been targeted for treatment, there is a need for additional information to be collected about its causes and characteristics. A behavioral assessment should result in a decision to intervene in the behavior as well as result in background information for determining an effective treatment procedure.

Biomedical Factors. Although a behavior has been selected for treatment, there still may be conditions that militate against its being treated with a formal behavior modification program. The first consideration is whether there is a specific biomedical factor that may be causing the behavioral disturbance. For example, a student may have an inner ear infection that leads to scratching at the ear. It would be misguided to set up a behavioral program to treat this problem when there is an underlying medical cause that is in need of remediation. Specific biomedical problems such as infections or skin diseases may lead to the display of aberrant behaviors. Thus, it is always necessary to consider the possibility of biomedical causes of the problem behavior. A physician should examine the student if such a cause is suspected. The physician may prescribe a particular medication, and observation then should be made of changes in the rate of behavior resulting from the medication. Before a behavior modification program is implemented, biomedical factors should be ruled out as possible causes or receive appropriate attention from a physician. After this step has been completed, the assessment process may continue.

One must consider the possibility of a *nonspecific* medical diagnosis of a behavior problem. Increasing attention has been given to the explanation and treatment of behavioral disorders such as hyperactivity through allergic and pharmacologic factors. Usually a specific biomedical factor such as eczema is not identified. Rather, an underlying metabolic or allergic factor is inferred to be the cause of the behavior problem. From this diagnosis, one of a number of possible treatments may be prescribed. These prescriptions may include pharmacologic agents such as Ritalin (methylphenidate) or a change in diet.

Such biomedical forms of treatment are in an experimental phase of development but are increasingly common in practice. The effects of dietetic and drug therapy may become evident over the long term (i.e., after months of treatment).The educational team must be prepared to work in conjunction with a medical professional whom the parent may have contacted for assistance. That is, the teaching staff may be carrying out behavior modification programs at the same time a physician is prescribing a pharmacologic treatment for the same behavior. Ideally, the educational and medical professions can coordinate their efforts for the benefit of the child. Yet, in the context of the assessment procedure we are outlining here, the check for medical causes is solely in the province of specific biomedical factors such as tangible infections and diseases. We are not recommending that inferred causes such as diets that require long-term treatment be investigated before behavior modification programs are tried. Still, the contemporary professional should keep abreast of developments in medicine and related fields. The teacher should share information with parents about recent developments in the allied health as well as educational fields. When the teacher observes certain presenting biological conditions in the student (e.g., a hand tremor), a referral should be made to an appropriate health professional.

Functional Analysis. After biomedical factors have been considered, the educational team should conduct a *functional analysis* of the problem behavior. That is, observations and recordings should be made to determine whether there is a pattern of antecedent and consequent events surrounding the target behavior. A successful functional analysis provides critical information for designing effective treatment procedures.

Figure 5.2 shows a recording sheet that can be used by teachers or parents in conducting a functional analysis of behavior. The left-hand column shows the date. The next column lists what antecedent event(s) preceded the behavior (e.g., the paraprofessional directed the student to sit in a chair). The next column provides a description of the behavior. The characteristics as well as the duration of the episode may be written (e.g., the child knocked over his chair and screamed for 5 seconds). The last column gives a description of what consequent event followed the behavior (e.g., peers laughed at the child, and the teacher ordered him to pick up the chair and sit at his desk). At the end of the day the teacher or parent can sum the number of incidents (and total duration) of the behavior. The number or duration of incidents per day then may be graphed and serve as a baseline before treatment is instituted. Most important, the recording sheet permits teachers and parents to conduct a functional analysis of the behavior.

After a couple of days of data collection, the sheets should be scanned to determine whether there is a pattern of certain antecedent events preceding the behavior or certain consequent events following it. The correlation of events in time leads one to believe that the antecedent or consequent event is a potential variable that maintains the behavior. The most common maintenance effects of antecedent and consequent events are escape and reinforcement operations, respectively. That is, problem behaviors often appear after an antecedent command has been given. The student engages in the problem behavior in order to escape or avoid doing the task at hand. The second condition, where persons around the student socially reinforce the problem behavior, is quite common. That is, the student's peers may laugh at him after he causes a disruption, and this contingent social attention may serve to reinforce the behavior and lead to its continued presence. The recording sheet enables teachers to conduct a functional analysis of behavior. The information gathered from the sheet produces rate, duration, and baseline data and sets the stage for the formulation of an effective treatment procedure.

Figure 5.2 Recording sheet for conducting a functional analysis of behavior.

Date	Antecedent	Behavior	Consequence
10/3	Paraprofessional said, "Sit in seat"	Knocked chair over and screamed (5 seconds)	Peers laughed, and teacher made him pick up chair
Total = 3	None	Screamed	Peers laughed
	Bumped peer	Poked peer in arm	Teacher scolded
10/4			

Characteristics of the Participants. The next steps in the assessment process involve considering the characteristics of the student and the individuals charged with carrying out the behavior modification program. Some behavior modification programs designed to manage high-rate behaviors require constant physical surveillance. One must assess whether the staff has the training and durability to carry out such demanding programs. If it is unlikely that they will be able to run the program, it is better not to institute the program at that time. An improperly run program can cause the student's behavior to worsen. A poorly run program results in inconsistencies in the delivery of commands (S^D's) and consequences (S^{R+}'s and S^{R-}'s). The success of behavior analytic programs, in terms of increasing skill behaviors or decreasing aberrant behaviors is based on the consistency of stimulus delivery. Particularly for students with serious learning difficulties, it is critical that stimulus events be presented consistently so that the individual can comprehend the regularity in the environment. The improper implementation of programs also can have an adverse effect on the staff. The staff person is likely to have an experience in which behavioral programming has failed. The experience of failure may shake the confidence of the professional and reduce his or her belief in behavioral procedures.

The assessment of the persons or mediators who carry out behavior modification programs is particularly critical when home programs are to be conducted by parents. Parents are more likely than staff members to be trained incompletely and to have numerous distractions that may prevent them from being consistent behavioral programmers. It is therefore necessary to determine whether parents or staff members can implement a program in the manner in which it was designed. It may be decided not to institute the program because of existing limitations involving parents or staff. The program may be simplified or run only for short periods of time so that it can be executed in an exact fashion. Whether it is decided to conduct, forestall, or modify a behavioral program, it is essential that an assessment be made of the mediators and their capability to implement behavioral programs.

Another consideration that often is overlooked involves the thoughts and feelings of the student toward behavioral programming. In most cases severely handicapped individuals are so intellectually delayed that they cannot make independent decisions related to their own welfare. For instance, such a student is unlikely to be able to decide whether to participate in and benefit from a particular program designed to help him. Legally, the individual is considered not competent, and a guardian is appointed to make programming and other decisions for him. In a minority of persons classified as severely handicapped, their higher intellectual capabilities enable them to make decisions that affect their lives. Professionals must be sensitive to the fact that some persons with severe handicaps are capable of making personal decisions, and we must help them in participating in decision-making processes such as IEP meetings. For example, a teenager with an IQ in the 50s and an expressive language of 2,000 words may have had numerous earlier experiences with behavior modification programs. He may have experienced these programs as being unsuccessful and dehumanizing. He therefore may have strong feelings against future participation in behavior modification programs. These feelings must be aired, and professionals and parents must discuss and resolve the matter of the teenager's participation.

Work with a variety of clinical patients has shown that when a client is not committed to participation in a program, the chances of success of the treatment package are seriously curtailed. Thus, if professionals feel strongly about implementing a program but the student is resistant to it, dialogue must occur so that the student changes her or his attitude to a positive one concerning participation. If the student continues to have a resistant attitude toward participation, staff members should seriously consider not implementing the program. In many circumstances the behavior is too severe (e.g., punch-

Figure 5.3 The behavioral assessment process.

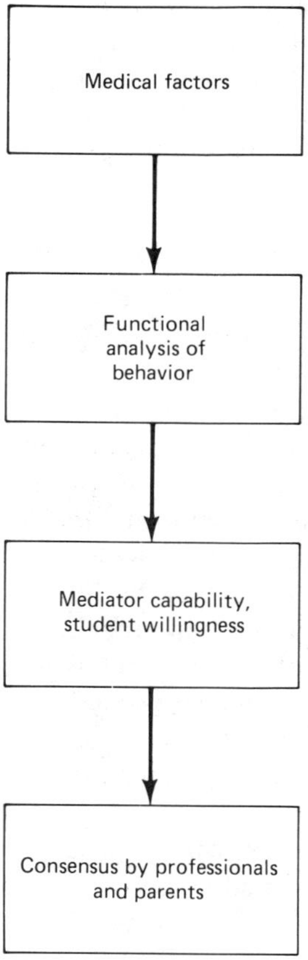

ing others) so that a program must be instituted regardless of the student's volition and feelings. Yet professionals must always be sensitive to the wishes of the student for both ethical and therapeutic reasons. In addition, there is a burgeoning field of self-control behavior therapy in which handicapped and other clinical populations regulate their own contingencies of reinforcement and become more independent in their daily lives (e.g., Sowers, Rusch, Connis, and Cummings, 1980).

Figure 5.3 presents a flowchart of the behavioral assessment process. Initially, medical factors are ruled out or treated. Next, a functional analysis of behavior determines the antecedents and consequences of the target behavior. The functional analysis also produces baseline data of the rate or duration of behavior. Next, a consideration is made of the mediator's capability and the student's willingness to engage in the behavior modification program. Finally, all relevant parties (professionals, parents, and possibly the student) must reach an agreement that there is a need for a behavioral program to be instituted.

The assessment information should facilitate the discussion of what type of program will be developed. In some situations a professional may write a behavioral assessment report that summarizes the information illustrated in Figure 5.3. The report should summarize medical, functional analysis, baseline, mediator, and client information. The report should end with an indication of a consensus reached about the need for a program and the general characteristics of the program.

Ecological and Curricular Variables

Behavior modification programs typically have consisted of the presentation of a baseline phase of sessions, followed by a treatment phase. Treatment has usually involved some manipulation of the consequences or antecedents—which led to a reduction of the problem behavior(s). The treatment most often consisted of a consequence package such as timeout or differential reinforcement. It is our feeling that the traditional behavior modification procedures that stress consequence manipulation have provided the richest research literature documenting how problem behaviors can be reduced. Yet before one begins a traditional behavior modification procedure, another set of factors should be considered. Ecological and curricular factors have not been investigated to the degree that consequence procedures have been. Yet there is a growing literature in research and practice that argues for the effects that ecology and curriculum can have on behavior disorders.

Just as medical factors are checked out first in the assessment process, ecological and curricular factors should be investigated and acted on when necessary before one proceeds to consequence procedures. Ecological and curricular factors are variables that a teacher normally will consider for typical classroom functioning (see Chapters 6 and 7). Thus, special postbaseline interventions may not be needed to reduce a problem behavior. However, specific ecological and curricular events have been known to trigger high rates of aberrant behavior (e.g., Rago, Parker, and Cleland, 1978; Weeks and Gaylord-Ross, 1981). The teacher should be aware of these events and correct the problem when possible. Data can be kept after the ecological change has been made to evaluate whether modification leads to a reduction in problem behavior.

Figure 5.4 shows a graph of baseline data. An ecological intervention was then instituted and a concomitant reduction in behavior resulted. The figure shows how an ecological intervention produced small changes in behavior. Next, a curricular procedure was attempted, and more substantive changes resulted. This repeated use of continuous measurement, intervention, and evaluation can be used to determine whether a sequence of interventions has reduced the rate of behavior from baseline and previous treatment levels.

Figure 5.4 Graph of treatment sequence.

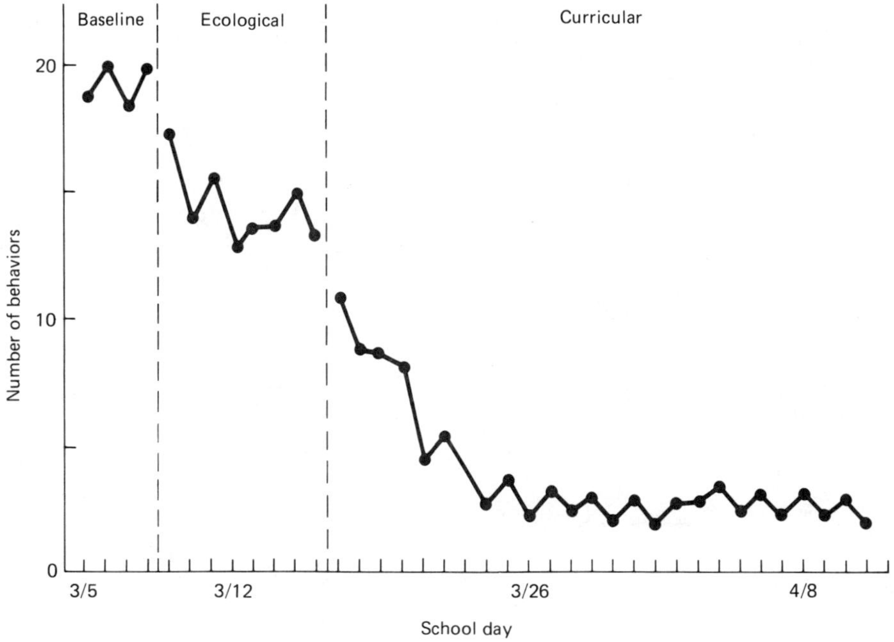

Ecological Factors. Three ecological variables may produce aberrant behavior. *Crowding* refers to a situation in which a large number of people occupy a relatively small amount of space. Research with animals has shown that crowded habitats produce a variety of psychopathologic behaviors. Unfortunately, in the past many classes for severely handicapped students were located in trailers, in back wards of institutions, or in partitioned rooms where there was overcrowding of persons. Overcrowding can produce increased levels of stress in both the students and the professional staff. Stress associated with crowding can lead to aggressive behaviors, low tolerance for frustration, and a general lowering of motivation and morale. A variety of aberrant behaviors may result from stress associated with overcrowding.

Figure 5.5 shows a flowchart of ecological variables. On the left-hand side are maintenance variables such as crowding that may cause or maintain the problem behavior. The professional should go down the left-hand column and consider whether each particular variable is a cause of the problem behavior. Observations, review of past records, functional analysis of behavior, and baseline data may indicate that a particular variable has caused or maintained the behavior. If such a conclusion is drawn, the teacher should move to the right-hand, or intervention, column. This column presents one

Figure 5.5 Ecological and curricular variables.

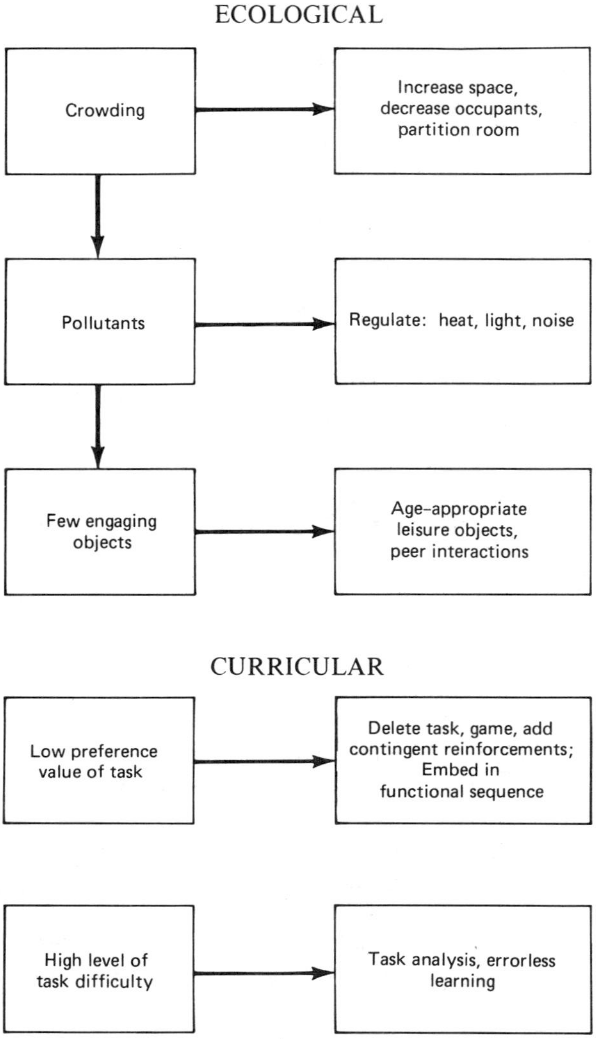

or more procedures that may remediate the behavior problem. For example, for crowding, the flowchart suggests increasing, changing, and partitioning spaces as well as decreasing the number of occupants in the classroom. Let us consider each of these interventions.

If crowding is defined as having too many occupants in too small a space, a sensible solution would be to obtain a larger classroom or reduce the number of occupants in the room. Unfortunately, teachers have relatively little influence in selecting a classroom. But if the room is clearly too small, the teacher should request a larger room by presenting the case to a supervisor. Sometimes a larger classroom may be obtained through such efforts.

A similar situation may exist when there are too many students in a classroom. Classes for severely handicapped students traditionally have been small in terms of the number of students, e.g., five to ten, in comparison to regular education classes. Yet because of budget cuts in local school districts, there has been a tendency to increase class size in order to balance the district budget. Again, a teacher may appeal for fewer students and have more or less success depending on the responsiveness of administrators and the effectiveness of parent advocacy groups.

The appropriate number of students may vary according to the type of students who constitute the class. Students with behavioral disorders or physical disabilities are likely to require much individual attention, with a smaller class size being more tenable, e.g., six to eight per class. When a large number of behaviorally disordered students are grouped together, there is likely to be a great deal of peer imitation of problem behaviors and an ascending level of noise and chaos resulting from deviant acts, but a class composed primarily of "higher functioning" students without behavior or physical disorders may reach an appropriate size of ten to fourteen. Thus, there is no magic number for class or staff size.

Another solution to overcrowding is to alter the space in the room by erecting partitions to create working areas or zones (see Chapter 7). The creation of zones through subdividing the classroom may prevent bodies from constantly bumping into each other and thus alleviate the sense of overcrowding. Another solution is to move students and staff out of the designated classroom to other sites throughout the school day. Chapter 7 describes ways to conduct instruction in multiple sites both on and off campus. Moving students and staff to different locales throughout the day may alleviate the oppression of the crowded classroom, and a reduction in associated aberrant behavior may result.

Environmental pollutants are a second set of variables that can have effects on problem behavior. Unfortunately, classrooms for students with severe handicaps are sometimes undesirable in terms of physical environmental characteristics such as heat, light, and noise. A room may be consistently too hot or too cold, with poor temperature regulation. There may be drafts from windows or ventilators. Sometimes there is poor lighting throughout the room or in certain parts of the room. Fluorescent lighting or blinking lights also may detract from visual attending efforts by the student. Also, some rooms become excessively noisy from adjoining areas or from radios, intercoms, or chatter within the class.

It should be remembered that our behavioral model of instruction is based on the student's attending to specific discriminative stimuli in the environment. These S^D's may take a visual, auditory, or tactile form. The presence of environmental pollutants such as noise may distract the student from an auditory S^D. Poor lighting can interfere with attending to visual S^D's. Excessive heat or cold can lead to body reactions that interfere with perceptual responses. Thus, environmental pollutants can create conditions that undermine effective instruction, lead to off-task behavior, and increase the likelihood of the appearance of problem behaviors. In addition, pollutants can cause discomfort and stress to students and staff, and this may result in more outbursts of behavior problems.

The presence of pollutants may be rectified in a fairly direct manner. Poor lighting may be improved through the purchase of more light fixtures or wire. Heating problems may be ameliorated through repairs of the furnace, air conditioners, or room insulation. External noise may not be amenable to improvement. Noise generated from within the class may be lessened through the use of room dividers and the careful monitoring of loud talking or music. Most of these alterations in the physical environment entail requests made to an administrator. Limited funds may undermine the removal of pollutants. Yet the serious professional must take the necessary steps to eliminate pollutants. If the existing classroom is beyond remediation, it may be necessary to request a different location.

The absence of *engaging objects* can lead to increases in the rate of aberrant behavior. Although all teachers attempt to decrease the amount of noninstructional, or "down," time, there still will be times between activities, at recess, etc., when students are left to their own resources. It is important to have leisure objects in the room with which the student can interact either alone or with peers during free play periods. Some students with behavior problems will display these behaviors when there are few objects or activities available. Social and leisure objects and activities may compete with the appearance of aberrant behavior just as instructional curricular activities do.

Thus, the teacher should enrich the class with a number of age-appropriate leisure objects such as toys, table games, and radios. In many cases the students will have to be trained in the proper functional use of these objects or be taught how to interact socially with the objects with a peer. In either case, the professional should consider the possibility that the absence of engaging objects may be correlated with the display of aberrant behavior. When this situation presents itself, the teacher should take the necessary steps to acquire leisure objects and train students in their use. The absence of leisure objects and its effect on aberrant behavior also may be observed in the student's home. In this case, the teacher should encourage the parents to acquire leisure objects and make sure the student uses them in the home.

Curricular Factors. Curricular variables are closely related to the notion of using leisure objects to reduce problem behaviors. As has been stated, when the student has no leisure or curricular activities in which to engage, there may be an increase in aberrant behavior. Thus, it is important to keep the student active and programmed in constructive behaviors. However, even when the student is engaged in a functional curriculum, additional variables may interact with the appearance of problem behavior. For example, when the student performs tasks that are of little interest, there may be a display of aberrant behavior as a preferred off-task response or as an escape response that may lead the teacher to terminate the instructional session. The functional analysis of behavior may show that certain tasks are associated with the appearance of a problem behavior. One reason why a task may be disliked is that it is at too high a difficulty level for the student. This may be indicated by a high rate of errors and the appearance of the problem behavior immediately after an error is made (Weeks and Gaylord-Ross, 1981). When a task has a low preference value for the student, a number of steps may be taken to increase its desirability. One step is to eliminate the task from the curriculum of the student. For example, a student's dislike of sorting papers into envelopes may be indicated by facial grimaces and occasional temper tantrums involving throwing the envelopes to the ground. Since the student has tantrums only when doing this task, it may be decided to exclude the sorting task from the student's curriculum. This deletion strategy may be appropriate for some tasks, but tasks such as toilet training or communication training may be too important to drop from the curriculum. Another possibility is to drop the task temporarily. This approach will cause the problem behavior to disappear once the task has been deleted. At a later time (perhaps in 3 months) it is possible that the task can be resumed without the problem behavior being in evidence. The behavior may have dropped out of the student's repertoire and may not reappear with the resumption of the task.

Another technique for increasing the preference value of the task is to introduce potent positive reinforcers that are contingent on correct performance. An assessment can be made of the reinforcement value of the consequences used in the task (see Chapter 2). It may be found that the consequences have little reinforcement value. Also, the task may have been delivered with no contingent reinforcement procedure. In these cases it may be necessary to institute a potent contingent reinforcement schedule. Another way to increase the preference value of a task is to insert it in a functional curriculum sequence chain (see Chapter 3). In isolation, the task may have little interest value for the student. Inserted within a longer natural chain, it may take on more appealing characteristics and decrease the likelihood of the appearance of correlated aberrant behavior. In a less theoretical vein, for years good teachers have had the knack of taking an uninteresting task and presenting it in a gamelike context so that it evokes the interest of students. These natural teaching practices should not be overlooked when one is attempting to increase the preference value of the curriculum.

A final way to alter the curriculum is to decrease the difficulty level of a task through task analysis and errorless learning procedures. As was mentioned in Chapter 2, task analysis breaks a task into a chain of responses in order to facilitate learning. The same process may be used for high-error tasks that are associated with the appearance of aberrant behavior. Similarly, errorless fading procedures break up an S^D into its component parts and introduces them to the learner in sequential steps. When stimulus control cannot be obtained with the complete S^D, an errorless procedure may be used to facilitate learning. When poor stimulus control is associated with the appearance of aberrant behavior, the errorless procedure may have the dual benefit of teaching the task and reducing aberrant behavior (see Chapter 10).

Figure 5.5 shows a flowchart in which ecological and curricular factors are considered as possibly maintaining aberrant behavior. When there is evidence that a variable such as task difficulty is leading to the appearance of aberrant behavior, the flowchart suggests methods for remediating the variable. Data can be collected repeatedly across intervention phases (Figure 5.4) to evaluate the effectiveness of the procedure. If the behavior continues to appear at a substantial rate, the professional should proceed to the next factor in the decision model and consider further treatment strategies.

Reinforcement

The major variables that maintain deviant behaviors are positive reinforcement and negative reinforcement. In positive reinforcement a professional or parent may consistently attend to a maladaptive response. For example, whenever a child repeatedly bangs her head against a table, the father may come over and hug her in order to comfort his daughter. Thus, a response (head bang)-reinforcer (hugs) relationship is established that maintains the behavior. Sometimes adults are not aware that they are reinforcing a behavior. For example, a teacher may scold a student for being disruptive. The teacher may think he is punishing the student's behavior, but the attention the student receives from the teacher through yelling serves as a positive reinforcer to maintain the behavior. Professionals and parents must not fall into the trap of inadvertently reinforcing a problem behavior through contingent negative attention. Negative attention can serve as a reinforcer because the behaviorally disordered student often receives a low rate of positive reinforcement (i.e., attention) from those around him. The troubled youngster is avoided because of his maladaptive acts. His needs for social interaction are met through the one way he knows how to obtain attention—maladaptive acts.

When a functional analysis of behavior has indicated that the problem behavior is being maintained through social reinforcement, two general tactics may be used to ameliorate the condition (see Figure 5.6).

Figure 5.6 Reinforcement variable.

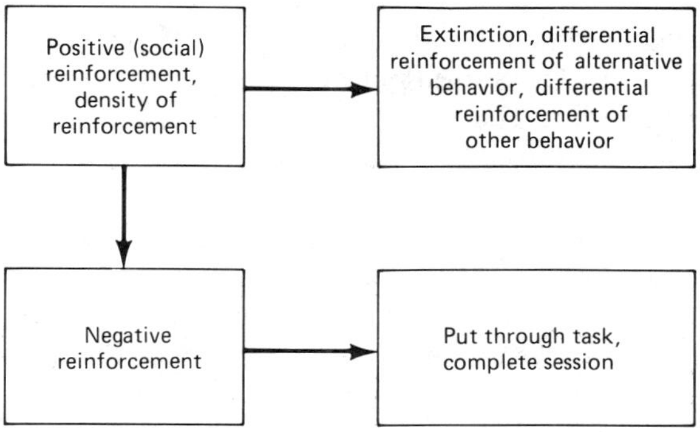

Extinction. *Extinction* is a procedure by which the persons who have been attending to the problem behavior contingently cease giving attention to the student after the behavior appears. Thus, the response-reinforcer relationship is broken. People must be consistent in ignoring the student for a fixed period of time (at least 10 seconds) after the response is emitted. If they are not consistent, there is a chance that the student will be placed on an intermittent reinforcement schedule (e.g., one reinforcer for every eight responses). Intermittent reinforcement schedules maintain behavior at rates higher than those resulting from continuous reinforcement schedules. Thus, the inconsistent implementation of extinction may worsen the problem. Another problem with extinction is that some behaviors introduce such danger to the environment (e.g., chronic assaults) that they cannot be ignored. In these cases it is not possible to implement extinction. Most problem behaviors do not lead to such imminent danger, and for these problems it is possible to use extinction.

Differential Reinforcement of Alternative Behaviors. DRA, as it is known, is another technique that can be used alone or in conjunction with extinction to eliminate problem behaviors. DRA essentially uses the same schedule as the contingent positive reinforcement of skill behaviors. That is, a response class of constructive behaviors is identified. Whenever the response occurs, the behavior is reinforced positively on a continuous or intermittent schedule. In the behavior management context, the differential reinforcement schedule serves to strengthen the appropriate response relative to the problem behavior. Then the appropriate behavior is more likely to appear in situations in which it has been reinforced, and inappropriate behaviors are less likely to appear in those same settings.

The DRA strategy attempts to identify as many appropriate behaviors as possible and contingently reinforce them. The more situations in which curricular responses can be reinforced, the more likely it is that aberrant behaviors will drop out of the person's repertoire. It must be remembered that behaviorally disordered students receive little reinforcement in their environment because they have alienated people by means of their abrasive behaviors. DRA changes this reinforcement pattern by building in reinforcement for appropriate behavior. The student then learns that she can get the attention of others not only through deviant acts but also through constructive behaviors.

DRA should be a procedure that is normally in effect in classroom programs. That is, throughout the school day a student should receive a considerable amount of positive reinforcement in instructional and free play settings. Figure 5.6 shows that the teacher should assess the amount or density of reinforcement received by the behaviorally disordered student throughout the school day. If the student receives a sufficient amount of reinforcement (e.g., one reinforcer every 1 to 5 minutes), it may not be necessary to institute a formal DRA program.

When insufficient reinforcement is being received, a DRA program may be established by identifying one or more appropriate responses that appear throughout the school day (e.g., working on task for 1 minute or initiating a play interaction with a peer). Whenever the student emits the behavior, there is contingent reinforcement with praise, edibles, tokens, etc. A response should be selected that the student already is emitting at a low rate or that can be brought about with minimal prompting. When DRA is successful, the appropriate response will increase in rate and the problem behavior should decrease concomitantly. Recording sheets and graphs can be used to monitor the rate of appropriate and problem behavior.

As was the case in developing preferred curriculum and an environment without pollutants, the appearance of a sufficient amount or density of reinforcement throughout the school day is a condition that should obtain in a contemporary educational program. Yet it is necessary to evaluate the reinforcement density as a possible variable that may be associated with problem behavior. When it is found that a low density is present, a formal DRA program should be established. It is relatively straightforward to use DRA in instructional settings. Correct responses are reinforced contingently as in a typical skill-building program. In free play settings, a social or leisure behavior is likely to be targeted, for example, handing a play object to a peer. Whenever the behavior occurs, a staff member will deliver reinforcement.

Differential Reinforcement of Other Behavior. Referred to as DRO, this technique is a variant of DRA. A time interval is used to key reinforcement. If the student does not emit the problem behavior in a given, fixed interval, e.g., 2 minutes, a staff person will deliver reinforcement. This procedure continues so that for consecutive 2-minute intervals reinforcement will be delivered if no problem behavior appears. If the problem behavior does appear, no reinforcement is given, and the interval is set back to run for another 2

Figure 5.7 Schedules of reinforcement.

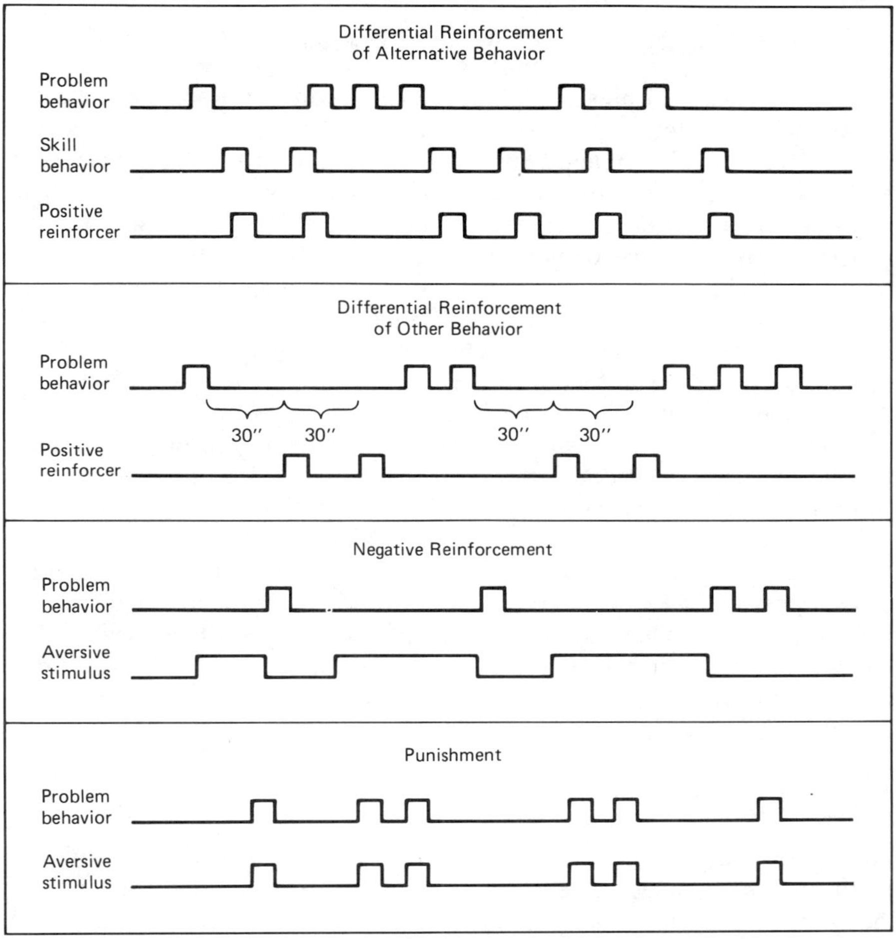

minutes. Figure 5.7 shows DRO and DRA schedules of reinforcement. When a student shows improvement so that a behavior occurs rarely during the DRO intervals, the length of the interval may be increased to, say, 4 minutes.

Do not increase the length of the interval in a frivolous manner. Never decrease the length of the DRO interval when the student displays an increase in response rate. If the interval is decreased under these circumstances, the student will learn that increased aberrant responding leads to shorter DRO intervals or an increased rate of reinforcement. Kitchen timers or stopwatches can be used to record DRO intervals. Kitchen timers are good because a bell rings indicating the earning of reinforcement. The number of problem behaviors and the number of reinforcers earned can be entered on a standard frequency recording sheet.

Many problem behaviors are maintained by negative reinforcement; that is, the student emits the inappropriate response to escape an unpleasant circumstance. Figure 5.7 presents a schematic of negative reinforcement; it can be seen how it differs from positive reinforcement. Most cases of negative reinforcement involve an adult giving a command for a student to perform a task. The student does not want to perform this task and emits a problem behavior such as a tantrum to avoid it. Some teachers may decide that the student is too upset that day and not require an effort by the student. The premature ending of the session or trial without completing the task reinforces the problem behavior negatively. Many students learn through their past history of negative reinforcement that if they emit certain problem behaviors, they can avoid doing tasks. In a sense the student is manipulating or controlling the situation through the aberrant behavior.

The main way to counter negative reinforcement is to put the student through the task at hand. Do not end the trial or session prematurely because of a behavioral outburst. Let the student finish the outburst, and then deliver an S^D to continue the next trial. Always try to end a session on a positive note in which the student receives reinforcement for correct performance. If possible, avoid ending a session with the occurrence of a disruptive behavior. If the student is put through the trial or session, he learns that aberrant behaviors do not enable him to avoid task performance. Over time, the problem behavior should decrease in rate because it no longer serves a negative reinforcement function.

Punishment

Our decision model for treating behavior problems entails that positive educative procedures such as ecology, curriculum, and reinforcement factors should be investigated first to reduce the rate of behavior. In many cases the manipulation of these variables will lead to successful behavior reduction. In some circumstances, however, a series of positive interventions may not lead to successful remediation. In these cases it may be necessary to institute a punishment procedure. For an alternative view, see the TASH Resolution on Intrusive Intervention (The Association for Persons with Severe Handicaps, 1981). Punishment is the contingent delivery of a stimulus that leads to the decrease in frequency of a problem behavior. Figure 5.7 shows the response-stimulus schematic.

Aversive Stimuli. One type of punishment involves the delivery of aversive stimuli like yells, seclusion, exercise, or slaps. Since these are quite unpalatable ways of treating people, they should be avoided except when absolutely necessary. At least one positive intervention should be tried before a

Figure 5.8 A treatment sequence.

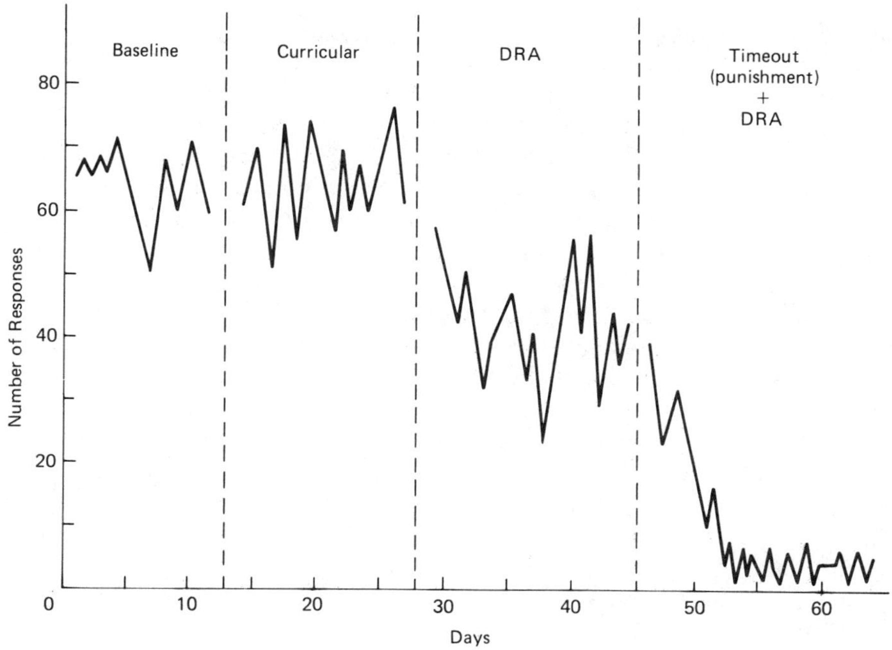

teacher uses punishment. When punishment is introduced, a DRA program should simultaneously be in effect. The DRA program permits the individual the choice of emitting appropriate behaviors and increases the likelihood of the appearance of those behaviors.

Figure 5.8 shows a graph of treatment sequence. Baseline data were collected initially. A curricular program was tried, and the rate of aggression did not change. DRA was used next, and the behavior dropped to about 50 percent of its original rate. Still, the student was emitting two or three aggressive acts per day, and this was presenting serious danger to peers and staff. It was decided to institute the punishment procedure of timeout, and the behavior dropped to a near-zero level.

Thus, punishment is an aversive procedure that should be used only when positive procedures have been tried and have failed to reduce the behavior to an acceptable level. Punishment should be used in conjunction with DRA, never alone. It probably should be used only for level 1 targeted behaviors, that is, problem behaviors that will lead to serious danger to the student or others or threaten the least restrictive placement of the student. The effects of punishment should be quite dramatic. If there is no substantive change in behavior after 2 weeks, the procedure should be discontinued. When the program has resulted in successful behavior reduction, strategies should be developed to thin out the use of punishment. The procedures for thinning out positive reinforcers that were presented in Chapter 2 can be used for thinning aversive stimuli.

A number of management procedures entail the delivery of more aversive stimuli. In the past an array of aversive stimuli were used that included electric shock, aromatic ammonia capsules, and slaps to the body. Most of these aversive stimuli have been banned from use in educational and residential facilities. If these or other aversive procedures are to be used, they should be screened by an ethics committee. Proper consent from guardians and professionals at the facility should be obtained. Exacting steps for monitoring treatment implementation must be followed. Timelines for reviewing treatment success and decision making to continue or discontinue the aversive program must be established. When the proper steps are followed, an aversive program may benefit the individual in a way that nonaversive programs cannot. The individual certainly has a right to a treatment that may rid her of a dangerous behavior and redirect her life in a promising way. The ethical and legal problem in using aversive procedures is that the severely handicapped individual is not competent to affirm his right to treatment. Therefore, some other group of adults must decide on treatment possibilities for him.

In considering the use of aversive procedures, a number of variables must be weighed. With more serious behavior problems it is likely to be critical that the behavior be suppressed so that further harm does not occur to the student and those around the student. When more palatable behavior modification procedures have been tried and have failed, it is often necessary to make a last ditch effort with an aversive procedure. There have been many documented instances in which contingent aversive programs were highly successful with difficult to treat behaviors (e.g., Lovaas and Simmons, 1969), but professionals should be aware of the potential limitations of aversive procedures. Most notably, punishment is not likely to generalize to other settings or persons so that when the program is discontinued, there is no response suppression to nontreatment settings. It is also possible that the aversive stimulus will harm the student physically or produce negative emotional side effects, for example, fear of teachers or other adults. But when proper administrative precautions are taken, punishment procedures are potentially effective programs that should not be denied to persons with severe handicaps.

Withdrawal of Positive Stimuli. A second type of punishment is withdrawal of a positive stimulus that leads to a deceleration in behavior. Removing a positive stimulus is generally a more palatable and acceptable procedure than delivering an aversive stimulus. *Response cost* is an example of this kind of punishment; it is a procedure in which the student loses positive reinforcers contingent on the appearance of the problem behavior. Token economies are well suited for use with response cost since the procedure clearly involves taking away a prescribed number of tokens from the student when the problem behavior occurs.

Timeout is a relatively mild aversive experience that removes the person from the situation in which the behavior has occurred. In *nonexclusionary* timeout, the student may have to turn her chair away from the group of students or stand in the corner for a fixed period of time. In *exclusionary* timeout, the student must go to an enclosed area such as his room or a booth for a fixed period of time. Care should be taken to make sure that the student does not harm himself in the secluded area. He should not be let out of the area while he is still being disruptive. Clear time limits should be set on the timeout interval so that it does not become an abusive experience. Overall, timeout is a very effective management procedure that usually involves little potential harm to the student.

Overcorrection and Contingent Restraint. There is another set of aversive procedures that do not have the noxious qualities of electric shock or corporal punishment. *Overcorrection* and *contingent restraint* are techniques that require the person to manipulate his or her body in a prescribed way after the deviant act has been committed. Contingent restraint requires that the person sit, stand, or lie in a fixed position with the hands at the side. If the person does not remain still in this position, one or more staff members restrain the person in the fixed position. As soon as the person begins to remain still, the staff person fades out the manual restraint. The contingent restraint interval usually lasts from 1 to 5 minutes. When the interval ends, the person resumes normal activity.

Overcorrection (Foxx and Azrin, 1973) is similar to contingent restraint, except that the person must go through a series of movements instead of remaining still. The movements may involve a series of exercises for correcting the troubled situation (e.g., cleaning up a room or cleaning soiled undergarments). The overcorrection period usually lasts from 5 to 20 minutes. When the person does not proceed voluntarily through the movements, a staff member provides manual guidance.

Positive practice overcorrection entails having the person repeatedly practice an alternative correct response to the problem behavior. For example, if a student has soiled her underwear, she may have to walk from different points in her house to the bathroom (perhaps ten consecutive times) to practice getting to the toilet in order to prevent accidents in the future. She also may participate in *restitutional* overcorrection, in which she must "undo" or correct the outcome of the problem behavior. For example, an incontinent person may have to wash his own and twelve other pairs of soiled undergarments. He is thus restoring ("restitutional") the object to its original state. Also, there is not just a correction but an *over*correction so that there is repeated practice of the behavior. Thus, an overcorrection program for incontinence could include 20 minutes of positive practice and restitutional overcorrection contingent on the appearance of a soiling accident. Overcorrection programs also include DRA so that when the person emits the correct behavior, e.g., defecating properly in the toilet, he is positively reinforced.

Although overcorrection has proved successful with difficult behavior problems, it may have certain negative characteristics. First, it is time-consuming. Second, if the person resists doing the behavioral movements, staff persons must physically guide him or her through the behaviors. These physical guides (prompts) can be exhausting to staff members and may lead to physical injuries if there is a confrontation between student and staff. Thus, proceed with caution when selecting and implementing overcorrection, but give it careful consideration when circumstances dictate.

Contingent restraint and overcorrection are moderately aversive procedures that have proved effective in eliminating very challenging behavior problems. Care must be given when a teacher is manually guiding the person through the movements, or physical harm may result. A verbal statement such as "No" or "Let's exercise" should be given at the beginning of these and other punishment procedures. Over time, the verbal statement may become a conditioned punishing stimulus. It then may be used to punish behavior or warn the student not to do the behavior. When professionals and parents gain verbal stimulus control over a student's behavior, there is less of a need to use the actual aversive events.

The Treatment of Tommy

Let us see how our decision model for treatment can be applied to the case of Tommy. Tommy displayed two problem behaviors: pica and head slapping. The behaviors occurred only during free play, with pica identified as a level 1 target and head slapping as a level 2 target. During target behavior selection it was decided first to treat the behavior at school and the pica at home; at a later time head slapping would be dealt with at home.

The assessment component was applied first. A number of physician's reports over the past 5 years demonstrated no relation between pica, head slapping, and biomedical factors. The functional analysis of behavior reported baseline data for 1 week. Pica took place once that week, during the 10 A.M. free play session. Head slapping occurred 105 times, dispersed throughout the four free play sessions that week. Only 3 of the 105 responses appeared during instructional sessions. The functional analysis also indicated that pica and head slapping occurred when Tommy was not involved with a play activity.

Next, environmental and curricular factors were considered. There did not appear to be overcrowding or pollutants present in the school environment. There were play objects present during the free play sessions, but

Tommy rarely engaged them. Since his problem behaviors seemed to be correlated directly with his lack of activity, an intervention was established by which Tommy would be taught a play activity. During the four free play sessions a paraprofessional taught him how to assemble Lego® blocks so that they would look like cars, buildings, etc. Tommy was taught how to attach the Lego® blocks and how to move the completed objects such as airplanes and cars. When he successfully learned Lego® assembly, the paraprofessional merely gave him the blocks at the beginning of recess and then left Tommy alone to play with them.

Figure 5.9 shows data from baseline and toy intervention phases. It can be seen that head slapping dropped to about fifty responses per week with the play procedure. Pica remained at one instance per week. It was noted that the play program led to playing with Lego® blocks after training was completed for about 40 percent of the recess sessions. At other times he put the blocks down and remained inactive. At these times he slapped his head and ingested objects. A second environmental intervention was considered: removing all potential objects that could be consumed in the recess areas. This was deemed impossible since there would always be some small objects present. (At best, care could be taken to avoid leaving dangerous materials around.)

The curricular factor was considered next. Tommy seemed to enjoy playing with Lego blocks and it certainly was not too difficult a task. But it was felt that a greater variety of play activities should be available to Tommy. This would prevent boredom and possibly increase the proportion of time he played during recess, concomitantly lowering his amount of aberrant behavior. A curricular intervention was established in which a paraprofessional taught him how to play: dart throwing, pinball, playing and listening to records, and shooting a basketball at a hoop. When the student learned each task, the paraprofessional faded out of the play session so that the student was merely given the play material at the beginning of each recess period. Figure 5.9 shows that head slapping decreased further to twenty-five instances per week, yet pica was still emitted once per week. It was noted that Tommy now played at recess about 60 percent of the time.

In order to decrease aberrant behavior further and increase play time, the reinforcement component was examined. It was decided to establish a DRA program. During every minute of recess the paraprofessional would observe Tommy. When he was playing with one of the designated play objects, the paraprofessional praised him verbally and gave him a raisin to eat. As the proportion of Tommy's play increased, the paraprofessional made checks every 2 minutes and ultimately only once during recess. Tommy's proportion of play time increased to 90 percent, and Figure 5.9 shows that head slapping decreased to five instances per week (one per day). At this time it was felt that the environmental, curricular, and reinforcement programs had been successful in reducing head slapping to a very low rate. It was de-

Figure 5.9 The treatment of Tommy.

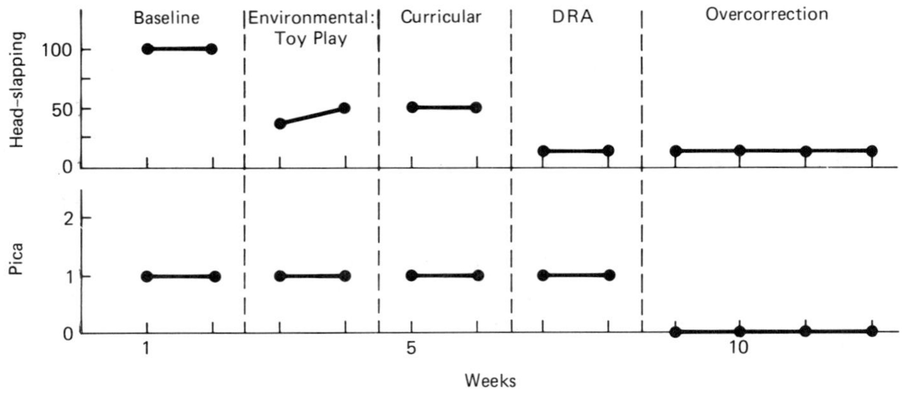

cided to continue these programs, with the prediction that head slapping would continue to decrease to a zero level.

Figure 5.9 shows that pica still did not drop below the rate of one instance per week. Although the training programs had increased play behavior dramatically, there were still inactive periods when Tommy would ingest an object. It was decided to try a punishment procedure in which pica would be consequated with an aversive stimulus. An oral overcorrection program was designed so that after every instance of pica Tommy would have to clean his mouth with Listerine for a 5-minute period. Before institution of the program, consent forms were signed by his parents, and measures were taken to monitor the program carefully. The paraprofessional guided Tommy's hand through the oral overcorrection procedure. With practice, Tommy did more of the mouth washing on his own, and manual guidance was faded out. Figure 5.9 shows that pica was eliminated after 4 weeks of oral overcorrection.

Summary

Serious problem behaviors are often prevalent among people with severe handicaps. In order to promote growth and development, it is imperative that these behaviors be eliminated or reduced to a tolerable level. Otherwise, problem behaviors such as self-injury will interfere directly with the teaching of constructive skills. A model for managing aberrant behaviors has been presented in this chapter. The model first targets the level of the problem behavior. It next assesses the etiological aspects of the behavior. Then a sequential treatment plan follows by examining ecological, curricular, reinforcement, and punishment variables. A case example was presented to show how the model may be implemented. The model has been implemented in a number of school settings and should be of assistance in managing the problem behaviors of handicapped students.

Chapter 6

Curriculum

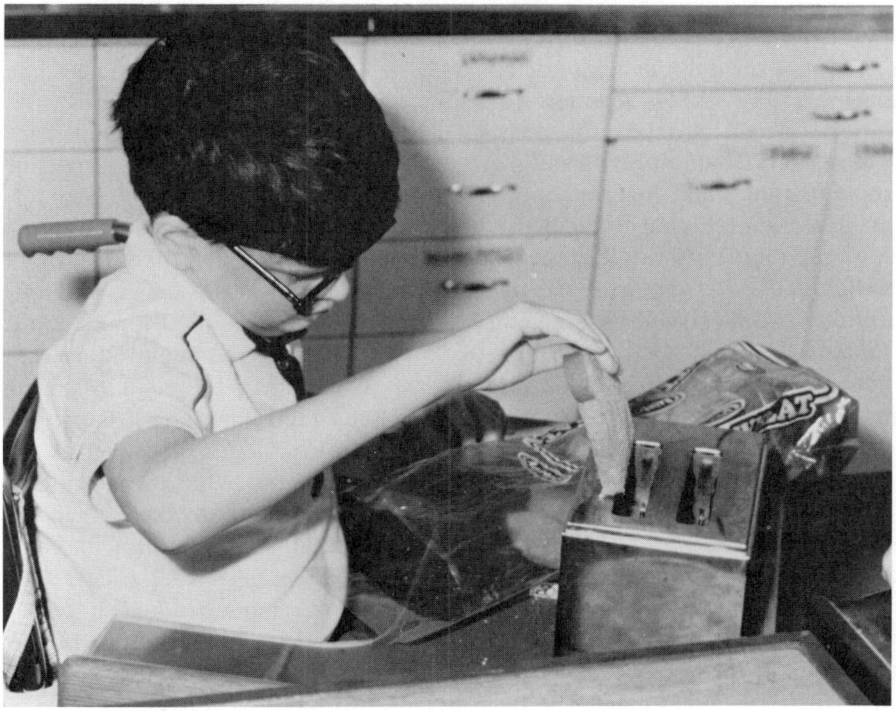

As a result of advances in our field, we can effectively deal with the issue of how to instruct students with serious impairments. Primarily through the principles of applied behavior analysis, a technology of instruction has emerged that enables teachers to instruct students successfully on a wide variety of tasks from motor skills to perceptual responses to cognitive operations. In Chapters 2, 3, and 4 we described the principles and means of implementing these instructional design techniques.

The issue of what to teach students with severe handicaps, however, is in a much more primitive stage of development. In Chapter 1 we described techniques for assessing students and formulating objectives for instruction. Although some useful assessment instruments have been developed, there remains the fundamental question of how to translate the acquired assessment information into specific target goals. The guiding principle in selecting curricular goals is the criterion of ultimate functioning (see Chapters 1 and 3 and Brown, Nietupski, and Hamre-Nietupski, 1976).

The criterion of ultimate functioning recommends that the activities identified for instruction should be keyed to future environments in which the student will reside, work, and play. Thus, educational goals can be set and carried out in particular apartments, factories, shopping malls, and restaurants of a community to prepare the student for more independent functioning in those sites as an adult. In terms of activities to be taught in the community, hundreds if not thousands of instructional objectives can be written for an individual student at a given time, but, an educational team must select a few (ten to thirty) objectives for the upcoming school year. After certain goals are selected, teachers may have second thoughts that instructional time should be spent on other activities of import that were not included in the IEP.

This chapter presents guidelines for selecting, implementing, and adapting curricula. The first section includes guidelines that outline selection procedures for teacher-generated versus commercially purchased curricula as well as recommendations for how to understand and implement curricula. The second section describes selected commercial curricula that have been shown to be effective with a number of severely handicapped students. Finally, there is a section on adapting curricular programs to the needs of the individual student.

Selecting Curricula

The process of curriculum selection is in many ways problematic. Numerous curricula have been written by educators in the field, yet when a teacher attempts to design an instructional program, it is not at all clear what steps should be taken to develop a task-analyzed curriculum. The most direct solution is to write a task analysis. Teacher-generated task analyses may fit the need in most cases, but the instructor should be aware of previously written task analyses and should select them for use when appropriate. Otherwise, teachers may spend undue amounts of time "reinventing the wheel." Selecting available curricula can save time as well as permit the utilization of programs that already have been validated with severely handicapped students.

Teachers almost invariably have to adapt a previously written curriculum for their own individual student(s). In many cases teachers may decide that the earlier written curriculum does not fit the needs of the students and then decide to write their own task analyses. In fact, with the increasing emphasis placed on teaching in natural environments, there is a greater likelihood that there will be idiosyncrasies in specific natural settings that limit the use of curricula from other settings. But the contemporary teacher should be aware of existing curricula and should build a library of task-analyzed programs. A cooperative library developed by a group of special education teachers in a school district would be even more sensible. The library should contain

1. Task-analyzed programs previously written by the teacher(s) in that district.
2. Commercially available curricula that may be purchased from publishers.

Guidelines

When a teacher reviews a commercially available curriculum, certain factors should be considered before deciding to purchase it and incorporate it into an educational program. Freagon, Rotatori, and Fox (1983) have advanced twenty-four criteria for evaluating curricula. We feel that certain of these criteria are more relevant than others in determining the value of the curriculum and considering it for one's personal use. Figure 6.1 lists the primary and secondary criteria for evaluating curricula. Let us list several of the primary criteria in terms of specific questions.

Figure 6.1

EVALUATION CRITERIA FOR A CURRICULUM

1. Who are the *curriculum designers*?
Are the curriculum designers teachers, supervisors, university personnel, grant personnel, or a combination thereof?

2. Is the curriculum *verified*, and on what *population*?
Are there success data (other than anecdotal) across a number of students to warrant inclusion in a disseminated curriculum?

3. Is the curriculum *handicapping-condition-specific*?
Is the curriculum geared to a specific handicapping condition (e.g., severely mentally retarded, severely physically handicapped)? Is the curriculum adaptable for *varying handicaps* within the severely and profoundly handicapping conditions? If the curriculum is designed for severely retarded students, can it be adapted to students who may also have a vision, auditory, or physical impairment?

4. Does the curriculum have a *philosophy* or a philosophical statement?
The curriculum philosophy should include an analysis and/or the concepts expressing fundamental beliefs. It should reflect the concepts and attitudes of the individual or group developers.

5. Does the curriculum include *curriculum objectives*?
The curriculum objectives should include the end toward which the effort was directed and/or continues to be directed.

6. Is the curriculum *functional*?
Does the curriculum emphasize the practical utility of its components or skills to be taught? Are the skills or components directly related to functioning in the everyday world?

7. Is the curriculum *developmental*?
Does the curriculum emphasize students' learning and growing along lines natural to nonhandicapped students' learning and growing?

8. Is the curriculum *comprehensive*?
Does the curriculum include commonly known curricular domains such as social, motor, communication, cognitive, self-help, and community?

9. Does the curriculum consider the students' *future ecological environments*?
Are post-21 environments considered for secondary-age students? Are secondary-school-age environments considered for elementary and middle-school-age students?

10. Does the curriculum consider the students' *present ecological environments*?
Does the curriculum provide for the students' present home, school, and community environments?

11. Is the curriculum *age-appropriate*?
Are the curriculum skills and components designed to assist a particular age group to function more like nonhandicapped students of the same age? Are the recommended materials of a nature that a nonhandicapped student of the same age might utilize them?

12. Is the curriculum *sequenced*?
Does the curriculum recommend a particular teaching of skills or components progression? The sequences should be verified by the reporting of student outcomes.

13. Is the curriculum *data-based*?
The curriculum should provide for continuous probe measurements of students' progress in curriculum skills or components.

14. Does the curriculum have a *teaching strategy or strategies*?
Does the curriculum provide information regarding teachers' verbiage in instruction, levels of assistance, positioning for specific tasks, etc.?

15. Does the curriculum include *prerequisite skills*?
The curriculum should account for and include student prerequisite skills necessary for teaching students more complex tasks.

16. Does the curriculum account for students' *acquisition, mastery, and maintenance of skills*?
Acquisition refers to the acquiring of the skill. Mastery refers to the ability to utilize the skill across persons, places, instructional materials, and language cues. Maintenance refers to the ability to perform mastery levels across time.

17. Does the curriculum provide for *interactions* with nonhandicapped students?
18. Does the curriculum describe *materials* that are *functional and age-appropriate*?
19. Are the curriculum *materials affordable*?
20. Does the curriculum describe *physical teaching environments*?
 The curriculum should include classroom floor plans, placement of equipment, stations, etc.
21. Does the curriculum provide *implementation strategies*?
 Does the curriculum give step-by-step procedures for implementation, things to do, and things not to do, based on the developers' experience?
22. Is the curriculum *compatible with curriculum designs for nonhandicapped school-age students*?
 Does the curriculum reflect age levels of implementation? Does it reflect a longitudinal process or have capabilities of being an early-childhood or elementary or secondary curriculum?
23. Does the curriculum have examples of *long- or short-term objectives*?
 These would be examples of objectives found in the Individualized Educational Program (IEP).
24. Does the curriculum reflect only *specific curricular domains*? Is it only a motor curriculum; a language curriculum; etc.?

Source: Adapted from S. Freagon, A. Rotatori, Jr., and R. Fox, Evaluation criteria for curriculum for the severely and profoundly retarded, *Journal for Special Educators* 19 (1983): 39–43. Reprinted with permission of PRO-ED, Inc., Austin, Texas.

1. Is the curriculum *handicapping-condition-specific*? Does it apply to a variety of severely handicapping conditions or does it apply to specific populations, e.g., deaf-blind or moderately retarded? A common flaw in interpreting published programs results from the population on which they were validated. The label "severely handicapped" covers a wide range of students, and what works with a moderately retarded person may not work with a profoundly retarded person.
2. Does the curriculum have *curriculum objectives*? The ultimate end or benefit to the student from engaging in that curriculum should be stated explicitly.
3. Does the curriculum have *long- and short-term objectives* that can be included in the student's IEP?
4. Is the curriculum *data-based*? Sample recording sheets or suggestions on how to measure pupil performance may be provided.
5. Is the curriculum *sequenced*? This is a cornerstone of curriculum, but some programs make better transitions from one component of the total curriculum to the next.
6. Does the curriculum have *teaching strategies* that provide information about prompting, reinforcing, etc.?
7. Does the curriculum provide *implementation strategies* with step-by-step suggestions for putting the curriculum into practice, deciding what to avoid, etc.?

The remainder of the criteria (see Figure 6.1) are important but probably not essential to the evaluation of a published curriculum. A teacher probably can adapt the commercial curriculum to assure that it is functional, includes interaction with nonhandicapped students, and relates to future environments when this information is not provided in the curriculum itself.

Commercially Available Curricula

In this section we describe four curricula that are commercially available. These curricula meet many of the selection criteria we have just described. The curricula have been used widely and have had a considerable degree of visibility. They were chosen from different domains in order to convey an idea of the types of tasks and activities severely handicapped children and youth can learn. The domains include communication, self-care, vocational, and leisure.

So far we have been using the terms "curriculum" and "task analysis" interchangeably. More precisely, a task analysis is the sequence of behavioral steps that constitute a single instructional program. For example, Figure 2.15, on page 76, shows the task analysis of a behavioral chain. In contrast, a curriculum consists of a number of task-analyzed programs. A curriculum tends to focus on a particular content domain such as self-care or communication. The curriculum may be sequential, in which case the student is taken from rudimentary skills in progression to more advanced skills, e.g., the Guess, Sailor, and Baer (1976) language training program. A sequential curriculum advances the student in a manner similar to the way mathematics is taught in regular education. A horizontal curriculum does not follow a sequential format. Rather, the student may learn one skill, e.g., shoe tying, which is not prerequisite to learning another skill, e.g., shirt buttoning. A number of skills in the curriculum may be taught at the same time. The self-help part of the Adaptive Behavior Curriculum (Popovich and Laham, 1981) contains task analyses of feeding, dressing, and personal hygiene, none of which follow a sequential order with the others.

Thus, a curriculum presents a whole package of programs that lead the student to acquire a set of skills in a particular domain. When the student completes the curricular program, his quality of life in the domain should have changed so that he becomes able, for instance, to speak in simple phrases, engage in recreation alone or with others, or display basic work skills.

Language Training. Guess, Sailor, and Baer (1976) developed a language training curriculum entitled Functional Speech and Language Training for the Severely Handicapped. This curriculum has a number of positive features that warrant its use with students who have limited language skills. The program is based on operant methodology, including careful instructions dealing with prompting and reinforcement procedures. Numerous recording sheets are provided with completed sample sheets so that the user should be able to

Figure 6.2

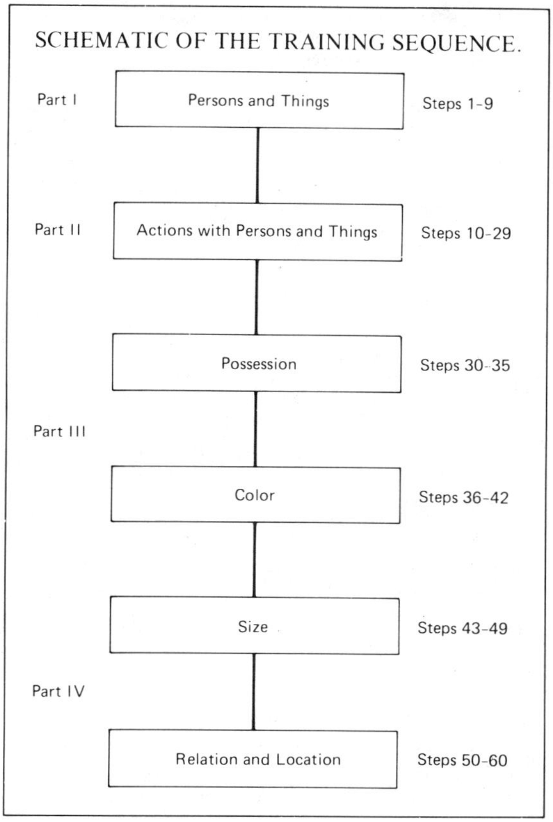

Source: Adapted from D. Guess, W. Sailor, and D. M. Baer, *Functional Speech and Language Training for the Severely Handicapped* (Austin, Tex.: PRO-ED, Inc.,1976), p. 2. Reprinted with permission of PRO-ED.

follow the program with few errors. The program is an exemplary model of curriculum sequencing. The four-part program sequences language acquisition into persons and things; actions with persons and things and with possession; color and size; and relation and location. Each of these four parts is broken down further into a series of program steps (sixty in all). Objectives and criteria are stated precisely. A flowchart summarizes the operations that the instructor must carry out to complete the program.

Figure 6.2 is a schematic presentation of the overall curriculum. Figure 6.3 shows how part 1 is subdivided into nine training steps. The figure also presents the primary cues to be delivered by the instructor and the re-

Figure 6.3

OUTLINE OF PERSONS AND THINGS CATEGORY

	Trainer	Student
STEP 1	(Show items) ask, "What's that?"	(correct labels); e.g., "ball," "nose," etc.
STEP 2	(Show items) say, "Point to (label)."	(correct point)
STEP 3	(Show items) ask, "What want?"	"Want (label)"; e.g., "Want milk"
STEP 4	(Show novel items)	"What's that?"
STEP 5	(Show mix of learned and novel items)	(correct labels) for learned items; "What's that?" for novel items
STEP 6	(Show novel items) "That is a (label)?"	"What's that?" / (correct label)[1]
STEP 7	(Show items) ask, "Is this a (label)?"	"yes/no"
STEP 8	(Show items) ask, "What do you want?"	"I want (label)"
STEP 9	(Show items) ask, "What is that?" Ask, "What do you want?"	(correct label) "I want (label)"[2]

[1]Student is trained to remember labels of novel items.
[2]Student is trained on a two-response chain.

Source: Adapted from D. Guess, W. Sailor, and D. M. Baer, *Functional Speech and Language Training for the Severely Handicapped* (Austin, Tex.: PRO-ED, Inc., 1976), p. 8. Reprinted with permission of PRO-ED.

sponses expected from the student. Figure 6.4 shows a flowchart of all the training operations for the programs in part 1. Figure 6.5 shows a completed recording sheet for the student, Dick. The number of correct responses for "ball" and "cup" was twenty-four, which translates to 38 percent correct (10 of thirty-one). This was Dick's performance during training sessions. These scores can be plotted on a graph.

A key advantage of this program over other language training programs is that it directs a teacher to instruct the student on the use of communicative forms that allow the student to operate or control the environment. For example, in step 3 of the part 1 program (see Figure 6.3), the student learns to say, "Want (object)," to the question, "What want?" In turn, the stu-

Figure 6.4 Training and correction procedures.

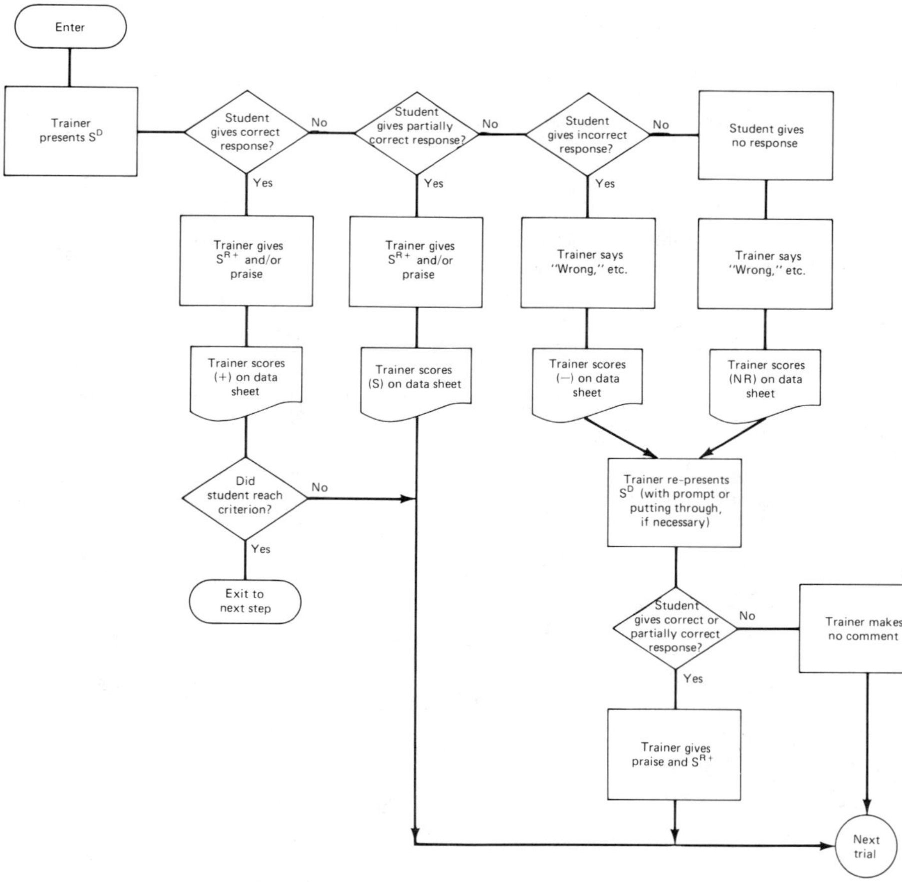

Source: Adapted from D. Guess, W. Sailor, and D. M. Baer, *Functional Speech and Language Training for the Severely Handicapped* (Austin, Tex.: PRO-ED, Inc., 1976), p. 6. Reprinted with permission of PRO-ED.

dent receives the object for a correct response. In the subsequent step, the student learns to say, "What's that?" when presented with novel items. Thus, the student learns to *mand* (make requests or commands) and make interrogative statements in the early phases of the program.

Many language programs spend a great deal of time at the beginning of the curriculum on receptive vocabulary training, i.e., pointing (not verbalizing) to a presented object. In contrast, the Guess, Sailor, and Baer program begins (step 1) with stating the name of an object to the instructor's question, "What's that?" Thus, even though the curriculum is behavior an-

Figure 6.5

SKILL TEST SCORING FORM FOR STEP 1

Student Dick Date 1/6/75 Session # 1

Trainer Bill

In blanks 1 to 16, list the sixteen items that are used in step 1; then list them again (not in the same order) in blanks 17 to 32.

	Item	Score		Item	Score
1.	Cookie	+	17.	Chair	−
2.	Pants	−	18.	Top	−
3.	Ball	+	19.	Nose	−
4.	Nose	−	20.	Cookie	+
5.	Chair	−	21.	Drum	−
6.	Pop	+	22.	Cap	NR
7.	Shoe	−	23.	Ball	+
8.	Car	+	24.	Pop	+
9.	Tummy	NR	25.	Mouth	−
10.	Table	−	26.	apple	+
11.	apple	+	27.	Pants	−
12.	Cap	−	28.	Shoe	−
13.	Top	−	29.	Spoon	S
14.	Mouth	−	30.	Table	−
15.	Spoon	−	31.	Tummy	NR
16.	Drum	S	32.	Car	+

Score trials as correct (+); incorrect (—); shape (S); or no response (NR)

Percent Summary for Test (based on thirty-two trials)

	+	—	S	NR
Score	10	17	2	3
Percent	31	53	6	9

Source: Adapted from D. Guess, W. Sailor, and D. M. Baer, *Functional Speech and Language Training for the Severely Handicapped* (Austin, Tex.: PRO-ED, Inc., 1976), p. 11. Reprinted with permission of PRO-ED.

alytic in theory and form, it contains many cognitive aspects from the work of Jean Piaget, in which the individual is taught to operate on his or her environment. The Guess, Sailor, and Baer program thus provides a good balance between the instructor gaining stimulus control over the student's performance and the student simultaneously learning to control or operate on the environment.

The program has other strengths in that it teaches the student "functional" words referring to objects that have been selected because they typically appear in the student's environment. Also, the program systematically builds in probes or skill tests to evaluate the student's progress intermittently. The program also gives suggestions to program for generalization to other people and settings.

Taken as a whole, the Functional Speech and Language Training for the Severely Handicapped curriculum has much to recommend it. It is comprehensive in scope, and it has been validated with a number of students in demonstration and research efforts (Guess, Sailor, and Baer, 1976).The curriculum stresses functional and operative language use. In addition, Waldo, Hirsch, and Marshall (1978) have adapted several parts of the program for teaching students to communicate with manual signs. This is an important adaptation for students who do not seem to make progress in the vocal modality.

Self-Care Skills. In the earlier days of educational programming for students with severe handicaps, most curriculum efforts were in the area of training for self-care skills such as using the toilet, feeding, grooming, and dressing. If a student's antisocial behavior was under control and he had learned some basic self-care skills, professionals considered their efforts successful. In the past 10 years this curriculum orientation has changed radically, with programming in natural environments leading to the development of curricula in the leisure, community, and vocational domains. Still, it is important not to forget programming for self-care and personal management skills. If a student is not toilet-trained or displays problem behaviors, he often will be excluded from participation in programs in more natural settings. With this in mind, let us examine one curriculum that focuses on self-care and other adaptive behavior skills.

The Adaptive Behavior Curriculum of Popovich and Laham (1981) is a comprehensive curriculum that offers hundreds of task-analyzed programs in the domains of self-help, communication, perceptual-motor, socialization, etc. The self-help section will be described here. This section is divided into feeding, dressing, and personal hygiene. Feeding includes the components of independent feeding and drinking. Dressing includes the components of garments and footwear. Personal hygiene has toileting and washing components. At the beginning of each section, e.g., independent feeding, there appears a developmental sequence of specific behavioral skills for

Figure 6.6 Task analyses for feeding skills.

TERMINAL BEHAVIOR

The student will chew solid food.

The student will

1. Allow the instructor to place a small bite-size piece of solid food between the student's back teeth (alternate food placement between left and right sides)
2. Retain food after the instructor has placed the food in the student's mouth
3. Close his teeth upon the food after the instructor has placed the food in the student's mouth
4. Open and close his teeth upon the food in an up and down motion, after the instructor has placed the food in the student's mouth
5. Allow the instructor to place the food in the pouch of the student's cheek (alternate food placement to left and right cheek with each piece)
6. Chew solid food with an up and down motion after the instructor has placed the food in the student's cheek

The student will chew and swallow solid food.

The student will

1. Allow a small piece of bite-size food to be placed on the center of his tongue
2. Move the food to the surface of his back teeth after the food is placed on the center of his tongue
3. Chew the food with a circular motion after the food is placed on his tongue (A circular motion is an up and down movement with diagonal and side-to-side motion of the lower jaw)
4. Chew and swallow solid food

Source: Adapted from D. Popovich and S. L. Laham (eds.), *The Adaptive Behavior Curriculum: Prescriptive Behavioral Analysis for Moderately, Severely, and Profoundly Handicapped Students*, Vol. 1, p. 8. (Baltimore: Paul H. Brookes, 1981). Copyright © 1981 by Macomb Intermediate School District of Mt. Clemens, Michigan. Reprinted with permission of Paul H. Brookes Publishing Co.

nonhandicapped students, e.g., swallow liquids (0 to 6 months) and suck liquids (0 to 8 months). The authors have task-analyzed each skill into a sequence of behavioral steps. For example, for swallowing liquids, the student will:

1. Allow liquid to be deposited in the mouth
2. Retain liquid in the mouth
3. Swallow liquid in response to a physical prompt
4. Swallow liquid

Figure 6.6 shows the task analyses for other feeding skills.

The Adaptive Behavior Curriculum merely presents the content or task-analyzed sequences of the program. In contrast to a curriculum such as that of Guess, Sailor, and Baer (1976), no explicit information is provided about behavioral objective criteria, recording procedures, instructional practices, or implementation steps. For a well-trained professional, it should not be too difficult to generate this information for a particular student. Many curricula, such as the Adaptive Behavior Curriculum, merely present the task-analyzed content. Other curricula have the advantage of spelling out every step needed to implement a program. A disadvantage is that many of the task analyses in this curriculum read like a sequence of behavioral objectives rather than steps in an instructional program. The Adaptive Behavior Curriculum is massive in having two volumes with hundreds of written programs. The two volumes serve as a curriculum library in their own right.

Vocational Training. In many respects vocational training is a most critical and exciting domain in special education. It is critical because if handicapped persons are able to obtain gainful employment, they can achieve a truly independent status and are likely to develop more of their human potential. If handicapped individuals cannot be employed, they are resigned to a dependent status and are likely to be perceived by society as welfare clients. When handicapped persons are employed, they are likely to be viewed in a positive way by others and by themselves.

In addition, much of what we have said about selecting functional objectives relates to the ultimate environments in which the disabled person must perform. An effective vocational preparation program should teach a wide range of skills that will enable the student to succeed in real work settings as an adult. These skills include the ability to learn new tasks, stay on a task for a long period, work at a high rate, and display general work skills such as getting to work on time, and socializing with coworkers. The difficulty with vocational preparation programs is that one rarely knows what specific job a person will assume as an adult. Therefore, the curricular content that should be selected is rarely self-evident.

It is possible to train *generic work skills* that probably will be applicable to all jobs. Generic work skills include punctuality, stamina, rate, and sociability. The specific job tasks such as assembly and maintenance are hard to predict, and so there cannot be training on specific tasks that will necessarily translate into a particular job. A vocational curriculum therefore must expose the student to a wide range of tasks and settings so that the skills needed to perform in adult jobs will be covered in the vocational preparation experiences. In order to ensure this exposure, the adolescent student should spend substantial amounts of time in real work settings. Vocational preparation conducted in classrooms can never approximate the work conditions found in actual job settings. Therefore, a vocational education program should move students to different real work settings during the secondary years.

When students are receiving training in an actual work setting, it is likely that the special education instructor will have to task-analyze the job tasks at the site so that the handicapped students can learn to perform them. When the student receives training in school, there is a value in conducting prevocational training for generic work skills. A prevocational training program can teach a number of task-related skills that should generalize to real work tasks in the student's future work placement.

The VOCSKILLS program (Vocational Opportunities Cooperative, 1982) is a prevocational curriculum that trains students in a number of basic skills involving the use of tools and machinery. The curriculum is organized into ten manuals that teach basic manipulation and concept skills as well as the use of specific tools. The basic skills manual teaches the following operations:

Manipulations
1. Twist
2. Arc
3. Squeeze
4. Precision placement

Concepts
5. Order
6. Package
7. Assembly games
8. Sort

Nine manuals teach the following specific tool uses:

1. Screwdriver use
2. Wrench use
3. Pliers use
4. Precision placement
5. Advanced assembly
6. Woodshop I
7. Woodshop II
8. Cleaning I
9. Cleaning II

Teachers following the basic skills manual take each one of the manipulations and concepts and have the student perform it with a number of different materials. For example, the arc movement with a wrench is done with a battery cable, a plumbing clamp, a wire rope clip, etc. The curriculum is committed to the *general case* model of programming for the generalization of skills. This model has the student practice a skill such as arc movement with a number of different materials that vary in shape, size, and color so that the student will generalize the skill to new materials. Figure 6.7 presents a page from the curriculum showing the arc movement with a battery cable. The display shows the

1. Place of purchase
2. Materials
3. Assembly sequence
4. Photographs or illustrations of the assembly sequence

Figure 6.7 Arc movement with a battery cable.

TITLE: Battery cable

PLACE OF PURCHASE: Hardware store

MATERIALS: Several battery cables of the same size
(Each cable should have bolts and nuts of two different sizes.)
A box end wrench that fits one nut size
An open end wrench that fits the second nut size

Assembly sequence: Note: When using wrenches, place the wrench *on the nut* and tighten it.

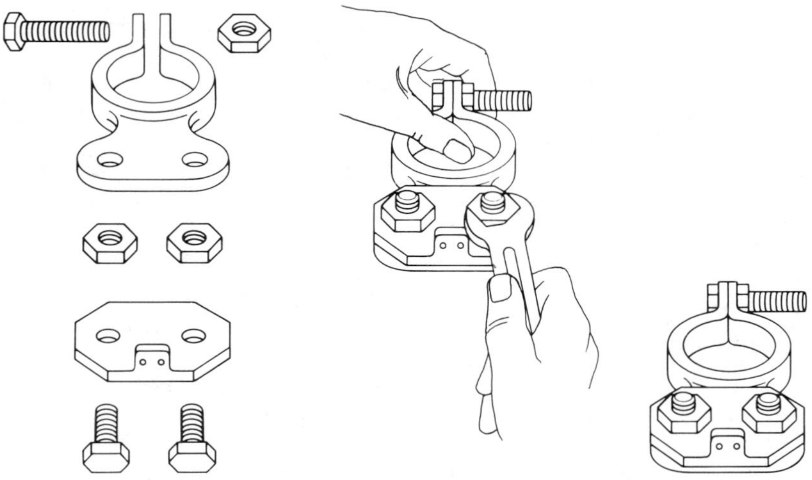

1 Task pieces

2 Align the flange. Place the nut and bolts with the wrench that fits.

3 Completed task

Source: Adapted from Vocational Opportunities Cooperative, *VOCSKILLS* (New Berlin, Wis.: Ideal Developmental Labs, 1982), p. 32. Reprinted with permission.

Figure 6.8 shows a more complex sequence for precision placement. It is apparent that the displays of the numerous tasks are clear and easy to follow. The tasks are not sequenced, and the instructors can pick out tasks at their discretion.

The VOCSKILLS manuals for tool use are even more comprehensive. They provide information on instructional strategies such as prompting and fading. There are excellent illustrations. Also, recording sheets and sequences for delivering instructions are given. Figure 6.9 reproduces a table from the curriculum that displays a lesson plan. The manual also describes common errors that should be avoided in tool use, e.g., the incorrect positioning of a screwdriver.

Figure 6.8 Sequence for precision placement.

TITLE: IC Connector with Resistors—Developed to Allow Practice with Nonconductive Tweezers

PLACE OF PURCHASE: Electronics store

MATERIALS: Nonconductive tweezers
Set of small resistors
IC connector

Teacher preparation

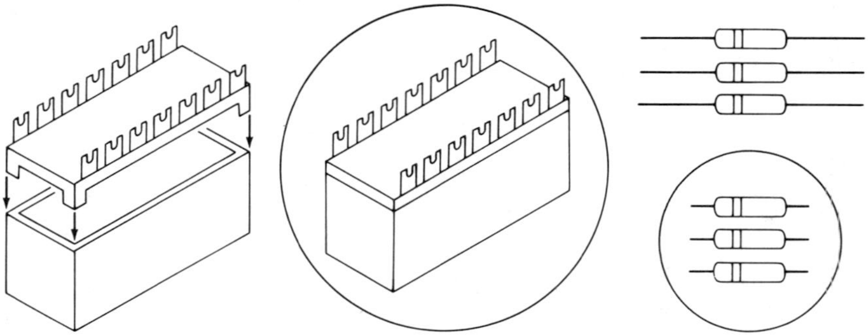

Remove top of connector and glue it underneath to cover the IC's.

Trim resistor leads to about ½ inch.

Assembly sequence

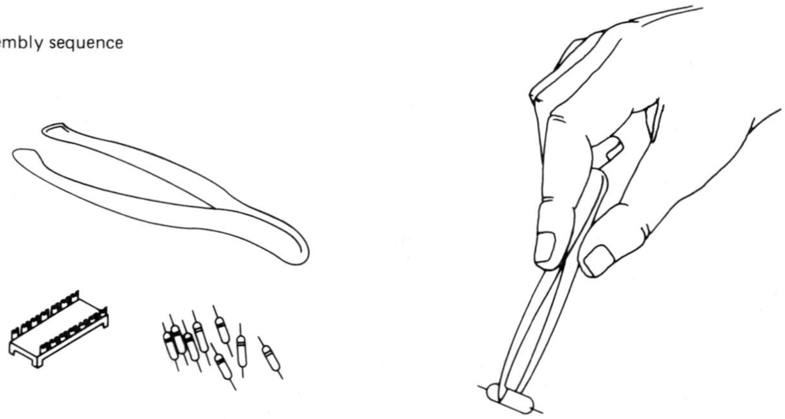

1 Task pieces

2 Picking up resistor with tweezers.
Hold the connector in the nondominant hand.

Source: Adapted from Vocational Opportunities Cooperative, *VOCSKILLS* (New Berlin, Wis.: Ideal Developmental Labs, 1982), p. 70. Reprinted with permission.

Figure 6.9 Lesson plan.

MATERIALS:

Teaching plate 14
Screw container
Screwdriver 14 square

CRITERION:

6 consecutive correct trials each of PLACE and TIGHTEN.

PLACE

Teacher sets plate 14 at a 0° plane.

Model: *"Watch me."*

Teacher points to a hole.

"Put a screw here."

Teacher places a screw in the indicated hole, using the sequence outlined.

Repeat once.

Cue: *"Your turn."*

Teacher points to a hole.

"Put a screw here."

Student places a screw in the indicated hole, using the sequence outlined.

REPEAT: 6 to 10 trials

Cue: *"Put a screw here."*

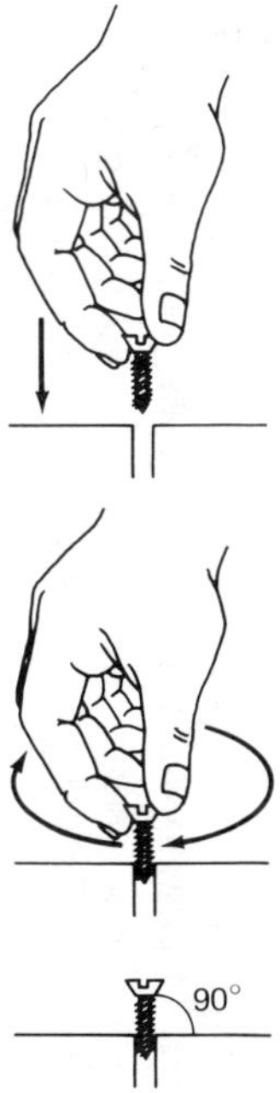

Student grasps screw by head, using thumb and first finger of dominant hand

and

positions the screw tip perpendicular to the indicated hole. . .

. . . inserts the screw tip perpendicular into the hole with a *simultaneous* turning motion . . .

. . . and gives the screw a turn or two just until it is secured.

TIGHTEN

Keep plate at a 0° plane.

Model: *"Watch me."*

Teacher points to screwdriver.

"Use the screwdriver and . . .

Teacher points to a screw.

"make it tight."

Teacher tightens the screw with the screwdriver, using the sequence outlined.

Repeat once.

Cue: Teacher points to a screw.

"Make it tight."

Student tightens the screw with the screwdriver using the sequence outlined.

REPEAT: 6–10 trials.

Cue: *"Make it tight."*

Student grasps screwdriver by handle

and

inserts the screwdriver tip perpendicular into the screw recess . . .

. . . turns the screwdriver a ¾ turn in a clockwise direction, maintaining a perpendicular alignment . . .

. . . loosens the grasp, using the fingers to balance the handle

rotates the fingers back to the original position . . .

. . . repeats until the screw is tight.

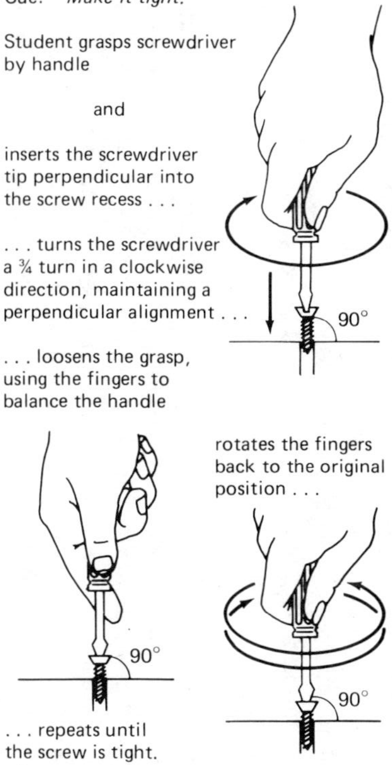

Source: Adapted from Vocational Opportunities Cooperative, *VOCSKILLS* (New Berlin, Wis.: Ideal Developmental Labs, 1982), p. 62. Reprinted with permission.

Thus, the VOCSKILLS curriculum is a comprehensive prevocational training program. It is presented in a clear fashion so that professionals can implement it easily with their students. The VOCSKILLS curriculum has been empirically verified with a number of students with severe handicaps (Bellamy, Rose, Boles, Wilson, and Clarke, 1981).

Leisure Skills. The development of leisure skills is another important domain of human behavior. The content of the self-care, vocational, and behavior management domains is essential in teaching individuals how to cope and adapt in their work and residential environments. The leisure domain addresses the issue of happiness and joy in life. A person may be programmed successfully at home and school but still may express little happiness in day-to-day routines. In fact, behavior analytic approaches have been criticized in the past for being too mechanical in method and producing robotlike responses. Therefore, there is a need for curriculum that explicitly teaches recreational behaviors. The behaviors can be performed in isolation or in a social context.

When persons with severe handicaps do not exhibit leisure behaviors in their idle time, there is a real chance that they will display problem behaviors such as self-stimulation, aggression, and self-injury. In addition, because of their intellectual limitations, when severely handicapped individuals are idle, they are not likely to self-initiate play activities. Rather, they tend to sit inactively or engage in aberrant behavior. Leisure behaviors present alternative response repertoires that the individual can emit in the place of less desirable acts. Finally, leisure behaviors tend to occur in less structured play settings where adults are not likely to prompt the behavior to occur. It is therefore important that when leisure skills are taught in structured learning settings, stimulus control be transferred to natural cues. Then the presence of equipment or of a peer can trigger the leisure chain to occur.

The Ho'onanea curriculum of Wuerch and Voeltz (1982) is an empirically validated curriculum that teaches severely handicapped learners a number of age-appropriate contemporary leisure activities. The curriculum was field-tested on fifty severely handicapped children and youth with a wide variety of disabilities. The chapters in the book show how to implement the programs. Of great importance to leisure programming is the book's presentation of procedures for selecting leisure activities that will be of interest to the student. Figure 6.10 shows a home leisure activities survey that asks the guardian to indicate the type of leisure activities in which the child has engaged in the past and the availability of the games and toys described in the curriculum. A leisure activity selection checklist (Figure 6.11) addresses questions of normalization, individualization, and environment. Specifically, the instructor responds yes or no to three activities from the curriculum for a particular child on the basis of criteria such as age-appropriateness, prosthetic capabilities, and durability. Activities receiving the

Figure 6.10

HOME LEISURE ACTIVITIES SURVEY

Student: Maile Date: 4/1/82 Completed by: Lynn Kahana (mother)

1. Please list any leisure activities available in your home, including other children's toys and games, in which your child has shown some interest.
   Lego, puzzles, Simon, toy piano, dolls.
2. What are your child's favorite leisure activities?
   puzzles, playing ball, swimming, going for rides in the car.
3. What does your child typically do during his or her free time?
   watch t.V., play with puzzles, listen to radio, scribble with paper and crayons.
4. Can you list some indoor or outdoor activities your family enjoys doing together? (Please list these by beginning with those you *most prefer*.)
   fishing, camping, horseback riding.
5. Are there any special *space* or *transportation* needs that we should consider in planning leisure or recreation activities for your child?
6. People resources: Are there other people in the home who spend leisure time with your child? Who and what would you like your child to be able to do with these persons? Maile's brother and 2 sisters play with her - I'd like Maile to be able to sit for maybe 15 minutes without breaking and grabbing toys. She also will tantrum and cry when she can't get her way, which makes her hard to get along with.
7. Which of these activities are available in the home?

✓ Lego	___ TV video games	___ Portable bowling	___ Marble rollway	✓ Target games
___ Pinball games	___ Lite-Brite	✓ Simon	___ Remote control toys	✓ Musical toys

8. Please assign a rating to each activity to indicate how interesting you think your child would find the activity.
   1 = not very interesting; 2 = somewhat interesting; 3 = very interesting

2 Lego	3 TV video games	1 Portable bowling	2 Marble rollway	1 Target games
3 Pinball games	2 Lite-Brite	3 Simon	3 Remote control toys	3 Musical toys

9. Which of these activities is your child permitted to play with?

✓ Lego	✓ TV video games	✓ Portable bowling	✓ Marble rollway	✓ Target games
✓ Pinball games	✓ Lite-Brite	✓ Simon	✓ Remote control toys	✓ Musical toys

10. Which of these activities do you feel are appropriate leisure time activities for your child?

✓ Lego	✓ TV video games	✓ Portable bowling	✓ Marble rollway	✓ Target games
✓ Pinball games	✓ Lite-Brite	✓ Simon	✓ Remote control toys	✓ Musical toys

Source: Adapted from B. B. Wuerch and L. M. Voeltz, *Longitudinal Leisure Skills for Severely Handicapped Learners: The Ho'onanea Curriculum Component* (Baltimore: Paul H. Brookes, © 1982), p. 17. Reprinted with permission of Paul H. Brookes.

Figure 6.11

LEISURE ACTIVITY SELECTION CHECKLIST

Student: Maile Kahana Date: 4/7/82 Completed by: Amy Selemister

	TV game Activity	Simon Activity	Bowling Activity
Normalization: A concern for selecting activities that have social validity and that will facilitate normalized play and leisure behaviors, as well as provide opportunities for movement toward increasingly complex interactions.			
1. *Age Appropriateness.* Is this activity something a nonhandicapped peer would enjoy during free time?	**yes** no	**yes** no	**yes** no
2. *Attraction.* Is this activity likely to promote interest of others who frequently are found in the youth's leisure time settings?	**yes** no	**yes** no	**yes** no
3. *Environmental Flexibility.* Can this activity be used in a variety of potential leisure time situations on an individual and group basis?	**yes** no	**yes** no	**yes** no
4. *Degree of Supervision.* Can the activity be used under varying degrees of caregiver supervision without major modifications?	**yes** no	**yes** no	yes **no**
5. *Longitudinal Application.* Is use of the activity appropriate for both an adolescent and an adult?	**yes** no	**yes** no	**yes** no
Individualization: Concerns related to meeting the unique and ever-changing needs and skills of handicapped youth.			
1. *Skill Level Flexibility.* Can the activity be adapted for low to high entry skill levels without major modifications?	**yes** no	**yes** no	**yes** no
2. *Prosthetic Capabilities.* Can the activity be adapted to varying handicapping conditions (sensory, motor, behavior)?	yes **no**	**yes** no	**yes** no
3. *Reinforcement Power.* Is the activity sufficiently novel or stimulating to maintain interest?	**yes** no	**yes** no	**yes** no
Environmental: Concerns related to logistical and physical demands of leisure activities on current and future environments and free time situations.			
1. *Availability.* Is the activity available (or can it easily be made so) across the youth's leisure environments?	**yes** no	**yes** no	**yes** no
2. *Durability.* Is the activity likely to last without need for major repair or replacement of parts for at least a year?	**yes** no	**yes** no	**yes** no
3. *Safety.* Is the activity safe, i.e., would not pose a serious threat to or harm the handicapped youth, others, or the environment if abused or used inappropriately?	**yes** no	**yes** no	**yes** no
4. *Noxiousness.* Is the activity not likely to be overly noxious (noisy, space consuming, distracting) to others in the youth's leisure environments?	yes **no**	yes **no**	**yes** no
5. *Expense.* Is the cost of the activity reasonable? That is, is it likely to be used for multiple purposes?	yes **no**	**yes** no	**yes** no
Area of Concern Scores			
1. Normalization	5	5	4
2. Individualization	2	3	3
3. Environmental	3	4	5
Total activity score	10	12	12

Source: Adapted from B. B. Wuerch and L. M. Voeltz, *Longitudinal Leisure Skills for Severely Handicapped Learners: The Ho'onanea Curriculum Component* (Baltimore: Paul H. Brookes, © 1982), p. 18. Reprinted with permission of Paul H. Brookes.

Figure 6.12

STUDENT INTEREST INVENTORY

Student: Maile Kahana

Instructions: For each activity, answer each of the questions below by placing the number of the description that best matches the child's behavior in the appropriate box for that activity.					
Activity	TV game	Simon	Bowling	music stick	Pinball
Date	4/10/82	4/10/82	4/10/82	4/10/82	4/10/82
Rater	Amy	Amy	Amy	Amy	Amy
A. For this child's usual level of interest in play materials, he or she is: 1. Not as interested as usual 2. About as interested as usual 3. More interested than usual	3	3	2	3	3
B. For this child's usual level of physical interaction with materials (pushing control buttons, turning knobs, putting things together, etc.), he or she is: 1. Not as busy as usual 2. About as busy as usual 3. Busier than usual	2	3	2	3	3
C. For this child's usual "affective" behaviors (smiling, signs of enjoyment, etc.), he or she seems to be: 1. Enjoying this less than usual 2. Showing about the same amount of enjoyment as usual 3. Enjoying this more than usual	3	3	2	3	3
D. For this child's usual level of "looking" or "visual regard" of an activity, object, or person, he or she is: 1. Not looking as much as usual 2. Looking as much as usual 3. Looking more often or longer than usual	3	3	2	3	3
E. Compared to this child's usual behavior during a short period of time with minimal supervision, he or she is: 1. Engaging in more negative behavior than usual 2. Engaging in about the same amount of negative behavior as usual 3. Engaging in less negative (or off-task) behavior than usual	2	3	2	3	3
Activity interest scores Total the numbers in each column	13	15	10	15	15

Source: Adapted from B. B. Wuerch and L. M. Voeltz, *Longitudinal Leisure Skills for Severely Handicapped Learners: The Ho'onanea Curriculum Component* (Baltimore: Paul H. Brookes, © 1982), p. 20. Reprinted with permission of Paul H. Brookes.

highest scores become likely candidates for inclusion in the student's educational program. Finally, a student interest inventory obtains indicators about the child's affect, perceptual tendencies, and preferences for a number of curricular games (Figure 6.12). This information is identical to the reinforcement preference test described in Chapter 2. Activities with the highest interest scores indicate that the child is likely to enjoy those activities and increase the probability that they will be included in the student's educational program.

The curriculum then describes the following ten task-analyzed leisure programs:

1. Electronic Music Stick®
2. Lego®
3. Lite-Brite®
4. Marble Rollway
5. Pinball games
6. Portable bowling
7. Remote-control vehicle
8. SIMON®
9. Target games
10. TV video games

In addition to the task-analyzed behavioral chains, information is presented regarding materials, entry-level motor skills, instructional setting and procedures, and game adaptations. Separate chain branches are presented for steps in which the student may have particular difficulty. There are excellent illustrations of handicapped students using the materials. The curriculum emphasizes the *principle of partial participation*. That is, there are some activities, e.g., pinball, in which the student may not ever be able to play at the level of a nonhandicapped student. Then the rules of the game may be changed or a simpler response strategy may be adopted. For example, in the game of pinball one normally moves the flippers when a ball is about to hit the flipper. This requires a good deal of eye-hand coordination. For students who cannot accomplish this task, a simpler strategy is to start moving the flipper as soon as the ball moves into the lower bumper area. This response strategy assures that the student will hit the ball on some occasions.

Finally, there are chapters dealing with generalization, instructional implementations, and parent involvement. Thus, the Ho'onanea leisure curriculum offers a comprehensive training package that can be used for a wide variety of students with severe handicaps.

Adapting Curricula

It is necessary to develop curricula for severely handicapped students because disabled persons typically do not learn skills such as self-care behaviors on their own or through the less intensive instructional procedures used in regular education. The main curricular strategy is to break down a skill into its component parts through the process of task analysis. If one then adds reinforcement, cueing, and data collection procedures, the systematic instructional format for a curricular manual will be complete. However, many

Figure 6.13 The use of curriculum branches to learn difficult behaviors.

BRANCH FOR STEP 8: PINBALL GAMES

Problem: The student does not track the movements of the ball after it leaves the shooter.

Instructional Objective: The student will visually track and locate the ball after it leaves the shooter.

Instructional Procedures:

1. Present the machine to the student with the power off.
2. Deliver an instructional cue indicating the ball's initial location, and deliver a verbal cue, "Watch the ball. After you show me where the ball is, we can play the game."
3. Pull the shooter so that the ball moves into play.
4. Lift up one end of the machine so that the playing surface is parallel to the table and the ball stops moving.
5. Have the student point to the location of the ball. If the student has been visually tracking the ball, he or she should be able to locate the ball within 5 seconds. If the student does not appear to be visually tracking the ball, shoot the ball into play, and without stopping the ball from moving, assist the student in tracing the ball's movement with his or her finger.
6. Reinforce the student when he or she locates the ball, and then begin to play the game.
7. This branch may be incorporated into ongoing skill acquisition training by implementing it at the beginning and end of the session as well as several times during the session.

Source: Adapted from B. B. Wuerch and L. M. Voeltz, *Longitudinal Leisure Skills for Severely Handicapped Learners: The Ho'onanea Curriculum Component* (Baltimore: Paul H. Brookes, © 1982), p. 86. Reprinted with permission of Paul H. Brookes.

students with serious impairments still will not learn many curricular programs successfully. In these cases it may be necessary to make adaptations to the programs to enhance the possibilities of success and participation.

Branching

Branching is a further extension of the process of task analysis. When a particular step in a sequence is not being performed well, a branching operation will break that step into a further sequence of steps. This new branch or sequence of steps can be performed within the total sequence or can be practiced in isolation. When the student can perform the branch correctly in isolation, it can be brought back and integrated within the total sequence. Figure 6.13 presents a branch from the Ho'onanea curriculum. Branching is a useful strategy that follows the general task analysis prescription: When learning is not successful, break the task into its smaller component behaviors.

Prosthetic Devices

Sometimes a student is able to learn a particular task but has a physical or sensory disability that limits involvement with the activity. In these circumstances an adaptive piece of equipment, or *prosthetic device*, may be used to increase the person's involvement. There are many examples of prosthetic devices.

1. In a self-feeding task, a student may have difficulty grasping a spoon. A curved spoon may be used to facilitate grasping, or a strap may be attached from the spoon around the hand to ensure grasping.
2. When a student has difficulty buttoning a shirt or pants, large-size buttons may be used to aid grasping. Another approach would be to use self-sticking tabs instead of buttons, thus requiring a simpler motor response to accomplish the same function.
3. A student able to play a video arcade game may have difficulty positioning his arm near the joystick. It is possible to build a small stand on which to rest the elbow. With the arm and elbow in the proper elevated position, the student can place his or her hand on the joystick and move it in an effective fashion.
4. A student may be able to swing a bat to hit a stationary baseball but lack the visual ability and perceptual-motor coordination to hit a ball thrown by a pitcher. A T-ball device can be used to facilitate hitting. A T-ball stand is placed on home plate. The ball is placed on the stand at the waist level of the batter. The batter then can take a swing and hit the stationary ball.

The number of prosthetic devices is limited only by the imagination of the teacher. Successful adaptations are invaluable because they enable the disabled person to engage in activities that would not normally be possible.

Partial Participation

When systematic instruction and prosthetic devices do not permit a student to engage in an activity, it is still possible to change the rules or operations of the task to permit participation. The principle of partial participation states that a student will engage in an activity with a simplified rule or operation or with the assistance of another person (to do some of the steps of the activity). In the previous example of pinball, a student could not accurately or successfully move the flippers to hit the ball in a coordinated fashion (Figure 6.13). Then the more gross perceptual-motor strategy of continuously hitting the flippers as soon as the ball descended to the lower plane of the board was taught to ensure successful strikes. Another example of partial participation would be in the game of baseball. Suppose a handicapped student could hit a baseball but was nonambulatory so that he could not run the bases even in a wheelchair. The game could be structured so that after he hit the ball, a nonhandicapped peer would run the bases for him. Partial participation also can occur in domestic chores. A student may have weak vision and lack the motor coordination to enable him to ignite and move pots on a stove. Partial participation in this activity could have the disabled person put some pots on the stove before a nonhandicapped person turns the stove on. A better solution, though, might be the use of an adaptive device, such as a microwave oven, where there is no danger of burns or fires and the oven can be set and activated precisely with digital controls.

As with prosthetic devices, there are numerous ways in which disabled persons can participate partially in activities. In both cases the alternative is no participation. It makes sense to attempt to develop adaptations that promote more independent functioning.

Summary

The curricula for students with severe handicaps have expanded greatly in recent years. The criterion of ultimate functioning has directed curriculum toward survival skills needed in the adult environments of residence, work, community, and leisure. This development has led to an emphasis on teaching functional skills and a deemphasis on teaching developmental tasks keyed to the normal developing child. The chapter pointed to the two paths for curriculum development: teachers writing their own task-analyzed programs and teachers selecting and adapting commercially available curricula. The chapter presented criteria for selecting a curriculum and then gave four examples of validated curricula in the areas of self-care, communication, vocational, and leisure. There are three ways to adapt curriculum for students with severe handicaps: branching, prosthetics, and partial participation. The following bibliography presents further examples of commercially available curricula.

Appendix: Commercially Available Curricula

These data are divided into the same headings we used earlier in this chapter. Each of these curricula meets most of the criteria suggested by Freagon et al. (1983).

Communication

Bricker, D. D. 1983. Early communication: Development and training. In M. E. Snell (ed.), *Systematic Instruction of the Moderately and Severely Handicapped*, 2d ed. Columbus, Ohio: Charles E. Merrill.

Lovass, O. J. 1977. *The Autistic Child*. New York: Irvington Publishers.

Spellman, C., DeBriere, T., Jarboe, D., Campbell, S. and Harris, C. 1978. Pictorial instruction: Training daily living skills. In M. E. Snell (ed.), *Systematic Instruction of the Severely Handicapped*, Columbus, Ohio: Charles E. Merrill.

Self-Care

Behavioral Characteristics Progression. 1973. Palo Alto, Calif.: Vort Corp.

Finnie, N. A. (ed.). 1975. *Handling the Young Cerebral Palsied Child at Home*, 2d ed. New York: E. P. Dutton.

Foxx, R. M., and Azrin, N. H. 1973. *Toilet Training the Retarded: A Rapid Program for Day and Nighttime Independent Toileting*. Champaign, Ill.: Research Press.

Project MORE. 1975. Bellevue, Wash.: Edmark.

Tawney, J. W. 1979. *Programmed Environmental Curriculum*. Columbus, Ohio: Charles E. Merrill.

Vocational

Rusch, F. R., and Mithany, D. E. 1980. *Vocational Training for Mentally Retarded Adults: A Behavior Analytic Approach*. Champaign, Ill.: Research Press.

Sowers, J., Lundervold, D., Swanson, M., and Budd, C. 1980. *Competitive Employment Training for Mentally Retarded Adults: A Systematic Approach*. Eugene, Ore.: University of Oregon.

Wehman, P., and McLaughlin, P. 1980. *Vocational Curriculum for Developmentally Disabled Persons*. Baltimore: University Park Press.

Social and Leisure

Cadigan, E., and Guess, A. R. 1981. *Sex Education—A Curriculum for the Deaf-Blind*. Watertown, Maine: Perkins School for the Blind.

Mikalonis, L., Haffman, J., Gaddy, M., Gillis, J., and Heater, G. 1974. *Leisure Time Activities for Deaf-Blind Children*. Northridge, Calif.: Joyce Motion Picture Co.

Wehman, P. (ed.). 1979. *Recreation Programming for Developmentally Disabled Persons*. Baltimore: University Park Press.

Chapter 7

Environmental and Classroom Organization

Thus far we have been interested primarily in describing the technology of teaching students with severe handicaps. We have described a stimulus-response-reinforcer model of learning that can assist the teacher in identifying what cues and consequences should be used in an instructional session. Emphasis has been placed on organizing controlled learning situations in which the student can process instructional stimuli without distracting events interfering with learning. As the student advances, the learning situation becomes more natural, with fewer artificial reinforcers and cues. Thus, the student is moved through a series of learning environments that ultimately approximate the natural environment of school, work, community, and residence. We have described this transition in terms of the instructional S^{D}'s and S^{R+}'s needed to facilitate learning, whether artificial or natural.

In this chapter the emphasis is on the environment that forms a backdrop for formal instruction. We describe the types of physical and social environments in which persons with severe handicaps spend their time and look at different types of schools and residences. An underlying assumption is that the types of environmental settings where students with severe handicaps are placed have a direct effect on their intellectual and social development. Illustrations of environmental contexts are presented, and suggestions are given for ways in which teachers may alter the physical and social environments of their students.

The Environment

The environment includes all the physical and social events that impinge on a person and that may potentially affect the person's behavior. The environment includes physical events such as heat, light, space, and materials. It also includes social stimuli such as verbal statements, smiles, touches, and other forms of human contact. All these events can influence the behavior of severely handicapped and nonhandicapped persons.

Past Lessons

In the past, educators working with severely handicapped students placed primary emphasis on controlling the instructional S^D's in the learning situation. Relatively little attention was given to the background environmental factors that can have a substantial impact on behavior. The main environmental strategy was to nullify the background environment by conducting instruction in a homogeneous setting in which one teacher worked with one student in a bland cubicle. The logic of this environmental strategy is to exclude distracting stimuli from the setting. This kind of environmental organization may be effective under certain circumstances, particularly when the student displays poor behavioral control or is distracted by other persons or events. Unfortunately, even today some teachers design the whole educattional program around the cubicle model and deny their students exposure to an array of environmentally stimulating experiences.

Methods for stimulating students with a variety of environmental experiences are presented in this chapter. The key point is that in any instructional situation there is usually one or a couple of S^D's presented to the student (e.g., the verbal instruction "Johnny, play with the car" and presentation of the car itself). In addition to the instructional S^D's and S^{R+}'s, there are stimuli that define the environmental context (e.g., the room, adults present, or noise). It is critical that the teacher give considerable attention to both instructional and environmental stimuli when designing an educational plan.

Instruction in Multiple Settings

A working premise in our educational model is that instruction should occur in multiple settings. For example, a teacher typically is assigned a classroom with a group of students who have severe handicaps. Because of their life experiences in regular education and exposure to past work in special education, teachers tend to assume that most of their time with the students should be spent in the special education class. This notion is reinforced further by the need to develop stimulus control. As was stated above, the success of the cubicle model in obtaining initial stimulus control over students has led some teachers to continue to use this isolated, one-to-one approach. It is important, though, that early in the student's education there be a steady exposure to many environmental settings. For some of the student's day it may be useful to work in a relatively quiet and isolated setting so that no distracting events interfere with difficult learning tasks, but the majority of the school day should take place in more natural circumstances within and outside the classroom.

The main reason for instruction in natural settings is to promote the generalization of learning to ultimate criterion settings such as group homes and workplaces. That is, if students are being taught to fold and sort clothes, they ultimately must show proficiency in that skill in the criterion natural setting, e.g., a laundromat or a bedroom. It is permissible to conduct initial instruction in the noncriterion classroom setting, but at some point instruction must occur in the ultimate natural setting. The proportion of learning occurring in the classroom vis-a-vis natural settings will vary according to the task, the student, and the practicality of moving students about in multiple natural settings. Ideally, almost all instruction should occur in the natural criterion setting. This ideal is limited by students who have major management problems, are under poor stimulus control, or are easily distractible, and by the practical matter of placing and supervising students in numerous situations. Our working assumption is that multiple-setting instruction is preferable because it promotes the generalization of learning to the criterion setting and provides a kind of environmental stimulation that cannot be reproduced in a classroom.

Besides the explicit learning that is geared toward meeting the student's IEP goals, multiple-setting instruction fosters the development of incidental learning. *Incidential learning* is unintended learning; it occurs in addition to whatever direct instruction is being conducted by the teacher. For example, a severely handicapped student may be taught how to play a game of Frisbee with a nonhandicapped peer. In addition to learning the Frisbee exchange, the handicapped student may learn how to posture, imitate styles of dressing, and reduce self-stimulatory behavior. These latter behaviors are examples of the incidental learning that results from interaction with a nonhandicapped peer. Diverse multiple environments permit valuable incidental learning to take place. Instruction that occurs solely in artificial, homogeneous environments may teach the designated skill, but it is unlikely to lead to generalization, incidental learning, or general environmental stimulation.

The Physical Environment

Institutions

In the past, severely handicapped persons lived in a variety of physical settings (Sarason and Doris, 1969; Wolfensberger, 1972). Some individuals were shut away in rooms or left to their own resources, and this often led to death, disease, or ridicule. The failure of communities to care for handicapped persons adequately led to a movement in the nineteenth century to create institutional residences.

Large institutions or state hospitals were constructed with the benign intention of providing a better place to live and a superior quality of professional care for handicapped persons. The facilities usually were located in remote rural areas and often were titled "colonies" because of their cloistered location. Institutions were inhabited by 500 to 5,000 handicapped residents. There usually was an equal number of staff members. Many institutions became self-contained communities, with staff members often living on the facility's grounds. In many cases the physical layout of the grounds had a charming pastoral quality.

On the surface, this appeared to provide a quiet, attractive, and supportive setting for handicapped individuals. Upon closer examination, though, there were many drawbacks to the institutional living model. The facilities created their own institutional life-style that was not comparable to patterns of living in community-based noninstitutional settings. The isolation of individuals in colonies did not prepare them to live in more normalized work and living settings in their home communities. Institutional patterns of behavior developed. Physically, beyond the pretty grounds, the actual living quarters were quite limited. Residents lived in barrack-style wards that were dehumanizing and did not prepare them for family or community living. The decor of the ward contained few items that could provide a personalized or homelike feeling. Walls were colored institutional green or blue. The ward was barren with few play or leisure objects. Worse, the residents spent almost all their waking and sleeping hours on or near the ward. Buildings for the more severely handicapped persons were often in the most remote locations of the hospital's grounds, had the poorest physical decor, and were the most crowded. Finally, in spite of infusions of millions of dollars as well as legal mandates such as consent decrees, institutions were unable to prevent abuse and dehumanizing treatment of the people who lived there (Blatt, 1973).

Because of the limited physical and social environment in institutions, a political movement to return persons from their institutional placement to the local community arose in the 1950s and 1960s. The deinstitutionalization movement has had varying degrees of success across the nation. In some cases specific state hospitals were closed down because their population dropped from thousands to hundreds of residents. The emptying of institutions is dependent on the number of community residences, such as group homes, that can be created to accept individuals returning to the community. Since the 1960s and 1970s, the rapid emptying of institutions has slowed. Most states now reduce their institutional population by preventing the initial institutionalization of the individual at an early age (Sontag, 1977). Again, the prevention of institutionalization is dependent on the existence of an adequate number of community homes that can serve as backup alternatives to natural family placements.

Community Placement

The placement of a handicapped person in a community residence does not automatically ensure that a stimulating physical environment will be provided. There have been instances of disabled persons being warehoused in barren hotel rooms with few services provided. A community-based residence, however, does provide the opportunity to expose the individual to a variety of physical environments such as stores, theaters, factories, and domiciles. This variety of physical settings provides stimulating and enjoyable experiences and prepares the person to function more independently in work, community, and residential sites. Again, the availability of multiple environments in community residences does not guarantee that the individual will receive substantive exposure to these varied settings. It is necessary for systematic programs to be implemented in community settings in order to guarantee such exposure and skill development.

An analysis of the residence (family, group home, foster care) should begin with an examination of the physical layout of the home. How many handicapped people live in the home? When there are more than six residents, the home may begin to take on an institutional quality; that is, the domicile feels less like a home and more like a facility where staff members come to work. Another issue related to physical environment is the layout of the home. Is there adequate space, or is there a crowded feeling with too many people moving about? No more than one or two people should sleep in a bedroom, or a barracks feeling may develop. There should be a recreation or family room that can serve as the focus for leisure activities. Without such a room, there can be too much milling about with few purposeful activities occurring. The family room should not be just a place for staff members and residents to watch television. The room should be equipped with a variety of age-appropriate leisure materials that individuals can engage alone or in small groups.

Next, examine the decor of the home. If, for example, adolescents live in the home, is it decorated for that age group? Too many homes (and classrooms) for handicapped persons are not designed with sensitivity to the issue of age-appropriateness. That is, homes for teenagers are decorated with dolls and wallpaper that are more appropriate for small children. Furniture, posters, toys, magazines, wallpaper, and bedspreads should be selected that are contemporary for the age group residing in the home.

Thus, a number of factors contribute to creating a normalized and stimulating residence. Specific things such as space, leisure objects, decor, and accessibility to the community must be organized so that a successful physical environment results. You can assess a home or class in a more subjective way by having strangers visit the residence and judge how homelike or depersonalized it feels. Ask them if they would be willing to live there or would permit their children to live there. The answer to this question often leads to suggestions as to how the environment could be improved. For example, bedrooms may be too cluttered with toys, a toilet seat may be cracked, the playroom may be barren of toys, or the kitchen may be in need of sweeping. There should not be separate standards for the environmental conditions of handicapped versus nonhandicapped persons. Asking a person what needs to be changed in the home for that person to live there comfortably tends to prevent the formation of separate standards.

The School Environment

The main intention of the book is to discuss educational programs in school or school-related settings. However, the points we have made about the physical environment in residential settings are directly related to environmental factors in school settings. The movement toward placing handicapped persons in community residences has had an impact on the type of school settings in which students with severe handicaps are taught. Students residing in institutions receive instruction in the most restrictive setting; that is, they are taught in the same setting in which they live. The physical limitations of institutional residences have been addressed. When education is conducted in the same setting in which a person lives, there is little opportunity for varied environmental stimulation or validation of skills in the criterion setting, e.g., factory or apartment.

A community placement does not guarantee environmental stimulation and skill validation, but it sets the occasion for them to occur. For instance, before the passage of P.L. 94-142 there was no guarantee that a handicapped student would receive an education. In many cases a severely handicapped child was denied an education in a public school. Students were educated either at home or at schools run by private nonprofit organizations like United Cerebral Palsy. In either case the student had a limited range of possible educational placements.

Segregated Schools. As more educational services have been provided for students with severe handicaps, there has been a range in the type of school sites in which special education classes are located. The most common site has been a segregated school building that contains all handicapped students. The school can be run privately or by the public school system. Segregated schools for the handicapped often differ in physical appearance from public schools. Private schools often are located in church annexes or basements. Since the outward physical appearance of the building may not resemble a school, people's attitutdes toward the students in attendance may be affected negatively (Wolfensberger, 1972).

The main effect of segregated schools is a social one; that is, the absence of nonhandicapped students offers no models for age-appropriate behavior to both handicapped students and their special education teachers.

Segregated sites tend to accentuate the handicapping condition rather than emphasize that the student is first a child who happens to have a disability. This sometimes can be seen in the titles of schools, e.g., These Our Treasures (segregated-handicapped) versus San Rafael High School (special class on an integrated site).

Integrated Classes. Integrated special education classes offer a wide variety of physical environments as well as opportunities for a range of social interactions. Particularly in junior and senior high schools, there are multiple settings to which the student with severe handicaps can be exposed. These areas include auditoriums, gyms, woodworking shops, industrial shops, typing rooms, cafeterias, and music and art rooms. As the students develop better behavioral control and more advanced skills, they can participate increasingly in these varied settings. Thus, a goal of the special education teacher is to expose students to a number of physical settings on the school campus. Contact should not occur only for the sake of exposure. Rather, a situation such as typing class should serve primarily as a site for skill building that also provides appropriate environmental stimulation.

In the case of typing, the student has to have the behavioral skills to sit and work in a chair for a 30- to 45-minute period. Before a student enters the regular education class, some preintegration work can be done to demonstrate that the student has the interest, fine motor dexterity, and ability to benefit from a regular class. Finally, a paraprofessional can accompany the student to the class to supervise the behavioral and skill aspects of instruction. Over time, the paraprofessional should be faded from the class, and then the student can continue to progress in an independent fashion.

Another possibility for multiple-setting instruction would be to train a student vocationally in the school cafeteria. One or more students will attend the cafeteria kitchen during a specific time of the day, e.g., 11:30 A.M. to 12:45 P.M. They can be trained on a number of skills, e.g., food preparation, dish washing, cleaning, and maintenance. The students will be under the supervision of both the cafeteria staff and the special education staff. Over time, the appearance of the special education staff member can be faded out so that the student can function more independently at the work training site.

Thus, a general strategy for multiple-setting placement is to supervise the student at the site initially and then fade the amount of supervision over time until there is not a special educator present. For some students the pace of fading supervision is fairly rapid (1 to 3 weeks). In other cases there may be a need to have a supervisor present for a long or indefinite period of time. The fading of the special educator should be keyed to the rate of progress of the student toward independent functioning. Individual considerations must be balanced with the practical logistics of placing and supervising students at many sites.

The amount of multiple-site placements that may occur is limited by the number of special education teachers, paraprofessionals, student teachers, related service professionals, and volunteers who can be organized to supervise students in different settings. When there are few staff members available, the number of multiple-site placements is limited. Similarly, when students require a long time to fade supervision, this ties up a staff member at that site and limits supervision of other students at other sites. The special education teacher must consider staff and student variables when planning multiple-setting instruction.

Off-Campus Activities. Another possibility for multiple-setting instructions is *off-campus activities*. In the past, off-campus activities usually entailed episodic field trips to a circus or store. In our educational model, off-campus activities involve ongoing visits to sites for the purpose of systematic instruction. A group of students may be taken to a restaurant to work on eating skills in public places. The students can travel to the restaurant on public transportation so that they also can work on bus riding and community mobility skills. The same instructional model of providing S^D's, prompts, and reinforcers is used in the community setting. Data are taken on pupil performance. In time, natural cues and consequences can control behavior so that the activities will take on a more normal flavor. The off-campus activities should be geared to the goals in the student's IEP. It is recommended that at least one activity be run off campus per week. The logistics of getting students off campus can be challenging. The teacher must organize the schedule, staff and students to maximize the opportunities for off-campus instruction. Anything less than one session per week would violate the formative instruction model for teaching. Intermittent off-campus visits take on the quality of field trips rather than training experiences in the criterion environment.

Another kind of off-campus activity is *on-the-job vocational training*. In this kind of training the student is placed in a real job setting in the community. The job site may be a factory, an office, a restaurant, etc. The student is placed at the site one or more hours per day and one or more days per week. The student engages in actual job tasks at the site, i.e., real work, not make-work. The goal of the placement is to have the student learn real work skills such as accurate and fluent performance of job tasks, working effectively for extended periods of time, displaying social skills to get along with co-workers, and being able to entertain oneself during break times. The performance of all of these skills must be validated in real work environments. Work experiences can be simulated in the classroom only to a certain extent. As with other cases of generalization, without training in the criterion environment we cannot expect severely handicapped students ever to perform the necessary vocational skills in real job settings. Therefore, it is imperative for 16- to 21-year-old students to have some kind of real work experience in the secondary years. This experience should facilitate their transition to successful employment during their adulthood.

Orchestrating the logistics of supervision is the main deterrent to conducting off-campus activities. In most cases a student cannot be placed alone without supervision from a special education staff member. In some cases the absence of a supervisor will be possible, and the placement will be comparable to a work experience placement in regular education. In these cases school insurance policies should cover liability for the student in off-campus sites. The teacher should make sure that liability and insurance guidelines are followed carefully. In the majority of cases a special education supervisor will be needed at the work site.

Who the supervisor is and what staff members remain in the classroom and at other community sites will depend on two variables: school policy and the number of available staff members. If school policy requires a credentialed teacher to be with students at all times, the extent of off-campus activities will be seriously limited. If paraprofessionals, student teachers, volunteers, or related service professionals can serve as supervisors off campus, there will be many more possibilities for these activities. If there are two special education teachers at the school, one can remain on campus and be administratively responsible for both classes. The other teacher then can go off campus to supervise students. Probably it will be most efficient to have two to four students located at an activity or work site. The number of hours spent at the site will depend on the nature of the job, the proficiency of the student, and the willingness of the employer to work with handicapped students for extended periods of time.

In any case, on-the-job vocational training is an invaluable educational experience for most students with severe handicaps (Brown, Shiraga, Ford, VanDeventer, Nisbet, Loomis, and Sweet, 1984). The logistics of organizing such a program will challenge even the best teachers, but contemporary professionals cannot renege on their responsibility to provide a comprehensive vocational training program.

An Example of Multiple-Setting Instruction

Let us present the case of Joan as an illustration of multiple-setting instruction. Joan is a 17-year-old student who attends a class for students with severe handicaps that is located on a regular high school campus. She has been labeled autistic and functions at the severe to moderate level of mental retardation. Although she used to have serious tantrum episodes, for the past 2 years she has displayed few behavioral outbursts. Joan has progressed so that she can work alone or in small groups of students successfully with no direct supervision. Based on a report from Joan's parents, she displays an interest in the family typewriter. The teacher decided to give her a few informal lessons on the typewriter in the classroom. Joan was able to match letters from a notebook by striking the typewriter keys. Since Joan had some rudimentary word attack skills, it was felt that learning to type could help her develop the personal management skill of copying lists of items to be purchased at food and other stores. Typing also could lead to occupational positions in copying letters, memos, labels, etc., in clerical or word processing office pools.

The teacher did some instructional programming on the typewriter, and Joan displayed notable progress. At that point, the teacher contacted the typing teacher at the high school and asked if Joan could attend typing class 3 days per week. The typing teacher agreed to a 1-month trial period. A paraprofessional accompanied Joan to the typing class. The trial period was successful, and over the next 3 months the extent of paraprofessional supervision was faded out gradually. From the full 45-minute period, the paraprofessional's time was decreased to 30, 15, 5, and then 0 minutes in the classroom. Eventually Joan walked to and from the class independently. She thus was integrated successfully into the regular education setting.

Later in the school year Joan's teacher made contact with an occupational education teacher at the high school. The teacher ran a French gourmet restaurant located on the high school grounds that was open to the public. The restaurant was a training site in culinary skills for regular education students. The special education teacher had trained Joan in food preparation and cleanup skills in the kitchen area of the special education class. The teacher communicated Joan's progress to the occupational education teacher and asked if she could attend the program to develop these skills further in a real life setting. An agreement was reached, and Joan attended the gourmet kitchen program on a daily 45-minute basis. A paraprofessional accompanied her to the restaurant but was faded out quickly over a 2-week period. Initially, Joan was engaged in cleaning and dishwashing activities in the kitchen. She then moved on to setting and clearing tables in the dining room. In the future it was planned that she would move on to rudimentary food preparation activities, for example, pouring, cutting, and mixing items.

Joan's two mainstreaming acitivites were typing and occupational education classes. In addition, she spent time outside the special education class in adaptive physical education, lunch in the cafeteria, and off-campus training. On a regular basis she and a group of special and regular students and staff members would go to food and department stores to develop shopping skills, restaurants to cultivate public dining skills, and buses and subways to foster travel training skills. The regular education students served as "special friends" and "peer tutors". Thus, Joan's typical school day consisted of about 40 percent of her time being spent in the special education class and the remainder of the time being spent in other settings.

The proportion of time spent inside and outside of the special education class varies from student to student. As the student advances through the secondary years, increasing amounts of time should be spent in multiple settings. Multiple-setting instruction promotes the generalization of skills and ensures that they will be performed correctly in the ultimate criterion environment. To conduct multiple-setting instruction, special efforts must be made by the special education teacher. It is simpler and requires less effort to carry out all instruction in the special education class. To move students out of the class entails receiving administrative approval, coordinating with the regular education staff, getting parental support, arranging for off-campus travel, and developing training relationships with off-campus individuals, e.g., employers, restauranteurs, and police. The efforts required for multiple-setting education are certainly demanding and challenging to the special education teacher but should result in a highly stimulating and satisfying program for both students and staff (Brown et al., 1984; Gaylord-Ross, Forte, and Gaylord-Ross, 1983).

Designing the Classroom

Although it is important to conduct instruction in multiple settings, students still spend a considerable amount of time in the special education classroom. In spite of the emphasis on out-of-class instruction, there exists a need to identify the important physical characteristics of a classroom for students with severe handicaps. In this section attention is given to the design characteristics of the physical environment.

The first general principle of physical design is that the appearance of the classroom should be geared to the appearance of a classroom for similar-aged nonhandicapped students. That is, a primary class for students with severe handicaps should have the look and feel of a class for primary-level nonhandicapped students. This principle often is violated in classes for handicapped adolescents, which may look like preschool classes with children's toys, puerile decor, and other infantile materials present. Special education teachers probably have designed classes in this manner with the assumption that their adolescent students are developmentally at the level of preschoolers, and therefore the classroom should take on the appearance of a preschool class. This error in design should be avoided. Use the age-appropriate rule as a guide in designing classrooms so that they aproximate classes for nonhandicapped peers. However, the nonhandicapped peer class should not always be used as a guide for classroom design. Regular education classes at the intermediate and secondary levels are often merely empty rooms filled with rows of desks and chairs. Such classes may be barren and unstimulating, and so they should not necessarily be the standard for classroom design. In addition, classes for students with severe handicaps often require special equipment such as prone standers or toilets so that they will of necessity differ in certain respects from regular education classes.

Areas and Zones. Let us examine the physical space of the class. If the classroom is rectangular in shape, it may be 20 by 30 feet, or 600 square feet. This amount of space may be ample for a class of six students, a teacher,

Figure 7.1 "Cubicle" model of the classroom environment.

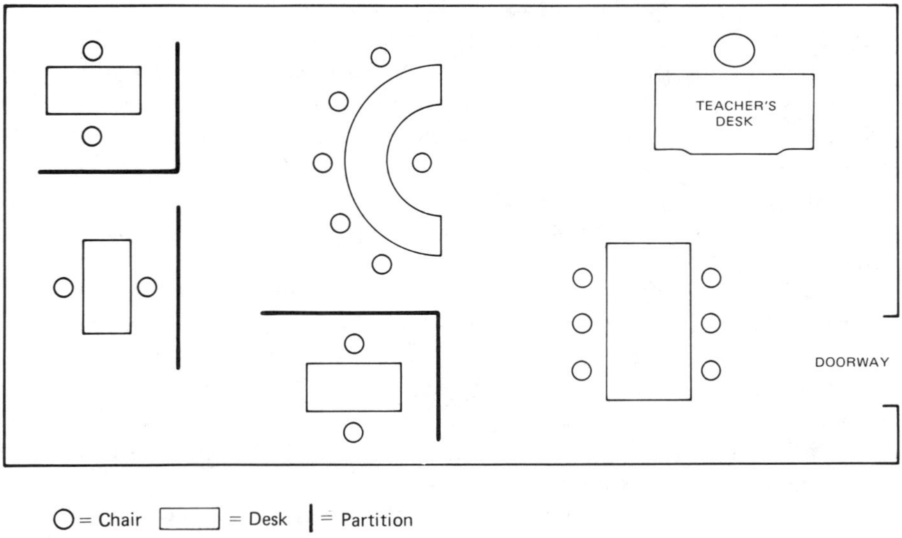

and a paraprofessional. The 600 square feet may lead to a sensation of crowding in a class of ten students, a teacher, and two paraprofessionals.

If the space is clearly inadequate, this should be drawn to the attention of a supervisor, and then some administrative arrangement can be made to obtain a classroom with an approprate amount of space. If one is stuck with a classroom that is too small, there are still changes that can be made to improve the spatial configuration. The use of multiple-setting instruction helps break the constricted feeling of being in a small, crowded room by moving people to different locations throughout the day. If your class is overcrowded, it will ultimately have deleterious effects on students and staff members. Students may emit more aberrant behavior; staff members may become more agitated, with crowding accelerating a drift toward staff burnout (Gaylord-Ross, 1980).

Although a classroom is an open space, it is useful to demarcate it into designated areas for instruction. The cubicle model breaks the classroom into a series of cubicles or areas for one-to-one instruction. Office or wall dividers are erected to cordon off the table where one teacher and one student sit next to or across from each other. At the completion of a session, staff members or students move to another cubicle for instruction. The cubicle area is usually barren in terms of materials designating an area such as "vocational" or "fine motor." As students develop better work habits and are less distractible, the dividers may be removed so that the tables and chairs openly face the classroom.

Figure 7.1 shows a configuration of cubicle areas in a classroom that comes with and without dividers. As students improve in performance and behavioral control, the class may progress so that small group instruction can occur. In this case two to five students may sit or be in a designated area with one staff member. Figure 7.1 shows a learning area where small group instruction takes place. A key factor in the cubicle model is that areas are designed for instruction without any theme for particular types of curricular activities, e.g., self-care or vocational. The instructor brings the necessary materials to the area. The student may be sitting, standing, or lying down. When the session is completed, students and staff members move to another area for learning.

In contrast, thematic *zones* reserve particular areas of the room for certain types of instruction. For instance, one part of the room can be designated as the vocational area. Here a variety of vocational materials are present for students to work with. For example, there can be pens to assemble, switches to sort, wires to loop, or screwdrivers to turn. The materials should be organized into neat compartments. Vocational materials often can be obtained from donations by citizens in the community.

Another thematic zone can be a leisure area. This area may contain materials such as magazines, record players (with headphones for quiet listening), squeeze toys that make sounds, table games, and hanging objects that can be examined or grasped. The leisure area can be used for a number of purposes. It can be used as a reinforcement area where students earn leisure time after completing their educational programs. For example, a student may be working on a vocational assembly task. For every bicycle brake assembled, a token is earned. When five brakes are completed (about 30 minutes of work), the five tokens are given to the teacher, and 5 minutes is spent in the leisure zone.

This example shows the contingent use of the leisure zone. The zone also may be used as a "holding" area for students when there are not enough staff members to conduct instruction with all the students in the class. For example, suppose there are nine students in the class and only one teacher and one paraprofessional present at a given time. Because of the physical and behavioral involvement of the students, it is not possible to conduct sessions with more than three students at a time. Thus, two staff members are working with six students at a given time, and three students are in "down" time. Such noninstructional time can be used more effectively if the students can be placed in a designated leisure area so that they can be engaged with stimulating materials. Students with severe handicaps who are left alone with nothing to do tend to spend their time sitting idly, self-stimulating, or emitting other rudimentary forms of behavior. A stimulating leisure area should contain age-appropriate materials that the student is likely to manipulate (e.g., a hand-held video game).

The third use of the leisure zone is to train students in recreational skills. In this instance instructional sessions are run in the leisure area to teach new

Figure 7.2 "Thematic" organization of a classroom.

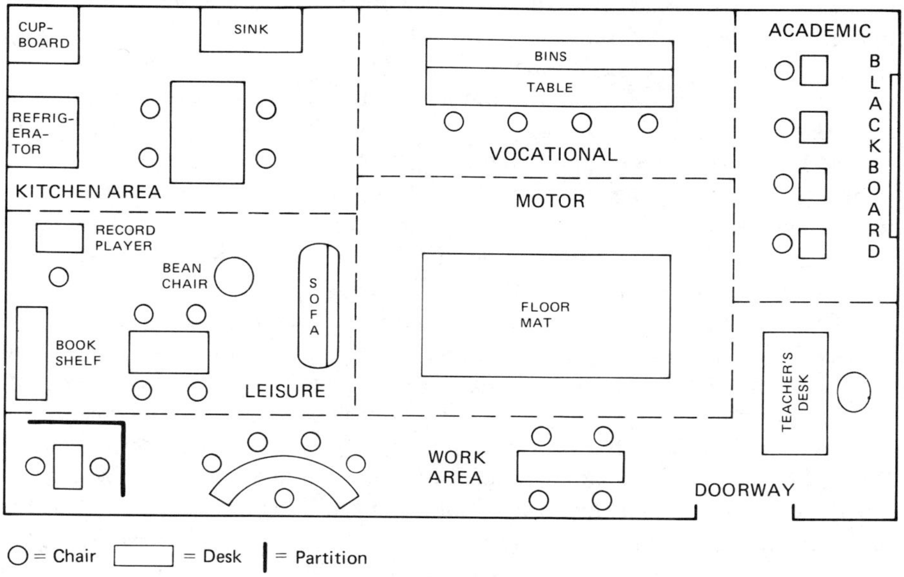

tasks, e.g., how to play a board game or throw darts. As with any other task, the instructor uses cues, prompts, and reinforcers to teach the leisure skill. The ultimate goal, though, is to fade out all artificial cues and reinforcers so that the student initiates the play activity on his or her own. Then the student can go to the leisure area or other recreational setting without adult supervision and engage in a leisure activity alone or with a peer.

There are other designated zones for the classroom. Toilet, sink, and locker areas are used for skill training in personal management. For classes of students with severe motor impairments there may be one or more zones containing sensorimotor equipment, e.g., mats and wedges. There can be one or more zones for academic instruction, e.g., reading or mathematics. A class for students with severe handicaps usually does not contain rows of desks, yet in some cases there may be a number of "higher" functioning students who benefit from the teacher lecturing at a blackboard. In this case a number of desks may be arranged near a blackboard for lecture and writing purposes. Figure 7.2 shows how a classroom may be organized into a number of thematic zones.

Decor. The aesthetic appearance of the classroom is another important aspect of the physical environment. The teacher should work actively to establish a pleasant, stimulating, and normalized decor.

One consideration is the odor of the room. Many students with severe handicaps are not toilet-trained and emit odors from urine and feces. Students who are not bathed adequately or whose clothes are dirty may exude unpleasant odors. One remedy is to train the students and their parents to bathe or toilet themselves in a better way. It is also possible to display agents that emit a pleasing odor. For example, air freshener vials emit pine, wintergreen, and other pleasant odors in a room. These fresheners can counteract the odors of feces and urine as well as the antiseptic agents used by janitors. Of course, one must keep the classroom clean. It is also advisable to grow plants in the room so that the visual and olfactory senses are stimulated more pleasantly. Be creative in selecting items that will produce an appealing odor for students, staff, and visitors.

The *color* and *lighting* of the classroom is another important factor. Some classes have poor lighting so that there are shadowy and dark areas in the room. Try to remedy this by adding more ceiling or table lights and replacing burned-out bulbs. Cubicle areas often are poorly lit. In some cases light rays can be so bright that they interfere with perception and performance. It may be helpful to change the angle of the light or shade the ray. Watch the students to see whether they are squinting to see things. Also, be alert to the development of headaches and fatigue when fluorescent lights are used.

Be careful that the room does not emit the bland colors of institutional green or blue. Try to select colors for walls, curtains, posters, and hanging objects that give vitality and variety to the room. Be sensitive to age-appropriateness. Do not pick light blues and pinks that may give an image of a preschool program for a class of older students. Place colorful materials on bulletin boards that reflect students' interests, holidays, and school activities. Use the same guidelines for selecting posters. Pick tasteful and age-appropriate furniture. Sometimes sofas and upholstered chairs can add to the domestic feeling of the room. It is desirable to have some kind of carpeting present. Carpeting gives warmth and intimacy to a room; it also tends to dampen irritating noises while being aesthetically pleasing.

In general, select materials for the room that are appealing to the eye and may stimulate the growth and development of the students. It is good practice to place objects around the room that your students can gaze at or play with. Mirrors, writing materials, and posters can be placed judiciously around the room. In designing the physical environment of the classroom, use the subjective guide, "Is this a room I would feel comfortable sending my own children to for an education?"

The Social Environment

In addition to looking at the physical aspects of a school environment, it is also possible to view the school as a social network. In our historical discussion of residences and schools for handicapped persons, it could be seen that segregated schools and institutions allowed handicapped persons to

Figure 7.3

PROGRAM SCHEDULE.

Activity Periods	Teacher	Paraprofessional	Related Services	Student Teacher	Other
8:30-9:00	Self-Care: Mel, Bill, Robert Morning circle	Self-care: Tom, Sue, Jim Morning circle		Self-care: Anna, Morris Morning circle	
9:00-9:30	Communication: Mel, Tom, Anna	Sensorimotor: Bill, Sue		Prevocational: Robert, Jim, Morris	
9:30-10:00	Communication: Jim, Bill, Robert	Sensorimotor: Tom, Anna	Speech therapy: Jim (Mon, Thur)	Academic: Sue, Mel	
10:00-10:30	Leisure and snack with special friends, all students	10:00-10:15 break 10:15-10:30 snack with students	Speech therapy: Mel, Robert, (Mon, Thur)	10:00-10:15 leisure 10:15-10:30 break	Special friends, leisure, snack
10:30-11:00	10:30-10:45 break 10:45-11:00 supervise	Prevocational: Bill, Anna, Robert, Sue	Physical therapy Jim, Bill (Tues, Fri)	Academic: Jim, Mel, Tom, Morris	Pioneers, Tuesday
11:00-11:30	Academic: Bill, Anna, Tom	Prevocational: Jim, Mel, Morris	Physical therapy: Mel, Robert (Tues,Thur)	Academic: Robert, Sue	Anna's Mom (Mon) Bill's Dad (Fri)
11:30-12:00	Academic: Jim, Robert, Mel	Social/leisure with special friends: Morris, Tom, Anna, Bill	Physical therapy: Mel, Robert (Tues, Fri)	Lunch	Assist teacher's groups, special friends 11:30-12:00
12:00-12:30	Toilet, Lunch, Recess, all students	Assist teacher		Assist teacher	Mel's Mom (Wed)
12:30-1:00	12:15-12:45 lunch	Lunch		Supervise students	Assist at lunch, recess
1:00-2:30	Community training: (travel, shop, eat, etc.) Mon, Wed: Mel, Bill, Robert, Tom, Morris 1:00-2:30 Tue, Thur: Anna, Sue, Jim 1:00-2:30 Friday: school assembly, all students 1:00-2:30	Goes with teacher on Mon, Wed 1:00-2:30 Tues, Thur vocational: Mel, Bill, Robert Tom, Morris Vocational 1:00-1:45 Tue, Thur social/leisure with peer tutors: Mel, Bill, Robert, Tom, Morris 1:45-2:30		Goes with teacher on Tue, Thur Mon, Wed vocational: Anna, Sue, Jim, 1:00-1:45 Mon, Wed social/leisure with peer tutors: Anna, Sue, Jim 1:45-2:30 Fri attend assembly 1:00-2:30	Peer tutors social/leisure Mon, Tue, Wed, Thur 1:45-2:30
2:30-3:00	Prepare to leave: toilet, press, etc. all students	Assist teacher		Assist teacher	

come in contact only with adult staff members and other handicapped individuals. For school-aged children and youth there were no nonhandicapped peers with whom to associate. The absence of appropriate peer models can have detrimental effects on the developing child. It is therefore important to consider the social ecology of the school world in which the handicapped student is placed. It is also useful to examine how the educational staff socializes within the school environment.

Scheduling

One of the first things a teacher must do at the beginning of the school year is set up a schedule. The schedule serves as a flowchart for where students and staff will be at different periods of the day. The schedule should be displayed openly on a wall in the room. It should be large enough in size and lettering that it can be seen from 10 to 15 feet. Figure 7.3 shows an example of a schedule.

Dividing the School Day. Basically, the school day is divided into a series of time segments in which different activities occur. The activities can be instructional sessions such as vocational training or communication. They also can include less formal instructional periods such as recess, lunch, breaks and toileting. The school day should flow from one activity to the next with students and staff being assigned to designated sessions.

Figure 7.3 shows a schedule for a primary class of students with severe handicaps. Along the top line of the schedule appear the names of the staff members and other persons who deliver instruction. There is a teacher, a paraprofessional, related service staff, a student teacher, and other participants (parents and special friends). There are eight students. The left-hand column breaks the school day into 30-minute sessions; this is an arbitrary time period that can be changed according to the program. The vertical and horizontal lines cross to form cells. In each cell the activity and the students participating in the activity are identified. It is more flexible to place the cell information on cards that can be replaced easily when changes in the session are made.

The first row in Figure 7.3 shows that from 8:30 to 9:00 all the staff members work with the students in taking coats off, using the toilet, and getting into a brief morning circle to greet one another. From 9:00 to 9:30 the teacher works with Mel, Tom, and Anna on communication. At this time the paraprofesional is working with Bill and Sue on sensorimotor stimulation. The student teacher is doing prevocational training with Robert, Jim, and Morris. No other persons are involved with instruction at this time. At 9:30 the students switch to different staff members at different locations in the classroom. At this time a speech therapist enters the room to work with Jim. At ten o'clock the speech therapist works with Robert and Mel and then leaves for the day. The therapist repeats this schedule on Thursday.

Figure 7.3 shows the schedule for one day. The cells and cards are large enough to indicate changes that occur from day to day within the week. For example, on Monday and Wednesday at 1 P.M. the teacher and paraprofessional go off campus for travel training with five students. The "related service" column shows the times when the speech therapist and physical therapist work with students. The "other" column indicates the program established by the teacher in which regular education students participate in play and instructional activities with handicapped students from the class. Regular education students enter the special education class at different times of the day. The "other" column shows when some parents of the students come to the class for 1 hour per week to participate in instruction with their own or other children. The "other" column also shows when volunteers come to the class on a regular basis. In this case, a member of the Pioneers group for retired telephone workers comes to the special education class. He adapts and tests electromechanical equipment that is used for communication and therapeutic aids. Thus, any person who provides instruction to the special education class on a regular basis is included in the schedule.

Key Factors. When a schedule is being designed, a number of factors must be taken into account. First, one must ensure that all the students' IEP objectives are being taught on a regular basis (at least once or twice per week). Second, different students must be placed into small groups for instructional sessions. It is not likely that all the students in a communication group, for example, will be working on the same tasks. Thus, students should be grouped according to the similarity of the tasks and the ease of implementing the session for the instructor. Third, it is important to consider the time of day when an activity is presented. A session requiring much attention and effort may not be scheduled after lunch, when a student has displayed a pattern of being drowsy. Fourth, it is important to examine the sequence of activities for each student and each staff member. For example, it is possible to schedule a staff member for three consecutive vocational sessions, but staff members may perform better when they vary the tasks and students they work with. Also, a student can be scheduled for two or three straight sessions on table tasks requiring quiet visual-motor attending. This may place undue strain on the student and hinder performance.

Go through the schedule and track the progression of activities for each student and each staff person. Make sure there are breaks and lunch for both groups. Try to obtain variation in the degree of motor activity across tasks for the students. Of course, giving instruction in multiple settings provides variation for everyone.

Group Instruction

We have discussed the need to move a student from a one-to-one cubicle model of instruction to more natural forms of teaching. The key objective of this process is to enable a student to function effectively with a group of peers.

For some students there is no probelm in working in groups of four to twenty-five students, for example, in a music appreciation class. However, many students with severe handicaps are incapable of working in a larger group without constant adult supervision. There are different reasons for this difficulty. Some students display a high rate of disruptive behavior so that a staff member must always be present to administer a behavior modification program or provide physical restraint to protect the student and others. Another problem is that the student has a such a short attention span that without constant adult interaction her attention is diverted to other materials or people who are unrelated to the instructional task. A similar problem occurs when a student may be distracted by the activity of other students in a group so that there is poor attending to the task at hand. For these reasons there is a need to lay out a systematic program that will lead a student from working in controlled cubicle settings to situations containing a larger group of people.

The starting point of a group transition program is to assess the student in groups of varying sizes. The student should be exposed to a repeated number of sessions in one-to-one (one student and one instructor), one-to-two, one-to-four, and possibly larger group settings. The student should be observed in these different settings to determine whether there is a problem in staying on task in the presence of other students. The teacher should determine the largest group in which the student can operate successfully. If the student does well in one-to-two but not one-to-four, systematic programming should begin with one-to-three or one-to-four.

Let us demonstrate such a program with a hypothetical student, Sal. Sal is a 7-year-old boy who has been labeled autistic. He is motorically active and has difficulty remaining in a chair for more than 2 or 3 minutes. He moves about a room rapidly, at times pushing objects down and sometimes slapping other students. Sal spends a considerable amount of time self-stimulating by twirling his hands in front of his face and mumbling undiscernible sounds.

Because of Sal's attentional and behavioral problems, his teacher began instruction in September by using the cubicle model of learning. All of Sal's sessions throughout the day were delivered in one of three cubicle areas in the classroom that were cordoned off by office dividers. Sal sat in a chair, and a staff member sat behind him to prevent his jumping out of the chair. The teacher exerted physical guidance to keep Sal in the chair when necessary.

After 3 weeks Sal was responding well to instruction. He was learning more discriminations and seemed pleased to earn reinforcers. The instructor rarely had to restrain him in his chair. At this point the instructor moved across the table from Sal during sessions; this was a more natural seating arrangement for student and teacher. Sal was positioned in the corner of the cubicle so that he could not run away easily. As it turned out, over the next two weeks Sal rarely had to be guided back into his chair during sessions.

At this point the teacher advanced Sal to the next step in the group instruction program. Another student from the class was present in the cubicle during sessions. The format for the one-to-two session had the teacher present a trial to Sal while the second student, Ira, sat idly. The trial lasted 20 to 30 seconds. Then the instructor ran a trial with Ira while Sal sat for a half a minute. This alternation procedure continued throughout the 20-minute session. The crucial interval was the idle time when Sal had to sit while the instructor was working with the other student. On trials in which Sal earned edible reinforcement, he continued to eat through most of the ITI. At times the instructor had to reach over and restrain Sal in his chair during the ITI. It also would have been possible to give him a toy to play with during the interval to prevent off-task behavior.

Over a 2-month period (November through December) Sal gradually reduced off-task behaviors to a zero rate during one-to-two instruction. In January the teacher decided to move Sal out of the cubicle area for some of his sessions. Six of his sessions were run in the cubicle, and two sessions were run in the open classroom (with no wall dividers separating students from the rest of the class). In the open area, one of his sessions was in a one-to-one and one was in a one-to-two. In the cubicle, three of his sessions were one-to-one and three were one-to-two. By the end of March all his sessions were moved out of the cubicle and into the open classroom. Progress was so impressive at that point (i.e., there were few off-task behaviors) that in April the teacher began Sal's sessions with three and four students present. Sal was now exposed to a variety of group formats: one-to-one, one-to-two, one-to-three, and one-to-four.

In May, the teacher began the first out-of-class instruction, in which Sal went to another class for music with a paraprofessional (twice per week) and went off campus with his teacher and another student for travel training sessions (once per week). Thus, Sal made substantial progress during the year in moving from the one-to-one cubicle mode to small group mulitple-setting instruction.

For some students this transition would have taken a much longer time. Whatever the time frame, special education teachers should be instrumental in moving their students to more natural group instructional modes. For more capable, self-regulated students the transition might be to much larger-size regular education classes containing twenty to thirty students. Whatever the size of the group, performing in a natural group setting is a valuable social skill that all students should obtain.

Social Integration

A key factor in social ecology is how students with severe handicaps are socially integrated with other persons in their educational programs. In our description of multiple-setting instruction a premium was placed on exposing the student to a variety of situations both on and off campus. However, training in multiple sites ensures only that contact will be made with nonhandicapped persons. Coming into contact with different individuals does not guarantee that any kind of sophisticated social interaction will take place. In fact, it has been shown repeatedly that when handicapped and nonhandicapped students are placed in proximity with one another, little social interaction takes place (Fredericks, Baldwin, Grove, Moore, Riggs, and Lyons, 1978). Thus, it is important to develop training programs that explicitly teach handicapped and nonhandicapped persons to interact with one another. Until such programs are implemented successfully, we can expect students with severe handicaps to isolate themselves from other individuals and display few prosocial behaviors. This section shows how the social skills of students can be developed through direct training efforts.

Social Play. Child psychologists have spent considerable time outlining the sequence in which preschool children develop social play behaviors (Fredericks et al., 1978; Parten, 1932). Although the normal developmental model often does not apply to severely handicapped persons, in the case of social interaction some instructive points may be learned from examining developmental social sequences. Essentially, three basic levels of social interaction may occur between two or more persons. The *asocial* level of play denotes the absence of social awarenes or social interaction. The individual may position himself so that he is completely inactive, engages an object in a repeated, purposeless way, or plays with an item in a useful manner. In all three cases the person does not display any awareness of or interaction with the people around him. Unfortunately, students with severe handicaps often spend disproportionate amounts of time in asocial play. They may sit idly and inactively. They may self-stimulate a part of the body, e.g., repeatedly wave the hands in front of the eyes. They may self-stimulate with an object, e.g., bang a toy car over and over on the ground. On a more positive note, the person may participate in a purposeful activity, e.g., shoot a basketball or play Perfection®, which involves no interaction with another person.

The next level of social play is *social awareness*. In social awareness play, the individual attends to or imitates other people around her. In the case of handicapped students, the child may intently watch other students play. The student may display a fixed gaze or smile when she observes something happen. The student may take the next step and imitate the actions of others. For example, one student may build a tower with blocks; the second student will observe this and start to build her own tower. Social awareness does not go so far as the next level of social play, which is called *direct social interaction*. In direct social interaction, an individual emits one or more behaviors that place her in immediate contact with another person. These behaviors can include the following:

1. An approach response is made in which the student walks or crawls up to another person.
2. A communicative gesture, e.g., a wave, is made to another person.
3. A verbal statement is made.
4. A person touches another individual.
5. A person hands an object to another individual.

All these behaviors are manifestations of direct social interaction. The interaction can become more advanced if reciprocation develops so that one person's response is followed by another person's response and a chain of alternating responses ensues. Direct social interactions may be spontaneous and unpredictable, as in the case of two friends casually meeting and conversing at recess. Interactions also may be more codified and follow a set of rules, as in the case of playing a game of tennis. In either case, students with severe handicaps have difficulty developing direct interactional behaviors. Students who have a tendency to be withdrawn, e.g., autistic students, have a proclivity for not interacting directly with others. However, task-analyzed programs to promote social interactions can be written in a step-by-step fashion. Figure 7.4 shows a task analysis of a direct social interaction

Types of Social Interactions. Figure 7.4 shows an interactional sequence in which one person gives a toy to another person, who plays with it for a little while and then returns it to the first person. This is one type of direct social interaction. It should be useful to catalog the various types of direct interactions that special education teachers can teach their handicapped students.

The simplest interaction is a greeting response. When a student approaches a familiar person, he or she can be taught to make some kind of "hello" or greeting. The nature of the greeting should be consistent with the norms of the nonhandicapped peers at the school. For instance, if the regular education students greet each other with phrases like "Hey" or "What's happening?" but not "Hello" or "What have you been doing?" only the former phrases should be taught as greeting responses. If a student cannot speak, some kind of gestural sign indicating "hi" can be given. The student should try to establish eye contact with the other person. The body should be positioned in a frontal (rather than sidewise) manner in relation to the other person. The student should not stand too close or too far from the other person. Also, the student should try to discriminate whom he greets so that he does not greet everyone he approaches. Rather, he initially should be taught to greet only familiar people.

Greetings are simple and often easy social responses to teach. The problem with teaching greetings to handicapped persons is that they lead to only brief interactions. It may take only 2 to 5 seconds for two persons to greet each other; after that, the interaction is likely to end. Nonhandicapped people tend to expand their interactions through conversation so that the duration of the interaction may last 1 minute, 5 minutes, or longer. Since persons with severe handicaps often have little or no expressive language, their potential for extended social interactions is limited.

An alternative to building interactions around conversations is to identify nonverbal play activities in which two or more persons can alternate turns in a reciprocal fashion. The play activities usually are geared around some object, e.g., a Frisbee® or a hand-held video game. The play object should be of intrinsic interest to both the handicapped student and the nonhandicapped student. If the latter student is not interested in the activity, any in-

Figure 7.4 Examples of direct social interactions.

BASKETBALL SHOOT AROUND

1. Ira positions himself near the basket.
2. Sandy grasps the basketball and stands about 10 feet from the basket.
3. Sandy shoots the ball at the basket.
4. Ira grabs the ball after it goes in the basket or misses.
5. Sandy moves to another position on the court. She moves 2 or 3 feet closer to the basket if she missed the previous shot. She moves 2 or 3 feet away from the basket if she made it on the previous shot.
6. Ira passes the ball to Sandy.
7. Sandy catches the ball and shoots it at the basket.
8. Repeat steps 4 through 7 until Sandy has taken five shots at the basket.
9. Sandy now positions herself near the basket.
10. Ira grasps the basketball and stands about 10 feet from the basket.
11. Ira shoots the ball at the basket.
12. Repeat steps 4 through 7 (with Ira shooting and Sandy retrieving) until Ira gets five shots at the basket.
13. Sandy and Ira may continue taking turns shooting and retrieving until they have decided they have had enough shoot around. Suggested time for shoot around: 10 to 20 minutes.

TOY EXCHANGE

1. Rafael grasps three Smurf® toys.
2. Jamie holds two puppets, one in each hand.
3. Rafael plays with the three toys (super, baker and skater Smurf®) so that toy characters interact with each other in an appropriate manner (wrestle, chase, etc.).
4. Jamie plays with the two puppets so that they interact with each other in an appropriate manner (e.g., speak, hug).
5. After five minutes of play by each child, Rafael hands Jamie the Smurf® toys and Jamie hands Rafael the puppets. The length of time the children play separately before exchanging the toys can vary according to the interests and attention span of the children.

teraction that ensues probably will be motivated by altruism on the nonhandicapped student's part.

Friendship rather than helping relationships should be the goal of social interaction programs. It is also useful if the activity is portable so that the handicapped student can play the game in a variety of settings. When training the student, you must teach both the skills required to play the game and the social skills needed to approach someone and initiate the game. Figure 7.5 shows a task analysis of a hand-held video game interaction. The stu-

Figure 7.5 Examples of social interaction sequences.

HAND-HELD PACMAN®

1. AS approaches NS.
2. AS establishes one m proximity.
3. AS establishes a face-forward orientation.
4. AS says, "Hi."
5. AS waits for response.
6. AS says, "Want to play."
7. AS waits for response. AS finds someone else if NS does not indicate willingness to play. AS then begins sequence at step 1 again.
8. AS turns game on.
9. AS hands game to NS.
10. AS watches NS play.
11. AS receives game from NS.
12. AS reads NS score.
13. AS turns game off.
14. AS turns game on to reset score to zero.
15. AS plays game.
16. AS reads own score.
17. AS offers game to NS. If NS accepts, play continues in alternating fashion. When NS indicates he or she is finished, AS takes game back.
18. AS says, "Bye."

SONY® WALKMAN

1. AS approaches NS.
2. AS establishes one m proximity.
3. AS establishes face forward orientation with NS.
4. AS says, "Hi."
5. AS waits for response.
6. AS says (and writes), "Want to listen."
7. AS shows radio to NS.
   a. If NS not interested in interacting, AS approaches another student (step 1).
8. AS turns radio on.
9. AS adjusts volume to level 6.
10. AS hands headphones to NS.
11. AS puts on headphones.
12. AS selects rock 'n roll station.
13. AS remains in proximity to NS until termination of interaction by NS.
14. AS says, "Bye."

Source: R. Gaylord-Ross, T. Haring, C. Breen, and V. Pitts-Conway. The training and generalization of social interaction skills with autistic youth, *Journal of Applied Behavior Analysis* 17 (1984), p. 229–47. Reprinted with permission of the Society of Experimental Analysis of Behavior, Inc.

dent approaches, greets, signals to play, plays the game in a reciprocal fashion, and bids farewell to terminate the interaction. It is possible to teach the game-playing skill separately from the social skills and combine them later in one long chain. It is also possible to teach the whole chain concurrently from the start.

Contexts for Social Interaction. We have described the three levels of social interaction: asocial, awareness, and direct. Most social skill training attempts to promote direct interactions. Awareness behavior is likely to occur incidentally as the handicapped student observes and imitates other persons in the multiple settings to which he or she is exposed. It is also useful to examine the kinds of social contexts in which the teacher may expect direct and awareness behavior to develop.

Peer tutoring is one type of context in which social interaction can take place between handicapped and nonhandicapped students (Alen 1976; Gaylord-Ross and Pitts-Conway, 1983). In peer tutoring, a nonhandicapped student teaches a handicapped student some task. The nonhandicapped student serves as an instructor. The peer tutor can be trained to deliver S^D's, prompts, and reinforcers just as a teacher would. The peer tutor also can collect data. In most cases the special education teacher will design the program, and the peer tutor will carry out the task-analyzed procedure. Instruction can occur in domains such as personal management, vocational, and leisure. Peer tutors usually conduct instruction in the special education classroom, but tutoring also may take place in other sites.

Peer tutoring has many advantages and some potential disadvantages. It brings handicapped and nonhandicapped students together in a rather structured situation. When these students come into contact with one another in free play settings, there is often little direct interaction. Peer tutoring organizes the situation so that there is an ongoing flow of behaviors between the students; that is, the tutor delivers cues and reinforcers, and the special education student emits various task behaviors. The predetermined structure of the session also fosters confidence in both students with respect to how they are supposed to behave when they encounter each other. Peer tutoring also has the advantage of increasing the ratio of instructors to students in the class so that a more intense level of instruction can be delivered. It is important that the peer tutors be committed to participate on a regular basis. If there is not steady attendance, few gains are likely to be made by the handicapped students.

The frequency of peer tutoring can vary. We suggest that primary-age tutors participate once or twice per week, whereas secondary-level peers may tutor four or five times a week. The peer tutoring experience also may be formalized further by making it part of a course requirement for the nonhandicapped student. This arrangement tends to ensure better attendance by the tutor.

The major drawback of peer tutoring is that it may hinder the development of friendship relationships. To some extent peer tutoring places the students in a professional-helping relationship. Students do not tend to become friends with their teachers. One therefore should be careful about the amount of peer tutoring to which a student is exposed. One way to make the peer tutoring interaction better approximate a friendship is to have the instruction occur in the leisure domain. Initially, the tutor will teach the special student how to play a leisure activity such as tennis or checkers. Over sessions the special student becomes proficient, and the students can play the game in a more natural and playful manner. That is, after task acquisition the interaction will evolve into a leisure exchange between equals rather than one between a tutor and a student.

A *student-centered* interaction is a second context for social contact among students. In the peer tutoring context, an adult teacher structures how the interaction will flow. In a student-centered interaction, the individuals are left to their own resources to interact. These interactions may occur at recess or at other break times. In the community they may occur in a house, on the street, or in a park. Ultimately, there is no adult present to shape the interaction. At first, it may be necessary for staff members to train the social interactions that will generalize to nonadult, unstructured settings (Gaylord-Ross, Haring, Breen, and Pitts-Conway, 1984).

Student-centered interactions are of vital importance because they enable students with severe handicaps to spend time with members of the nonhandicapped peer culture. In the past, social environments often were created in which handicapped students interacted only with adults such as parents and professionals. Student-centered interaction permits handicapped students to learn that their peers are important persons too. Through awareness and direct interactions, the handicapped individual may begin to develop prosocial behavior patterns. The importance of imitating nonhandicapped role models cannot be underestimated. Normal children develop almost all their social skills through imitating others, not through formal instruction. We therefore must provide ample opportunities for handicapped students to benefit from prosocial role modeling.

The *special friends* program can be used to facilitate student-centered interactions. For a 6-week to 6-month period a pair of students can be designated special friends. The nonhandicapped student is likely to be a volunteer from a regular education class. The students meet on a regular basis (two to five times per week) to participate in leisure activities. The interactions can occur on the playground, in the special education class, off campus, or at some other site on the school grounds. Examples of special friends leisure interactions could be video games or electric racing cars. Initially, the severely handicapped student may not have the skills to participate in the leisure interaction. It may be necessary for a teacher to be present to prompt and reinforce leisure interactions. When criterion has been reached on the interaction task, the teacher can be faded out of the situation so that the handicapped and nonhandicapped students can be left to interact in a student-centered manner.

Figure 7.5 shows an example of a social leisure activity—Walkman® radio listening—that can be trained and ultimately lead to a student-centered interaction. Listening to a Walkman® radio can be an isolated activity, but Gaylord-Ross et al. (1984) found that when it was trained in a social context, students exchanged the headphones and expanded conversations into genuine social interactions. Thus, we can see that special friend relationships can have great value. They tend to build a "buddy system" in which true friendships can develop. They help develop social leisure skills. They tend not to leave the handicapped student isolated in free play situations. Such students now have friends they may approach for purposes of interaction.

Summary

The chapter described how the environment plays a part in shaping the behavior of students with severe handicaps and those around them. Historically, persons with severe handicaps were placed in isolated and debilitating environments that tended to exaggerate their disabilities. Our belief is that handicapped students should be educated in integrated school sites. Ways to make the classroom environment more normalized and stimulating were examined. The importance of conducting instruction in multiple sites was elucidated because of its impact on promoting generalized learning and providing varied environmental stimulation. Practical ways to schedule students, staff, and activities were presented. Finally, methods were illustrated to better socially integrate students with severe handicaps in educational settings.

In the past, educators tended to ignore the physical and social environment. Instruction often was provided in segregated schools, in cubicles, and with one-to-one adult-child interactions. The educational model proposed here is much more diverse. Ideally, education should occur in integrated schools where concerted efforts are made to maximize the contact and interaction between handicapped and nonhandicapped persons. The student is educated in a variety of settings in which the size of the group of students and staff varies. Social skills are taught explicitly through various means so that prosocial behaviors develop and enduring acquaintanceships and friendships evolve between students. This educational model is not hypothetical. It has been used by a number of teachers in different parts of the world. It is up to you to try to implement the model with your students.

Chapter 8

Home-School Interactions

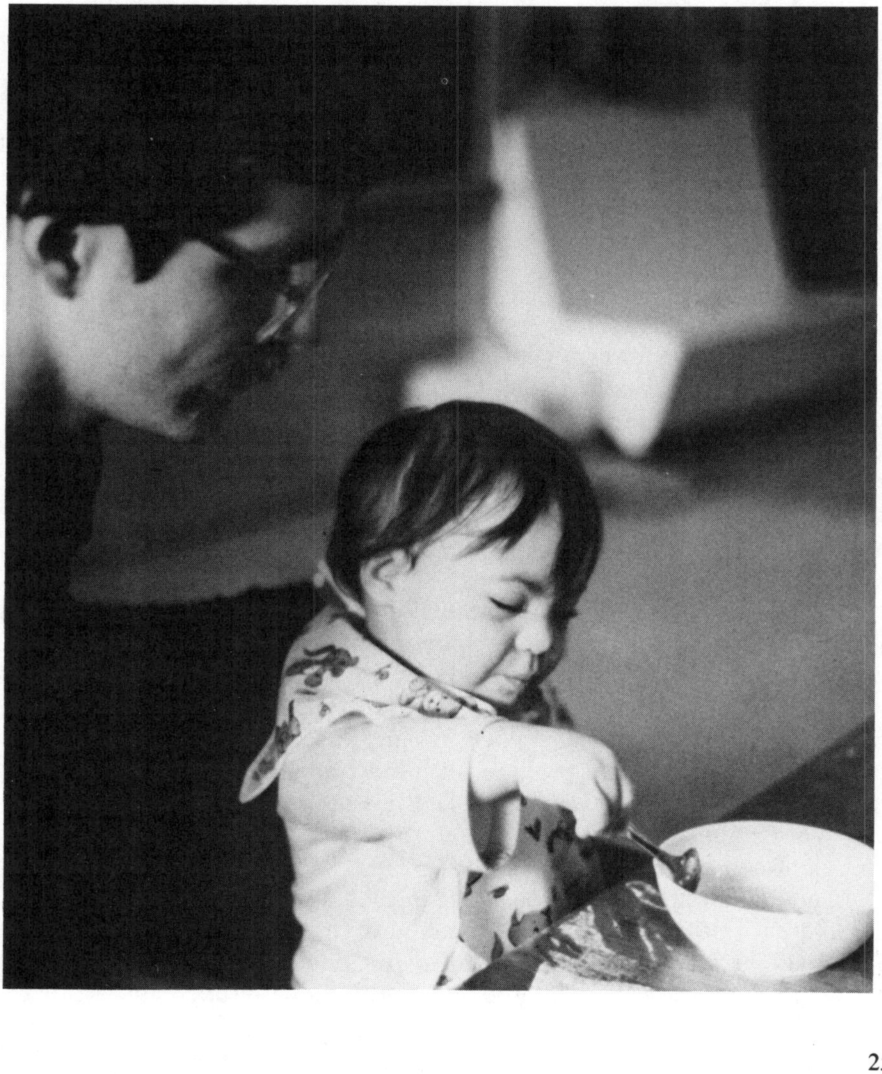

The emphasis so far has been on school-based instruction that takes place on or off campus. At other times of the day the student is involved primarily with his or her parents. The role of the family is critical in educating students with severe handicaps; therefore, it is important that teachers establish ongoing communication with the parents of disabled students. The chapter describes a parent involvement program that facilitates the generalization of acquired skills to the home and school settings.

Being a Parent

In the past the family was a stable, predictable entity in one's life. People tended to marry and live their adult lives in the same community (or a nearby community) in which they were brought up. An extended family of relatives existed to provide nurturance and support. One's economic life could be predicted from one's family background and type of education. Getting married and bringing children into the world was a given in most people's lives. The responsibilities of being a parent were assumed to be part of the individual's destiny.

In today's society people are more likely to be on the move. Job possibilities exist worldwide and nationwide. Our society is more transient as people change employment in a rapid fashion. The old neighborhoods and extended families are not present to provide support to parents and their children. Families tend to be "nuclear" in the sense that the parents and children live together and provide for almost all of one another's needs. Grandparents, uncles, and old school chums are not present. The nuclear quality of families tends to place more pressures on spouses and parents to meet all of one another's wants and desires.

In addition, our society is changing in such a way that marrying or having children is no longer an unquestioned presumption. There is a tendency to think of one's personal needs first. The individual-centered life-style runs counter to the responsibilities brought about by long-term commitments to spouses and children. Therefore, our society has developed to a point where it is no longer considered deviant to remain single or not have children. A value is placed on options and pluralistic life-styles. Although this cultural trend may lead to greater personal emancipation, it also has led to a devaluation of the central importance of families and children. Without the supporting systems of culture and family, it may indeed be more difficult to raise children and maintain a marriage.

We have described this difference between current and past times to give the reader a sense of the support system needed to maintain a successful family life. The need for a support system may be even more acute for a family raising a child with handicapping conditions.

Parental Demands

Being a parent places very direct responsibilities on the individual. One's time is circumscribed as a parent who must provide care and supervision for the child. One cannot always decide spontaneously to go here or there without first considering whether the activity fits into the child's schedule. Activities often must be planned around baby-sitters and children. Also, the addition of children to a family places monetary demands on the parents. Food, clothing, and other costs projected over 20 years place many long-term and short-term pressures on the family. In addition, the rising cost of housing has made home ownership an unattainable dream for many new families. Thus, economic forces can mitigate against the development of stable family units.

The presence of a handicapped child in the home adds many additional responsibilities and costs for the family. The additional costs may include special equipment that must be purchased for the child, e.g., wheelchairs or the cost of respite care. Since some students with severe handicaps require constant supervision, a time and cost pressure is placed on the parents. For a single-parent family or a family with low income, the fiscal and psychological pressures can be heightened further. A real hardship is envisioned when a projection is made into the future. That is, when the child is likely to require constant care through the school and adult years, a rather imposing psychological and fiscal burden is placed on the parents.

The Brighter Side

We regret having to begin a chapter in such a negative manner, yet the reader should be aware of the realities and pressures of raising a handicapped child. When these demands cannot be dealt with adequately, parents may seek placement elsewhere. Where community-based placements are not available, this may mean placement in a state hospital.

On the brighter side, handicapped children are children like all others. They are capable of giving and receiving love. Parents develop strong, affective relationships with the handicapped child. Out of this love a commitment to maximize the growth and development of the child may emerge. When parents have the resources, they can learn a number of specialized skills that will increase their effectiveness in working with the child. The skills of being a parent of a normal child usually are not taught in a formal manner (although parent training is often appropriate for this population, too). Parenting skills should be taught to the parents of a severely handicapped student if the student is to develop to his or her maximum potential. It is the purpose of this chapter to describe the kind of parent training program that is needed to promote the development of these skills.

In this program the special education teacher plays a leading role. The teacher should motivate parents to make an effort to modify their parenting behavior. The teacher should establish an effective communication system between parents and professionals so that cooperative efforts can be engendered. Next, the teacher must institute a parent involvement program in which the parents become key members of an educational team. In some cases the parents are taught specific skills in dealing with their children, e.g., behavior management. In other cases the parents take the lead in providing information about how their child's needs can best be served.

In all cases, though, a parent involvement program should not establish a hierarchical relationship between parents and professionals. Too often in the special education field parents are put off and feel inferior to professionals. Sometimes this is the fault of the professional. The professional must feel confident about having the skills and knowledge to impart to parents yet not project an air of superiority that will preclude two-way communication.

Communication

One of the major reasons for the failure of parent involvement programs is inadequate communication between parents and professionals. Before we mention the types of communication procedures that can be utilized, let us consider the individual characteristics of the parents and the teacher.

Interpersonal Dynamics

Poor interpersonal communication may result from the different backgrounds and value systems of the individuals. For example, the teacher may be from a middle-class background and the parents from a lower social class. Parents may speak a foreign language that the teacher does not understand. There may be significant age differences that undercut a common perspective. The family may have a different cultural background and perspective than that of the teacher. When differences in beliefs and values related to child raising, teaching, and other matters exist, it is up to the professional to close the gap so that an effective parent involvement program may develop. The teacher may have to learn some key phrases in the foreign tongue or may have to take a course or complete readings to understand the cultural perspective of the families being worked with. Such efforts should pay off in terms of the parents appreciating the teacher's attempt to reach out to them. In turn, the parents are likely to become more involved and committed to working with professionals in order to help their children.

Probably more important than cultural and value differences are the differing perceptions of the parents' role that professionals and parents are likely to have. Professionals who have been trained in a curriculum and systematic instruction model are likely to view parents as individuals who can provide more instruction in the home setting. The role of parents as skill builders may not be consistent with the perception parents have of themselves. Parents are more likely to see themselves in a caretaking rather than an educational role. For example, a teacher may be spending much effort on teaching self-feeding skills to a student. The parents may want the child to improve in feeding skills but are more concerned that the child will consume enough food during the self-feeding program so that there will be no weight loss. Parents may support the idea of more independence through self-feeding or self-grooming, but not at the expense of not consuming sufficient amounts of food or looking sloppy in public. Parents are sensitive to the health needs of the children and to how others view the child. It is therefore important that educators not impose instructional roles on parents when the parents are not receptive. Rather, the professional should identify the roles that parents perceive for themselves and build child-parent activities around those roles.

Establishing a Communication System

The professional must use certain informal techniques to cultivate relationships with families. These techniques include being friendly, offering help when needed, and learning the cultural perspective of the family. Beyond these informal, interpersonal techniques, there is a need to establish a formal communication system between parents and professionals. The communication system ensures that both parties will be continuously aware of each other's efforts in dealing with the child. The communciation system helps coordinate the joint actions of the parent involvement program.

The Initial Contact. Within the first month of the school year or directly upon receiving a new student, it is critical that the teacher make direct contact with the parents. The best kind of direct contact is face-to-face interaction. The parents should be invited to visit the class in the first month. This will give them an opportunity to observe the kinds of activities taking place at school and will enable the teacher to explain the nature of the program fully. If the parents cannot visit the class in the first month, the next best alternative is for the teacher to visit the home of the student. Ideally, a home visit is made at least once during the school year. It is a good idea to make this visit in the first few months. Since it may not be possible to make the visit in the first month of classes, it may be necessary to use a phone call as the direct contact in the first month.

When making the phone call, or school or home visit, try to have both parents present. There is a strong tendency in special education to have contact only with the mother. Try to avoid this tendency by getting the father involved as much as possible. Be sensitive to parents' schedules. Sometimes the meeting may have to be at a time that is inconvenient for the teacher or the parents.

During the intial direct contact, a number of things should be accomplished. Of course, good rapport should be established. Being friendly, enthusiastic, and professional and showing your concern for the child should go a long way toward building rapport. The teacher must be a good listener with parents. The teacher is eager to explain his or her program to the parents. This is certainly an important aspect of the initial meeting, yet the teacher must listen and probe to find out what is important to the parents. The professional's goals and methods may be inconsistent with the parents' view of child raising and education. For example, the parents may be of an artistic or humanistic bent and find behavioral procedures unsuitable for their child. The teacher must listen to these views and then offer alternative positions that show, for example, that behavioral procedures are not incompatible with humanistic goals.

The key thing is that the initial contact should establish a general agreement between parents and teacher in regard to the values and basic ways in which the student will be educated in the coming year. Until a consensus is established, the teacher should not proceed to enter actively into a description of the program. When parents are not committed to the goals of a program, one can expect little effort on their part in terms of cooperating with the program.

When talking to parents, the professional must be aware that parents' main concern is the family as a systemic unit. In contrast, the professional's main concern is the individual child. The professional may wish to set up home programs that will benefit the handicapped child but may, for example, take time away from the parents' interaction with their nonhandicapped child. For this reason the parents may resist or not participate in the program. The professional must be sensitive to the family as a system and proceed with programs with an awareness of how they are going to have an impact on the various roles family members must play.

Building on Parents' Roles. When discussing activities in which parents can participate within a parent involvement program, the professional should build on the roles that parents carry out already. For example, at the preschool level the main emphasis should be on supporting what parents already are doing well. The teacher may find out that a parent is doing an excellent job of providing a well-balanced diet and that both parents are spending much time taking the child to cultural and recreational events. The professional should praise these efforts in order to foster other efforts and develop a positive parental self-concept. At the preschool level, less effort may be spent on parent education with respect to teaching contingency management and other specific skills.

At the grade school level, a greater emphasis should be placed on educating the parent with regard to skill-building activities. Care should be taken not to burn out the parents. One or more simple programs that may be carried out in the home can be introduced. Again, support should be given to activities that parents already are doing well.

At the intermediate school level, parents should be made aware of ultimate adult environments and the need to prepare the child for functioning in these residential and vocational settings. At the intermediate level, skill-building programs may be geared to the community as well as the home setting, e.g., shopping in stores.

At the secondary level, parents must give considerable attention to postschool environments. Discussion should begin in regard to what kind of vocation the student will be suited for, e.g., assembly-line work, technical, or janitorial. Parents should participate in vocational assessment and training decisions. They also should be made aware of residential options in adulthood, the establishment of trust funds, etc. Parents of secondary students also may participate in supervision of "homework." Some parents who do not see themselves as playing a direct instructional role may view supervising homework as part of their parental responsibility. The teacher may send home tasks (e.g., worksheets or leisure activities) for the student to complete at home, and the parent will oversee the homework task and make sure it is completed.

The key point is that parent involvement will change over the different phases of development, and the professional must alter the nature of parent participation accordingly. The professional also must listen to what parents are saying about the child and determine how the educational program must change to benefit the student. Parents often make invaluable suggestions related to what materials or methods will work best with the child. The teaching staff may spend months finding out what reinforcer or management technique works best with a student. If they listen to the student's parents, they may be able to obtain this information within a few weeks. Much of the information presented in this chapter may make it appear as if professionals were constantly trying to change parent behavior. The teacher should present the framework of the school program but be open to constant parent input to modify the actual program delivered to the student.

Using Demonstrations. In describing a program to parents, demonstration works best. If the initial meeting is held in the classroom, the teacher can demonstrate the instructional techniques with actual students. When parents can observe an effective instructional technique, they are likely to become excited and see how similar techniques can benefit their child. If the initial meeting is held in the home, the teacher can demonstrate a particular technique with the child.

The central aim of the parent meeting is for the teacher to explain the educational program. The parents should be "walked through" the systematic instruction process; that is, it should be explained to them how long-term and short-term goals are set. Examples of task-analyzed programs should be described and modeled. The use of positive reinforcement should be emphasized. An example of a typical day's activity for a student can be illustrated. The teacher should be more or less technical in the program description depending on the interests and intelligence of the parents. Some parents are able and motivated to become partners in designing and running instructional programs. For most parents a "train and generalize" model will be used; that is, the initial acquisition training will be conducted by the teacher. When the student learns the skill with his teachers, he then is taught to generalize the skill in the home setting. This training model is described in more detail below.

After a description of the teacher's educational program is made, the parents and teachers should begin to discuss educational goals for the student. This discussion is likely to take place in more detail at another meeting, but at the initial meeting the parents should be oriented to the importance of functional goals that will meet the long-term vocational and residential needs of the student. They should be told that the development of the IEP is a joint venture for parents and professionals. They should be told that they will be asked to fill out an environmental inventory (Brown, Branston, Hamre-Nietupski, Pumpian, Certo, and Gruenewald, 1979) that will determine partially what will be taught to the child in the coming year.

Thus, the initial meeting should accomplish a number of things. Rapport is established. A discussion of values and education is made, with a consensus reached on educational approaches. Next, an exploration and demonstration of systematic instruction is made. Subsequently, a beginning discussion of the educational goals of their student is conducted. The meeting should end with a discussion of what type of involvement the parents will have with the school program. Commitments may not be made at this meeting, but both parties should begin to think about how much time and effort the parents can devote to collaborating with the school staff in working with the child. The sequence of activities that take place in the initial parent meeting are as follows:

1. Establish rapport.
2. Exchange educational values.
3. Demonstrate systematic instruction.

4. Discuss educational goals.
5. Explore parent involvement.

Maintaining Parent Involvement

A successful initial contact with parents should take place. The success of this contact sets the stage for ongoing communication and cooperative efforts between the parents and the teaching staff. A system for maintaining ongoing communication must be established immediately. The nature of the communication system will vary according to the motivation and abilities of the parents, but a minimum degree of ongoing communication must be maintained with all parents.

The Daily Log. A simple device for mutual correspondence is the *daily log*. A notebook is set up so that at the end of the day the teacher writes a few sentences describing the student's behavior at school that day. Notations may be made about performance on instructional tasks. Comments can be written to describe the child's mood or behavior problems. The teacher also may describe health, diet, or other medical matters. If, for example, the teacher and parents are trying to increase the student's weight, comments can be made about how much was eaten at school that day and whether there were any instances of vomiting. Figure 8.1 shows an example of notes written by a teacher and a parent for a series of school days.

At the end of the school day the notebook accompanies the student back to the home for the parents to read. Before the child leaves for school the next day, the parents write a few lines about the child's behavior, health, and related matters. For example, the parent may write that the child ate a large dinner but refused breakfast and wound up gaining a pound since the previous day. The notes also can contain affective statements about the progress of the student. For example, the teacher may write that Billy is really making progress in using the toilet and that many of the gains are due to the parents' efforts. This kind of comment points to the student's progress and positively reinforces the parents' behavior.

A key factor in an effective parent involvement program is the degree of participation by the parents. To increase their participation, teachers should make reinforcing comments in the notebook. Such positive feedback, as well as face-to-face interactions, goes a long way in motivating parental cooperation. Conversely, parents may write reinforcing comments about the teacher's efforts. In fact, a mutual reinforcement system of praising each other's efforts should be used as much as possible. When parent-teacher communication has been established within a mutual reinforcement system and disagreements arise, they are likely to be resolved through constructive discussion. The absence of mutual reinforcement increases the

Figure 8.1

PARENT–TEACHER DAILY LOG

3/2 Bill did well at school today, particularly in communication. His nose continues to run, but his cold seems better than last week.

3/3 We stopped giving Bill his medicine for his cold, so we did not send it to school with him. Tomorrow we will resume the dressing program.

3/3 The class went to the circus today, and Bill seemed to enjoy himself. I have sent home some recording sheets for the dressing program.

3/4 Bill only got 3 out of 9 steps correct on his dressing Program. Ugh! He seemed happy with his circus paraphernalia.

3/4 Bill urinated in his pants today. That's the first time in 3 months. Have you noticed this at home? Otherwise, he had a fine day at school, especially in Speech therapy.

3/5 Bill hasn't had any toileting accidents lately. Glad to hear he's doing well in school.

3/5 Bill continues to progress in prevocational and communication. I have sent home copies of his graphs. Let's set up a parent meeting for next month.

parents' and teacher's sense of isolation, and this is likely to place them in an adversarial position when disagreements arise.

The daily log facilitates continued communication with a minimum of effort. It gives both parties the sense that they are in constant contact with each other. In some cases, though, it may not be possible to maintain daily communication. Parents may be working two jobs, have an unusual schedule, or be so disorganized in their own lives that they do not keep up the daily log. In these cases the notebook may be exchanged on a weekly basis. Almost any parent should be able to write a few lines once a week.

Another potential problem deals with language and literacy. Some parents do not speak or write English. If the teacher is not bilingual, there is no basis for notebook exchanges. Another potential problem occurs if the parents are illiterate or semiliterate so that they cannot make entries into the log. In these cases it may be possible to design a recording sheet on which the parent and teacher enter pluses or minuses to indicate the student's performance on certain behaviors that day. Figure 8.2 shows a simple recording sheet that can be exchanged between parent and teacher. Once the sheet is explained to the parents (possibly through an interpreter), they can make simple plus or minus entries. Similarly, they then will be able to understand the plus and minus entries made by the teacher.

Figure 8.2 Home-school recording sheet.

Date	Putting on Coat Without (+) or With (−) Physical Assistance from Adult: HOME	SCHOOL
4/3	+	+
4/4	−	−
4/5	−	+
4/6	+	+
4/7	−	−
4/11	+	+
4/12	−	+
4/13	+	+
4/14	+	+

Parent Visits. The most intense and potentially beneficial contacts between people are face-to-face interactions. Trust tends to develop when individuals have continued contact. Negative stereotypes about others are likely to be broken as a result of ongoing interaction. Thus, it is advisable to set up as many direct interactions between parents and teachers as possible. Ideally, parents should visit the child's class on a weekly or monthly basis. In many cases parents have work and other responsibilities that preclude this rate of visiting. Some agreeable rate of visits should be set at the beginning of the school year, e.g., monthly or bimonthly. If parents are truly to learn instructional skills, there must be a minimal level of direct contact, probably once per month by one of the parents.

Once a visitation rate is agreed upon, the parents must formally commit themselves to it. A behavioral contract may be drawn up that specifies their involvement. Figure 8.3 shows such a contract. The degree of involvement is stated, and both the parents and the teacher sign the contract.

The contract, of course, has no legally binding power. It is used to solidify the commitment of both parties to work with each other. The teacher should use good judgment as to whether a contract will fit the behavioral styles of the particular parents and whether it actually will motivate them to make the visits and work with the child at home.

When parents visit the school program, a number of activities may take place. If the visits are infrequent, e.g., once or twice a year, they will consist mostly of observation and conferences describing the progress the student has made. When visits are more frequent, a substantive emphasis can be placed on cooperative instructional efforts. At these sessions a review of

Figure 8.3 Parent involvement contract.

We the parents of ________________________
Student's name

agree to participate to the best of our abilities in the Sherman School Special Education Parent Involvement Program.

____
Mother's signature

____
Father's signature

I, Mrs.________, as the teacher of ________________________
Student's name

will give my fullest effort to make the Parent Involvement Program successful.

____
Teacher's signature

the data of past programs can be made. The teacher can demonstrate new instructional techniques. The parent can run a new or previously learned program with the child. The teacher then can give feedback to the parent concerning the delivery of S^D's, prompts, and reinforcers. If parents are more resistant to direct instruction, they may be assigned roles as "room parents." By becoming familiar with the program in this noninstructional role, they may gradually increase their interest in teaching procedures.

In reviewing student progress, a discussion can ensue through which changes in instructional programs can be made. For example, the student may behave quite differently in an activity like toothbrushing across the home and school settings. The parents and teacher can examine these differences and recommend changes so that there is more consistency between home and school. Since parents have spent so much time with the child in the past, they may suggest unique reinforcers that will be motivating. There may be special prompting procedures they have developed that facilitate performance with the child.

Thus, it can be seen how a mutual sharing of information can occur during parent visits. Both participants need the knowledge and know-how of the other. When the discussions are of a more technical nature, the teacher probably should take the lead because of his or her expertise and training. Yet professionals must never dictate what will be taught and how it will be taught. A two-way flow of communication must take place.

Although this book has focused on educational efforts in integrated school settings, many students with severe handicaps reside in segregated residential settings, e.g., state hospitals. It is important for the teacher in these settings to develop a communication system with parents, who may live many miles away. The teacher should write a letter at the beginning of the school year introducing himself and providing a brief description of the educational program. Thereafter, the teacher may send home examples of the student's work and indicators of progress on a monthly or quarterly basis.

During the year the parents are likely to make one or more visits to the facility. The teacher should find out when these visits will take place and invite the parents to examine the school program. During the visit they can observe the child, and the teacher can show through demonstrations and records how the student is progressing. Some students make home visits, and the parents can be shown how to carry out self-care, leisure, and other activities with the child during these visits. Although coordination with parents of institutionalized students presents difficulties, it may lead to benefits for the student and the parents. If the child has successful home visits, it may move the parents to consider a permanent placement in their home.

Setting Goals. A key feature of a special education program is the development of the IEP. As stated in P.L. 94-142, parents should play an active role in developing the IEP. Parents can make their greatest contribution in determining what will be taught. In general, professionals have greater expertise in designing techniques for teaching particular tasks. Parents, though, often have strong feelings about what they would like the child to learn. For example, some parents have expectations that their severely handicapped child will learn to read. In some cases this may be a realistic expectation, but in other cases the student's cognitive impairment is so extensive that reading is not a reasonable goal. In these cases the parents' and teacher's ability to resolve differences will be put to the test. The teacher may present months or years of data showing the student making little progress in prereading skills, but the parents may not relent in their insistence that substantial portions of time be spent in teaching the student to read. Fortunately, in most instances there will not be such divergent opinions about what should be taught. In this case the parents and teacher simply need to meet to develop instructional goals for the student. This process should occur before the formal IEP meeting.

The best way to select goals and objectives is to apply the environmental inventory strategy (see Chapter 1). The thrust of the approach is that the parents and the professional enumerate skills that are needed to succeed in the next environment and in ultimate environments. The parents' preferences and beliefs about future vocations for the child are shared with the teacher. Long-term goals and short-term objectives are established after agreement has been reached concerning the thrust of the educational program. Parents are most knowledgeable about their child in the domestic, community, social, and leisure domains. They therefore may play a larger role in determining goals and objectives in these areas than in the vocational and academic domains.

Parents differ widely in the degree to which they participate in discussions with professionals. In far too many instances parents are in awe of professionals and feel that they can contribute little to educational planning for their child. In these cases the teacher must take a facilitative role in getting parents to speak out and voice their opinions about objectives and teaching techniques. With reserved parents, the teacher must be more nondirective and make sure to listen to what they have to say. When parents do speak out, they must be strongly reinforced and encouraged to continue their participation.

Another way to increase parent participation in goal setting is to have them engage in an assessment of the child with a professional. They can help fill out, for instance, the AAMD Adaptive Behavior Scale. Parent involvement in assessment lets the professional learn more about the student, parent attitudes toward the child, and parental willingness to work on instructional programs.

Other parents feel that they are the only ones who know what is best for their child. In these instances the teacher must be firm in explaining instructional programs and curriculum preferences. The teacher should try to identify areas in which there is teacher-parent agreement. Areas of agreement should be emphasized to assure that the relationship does not become an adversarial one. In the areas of disagreement, e.g., how much time should be spent on reading, the issue should be specified clearly in a face-to-face meeting. The teacher should present all the objective data to support her position and ask the parent to do the same. Both parties should be objective and let the data dictate a resolution to the problem.

In many cases emotions will cloud the issue, and scientific data will not tilt the scale toward an easy resolution. During these discussions, make sure to emphasize that both sides are arguing for what is best for the child. Actively search for compromises. Most conflicts are resolved by both sides giving in from their original positions. For example, the teacher may agree to work on reading in a functional context. That is, the student can be taught to read or discriminate survival signs such as "men's room," "stop," etc. When no agreement can be attained, the teacher must be prepared to stand her ground on the issue. This may mean going to a due process hearing so that a third party can resolve the matter.

The step to judicial mediation is unfortunate because it tends to harden the lines between parents and professionals. Regardless of who wins the due process decision, both parties must continue to work with each other after mediation is completed. The bad feelings that persist after mediation hearings are not easily undone and may interfere with further communication. But if the matter truly affects the development of the student, the ony recourse that the teacher or parent may have is third-party mediation. Thus, proceed with caution. Try to use all your interpersonal and professional skills to resolve a matter with a parent.

Parenting Skills

A parent involvement program establishes an ongoing communication system, which in turn sets the stage for cooperative instructional ventures between home and school. When parents and teachers have face-to-face contact at least once per month, it is possible to initiate systematic efforts in upgrading parenting skills. If parents cannot come to school as often as once a month, it is possible to maintain this rate of contact through phone calls or home visits by the teacher. For parent skill-training efforts to be minimally successful, there is a need for at least one conversational interaction per month between teacher and parent.

When approaching the topic of parent skill training, the teacher should be careful to explain that he does not have all the answers for parenting a handicapped child. The things parents are already doing well should be emphasized. The teacher should point out that there are certain ways in which they can improve their interactions with the child.

Stimulation

The first set of skills that can be taught to parents is presenting a stimulating home environment. In Chapter 7 the important aspects of the physical and social environment in the school were described. Similarly, it is important to communicate to the parent that the home is a source of physical and social stimulation for the child. They should be told how active stimulation of the child's body and mind is one of the most important ways to promote positive growth and development. When the teacher makes a home visit, an assessment of the physical and social characteristics of the home should be made in terms of how they are stimulating the child.

Physical Stimulation. An assessment should be made of objects in the home that can serve as sources of stimulation for the child. What kind and number of toys are present? Are they available for daily use, or are they locked away somewhere? Are the toys appropriate for the age and developemental level of the child? As in school settings, one often can find infantile or preschool types of toys in the home of a handicapped youth. Encourage the parents to purchase toys and leisure items that are age-appropriate, cognitively stimulating, and of interest to the child, for example, video games. There should be a variety of toys present that stimulate different attributes of the child, e.g., items to read or visually scan, table games, balls or Frisbee® saucers, that lead to reciprocal interactions. The parents must teach the child that there are certain areas of the home where play can occur and other areas and items that are off limits. For example, the living room and the family's stereo equipment may be places where free play is forbidden. This matter should be presented as a discrimination learning task in which play in certain areas is reinforced and play in other areas is censured.

The teacher should examine the play equipment in the backyard or at a nearby playground. The handicapped student should have access to this equipment. Are there pets in the home that can be sources of stimulation? Are radios and televisions present, and has the child been taught to manipulate them? Does the child spend excessive amounts of time watching television or rocking to the music on the radio? These are all questions that should be examined, with practical suggestions given to the parents to improve the physical environment in the home.

Social Environment. A key concern is how parents interact with the child. A gross measure of interaction is the amount of time the parents spend emitting vocalizations or gestures with the child. Unfortunately, the fathers of both handicapped and nonhandicapped children often spend just a few minutes a day interacting directly with the child.

It is possible to examine the types of interactions that take place between parent and child. A considerable portion of these encounters probably involve the parent providing assistance to the child, e.g., bathing, propping, and giving commands to do something such as sitting quietly or buttoning a shirt. Although it is important to provide assistance and give directives, there are three other kinds of interactions that need to occur but often appear at a low rate. Parents must be effective *instructors* in order to get the child to learn new skills such as grooming, dressing, and chores. Parents must have *leisure* interactions with the child. As the child gets older, parents must try to facilitate play encounters between the child and the child's peers. Finally, parents need to communicate *intimacy*.

A considerable part of the parent skill-training program focuses on making parents better instructors. Given a reasonable effort on the parents' part, success can be expected in improving their teaching skills. In the area of leisure interactions it is important for parents to set aside certain times of the day or week when they will play directly with the child. Without such scheduling, parents may get caught up in their own routines and concerns and tend not to spend time in recreation with the child.

Intimacy is a key factor in all parent-child relationships. Many adults have difficulty making outward displays of affection. When the teacher meets with parents in the presence of the child, the teacher should note whether the parents talk to the child, kiss or hug the child, tell him they love him, etc. Affectionate behavior is most likely to be observed in the home setting. When parents do not appear to display affection to the child, the teacher should tell them tactfully that affective displays are an important part of constructing a trusting social climate in the child's world. It may be necessary for the teacher to informally model intimate behavior such as hugs, cooing, and endearing verbal statements. In some cases and in the right context, the teacher may praise outward displays of affection directed by parents toward the child.

An area of the social environment that often is overlooked involves the siblings of handicapped students. As was stated earlier, professionals sometimes forget the effects of home programs on the family unit. One member who is likely to be overlooked in professional efforts is the sibling of a handicapped student. So much effort and attention may go into compensating for the deficiencies of the handicapped child that siblings receive relatively little attention and nurturance from their parents. There are a number of ways to avoid this problem. One way is to avoid designing programs that involve a disproportionate amount of the parents' time. A second way is to devise programs, e.g., leisure activities, that can involve both the handicapped and the nonhandicapped siblings. A third method is to permit older, willing siblings to play the role of instructor in home programs. This will get the nonhandicapped sibling involved with the specialized programs.

Behavior Management

After stimulation, a key aspect of the parenting process is behavior management of the child. A major reason why children with severe handicaps are removed from the natural family placement is problem behavior. Besides the extra demands of parenting a handicapped child, many parents cannot cope with children who are chronically destroying property, injuring themselves, or attacking others. Fortunately, the behavior modification techniques described in Chapter 5 can be used by parents in the home setting in order to reduce disruptive actions.

The teacher may take the lead in setting up home programs and teaching parents how to implement them. Often there is a community service system that can provide a psychologist or social worker to serve as a behavior modification consultant to the home. In many cases parents may become quite adroit in behavior modification and be able to design their own programs. In most cases the lead must be taken by the professional in designing and monitoring the program.

The procedures used to establish home programs are identical to those discussed in Chapter 5. When designing a program for the home, the teacher first must observe the parents interacting with the child and pool that information with what is known already about the management of the student. Observe the parents' reinforcement strategies. Do they reinforce appropriate behaviors? Do they reinforce inappropriate behaviors? Are they nonreinforcing? Also examine how they punish and prompt the child's behavior.

Be on the lookout for inconsistencies in how each parent treats the child. One parent may be very nurturant but a poor disciplinarian, and the other may be aloof but a good behavior manager. Draw conclusions about the parents' behavioral style and bring this to their attention at the appropriate time.

Delivering Instructions and Reinforcers. A parent behavior training program has two components. The first component deals with the delivery of instructions and reinforcers; the second deals with the delivery of aversive consequences. In the first training component, the value of positive reinforcement should be explained to the parents. Readings may be offered from such primers as that of Patterson and Guillan (1968). The teacher should explain how contingent positive reinforcement is a powerful way to motivate human behavior. Examples should be given of how the rate of appropriate behaviors can be increased through positive reinforcement. The teacher should model this process with the child or through role playing.

Next, feedback should be given about how the parents may be reinforcing undesirable behaviors. From observations, the teacher can point out how the parents are reinforcing a behavior such as playing with the sugar bowl at meals. Directions may be given about how the parents may ignore that behavior or redirect the child to an appropriate activity, e.g., correct use of utensils. Again, examples and demonstrations should be provided that show how adult attention (reinforcement) of maladaptive behaviors can maintain those behaviors. Ample practice with the child should occur, with the teacher giving feedback so that the parents can learn to be reinforcing agents for appropriate behaviors and nonreinforcers of problem behaviors.

After the parents have learned how to reinforce or ignore selected behaviors, they should be taught how to deliver instructions to the child. Parents of children with behavior problems are notoriously poor in giving commands to the child. They may give general commands like "Be a good boy" that have no referent to a specific behavior the child can do. Another poor type of manding (commanding) is giving a command and not allowing the child enough time to complete the request. For example, the parent may say, "Clean up the toys on the floor." Within 5 seconds the parent may start cleaning up the toys before the child has a chance to do so. Thus, the child does not have a sense of task completion and does not have an opportunity to learn that following instructions earns reinforcement. Parents often are tempted to complete the task for the child because it is easier than waiting for the child's response, prompting it, or reinforcing it. In the short run it is often easier to complete the task for the child rather than waiting for the child to do so. Unfortunately, in the long run the child will never learn the skill if the parent is always finishing it prematurely. A rule of thumb is, "Do not give a command to a child to perform a task if there is not time for him to complete it." If the parent must complete the task for the child because of time constraints, the command should never be given in the first place. Another kind of erroneous command is to give a series of statements that switch the topic from second to second. For example, a parent may say, "Brush your teeth" (2-second pause), then "No, clean your face, it's so dirty" (5-second pause), then verbally prompt too soon, "Now clean your lips better than that." The child is bombarded with a sequence of verbiage that is confusing and does not permit the completion of a successful response. Poor instructors have a tendency to talk too much and change the thrust of their statements in a rapid fashion.

Inform parents of the characteristics of good commands and prompts. The command should be short and discrete, e.g., "Pull up your zipper." State the command in a firm but warm voice. Give the child an adequate opportunity (latency) to complete the task. The length of the latency (5, 10, or 20 seconds) is determined by the characteristics of the task and the student. Do not intercede with prompts too swiftly. The manner of prompting the child, e.g., verbal, model, or physical, should be predetermined. When the child succeeds in following the command, be reinforcing with an effective consequence. Parents should practice delivering mands, prompts, and reinforcers with the child in the presence of the teacher. The teacher should give feedback to the parents to improve these skills in the hope that the parents will perform them successfully when the teacher is not present.

Delivering Aversive Consequences. The second component of the parent behavior training program addresses the matter of delivering aversive consequences. The first component of delivering cues, prompts, and positive reinforcers applies to both behavior problems and the learning of skills. The delivery of aversive consequences relates only to the suppression of problem behaviors.

When the parent and the teacher design a behavior modification program for the child, they should follow the decision model described in Chapter 5. Their initial program attempts should contain manipulated curricular and positive reinforcement variables. If these positive approaches fail, it may be necessary to consider and then implement a procedure that uses aversive consequences. A thorough discussion should be made with the parents concerning what kind of aversive consequences if any they will be comfortable using.

The first procedures to be considered are response cost and timeout. Other procedures that may be considered are overcorrection and contingent restraint. When a procedure has been selected, the parents and the teacher should carefully role-play the use of the behavioral technique. The teacher can demonstrate its use with the child. Finally, the parents should use timeout, for example, with the child, and the teacher should give feedback to them in relation to its proper application.

Aversive procedures have the potential for abuse, and so they must be monitored carefully. The timeout or overcorrection period must not extend beyond its prescribed interval. The parents should administer the intervention in a neutral, affective manner so that the interaction does not become emotionally charged and abusive. Data must be collected carefully to evaluate whether the procedure is working. If behavior has not been reduced significantly within a week or two, the procedure probably should be dropped or modified substantially. The problem behavior should be reduced to an acceptable or zero rate within a month or two so that the aversive intervention can be discontinued from the parent involvement program.

Data Collection

When parents are serving as instructors for the child, there is a need for them to collect data on student progress. The amount of data collected by parents varies from family to family. In Chapter 4 we stated that the teacher should develop a measurement system that will meet the program's needs and not overwhelm the staff with recording activity. As the measurement system begins to run smoothly, additional data collection requirements may be added. With parents, the initial data collection system should be very simple and should minimize excessive recording. Parents have multiple demands in their numerous roles as spouse, provider, homemaker, and parent. A simple system should be selected that can be implemented successfully. If the recording system is too demanding, parents will not use it, and their role as data collectors will cease.

Figure 8.4 shows a simple data sheet in which the number of problem behaviors appearing is recorded in a checkoff fashion each day. Whenever the behavior occurs, the parents consequate it with their behavior management program and record the event on the data sheet. The completion of skill tasks can be recorded similarly on a sheet that lists the date and the task. If parents get more proficient at data collection, they can run actual training sessions in which data are collected on a trial-by-trial fashion or entries are made for each response in the task-analyzed chain (see the figures in Chapter 4).

Again, parents must not be overloaded with too much programming activity. It makes sense to start with having the parents record just one behavior. As the parent involvement program progresses, this number may be increased. Similarly, behavior management programs should start with modifying just one behavior. If the behavior is at a fairly low rate of five or fewer incidents per day, the parents should have little trouble consequating and recording it. With skill-training programs, a separate time must be set aside to run the trials in a session. The parents must fit this 5- to 30-minute session into their existing schedule. For some parents this will present little difficulty, but for many others one should be sensitive to what would be a reasonable number of skill-training sessions for parents to complete. Of course, the more the learning sessions can fit into the naturally occurring

Figure 8.4 Home recording sheet of the frequency of aberrant behaviors.

Date	Tally	Total
5/11	✓✓✓✓✓	5
5/12	✓✓	2
5/13	✓✓✓✓✓✓✓✓✓	9
5/14	✓✓✓✓✓✓	6
5/15	✓✓	2
5/16	✓	1
5/17		0
5/18	✓	1
5/19		0
5/20	✓✓✓	3
5/21	✓✓	2

events of the day, e.g., a toothbrushing session or a parent-child play session, the easier they will be to carry out.

The Parental Involvement Model

As we have seen, the main characteristics of a parent involvement program are a communication system and a parent training system in which parents learn the skills to be effective instructors, stimulators, and nurturers of the child. The thrust of the program is to establish a balance in the flow of communication between parents and professionals. Two-way communication must occur in the areas of the philosophy of educating a student with severe handicaps and in determining what educational goals are to be set for the particular student. In the area of the technology of teaching the student, it is to be expected that professionals will take the lead in designing teaching strategies to attain the IEP goals.

Coordinating Home and School Endeavors

A training and generalization model for teaching can be useful in many cases of home-school endeavors. The model states that the initial acquisition of a skill is accomplished by the teaching staff. Students with severe handicaps often require hundreds of trials to learn a new task. Exact prompting procedures may be needed to facilitate mastery of a skill. The time and preci-

Figure 8.5 Graph of shirt buttoning program with instruction initiated in school and extended to the home.

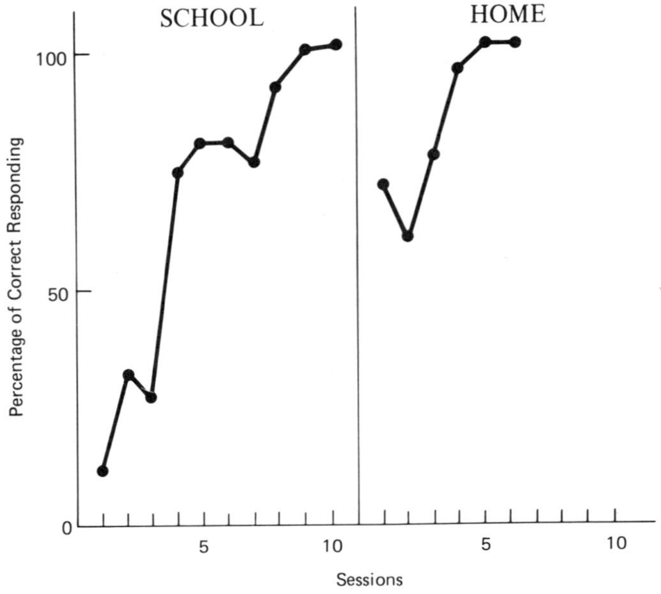

sion needed to teach tasks may be too demanding for parents to do in the home. Professionals have the training and time to succeed in the acquisition phase of learning. When the student has been brought to acquisition criterion, the parents can begin practice in extending that skill to the home setting.

This generalization training is done in conjunction with the teaching staff. The teacher should explain and model the program to the parents. After acquisition, the student should be easier to work with for the parents. Fewer prompts should be needed. Since the student can perform the skill in a smooth manner, the main focus of generalization training is to get the new, natural cues of the home to be discriminative for the child. Suggestions for attaining generalized responding appear in Chapter 3. Figure 8.5 shows a graph demonstrating how a child learned shirt buttoning at school before sessions were moved to the home.

Thus, the training and generalization model introduces home training after school acquisition training is completed. It is not necessarily true that all cases must follow this sequential approach. Some parents become quite skillful running programs and do not have to wait until the teacher has succeeded before home instruction can begin. Instruction may begin simultaneously in the home and at the school. Figure 8.6 shows a graph of a coordinated home-school program in which instruction began simultane-

Figure 8.6 Graph of home-school program begun simultaneously in both settings.

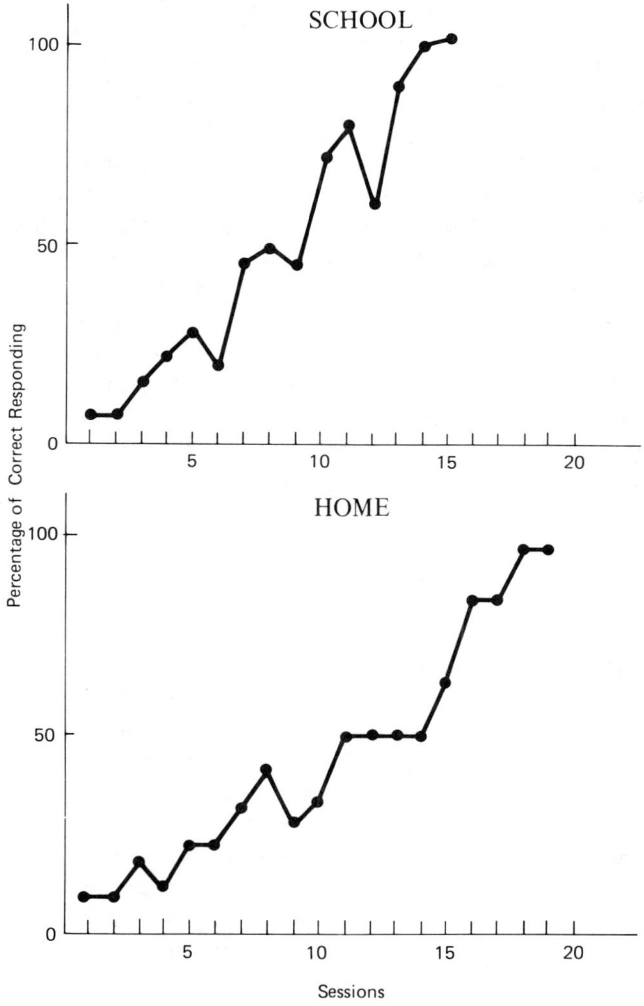

ously in both settings. In other cases it may not be possible to teach the task at school. For example, suppose a youth is expected to learn the domestic chore of depositing garbage from the interior of the house into garbage cans outside. There is likely to be no replica of this activity at school. Acquisition training can be carried out only in the home. It is important for the teacher to help design the program and give assistance in showing how the program can be conducted.

Home-school instructional endeavors are likely to be in the domains of personal managment, domestic, community, social and leisure. There should be less coordinated instruction in the academic and vocational domains since these domains are primarily the province of the school. In general, a contemporary program of multiple-setting instruction will have many areas of overlap between the home and the school for cooperative efforts. The training and generalization model constitutes a realistic approach to obtaining the generalization of learned skills.

It may seem that we have placed too much emphasis on minimizing the demands and efforts involved in parent participation. These concerns have come from our experience with and sensitivity to the daily pressures that parents of handicapped children face. It is always safe to start with a nominal requirement for participation on the parents' part, e.g., recording the frequency of one behavior for 1 hour. As the teacher monitors the program, there can be an increase in the amount of teaching and data collection the parents complete. In some cases the parents will become highly motivated and display the ability to design and implement numerous programs. In that case the parents and the teacher become instructional colleagues. Usually the teacher takes the lead in designing and implementing programs, and the training and generalization model should work well.

Providing a Support System

A parent involvement program facilitates communication between the home and the school and enables parents to become effective instructors of their children. Beyond these specific objectives, a parent involvement program provides a support system for the student's family. At the beginning of the chapter we examined the special demands and pressures placed on parents of handicapped children. One major stressing event is their tendency to feel isolated from people in the community.

A parent involvement program can alleviate this sense of isolation in a number of ways. First, by having ongoing communication between home and school, the parents get a sense that someone out there cares about the family. Just being a good listener communicates to the parents that the teacher cares about their problems. Second, as the parents learn how to instruct the child, they may gain a sense of having the ability to control the learning and destiny of the child. Because many parents are ineffective as teachers, they develop a sense that their children will never grow up, learn, or amount to anything. An effective training program will manifest the learning potential of the child to the parents and show them that they can manage behavior and teach new skills to the child. As a result, parents should become more optimistic about the child's future and their ability to influence it. Third, teachers can play an important role in connecting parents with other potential support groups in the community. The teacher cannot take on the role of a social case worker but can direct parents to other resources.

The first potential support group is other parents. Often there is a back-to-school night during which parents can get to meet one another. Parents should be encouraged to exchange phone numbers and addresses and to continue communication. Perhaps cooperative child care can be organized among the parents. A parent group for special education students in that class or school often can be formed. Such a group can help obtain further services for the students at the school and in the community. Parent groups can run benefits to raise money. They can help bring favorable publicity to the accomplishments of the special education program. The parent organization also may play an advocacy role in due process hearings and in lobbying for bills beneficial to handicapped persons. Most important, a parent group provides a network of familiar persons who truly understand the problems of the individual parent because they are in the same position. It is thus possible for parents to share experiences and counsel with other parents.

Of course, parents of handicapped children should not isolate themselves from the parents of nonhandicapped students. The former group should be encouraged to join the school's PTA and participate actively. Participation in regular education activities reinforces the parents' view of their child as another human being instead of always associating the handicapped label with their child and parental role. Interacting with parents of nonhandicapped students also provides a vehicle for promoting integration experiences at school between regular and special students.

The teacher also can put parents in touch with existing community agencies. Many states have agencies for the developmentally disabled that provide extensive services during nonschool hours. Such services may include respite care, physical therapy, counseling, and special equipment. In many cases it is necessry for the parents to register the child as a client of the agency in order to qualify for services. Many parents are not even aware of the existence of such agencies, e.g., legal advocacy groups and the state department of rehabilitation. Teachers can inform parents of the existence of such agencies. There are also national organizations with local chapters in which parents may wish to participate (United Cerebral Palsy or Easter Seals). These groups often are organized around a particular disability group. The major organizations related to students with severe handicaps are the National Association for Retarded Citizens, the National Association for Autistic Citizens, the Association for Children with Down Syndrome, the Association for Persons with Severe Handicaps, the American Association on Mental Deficiency, and the Council for Exceptional Children.

Teachers can disseminate information to parents that will improve their skills as instructors and parents. There are manuals and books written especially to help parents improve their behavioral skills (Patterson and Guillan 1968). Finnie (1975) has written an excellent text on caring for physically disabled children. Hanson's (1978) work on caring for Down syndrome infants is an informative volume for parents. Teachers may be able to give or lend copies of such books and manuals to parents or inform parents where they may be purchased.

An Example: The Jones Family

Let us take as an example a family with a severely handicapped student who participated in a parent involvement program. The Joneses represent just one type of family that may engage in such a program. The example illustrates the main characteristics of the parent involvement process.

Martha and Bill Jones were middle-class people who lived in a small town outside a large city. Bill worked on the assembly line at a nearby auto plant. Martha worked part-time as a bookkeeper at a local appliance store. They had three children: Bill Jr., Susan, and Todd. The children ranged in age from Bill at 13 to Todd at 8.

Todd was severely mentally retarded with no major physical or behavioral disabilities. He was lethargic most of the time, displaying little effort when working on school or domestic tasks. He learned at a very slow rate and had mastered only two of his twelve IEP objectives the previous school year. His teachers had not applied the principles of systematic instruction outlined in this book in a rigorous fashion. Thus, when Ms. Adele Lamotta, Todd's new teacher, described her program to the Joneses, it sounded different from what they had experienced in the past. Adele had received training in behavior analytic procedures during her credential work at the state university.

On the first day of classes Adele sent a flier home with Todd that introduced herself and stated that a parent meeting would be held during the first month of school. In that month the Joneses noticed that Todd brought home sheets of paper that had grids filled with pluses and minuses. They saw numbers like 87 percent on the sheet that seemed familiar, but they were not quite sure what to make of them.

Mr. and Mrs. Jones had some time off from work, and so they both attended the parent meeting with Ms. Lamotta on a Tuesday afternoon. The teacher explained her program and emphasized the precision aspects of instruction. They all observed a paraprofessional teaching Todd and two other students. Adele pointed out the precise way the aide delivered cues and reinforcers to the students. She stressed that unless such care is given in teaching students like Todd, the child is unlikely to learn. Martha Jones asked what the aide was writing down on the sheets. Adele began to explain the rudiments of systematic instruction, describing how activities are task-analyzed and how motivating reinforcers are used. The importance of keeping careful records to monitor pupil progress was emphasized, and Mrs. Jones was able to relate this practice to her own vocation of bookkeeping.

After 15 minutes of observation and discussion, Ms. Lamotta asked the

Joneses if they would like to try the systematic teaching procedures with their son. They both were a little cautious, but Mr. Jones said that he would give it a try. The teacher explained how he should give the cue "Set the table." When Todd placed the fork, spoon, knife, and plate in their proper positions, Mr. Jones was told to praise him and give him an edible (a raisin or a piece of dried apricot). Adele then showed him where to mark a plus or minus on the recording sheet. Mr. Jones ran a few trials and was very pleased to see Todd be so responsive to him. Susan then tried a few trials with Todd and was equally enthusiastic about this success and her own accomplishment.

Ms. Lamotta went on to explain that there were a number of things to learn about systematic instruction and other skills related to parenting children with severe handicaps. She asked the Joneses if they would be interested in participating in a parent involvement program. She told them that it entailed keeping in constant communication through the daily log and intermittent phone calls. It entailed one parent visiting the class at least once a month for skill-training sessions. It also involved their working with Todd on programs at home and keeping records of his progress.

The Joneses were enthusiastic about the parent involvement program. They stated that they both worked, had two other children, and had a number of responsibilities, but they would give the program an earnest try. Ms. Lamotta produced a paper, stating that the Joneses and the teaching staff would sign a contract for their cooperation in Todd's parent involvement program. Ms. Lamotta then explained that she and her staff were assessing Todd and that they soon would be formulating goals for his IEP. She showed the Joneses a copy of the parent environmental inventory form. She went over it with them and asked them to fill it out at their leisure. She told them that she would be making a home visit within the next 6 weeks. At that time they could go over their responses on the form and begin to set IEP goals for Todd. She also gave them Patterson's book to read. They concluded the 45-minute meeting with mutual enthusiasm about working together in the future.

During the next month the Joneses and Ms. Lamotta exchanged points of information through the daily log and one phone call, which mainly concerned the medical treatment of Todd's case of hives. The following month Ms. Lamotta made her home visit. She reviewed Todd's progress and her own conclusions drawn in her assessment. The Joneses explained to Adele their responses on the environmental inventory form. A discussion ensued, and they began to hone in on actual goals that would appear on Todd's IEP. Ms. Lamotta said that she would take these goals and objectives and write them in more precise detail. She told them that there would be other objectives, particularly from the academic and vocational domains, that they had discussed briefly and that she would be completing. She then spoke more about the principles of systematic instruction and discussed Patterson's book. The 95-minute meeting ended with them setting up a class visit by Mr. Jones in 2 weeks.

At the next school visit Mr. Jones and Ms. Lamotta discussed an actual instructional program that they had been working on at school and that the parents could use for generalization in the home. The teacher demonstrated with Todd the sweeping program in which Todd had to sweep up the classroom floor and deposit the residue in a garbage can. Mr. Jones agreed that this would be a useful chore for Todd to do at home. He then ran a trial with Todd and reinforced him properly. The teacher showed the parent the recording sheet and gave him some feedback on how to correct errors. Mr. Jones stated that they would run the program at home on 4 specified days a week. The father would explain the program to his wife, and they would give each other feedback concerning the implementation of the program. They then ran the program in a successful manner three times a week.

The following month Mrs. Jones made a school visit. At the meeting Ms. Lamotta briefed her on Todd's general educational progress. Mrs. Jones reviewed Todd's progress on sweeping and shared the data sheets with the teacher. She then ran a sweeping trial, and the teacher generously praised her for her instructional techniques. Ms. Lamotta told her of a parent group for the class and gave Mrs. Jones the phone numbers of other parents she could contact. Martha indicated that she would be interested in participating in such a group. She went on to say that Todd was beginning to have a problem wetting his bed at night. The teacher set up a data sheet in which the parents could collect baseline recordings of when and with what frequency the enuresis was occurring. At the school visit the next month they would set up a toilet-training program for Todd. If the matter necessitated more immediate attention, they would discuss the program over the phone before then.

The parent involvement program continued in this manner during the school year. Phone calls, logs, and monthly meetings kept the parents and teacher in communication. The monthly visits tended to focus on the review and establishment of instructional programs. Over the months the parents increased their number of home programs to three at a time. Some programs were run daily, and others only a few times per week. The Joneses became active participants in the class parent group and became active in a national parents group for handicapped persons. They were successful and enjoyed working on the home programs but never designed new programs of their own. They tended to follow and generalize programs already validated by the teacher. They did learn more about the home physical environment and added a number of new age-appropriate toys in both the interior and the exterior of their house.

The Joneses also became much more nurturant in their social interactions with Todd. They had come to understand the power of positive reinforcement in motivating Todd to learn and perform through their own teaching experiences with him. As an outgrowth of this, Ms. Lamotta noticed that the parents were much more affectionate and interactive with Todd. They seemed to display more confidence in their exchanges with him and generally felt more positive about being the parents of a child who had handicapping conditions.

Summary

This episode gives a description of a typical parent involvement program. The program was generally successful in facilitating communication between parents and teaching staff, getting the parents to be more effective instructors, and connecting parents with other support groups and resources in the community.

Each parent involvement program takes on its own characteristics. Some parents become extremely active participants, making visits to the class at least one time per week. Other parents are never able to run even one program at home successfully. The teacher must become skillful in adapting the nature of the parent involvement program according to the needs and abilities of the individuals. Always try to improve the skill level of the parents in some way while making the parents feel better about themselves in their parental role. If instructional sessions cannot be conducted in the home, give the parents suggestions so that they can improve the physical environment of their house or apartment. Give them pointers about how they may be more nurturant, stimulating, and disciplined with their children, i.e., improve their soical environment. Sometimes the parents can offer little participation but a mature sibling may play the major role as an instructional mediator. The teacher must be resourceful in devising ways to make the home environment a source of stimulation and support for the student and a setting that can further enhance gains in learning made in the school context.

Chapter 9

The Many Facets of Being a Teacher

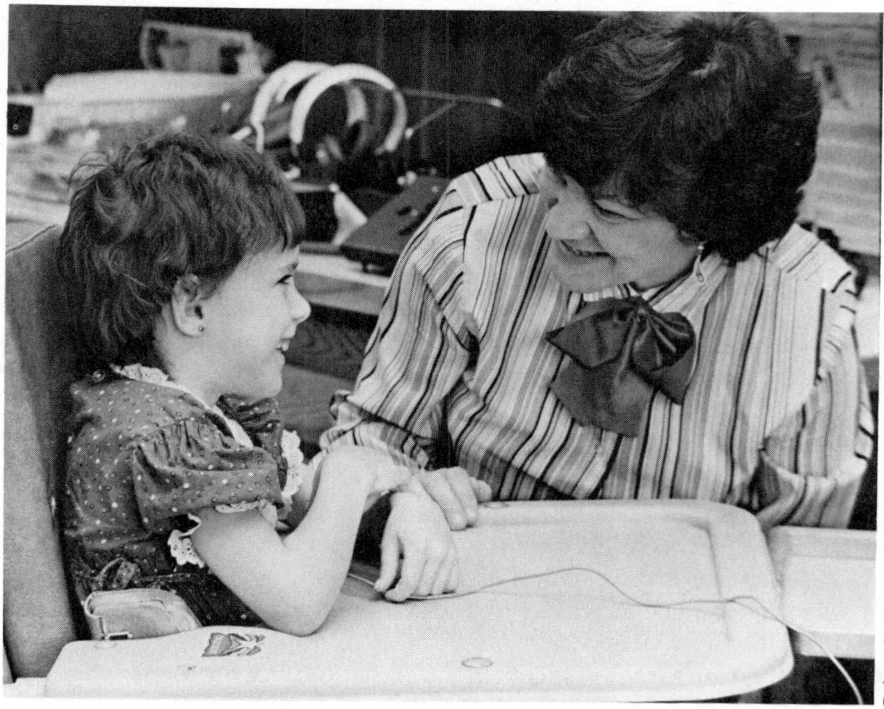

Dolores Jenkin

The role of the teacher of severely handicapped students is very complex; it is not a single entity but rather a collection of roles. These roles evolve from the expectations of others and may be accepted or rejected by the individual teacher. Individual teachers assign different weights, or values, to the different facets of the job. For example, one teacher may devote a large proportion of time and energy to instructing paraprofessionals, whereas another will devote the same amount of time to working with parents. Although such individual variations are inevitable, some people will view a person as a poor teacher if their role expectations are not met. Although the old maxim that you can't please all the people all the time is certainly true, many teachers' careers are jeopardized because of their ignorance of the roles they are expected to play. In this chapter we shall clarify some of the major roles, thus allowing the reader to make an informed choice about how to apportion time and energy.

Some of the major roles the teacher of severely handicapped students may be expected to fulfill are as follows:

1. An educator of severely handicapped learners
2. A liaison between the parents and the school district
3. A supervisor and teacher of paraprofessionals
4. A member and coordinator of a team of professionals who will be working with the students
5. An advocate for the students in the classroom and for the severely handicapped population as a whole

Specific Roles

The teacher is expected to demonstrate certain skills within each role category. Some of the expectations are formal and are spelled out explicitly in teacher handbooks, by administrators, or by state laws or federal regulations. Others are conveyed informally through discussions or unexpected disagreements with experienced teachers, parents, paraprofessionals, and administrators. We shall focus on specific skills that often are expected of teachers who work with severely handicapped students.

Educator

The educator of severely handicapped students is expected to be skilled in a variety of teaching techniques that will help the students acquire new behaviors and decrease their inappropriate behavior. Such skills have been discussed in detail in Chapters 2, 3, 5, and 6. The teacher is expected to know how to assess a student's educational needs, write instructional programs that meet those needs, and regularly monitor the student's progress. These skills have been addressed in Chapters 1, 2, and 4. An educator also is expected to schedule learning experiences in such a way that the students will not become frustrated, bored, or overly fatigued. It is expected that classroom time will be used efficiently so that each student is exposed to the maximum number of learning experiences. Scheduling was addressed in Chapter 7.

But the educator's role does not stop at this point. There are numerous other duties that will influence others' perceptions of the educator's effectiveness markedly. One of the most important duties is the physical organization of the classroom. The appearance of the classroom is extremely important to administrators, parents, and other teachers, particularly at the preschool and elementary levels. In particular, a teacher of severely handicapped students needs to figure out ways to make the room appear clean, banish unpleasant odors, arrange materials and equipment in ways that do not make the room seem cluttered, and arrange attractive bulletin board or room displays. Although these efforts take quite a bit of time, the results are worthwhile. Teachers working in facilities that serve both handicapped and nonhandicapped students will find that other students and teachers are more likely to drop in and interact with the handicapped students if the room is physically appealing.

A related duty is the repair or maintenance of adaptive equipment. In some schools this is handled by the therapists or the custodial staff, but often the teacher has to do it. Having good tools (hammer, screwdriver, pliers, drill, and socket set) can ease these responsibilities and ensure that the students will not be in danger from broken or outgrown equipment. Be sure to consult parents and therapists before making any equipment modifications. If there is a great deal of equipment building or rebuilding to be done, it is sometimes possible to make arrangements with an industrial arts teacher at the high school to have the high school students do the needed work; however, this must be arranged before the school year begins.

Another critical duty is the keeping of records, especially attendance records and report cards. Sloppiness in this area will make a negative impression on administrators.

Other duties that may be expected include attending PTA meetings; supervising students from other classrooms in the lunchroom, playground, or homeroom; and serving on school committees. Undertaking these duties willingly will help other teachers view you as a competent professional.

Parental Liaison

As was indicated in Chapter 8, a teacher of severely handicapped students is expected to interact extensively with the students' parents. Generally, the teacher is expected to meet with the parents at the beginning of school (particularly if the parents have not worked with the teacher before) to determine the family's educational priorities. It is expected also that the teacher will meet with the parents regularly to keep them updated on the child's progress in school. Such contacts are required of all teachers regardless of the population they teach. Teachers of severely handicapped students, however, often are expected to take on additional responsibilities in their role as school-parent liaison.

Training parents to use specific techniques with their children or to carry out certain educational programs is a responsibility that falls to the teacher in many school districts. This can take the form of formal classes for parents, inviting the parents to help in the classroom, regularly scheduled home visits, frequent telephone calls, or simply sending home instructional programs and requests for information. Formal parent training is more likely to be a part of the teacher's job in preschool and elementary settings than it is in junior high and high school settings. Informal training and information exchange, however, is expected in all settings.

The teacher usually is expected to invite the parents to become part of the assessment effort and to encourage their involvement in the IEP process and the planning of long-range goals for the child. This may involve sending home materials that the parents can fill out, telephone discussions, or face-to-face discussions. Basically, the teacher is expected to treat the parents' ideas and requests for information with tact and respect. It is important to remember that they probably have dealt with the child longer than any teacher and will have to continue to deal with him long after he has left a class. Thus, they generally know more about the child than the teacher does and also have more insight into what is needed by the family as a whole. It is critical not to shut off communication by ignoring parental input or requests.

But the most important duty the teacher has in the role of school-parent liaison is the ability to listen to the parent. Most parents of severely handicapped children feel isolated. They cannot brag about their child's accomplishments to the neighbors. They cannot freely express their frustration about the child's lack of progress to others. They desperately need to be able to talk to someone who knows and understands the child but who has a more objective outlook. Sometimes they just need to have someone listen. Often they need support for their own perceptions or proposed plans, and at times they need help in determining a plan of action. They may call on the teacher for help in any or all of these areas.

This does not mean that a teacher has to be at a parent's beck and call 24 hours a day or that the teacher should agree with parents who have markedly unrealistic views of their child's handicap. It simply means that the teacher needs to recognize that many parents need to feel free to discuss personal matters that are not connected directly with the child's education. Obviously, such discussions should be held in strictest confidence and should not become a part of the school records unless the parents agree.

Occasionally a teacher will encounter a parent who needs more support than the teacher can give. It would be appropriate to suggest counseling services to such parents. If they do not respond to such suggestions and continue to "harass" the teacher, it may be necessary to sever discussions of personal issues.

The teacher should be especially cautious when dealing with parents who are unhappy about another professional's handling of their child or parents who are involved in some type of dispute with the school district or the special education administrators. A teacher's job can be in jeopardy if administrators or other professionals feel that the teacher is being unprofessional in statements about the district or other professionals. Of course, teachers should not feel that they have to compromise their principles to avoid problems with the district if the issue is of great enough importance. Caution and documentation are advised in such situations, however.

Most parents expect that a teacher will keep them informed about any changes in the child's sleeping, eating, or toilet habits. They also need to know if a medication has not been given, if the child has had an epileptic seizure, and if any health or dental concerns have arisen. They should be informed if there are changes in the staffing of the classroom or major schedule changes since these factors may be reflected in the student's behavior at home.

Overall, the teacher's job as a liaison can be summed up in three words: Keep in touch.

Supervisor of Paraprofessionals

Most teachers of severely handicapped children will be assigned at least one aide or paraprofessional to help in the classroom. The types of jobs that can be assigned to this person differ from state to state. Therefore, the teacher should check with the district personnel office and the state department of education to determine exactly what duties can be assigned to paraprofessionals.

In most states paraprofessionals can be involved in preparation of materials, room maintenance, custodial tasks (such as toilet use and dressing children), supervision of mainstreaming efforts in which the special student spends part of the day in a less restrictive classroom or community setting, and conducting educational programs under the direct supervision of the teacher. In most states a paraprofessional cannot (1) be solely responsible for a classroom, (2) select assessments or interpret the results, (3) develop or conduct educational programs without supervision, or (4) be employed as a substitute teacher.

In general, newly hired paraprofessionals have had very little experience with disabled children. In addition, few have had formal training in how to teach. Often the new paraprofessional pities the children and finds it difficult to watch the child struggle to learn new tasks. Because the pay for paraprofessionals is usually low, people with poor work habits or little education may be the types who apply for such jobs. Thus, the teacher may need to spend a considerable amount of time teaching the paraprofessional.

It is best if such training occurs at the beginning of the school year. Unfortunately, most school districts do not provide ample time for such training. This means that the teacher must take time from the busy class schedule to train the paraprofessionals. Some teachers are able to do an excellent job at this; others are much less successful. Most teachers who do an excellent job confess that they sacrifice some student teaching time in the first 2 to 3 weeks of school in order to train their paraprofessionals. They feel that it is more effective to take the time to train and supervise the paraprofessionals adequately at the beginning of the year than to spend time throughout the year trying to break bad habits that have been established through lack of training.

Most paraprofessionals also seem to require a clear definition of what is expected of them and training in how to carry out these duties. They do not feel it is fair for the teacher to assign them students, give them a written program or data sheet, and simply expect them to begin. Failing to spend time teaching the paraprofessional how to conduct instructional programs properly can result in one of two bad situations. In one situation, the teacher feels that the untrained paraprofessional cannot be given the responsibility of conducting educational programs, and so the paraprofessional is expected to do most of the custodial and maintenance work. Some paraprofessionals are offended by this division of labor, feeling that they are being stuck with all the dirty work. In the other situation, the teacher divides educational and custodial tasks more equally, even though the paraprofessional has not been taught to conduct instructional sessions properly. This often results in poor teaching, which in turn results in the students failing to progress and increasing their behavioral problems. This combination usually makes the job very nonreinforcing to the paraprofessional, and problems such as absenteeism, negativism, and difficulty getting the paraprofessional to conduct the sessions begin to emerge.

Most teachers recognize the need for supervision and training of paraprofessionals but may not realize how many areas require training. For general purposes, a teacher should assume that a beginning paraprofessional will need training in the following areas:

1. Understanding exactly what the job is and how it relates to the jobs of their associates
2. Coping with negative emotions and stress
3. Listening and communicating effectively with other professionals and parents
4. Information about the students, particularly in the areas of epileptic seizures, cerebral palsy, and other types of physical disorders that may make them feel uncomfortable
5. Basic first-aid methods, as well as ways of dealing with life-threatening situations such as choking, status epilepticus, and severe bleeding
6. Techniques used to teach particular programs and control persistent behavior problems
7. Techniques for positioning and moving the physically handicapped person that ensure the well-being of both the student and the paraprofessional
8. Using audiovisual and office equipment

Although the personnel office should inform paraprofessionals of their professional responsibilities, the teacher also may wish to discuss such topics as (1) evaluations, (2) calling in if late or ill, (3) cooperating with other staff members, (4) conducting programs that have been assigned, (5) confidentiality of records, (6) absentee and tardiness policies, and (7) asking questions when instructions are not clear. It is far better to discuss these topics openly at the beginning of the year and to remind the paraprofessional of certain items periodically than to bring up these subjects only when a problem develops.

Although some paraprofessionals are well educated and can follow written instructions well, it is important to present most information verbally and to demonstrate or role-play desired teaching techniques. It is often a good idea to give paraprofessionals a short set of written instructions to help them recall what has been demonstrated or discussed, but this should not take the place of clear person-to-person instruction and supervision.

Three experienced teachers of severely handicapped students were asked to describe how they saw their roles in relation to the paraprofessionals. Their remarks are summarized below:

Teacher 1. My primary role is to provide a good model of work behavior and a positive attitude toward handicapped students. I need to teach the paraprofessionals how to run instructional programs properly and show them how to treat the kids gently and with dignity. Most of the time they need to be taught how to be positive with all the children—I guess this is what I work on first and spend most of my energy doing. I also try to change their perceptions of the handicapped person by showing them how to apply the golden rule and teaching them to observe the signs that show that these kids have feelings too. A secondary role I have is to be sure nobody, kid or paraprofessional, gets bored, because boredom means that they are not learning.

Teacher 2. I think the most important thing that should be done with paraprofessionals is to be sure that they really understand the characteristics and disabilities of the individual students under their care. Once they get to know the strengths and weaknesses of their students—you know, get to know them as people—then they are ready to learn to teach them. I also think it's essential to teach them emergency and safety procedures very early. I do this in person and also give them written instructions. The written instructions are important from a legal standpoint, so I make sure that I do both. I supervise this very closely. I also show them how to do the programs, observe them when I can, and answer questions at any time. If they have worked with this population before, I try to talk with them a little about a general philosophy that these kids can learn and are very worthwhile people—we talk about how the programs can help them be more independent, even if some of them will never be able to live or work in a nonsheltered environment.

Teacher 3. I think I usually try to teach them how to be a teacher. They need to be taught how to conduct behavior programs, because if they aren't, they'll get frustrated and use punishment. They also need to be taught how to communicate with the children and the other staff. They have to be told over and over that it is all right to ask questions. I try to teach them respect for the children, mostly through modeling and feedback. Lastly, I teach them how to help the children become more independent in self-help tasks; new paraprofessionals always seem to want to do things for the children rather than teach them how to do them by themselves.

All three teachers also mentioned the importance of allowing the paraprofessional some input into the classroom schedule. Some suggested ways of doing this were to (1) determine when they prefer to take their breaks and lunchtime, (2) try to schedule more sessions with their favorite student(s) than with less-preferred students, (3) give them responsibility for developing and conducting a weekly group activity such as an art project or a nature walk if they seem interested, and (4) consistently ask them how they think the individual programs are working and then use this feedback to improve the sessions.

Occasionally conflicts arise between the paraprofessionals and other staff members. Such conflicts can involve duties, absenteeism, poor work habits, or failure to follow instructions. When such conflicts occur, it is critical that the teacher sit down with the paraprofessional and discuss the problems. This is not a pleasant task, but it is part of the supervisory role. During this discussion the teacher should explain what the problem is and why it is a problem. The teacher should listen to the paraprofessional actively and responsively in order to determine his or her views on the subject. If there is room for negotiation, both parties should try to reach a compromise position that satisfies both. If there is no room for negotiation, the teacher should state exactly what changes are expected and explain to the paraprofessional that if such changes cannot be made or seem to be too demanding, both the teacher and the paraprofessional can meet with the appropriate administrator.

If the paraprofessional agrees to make changes but the changes are not made, another meeting should be held with the paraprofessional. This meeting should be documented and followed by a meeting of both parties with an administrator. Points that are of importance included the following:

1. Always talk to the paraprofessional before making complaints to administrators.
2. Talk to administrators with the paraprofessional present.
3. Keep written documentation of when meetings occur and what topics were discussed, especially if the problem has been discussed before.
4. Do not make negative comments about the paraprofessional to other staff members (even if they initially brought the problem to your attention).
5. Never involve the parents in this type of conflict.

In summary, the role of the supervisor involves telling paraprofessionals what is expected, teaching them how to meet these expectations, giving them feedback on their performance, and preventing or resolving conflicts between members of the staff.

Member of a Multidisciplinary Team

Almost every special education teacher works as part of a team of professionals from different disciplines. This team may be called multidisciplinary, interdisciplinary, or transdisciplinary. Regardless of the title, the purpose is the same: A team is established in order to provide the best overall education and habilitation programs for a particular child.

It is important that the teacher know the roles of each member of the team and know what services each can be expected to provide. Although team composition differs from district to district, the following professions are often part of the educational team.

Occupational Therapist. The occupational therapist traditionally is considered an expert in the area of fine motor skills and the skills of daily living. This team member can provide information about normal child development and adaptive or prosthetic devices that assist in the learning of such skills as self-feeding, hygiene, dressing, and toilet training. The pediatric occupational therapist provides expertise in the areas of abnormal reflex inhibition, sensory integration techniques, procedures for inhibiting abnormal reflexes and facilitating normal eating patterns, and the training of fine motor skills such as reach, grasp, release, and hand-to-hand transfer.

Physical Therapist. The physical therapist also deals primarily with the motor domain but usually has had more training in gross motor skills, mobility training, and regulation of posture. Thus, the physical therapist can provide information relating to proper ways to lift, carry, or position physically handicapped students as well as design and order adaptive equipment to prevent deformities and improve the student's ability to move around in the environment. This expert can provide direct training to the student and staff in the correct use of adaptive equipment such as scooter boards, canes, walkers, wheelchairs, prone boards, and standing tables.

Speech and Language Therapist. The language therapist can provide valuable information related to normal and abnormal language development, the interplay between receptive and expressive communication, and alternative communication systems for students whose oral language capacity is severely limited. This therapist can help design communication boards and choose words or sounds appropriate for a particular student's ability. In addition, this expert can provide services directly to the student in the areas of articulation, vocabulary expansion, prelanguage activities and stimulation, oral-motor exercises, and correct use of adaptive aids such as communication boards. The teacher should be aware, however, that only in the past 5 years have speech and language therapists been trained to deal with severely handicapped students who function at the presymbolic level. For this reason, most therapists currently in the field are still in the process of learning, primarily though trial and error, which techniques will work with these students.

Psychologist. The school psychologist usually can provide a great deal of information related to normal child development and assessments that are available to measure intellectual functioning and adaptive behavior. The psychologist can be a big help when changes in placement are being considered or in developing an educational program designed to move the student to a less restrictive environment. This expert also can provide information about and training in how to work with a student who exhibits a great degree of maladaptive behavior. The teacher should not necessarily expect the psychologist to provide direct services in areas other than assessment. In most districts a psychologist provides consultation and follow-up in the area of behavior management rather than direct services. The psychologist also may help with the environmental inventory, work with certain families (especially those in need of support and counseling), and help plan for instruction in the various social skills needed for community competence.

Nurse. The school nurse usually is included in the educational team. This professional can give the staff information related to the student's diagnosis, the types of medication the student is receiving, how to handle emergencies, nutrition, recognition of child abuse or neglect, and management of epileptic seizures. The school nurse often can arrange for staff training in cardiopulmonary resuscitation (CPR) and the Heimlich technique. If the student has special medical equipment, such as an ostomy bag, the nurse can train staff members in maintaining such equipment properly and recognizing emergency situations. If the student needs special medical services such as tube feeding, the nurse should determine whether such services can be carried out legally by classroom personnel. If not, the nurse probably will have to provide these services. The nurse also may have valuable insights into toilet-training programs. In addition, the nurse can provide services designed to reduce the risk of health problems in both staff and students, detect the onset of health problems, and help determine when a child needs to be sent home because of illness.

Other Educational Specialists. Other educational specialists, such as music educators, adaptive physical education teachers, and teachers of visually and hearing impaired students, may be included in a team. Some of these, such as the adaptive physical education teacher, may provide direct services to the students on a regular basis. Others, such as a teacher for hearing-impaired students, may be able to give the teacher helpful hints in dealing with a severely handicapped student who has a hearing impairment.

Audiologist. The audiologist usually is included in the team whenever the child has a suspected or identified hearing loss. In addition to testing the student to identify a hearing loss and then measuring the degree of that loss, the audiologist also can provide guidelines on equipment and procedures that may help the student compensate for this loss. This expert can provide information on the care, testing, and maintenance of hearing aids. Before a student with severe handicaps can be tested by an audiologist, it may be necessary to teach that student to make some kind of consistent response to sounds. Usually the audiologist will request that the educational staff provide this training. The audiologist should show the teacher exactly what is required and suggest methods that have been used successfully in the past.

Administrator. The administrator should be looked upon as an important part of the team. This specialist helps ensure smooth transitions as the student moves from level to level (e.g., elementary to middle school) and from teacher to teacher. The administrator also can provide input related to provision of equipment, transportation, and needed services. The better informed the administrator is about the needs of the students and the program being provided, the more likely the administrator is to make correct judgments and decisions about the program as a whole. Even if the administrator cannot arrange for the district to provide needed services during the current school year, it may be possible to set the wheels in motion so that such services will be available the following year.

Parents. The parents are an integral part of every team. They need to know exactly which services will be provided and the details of how each service will be provided. From this information they will be able to provide a continuum of services from the school to the home. They also can provide information related to the child's medical and educational history as well as a description of whether proposed programs or adaptive aids will fit into the family constellation.

Lyon and Lyon (1981) have pointed out that members of a team can serve in a number of roles, including (1) providing information, (2) training other staff and parents, (3) assessing the student, (4) providing consultation and follow-up, (5) observing and evaluating instructional programs, and (6) providing services directly to the student. The role(s) chosen by a particular team member will be based on the team member's expertise with that type of problem, the needs of the child, the team member's schedule and other responsibilities, and the perception the team member has of the competence and desires of the other team members.

Generally, problems with other team members come from one of three sources. One type of problem occurs when a teacher believes that a student needs more intensive services than the other team member has decided to provide. For example, the teacher may feel that a particular student needs direct occupational therapy services, whereas the therapist has elected to provide assessment and consultation to the teacher. This type of problem requires delicate handling because the team professional may feel that the teacher is questioning his or her professional judgment. Skills in listening and negotiating combined with a clear focus on how to serve the student best are needed when this type of problem comes up. Furthermore, the teacher must realize that most ancillary personnel, such as therapists, usually are scheduled to serve far more students than they can see in individual sessions. Sometimes consultation is all that can be given unless their case load is lightened. Changes in case load can be made only through the administration.

A second problem occurs when some of the team members are not providing the services they have agreed to provide. For example, a music therapist may be meeting with the students only once a week instead of twice a week as was agreed in an earlier meeting. If this occurs, it is important for the teacher to speak directly with the person who is supposed to be providing the service and try to ascertain why there has been a change. If the problem cannot be resolved to both parties' satisfaction, both the teacher and the other professional must meet together with an administrator to determine exactly what to do. Again, conscientious attempts to negotiate may be required in order to resolve the problem without antagonizing the other professional.

The third problem occurs as a result of poor communication or follow-up. It is important to talk with all the other team members when making any major changes in a student's educational program. It is also considered highly unprofessional to alter another team member's prescribed instructional program without consulting that team member. Failure to discuss proposed changes with other team members will cause dissension and distrust among the team members that eventually will be detrimental to the student's education.

The teacher's role on the team is usually one of educational synthesizer (Bricker 1976). The teacher must discover what each of the other professionals feels the student needs and find a way to meet those needs. Sometimes this entails adjusting the student's schedule so that each professional who desires to do so has the opportunity to work directly with the student. Sometimes it involves learning new skills and having the appropriate professional observe and give feedback as the new skills are applied. At other times it requires information exchange in which the teacher informally discusses the student's progress or lack of progress with the appropriate professional and asks for suggestions.

Because the teacher usually plays the role of educational synthesizer, the teacher often assumes the role of team leader. This means that the teacher is expected to inform the team members of changes in the student's program and arrange meetings among the team members. The teacher also is expected to inform all team members when it is time to assess a student and when an IEP meeting is scheduled. Since most of the people on the team tend to be very busy, it is sometimes quite time-consuming to try to arrange team meetings. It is imperative that such meetings be conducted efficiently and effectively. Also, although the teacher usually is given the apparent leadership function of the team, this does not necessarily mean the teacher has the final say when conflicts arise. For example, in regard to a student who has a severe health disorder, if a conflict arose between the student's educational needs and medical needs, the team might decide to give the school nurse's input priority over the teacher's. Thus, the school nurse might decide that the student needed an afternoon nap more than a particular educational program. Frank discussion and negotiation are far more productive than power struggles in such situations.

In summary, the teacher serves both as a team member and as the coordinator of the team. The skills required are diplomacy and tact as well as the ability to listen carefully and negotiate solutions to problems. A well-run team will make great contributions to a child's education, but a poorly run team can be worse than no team at all.

Advocate for Persons with Severe Handicaps

The teacher of severely handicapped students is expected to serve as an advocate both for the students in the classroom and for the severely handicapped population as a whole.

Gardner (1979) stated that "an advocate is a person who pleads a cause, and acts at all times to promote or maintain that cause as if it were his or her own." Advocates for developmentally disabled individuals generally work in accordance with the following principles:

1. Each person has value, no matter what his or her handicap.
2. Each person is capable of growth or learning regardless of the severity of his or her handicap.
3. Insofar as possible, each person should be given the opportunity to partake of the same experiences and to live and function in the same environment(s) that he or she would if he or she were not handicapped.
4. The consumer of services (in this case, the handicapped person) knows his or her needs best and should be involved to the maximum extent possible in the determination of what and how such services will be offered.
5. Handicapped individuals are citizens and have the same rights and responsibilities as any other citizen of the same age. Any restriction on these rights or responsibilities must come under very close scrutiny.

A teacher's advocacy effort can be conceived of as occurring on three levels: (1) personal, (2) schoolwide, and (3) communitywide.

The Personal Level. Teachers must make every effort to treat their students with dignity and respect. They must make efforts to keep up with new developments in the field in order to provide the best education possible. Most personal advocacy efforts, however, are made internally. These involve examining one's assumptions and beliefs to see whether they are consistent with the role of an educator of persons with severe handicaps. It may be necessary to confront one's beliefs about exactly what constitutes a "worthwhile" life and what contributions intellect makes to being "human." It may be necessary to reassess one's religious and moral stances periodically in regard to such issues as euthanasia, abortion, amniocentesis, surgery in utero, and gene manipulation. A careful study of issues and problems related to aversive treatments, drug therapies, and surgeries used to control unacceptable behavior is pertinent. Personal decisions about institutionalization versus deinstitutionalization and sheltered versus competitive work placements will have to be made. Only when a teacher has agonized over these and similar issues can he or she claim to be an advocate.

The School Level. To function as an advocate on the school level, the teacher must be clearly informed about the laws that protect the rights of handicapped children and their parents. Two federal laws that have strengthened the rights of handicapped children are Public Law 94-142, the Education for All Handicapped Children Act of 1975, and section 504 of Public Law 93-112, the Rehabilitation Act of 1973.

Public Law 94-142 was passed by Congress to ensure that all children, regardless of handicapping condition, have available a free, appropriate public education. In simple terms, the law entitles the handicapped child to the following (Michaelis, 1980):

1. All children ages 6 to 17 are entitled to go to a public school free of charge. If the state provides free public education to children under the age of 6 (e.g., kindergarten) or over 17, this also must be provided for handicapped children.
2. As far as possible, a handicapped child should be educated in a school close to home with nonhandicapped children of the same age (least restrictive alternative).
3. If the child's handicaps are such that the child will need extra help in order to learn, the school should arrange for the child to have that help (special education and related services).
4. Before arranging such help, however, the school must discuss with the parents the types of help that are available and the methods that can be used to determine what type of help would be most suitable (notice of intent to evaluate and provide special services).
5. The parents must agree with the school on the methods to be used to determine the type of help provided, and the results of these evaluations must be discussed with them (consent to evaluate and parent understanding of evaluation).
6. After the parents and the school have finished the evaluation, they should plan together what services will be provided and exactly what will be taught to the child (IEP meeting).
7. The school must provide the parents with documentation of how well the child is learning the skills discussed at the IEP meeting (review of IEP).
8. Any time the IEP does not seem to be working, the parents and the school should get together and formulate a new plan (voluntary amendments of the IEP).
9. If the school and the parents are unable to come up with a mutually agreeable plan at any time (during the evaluation process, the placement process, the IEP meeting, or the IEP amendments), another person or agency with no personal or professional interest in the child can be called in to help determine what is in the best interest of the child. (due process hearing).
10. All the records and reports that the school writes about the child are for the parent to read. If the parent does not agree with the information in these records, the parent has the right to place a written disagreement

in those records. Permission must be granted by the parent for anyone else to read the school records. (free access to records and confidentiality).

Section 504 of P.L. 93-112 was enacted to ensure that "no otherwise qualified handicapped individual in the United States shall, solely by reason of his handicap, be excluded from participation in, denied the benefits of, or be subjected to discrimination under any program or activity receiving federal financial assistance." This law allows a handicapped person to participate in vocational rehabilitation services, live in federally subsidized housing, and enter into many competitive jobs. It also spells out several provisions related to preschool, elementary, and secondary education that are very similar to those in P.L. 94-142. This law is probably of more interest to people serving the adolescent or adult population than to people serving preschoolers or elementary students.

Another step a teacher can take to be an advocate at the school level is to become informed about child abuse and neglect. A handicapped child is often at greater risk for abuse or neglect than a nonhandicapped child (Howell, 1977; Kline, 1977) since such a child places extra stress on a family. The teacher and paraprofessionals are in a position to observe the health and behavior of their students on a daily basis and thus may be the first to suspect child abuse or neglect. Some indicators that a child may be in need of protection from the family include the following (Halperin, 1979; National Center on Child Abuse and Neglect, 1975):

1. Frequent injuries such as welts, cuts, burns, more than one broken bone, or strap marks
2. Injuries in different places on the body
3. A combination of fresh and healing injuries on the same area of the body
4. Reluctance to leave school
5. Frequent and severe mood shifts
6. Constant fatigue
7. Fearfulness of adults or persons of one sex
8. Begging and stealing food
9. Untreated injuries
10. Improper clothing for weather conditions
11. Extremes of emotion such as aggression, passivity, or need for affection
12. Frequent tardiness or absenteeism
13. Frequent crying or other annoying vocalizations

None of these signs is an absolute indicator of abuse, especially in children with severe handicaps, since such children are more prone to injury resulting from motor and cognitive problems. Nonetheless, teachers should keep the possibility of abuse and neglect in mind as they observe their students. If there is any indication that the child's injuries, malnutrition, or behavior could be due to improper care or actual abuse, the school nurse should be informed and asked to observe the injuries or behaviors. Written documentation of injuries or improper care (e.g., coming to school without a coat when it is snowing) should be kept by both the teacher and the nurse. It is important that such documentation include the date of observation, the signature of those persons who observed the injury or behavior, and a clear description of what was observed. Descriptions of injuries should include the location on the body, the approximate size (measure if at all possible), the type of injury (e.g., bruise or cut), and whether the injury appears to be new or old. Photographs of the injuries sometimes are needed to document abuse. Descriptions of behavior should include the setting and a narrative of exactly what occurred and how it was handled.

It should be noted that forty-three of the fifty-four states and territories of the United States require educators to report suspected child abuse and neglect (Council for Exceptional Children, 1979). Since the policies and procedures for doing this, as well as the penalties for not reporting, differ from state to state, it is important that teachers contact the state maternal and child welfare office to determine exactly how to proceed. It is best to do this at the beginning of the school year rather than wait until abuse is suspected. This way, the teacher will not need to wait for this information at the critical time. Some school districts, primarily large ones, have established clear procedures for reporting suspected abuse or neglect. Before doing any other type of report, be sure that such procedures are followed.

Every state that requires reporting of child abuse also provides legal protection for the person who does the reporting. This usually includes freedom from being sued for libel, slander, or invasion of privacy.

Lehr (1982) has pointed out the fact that teachers of severely handicapped children also can help prevent abuse of their students. This can be done through maintaining contact with the parents, providing support in accepting the child's handicap, developing realistic expectations for the child, obtaining respite care, obtaining financial assistance, and helping the child learn skills that will make him or her easier to care for.

The teacher also should know where the family can obtain help if they seem to be in a particularly stressful situation. Names and addresses of people who can provide respite care and of groups such as Parents Anonymous that provide direct counseling for parents who are abusive or are afraid they may become abusive should be given to every parent.

Yet another way to serve as an advocate on the school level is to arrange ways for nonhandicapped students and staff members to learn about your students. This can be done formally by devising specific teaching units for other classes. If a teacher does not have the time to teach such a unit, perhaps a parent can do it. If this is not possible, arrangements may be made to have a student or professor from the special education department at a nearby university do it. Less formal but equally effective is the technique of arranging opportunities for handicapped and nonhandicapped students to work and play together. This can be done by keeping the students together during music, art, physical education, some field trips, recess, and lunch. Students also can spend time in one another's classrooms. The teacher should be aware, however, that mere proximity will not overcome nonhandicapped children's prejudices and fears. The teacher will have to be alert to point out similarities between the students and give the nonhandicapped students the facts they need to know in order to interact effectively with the special students.

Information provided to the other teachers is equally important. They need to know what types of skills are being taught and why these are valuable. They may feel jealous of a teacher who has such a small class and a paraprofessional while they struggle to get the job done alone with many more students. They may question overtly or covertly whether such students belong in a school setting and may wonder why such children are not institutionalized. They often are not aware that some of these students have the potential for competitive employment and community living. Such information can be disseminated without fanfare during conversations in the teachers' lounge or before and after school.

It is important to realize that serving as an advocate at the school level can be a very subtle process. In essence, the teacher's every action may serve as a model for others to copy. Therefore, it is of the utmost importance for a teacher to provide an exemplary model of how one interacts with persons who have severe disabilities. This would include such things as not talking about the children in their presence as if they were not there and not moving or repositioning the students without telling them what is going to happen or where they are going to be taken. It also would include allowing them to make choices insofar as they are able and talking to the children about events or persons in their environments that would be of interest to any child.

The Community Level. Advocacy on the community or national level can take many forms. Some teachers do not want to get involved in community advocacy activities because they can be quite time-consuming. Others feel that such activities are perhaps even more important in the long run than what takes place in the classroom. One form of community advocacy involves arranging opportunities for one's handicapped students to participate in community activities enjoyed by other children of the same age. For example, the teacher may arrange regular trips to a fast-food restaurant where the students can practice ordering food, paying for food, and several self-care skills. Such trips serve to educate not only the handicapped students but also the general public and those persons (e.g., waiters and waitresses) who need to learn how to interact with persons who may be using alternative language systems.

In planning such activities, it is important to keep the aspect of community education in mind. Giving some advance notice of what to expect from your students and arranging practice opportunities so that they are brief and do not occur at the busiest time of the day also will help make such encounters instructive rather than aversive to the people serving the students. In addition to community activities, the teacher of adolescents may need to talk with business leaders and try to locate community-based job-training sites. If such sites are located, the teacher has a commitment to see that they are used in a way that will encourage continued participation and support. This may entail sending a paraprofessional or training a volunteer to go with the students and help them fit smoothly into the routine. Obviously, the arrangements for community activities or community job training are time-consuming and usually must be done after school.

Another way to approach community advocacy is to serve as a citizen advocate for a handicapped individual (usually this individual will not be a student in the classroom). According to Gardner (1979), citizen advocacy involves a one-to-one relationship between a person who volunteers to be an advocate and a person who needs an advocate (known as the protégé). A citizen advocate can serve as a friend, providing companionship, social interaction, and emotional support. A citizen advocate sometimes takes on the role of unpaid teacher or counselor for a specific individual. Most citizen advocates provide some transportation for the protége; many also take legal action on behalf of the protégé. Such advocacy efforts can be undertaken on one's own or under the auspices of a group such as the Council for Exceptional Children.

A third type of community advocacy entails involvement in the local and national political scene. As a first step, a teacher should stay informed of legislation that pertains to the education, vocational status, financial benefits, or living arrangements for people with disabilities. In some cases the teacher may wish to contact legislators or other politicians to discuss proposed legislation. The teacher may want to circulate petitions or literature to other school personnel or within the neighborhood. Sometimes teachers are asked to testify in court cases involving the educational rights of students with severe handicaps. Some teachers become quite active in coalitions or advocacy groups that strive to obtain services such as respite care and group homes.

Many parents expect that their child's teacher will be involved in some political activity related to rights for handicapped persons. However, if a teacher works for a state agency rather than a local school district, there may be difficulties involved in serving as a political advocate. In order to avoid conflict of interest situations (a potential legal problem), most state agencies put limits on when and how a state employee may lobby or engage in other political activity. Some school districts also get nervous if a teacher becomes overtly active in the political scene. Be aware of these pitfalls and try to ascertain the agency's rules ahead of time.

In summary, the teacher's role as an advocate involves trying to obtain optimal services and opportunities for persons with severe handicaps. This can be done within the classroom, within the school, and within the community. It primarily entails educating others, giving them the opportunity to become comfortable around persons with handicaps, and arranging ways for handicapped and nonhandicapped individuals to work and play together.

Key Skills

It should be obvious from our discussion that a teacher needs to develop a wide variety of skills in order to fulfill a multiplicity of role demands. There are, however, certain skills that are needed in several roles. These skills relate to getting people to work together effectively. Three such skills that seem vital to teachers are (1) being able to listen attentively and responsively, (2) being able to conduct meetings efficiently and effectively, and (3) knowing how to negotiate.

Attentive and Responsive Listening

One of the most important skills a teacher can have is the ability to listen. Listening actively allows a person to respond to others in a supportive and nonjudgmental way. It can keep a person out of trouble with those in authority. It can allow one to sense when problems are emerging, enabling one to work on solving them before they become insurmountable. Active and responsive listening is a tool that sets the stage for cooperation and teamwork by letting all members of the team (parent, paraprofessional, ancillary staff, teacher, and administrator) know that their ideas have been heard accurately and that their views are understood and valued.

Probably no interpersonal skill is more needed and less practiced by teachers and other professionals than active listening. This is the case because most people assume that listening is automatic and never give much thought to it being a skill that needs to be practiced and learned. Active listening differs from simply hearing and is far more demanding and difficult. As John DiGaetani (1980, p. 40) explains:

> One reason [listening is difficult] is that people are usually absorbed in their own lives and activities and really listening to someone else becomes boring and painful for them. Only when the other person is through and we can start talking do most of us enjoy the conversation.

Another factor that makes listening difficult is the discrepancy between the rate at which the brain can process speech (about 800 words per minute) and the rate at which most people talk (about 200 words per minute). It is very easy to fill in the spaces by thinking about other things instead of concentrating on what the other person has to say.

But what is active listening? *Active listening* is a term coined by Carl Rogers (1970) to describe a type of listening in which the listener has definite responsibilities. The listener does not "half listen" but concentrates on what the speaker is saying and tries to understand what the speaker is feeling. In other words, the listener is not passive but actively tries to hear the facts and understand the way the other person feels about these facts.

Active listening does not imply that the listener should only listen, nor does it mean that the listener has to agree with the speaker. It simply means that the listener works to try to understand exactly what the speaker is trying to communicate. Thus, active listening requires a number of skills: concentration (the ability to focus the brain's attention), a desire to understand the other person's point of view, an awareness of what is meant as distinguished from what is being said, and judgment about how to act on this information (DiGaetani 1980).

But active listening is not enough. It is equally important that the listener demonstrate unequivocally that the speaker's point of view has been heard and understood. This is called *responsive listening* because the listener makes responses that demonstrate that he or she has heard the content and understood the feelings behind the content.

Some Guidelines. How does a person become an active and responsive listener? There is no magic formula, but several guidelines have been proposed by experts in interpersonal communication (DiGaetani, 1980; Fuller, 1983; Rogers, 1970). These include the following:

1. *Try to generate a genuine interest in what the other person has to say.* Remind yourself that this person would not be talking to you unless he felt that the information he was giving was important. As you listen, try to determine why the things he is saying are important to him.
2. *Give the person nonverbal cues that you are listening and interested.* Sitting down, looking at the speaker, and leaning slightly toward the speaker are nonverbal cues that signal attention and interest.
3. *Use paraphrasing occasionally to ensure that you are hearing what the speaker actually intends. Paraphrasing* is defined as rewording what has been said before. In active and responsive listening, paraphrasing is done in order to give the speaker a chance to see whether she is communicating what she wanted to communicate. The emphasis is on letting the speaker ascertain what her statements meant to you, the listener. Therefore, a paraphrase not only should restate what the speaker said but also should indicate what it meant to you. For example, if a paraprofessional says to you, "I just can't stand Johnny's drooling anymore," you might paraphrase this by saying, "Apparently Johnny's drooling program isn't working?" Then if the paraprofessional was concerned not about the drooling program but about some other aspect of Johnny's drooling, it would be easy for the paraprofessional to make a clarifying statement such

as, "It's not the program that I'm worried about. It's probably working, but he's ruining the materials, and I have to remake the communication cards every day." This clarification would allow the listener to make the necessary adjustments in his perception of the problem.

4. *Listen to the content but also try to ascertain the speaker's feelings about the content.* As you listen to what the person is saying, look at the speaker's body language. Try to determine how that person feels about what is being said by attending to facial expressions, gestures, and posture. A paraprofessional who says, "I just can't tolerate Johnny's drooling anymore" while slumping in his seat and wringing his hands is giving a somewhat different message than one who says the same thing but accompanies the verbal message with an aggressive posture and clenched fists. The listener also must be sensitive to the way the speaker words things. For example, a person who says, "I've finished graphing Esme's data," is probably informing you simply that the assigned work is done and that the person is ready for another job. But the person who says, "I've finally finished graphing Esme's data," is providing information about his feelings about that task. Sensitivity to the feeling component of communications is a very difficult task but generally will improve with practice.
5. *Try to identify "trigger" phrases or attitudes that cause you to stop listening and react instead.* Every person considers certain ideas, concepts, or words totally unacceptable. A speaker who uses such words or defends such ideas generally will be tuned out. This reaction is almost reflexive in most adults. A good listener tries to be aware of his or her own triggers and makes a special effort to listen actively in spite of a gut-level reaction. Again, active and responsive listening does not imply that one accepts what the other person is saying. Instead, it is a way of getting the maximum amount of information from other people. Being able to listen instead of react when emotionally laden issues are being discussed is critical if one wishes to be a successful advocate for students.
6. *Learn to listen to differing views and statements without trying to change the speaker's attitude or mind.* Generally, when a speaker expresses a view that is different from the one held by the listener, the listener begins formulating arguments that can be used later in the conversation to convince the speaker that such views are totally erroneous. Unfortunately, while this internal fact gathering is going on, the listener stops listening. Thus, the listener loses the opportunity to learn the reasons and facts that have influenced the speaker to take his or her position. Similarly, when the speaker tells you of a problem he or she is facing, the general reaction is to begin trying to solve the problem for that person. Sometimes this is perfectly legitimate, but if the listener stops listening in order to brainstorm, active listening is not occurring. Many people can solve their own

problems simply by having a noncritical listener who uses good questioning techniques, paraphrasing, and perception checks well. But if the person needs help solving the problem, it is likely that advice will be more useful and pertinent if the listener has listened actively and has an accurate perception of exactly what the problem is and how the speaker feels about it.

Conducting Meetings

A teacher often finds it necessary to meet with paraprofessionals in order to determine how well students are progressing on certain instructional programs and to communicate changes in programs and duties. The teacher often will find it necessary to attend or hold team meetings with therapists, social workers, and a variety of other professionals. As noted in Chapter 8, the teacher also will meet several times each year with every student's parents. It is a general rule that most meetings teachers have with others have to be conducted within a fairly short time period. This is the case because school days are organized around the actual teaching of students, and very little time is allotted for preparation or consultation. Because of this, meetings must be conducted efficiently if the necessary information is to be gathered and imparted. Of course, the teacher must be sensitive to the feelings of the other participants and make sure that each feels that there has been an ample opportunity to communicate relevant information and to fully understand (and in some cases differ from) any decisions that were made. It can be difficult to be both efficient and sensitive during meetings. Businesspeople have realized this for many years, and business journals are filled with articles outlining methods for conducting effective meetings. Although educational meetings may not need to be quite as organized as business meetings, much of the information in these articles can be quite useful.

Steps to Improve Meetings. Some of the steps that have been described (Bradford, 1978; Hengel, 1979; Raudsepp, 1983) as important in improving meetings include the following:

1. *Plan an agenda.* Before calling a meeting, it is crucial to determine exactly what will be discussed. It is particularly important to determine for each item on the agenda whether it is (a) information that needs to be disseminated, (b) a problem that needs to be solved, (c) a decision that needs to be reached, or (d) a plan that needs to be made. Each of these requires a different type of group process. Time can be saved if it is made clear, either in the agenda or as each item is introduced, whether listening, problem solving, decision making, or planning is desired.
2. *Schedule the meeting in a conducive atmosphere.* Try to have the meeting in a room where everyone can see easily without discomfort. If you

expect disagreement between certain participants, try not to seat them across from each other (adversarial positions). Instead, arrange the seats so that they must sit on the same side of the table or all face a chalkboard on which the problem(s) can be written. Try to pick a room with a comfortable temperature and adequate lighting. Shut the doors if there is any chance that there will be distracting noises or interruptions.

3. *Be sure the right people are there.* Although it is sometimes impossible to get everyone to a meeting who needs to be there, do not hold a meeting unless the critical personnel are there. If a problem is being discussed, critical personnel are those people who are directly involved in the problem. If a decision must be made, critical people are those whom a decision will affect. If a plan must be formulated, be sure the people who must carry out the plan are present. Although it may seem simpler to invite everyone to a meeting, it has been found that small groups (eight or fewer people) are more efficient and effective.
4. *Facilitate rather than dominate.* Group leaders should be careful not to make long-winded presentations, especially at the beginning of a meeting. A careful description of what needs to be done and a short summary of the known facts that must be considered is generally adequate. From that point on, the leader's job is primarily to clarify any points that have been made by other members of the group. Obviously, there are some exceptions to this rule. If a meeting has been called to impart certain information, such as changes in a student's schedule, the leader will be expected simply to give that information and answer questions.
5. *Avoid behaviors that impair communication.* It is particularly important for a group leader to be aware of and avoid behaviors that provoke hostility or defensive communication in others. This is particularly true when the participants in the meeting have very different views on the item being discussed. Faules and Alexander (1978, p. 111) have described eight behaviors that impair communication: (a) labeling other people or calling them names, (b) interrupting others as they are about to make a point, (c) anticipating an argument with a counterargument, (d) implying an ulterior motive, (e) contradicting others, (f) listening with an air of incredulity, (g) using laughter to derogate ideas, and (h) conveying a mood of dismissal.
6. *Summarize the main points.* At the end of the meeting, the leader should take the time to summarize the decisions that were reached, who has agreed to do what, and what follow-up will be needed. Such a summary will give all participants a sense of accomplishment and will end the meeting on a positive note.

Teachers desiring more information on the art of conducting meetings are referred to business journals such as *Training, Supervision, and Supervisory Management.*

Negotiating

A third skill that is often useful to the teacher of severely handicapped persons is the ability to negotiate successfully. It is often necessary to negotiate with administrative personnel in order to obtain needed supplies or building modifications or to make changes in the general curriculum (e.g., adding more community-based training). It is sometimes necessary to negotiate with parents whose views of their child's needs or potential may differ greatly from your own. Furthermore, negotiation is a critical skill if you are to be an effective advocate for your students on the community and political fronts.

There are many books available that purport to teach negotiating skills, for example, *You Can Negotiate Anything* (Cohen, 1983), *Power Negotiating* (Ilich, 1980), *The Negotiating Game: How to Get What You Want* (Karras, 1970), *The Art of Negotiating* (Nierenberg, 1981), and *Negotiate Your Way to Success* (Seltz and Modica, 1981). Although each of these is potentially valuable to a businessperson or a person in a position of authority, it is important for the teacher to remember that there are certain critical differences between education and business. Books advocating a hard-line approach are likely to be counterproductive for the teacher, particularly when dealing with administrators or parents. Manuals that advocate a less aggressive approach contain information and suggestions that can be quite beneficial in helping the teacher attain his goals without antagonizing others.

One manual that several educators have found useful is Roger Fisher and William Ury's *Getting to Yes: Negotiating Agreement Without Giving In* (1983). These authors use a technique they call *principled negotiation* that essentially consists of four basic components:*

1. The participants must come to see themselves as working together to attack a common problem rather than attacking one another.
2. The participants must endeavor to find out the other side's needs, desires, concerns, and fears (in relation to the problem) as well as effectively articulate their own. This will allow both sides to begin a problem-solving venture rather than simply stating and holding to a hard-line position.
3. The participants then need to brainstorm and come up with several options, particularly trying to find some that will result in mutual gain (i.e., satisfaction of at least some of the interests of both sides).
4. The participants must mutually decide on some objective criteria, such

* Roger Fisher and William Ury, *Getting to Yes: Negotiating Agreement Without Giving In* (New York: Penguin Books, 1983). Copyright © 1981 by Roger Fisher and William Ury. Used by permission of Houghton Mifflin Company.

as professional standards, moral standards, equal treatment, cost, tradition, or efficiency, on which the final decision will be based.

However, simply reading about negotiation techniques will not make a teacher a good negotiator. Good negotiation skills, like most interpersonal skills, must be learned through practice. In addition, successful negotiation may depend on how well you have fulfilled your many roles. You will be negotiating from a more powerful position if the other party sees you as a competent professional.

Summary

Overall, the teacher of severely handicapped individuals has an extremely challenging set of roles. An honest attempt to meet the expectations of these roles will make the job more stimulating, fulfilling, and interesting. The teacher may emphasize certain roles more than others. Most teachers enter the educational field because of their delight and fulfillment in interacting with students. The professional teacher, though, must play multiple roles in addition to being a direct instructor of students. These roles include being an educator, an advocate, a parental liaison, and a supervisor of paraprofessionals. In addition, the teacher is part of an educational team. The teacher should be familiar with the roles of other members of the team such as physical therapists, nurses, and administrators. The teacher often must take a leadership or synthesizing role in coordinating the efforts of the educational team. In order to participate effectively in multidisciplinary and other group activities, it is important to display a number of human relations skills. The teacher can learn to be an attentive and responsive listener and an effective negotiator. A teacher's ability to participate in and provide leadership in decision-making groups ultimately should lead to a superior quality of education for students with severe handicaps.

Chapter 10

Past, Present, and Future Directions

Dolores Jenkin

In this last chapter we shall tie together developments in the education of students with severe handicaps. We shall summarize past trends, current model demonstration efforts, and future directions. Additionally, a review of selected research about persons with severe handicaps will be included.

Past History

It is not an understatement to say that the education of students with severe handicaps has come a long way. Not too long ago (and unfortunately in isolated cases to this day) it was the practice to sequester a severely impaired child in the confines of a home, a room, or even a closet. Society had no expectations that the disabled individual could amount to anything, and in some cultures it was believed that the disabled individual was diseased or had satanic qualities. In some cases this led to euthanasia, abandonment, or ostracism. At best, the severely impaired individual was relegated to a deviant status and was not included in the mainstream of society's activities (see Wolfensberger [1972] for an expanded discussion of the history of treatment of disabled individuals).

From this benign neglect or malevolent treatment of disabled persons, an awareness eventually developed in the nineteenth and twentieth centuries of the need to improve the treatment of mentally and emotionally impaired persons. As was stated in Chapter 7, this concern typically was translated into the creation of institutional enclaves where supposedly best-care practices could be provided by teams of professional specialists. With the onset of the 1950s and 1960s, many professionals, parents, and consumers questioned the benefits of such cloistered treatment facilities. The deinstitutionalization movement originating in the mental health field gained momentum, and many disabled individuals were moved to community-based treatment facilities, e.g., group homes, foster care, and consumer-run apartments.

Normalization

The philosophy of *normalization* of human services argued that in the vast majority of cases the most effective treatment program could be provided in circumstances that best approximated natural living, work, and leisure environments. Thus, the notion of the *least restrictive environment* emerged, which stated that the individual should be placed in settings in which he or she was capable of functioning most independently. For example, in the residential sector some persons, because of their physical or behavioral disabilities, may require constant 24-hour supervision in a group home. Other individuals may require more intermittent supervision in a board and care home for disabled individuals. Others may function more independently in their own homes with only occasional monitoring from social service workers. When a placement decision is being made, the least restrictive principle dictates that the individual reside in the type of environment in which he is capable of the most independent functioning. Some people cannot live in an unsupervised apartment but can succeed in a board and care residence. For such an individual, a 24-hour supervised group home would be too restrictive, and an unsupervised apartment would be inappropriate because of its lack of proper monitoring. It is hoped that over time and with programming that facilitates greater independence, the consumer can progress to a residence that allows for more freedom.

Mainstreaming

Interestingly, a similar, parallel movement developed in special education, where the notion of *mainstreaming* became the key term to describe normalized, least restrictive programming. In contrast to residential programming, though, educational services did not start from the position that the disabled person was already receiving an education. In residential services the person was being cared for in a facility, whether a state hospital, a nursing home, or a group home. The issue was one of finding the best setting to serve the individual.

In the educational sector the first issue was that many disabled persons were not receiving any educational program. Public school districts assumed that children with severe handicaps were too disabled to benefit from an educational program. Thus, severely disabled children were excluded from a free public education. Parents were left with the choice of keeping their children at home, sending them off to an institution, or paying the tuition for a private school program. In the latter case many private, parent organizations such as the Association for Retarded Citizens did fund raising to support their school programs.

Obviously, the landmark legislation that radically changed the state of educational affairs was P.L. 94-142. The Education for All Handicapped Children Act reversed the previous philosophy by stating that all children, no matter how severe their impairment, had a right to a free, appropriate education. Since the passage of this law in 1975, public school districts have begun to serve all school-age special education students no matter how severe their impairments. Legislation has led to the placement of tens of thousands of severely handicapped students who previously were unserved but who now attend special education classes.

Large-scale efforts were made by local and state governments to search for all students who were not receiving an educational program. Extensive teacher training efforts have been made by universities to prepare personnel to work with this population. Large sums of money have been allocated for professionals to serve severely disabled students. The public law also built in due process mechanisms so that parents and advocates could appeal decisions made by school administrators related to placement, instruction, and assessment. Finally, federal funds were allocated for research and demonstration projects to investigate the best educational practices and the learning mechanisms of severely impaired students.

Thus, during the past decade there has been a veritable revolution in society's view of educating severely handicapped children and youth. Some school districts have been particularly innovative in demonstrating the best educational practices for severely handicapped students. In the next section we shall describe a few of these programs so that the reader can incorporate some of their characteristics in their own educational programs.

Model Programs

The Madison Preschool Program

Dr. Lizbeth Vincent of the University of Wisconsin has coordinated a program with the Madison Metropolitan School District that has provided exemplary services for preschool severely handicapped children. The program (Vincent and Broome, 1977) serves children from birth to age 5. It places an emphasis on parent involvement, contact with nonhandicapped peers, and the teaching of functional skills. The program is divided into infant and toddler phases. With infants, contact with the program begins immediately at birth, when a physician may determine that the newborn is at risk. A coordinated referral system has been developed in which the obstetrician or pediatrician will refer the high-risk infant to personnel from the special education preschool program within hours after birth. A representative of the program will be immediately in touch with the parents. Personnel making the initial contact orient the parents to the prospects of having a handicapped child. The positive aspects of parenting a handicapped child are emphasized. This approach is in contrast to some pediatric orientations that emphasize the defects of the child and the need for institutionalization. In the following weeks a schedule for contacts with the program is established.

In the infant phase of the program, an emphasis is placed on teaching the parents skills in caring for their child. Visits are made by parents with their child to the program. Also, program workers make visits to the home to provide services. Parents are taught skills in feeding, handling, playing with, and stimulating the child. Although the parent training imparts skills from professionals to parents, the program is not seen as a one-directional process. That is, each parent is viewed as presenting particular attitudes and skills that are potential assets in dealing with the child. The parent training program does not deliver a singular package of skills for the parents to acquire. Rather, skills and approaches that the parents use are combined with the procedures espoused by the professional program.

The toddler phase of the program is school-based; that is, the handicapped child attends a classroom program located at a public school on a daily basis. A special education teacher trained in early childhood education leads the class. The class is composed of both handicapped and nonhandicapped students. Many activities promote the social skill development of students through interaction with their peers. In such an integrated class, the handicapped students can model prosocial behavior from their nonhandicapped peers. Also, the nonhandicapped students can learn about disabled students, be taught how to interact with them, and develop positive attitudes toward disabled persons. Personnel from the integrated preschool classroom encourage parents to attend the classes in order to assist in instruction and learn additional parenting skills.

The directors of the Madison preschool program place a high priority on teaching functional skills for future environments. Dr. Vincent has identified the skills needed by handicapped students to succeed in regular kindergarten and first grade classes (Vincent, Salisbury, Walter, Brown, Gruenewald, and Powers, 1980). She and her colleagues have found that preacademic skills such as reading and arithmetic are not essential to success in kindergarten. Rather, prosocial skills such as taking turns, listening, and waiting in line are the keys to success in the early elementary grades. Following is a list of the critical behaviors or ''survival competencies'' (Vincent et al., 1980), the preschool student needs in order to be prepared for success in early school years:

1. Initiates interactions with adults and peers
2. Interacts with adults and peers when not the initiator
3. Demonstrates appropriate isolated play skills
4. Makes choices from visible and invisible referents
5. Executes at least one task from start to finish
6. Listens and attends to a speaker in a large group
7. Follows at least a one-component direction

8. Demonstrates turn taking in a small group
9. Demonstrates mobility from place to place
10. Manipulates small and large objects
11. Demonstrates appropriate attention-getting strategies
12. Adapts to working in more than one room with more than one adult
13. Demonstrates simple dressing and undressing skills
14. Attends to task for minimum of 15 minutes
15. Adapts to transitions between activities across the day
16. Expresses ideas to others
17. Communicates with peers and adults
18. Toilets independently
19. Responds to social reinforcement
20. Asks questions of others

This information sets the stage for the kinds of skills that are emphasized in the Madison program.

Overall, the Madison program is exemplary because it begins a longitudinal service delivery program for disabled persons. It places emphasis on the positive development and potential of disabled persons. Additionally, parents are key partners in the child's program, there is much social interaction between handicapped and nonhandicapped peers, and much instruction is given to learning functional skills for subsequent environments.

The Madison Secondary Program

There are many exemplary programs for students with severe handicaps. The Madison, Wisconsin, school district has been in the forefront in developing innovative educational programs. A key feature of the district's special education program is that longitudinal services have been designed that have an impact on the student from birth to the adult years. Thus, we saw how personnel from the Madison preschool program made contact with parents immediately after the identification of an at-risk neonate and continued the intervention process so that the student could achieve maximum integration into regular elementary education.

The primary programs in Madison continue the emphasis on teaching functional skills in multiple, integrated settings. The self-contained special education classes are located on public school campuses. The severely disabled students receive instruction in multiple sites on the school campus, e.g., the cafeteria, as well as some training excursions into the community. These experiences not only permit the teaching of functional skills in natural settings but also foster social interactions between the disabled students and a variety of nonhandicapped persons.

At the secondary level, the emphasis on off-campus instruction increases. Dr. Lou Brown of the University of Wisconsin has developed a model for secondary special education that places the primary site for instruction in the surrounding community rather than the school (Brown et al., 1979; Brown et al., 1984). If the primary student spends 20 percent of his time off campus, the secondary severely handicapped student in Madison spends at least 50 percent of his time in off-campus settings. Instruction in the community is keyed to goals established from environmental inventories generated from domestic, community, vocational, and recreational settings. Students learn to shop in stores, cross streets, use mass transportation, bowl in bowling alleys, and learn a vocation in real work settings.

Probably the greatest emphasis of the secondary program is on placing students in real work settings to receive vocational training. A cornerstone of Brown's model is that the student engage in meaningful work. Meaningful work involves activity at a job site that normally would be done by employees. Meaningful work is not portions of tasks or activities that normally would not be done as part of a job of a nonhandicapped employee. Through training on meaningful or real work, the student is prepared to assume actual jobs upon graduation from school.

A second characteristic of the vocational training is that students are placed on individual jobs at the work site rather than in groups or in enclaves of disabled persons. Figure 10.1 shows the types of training sites and the types of tasks performed by disabled youth. It can be seen that the students spend about 2 to 3 hours of training a week at the respective sites.

The professional supervising the vocational training is not the student's special education teacher. Rather, a community vocational teacher spends all his or her time monitoring students at the community training sites. When the student first is placed in the training site, the community vocational teacher stays continuously with the student. The teacher makes sure that the student learns the job tasks and acquires the generic work skills of punctuality, stamina, grooming, and socialization with coworkers. As the student learns these skills and begins to function more independently, the teacher decreases the amount of time spent supervising the student at the work site. The decrease in supervision time uses the transfer of stimulus control strategy (Chapter 2) by which supervision (the S^D) changes hands from the community classroom teacher to the employees and other natural cues at the work site. When the transfer is complete, the teacher makes only intermittent visits to the work sites to monitor pupil progress.

One of the strongest points of the Madison secondary program is that it is coordinated with adult service programs in the community. Specifically, there is a private nonprofit agency that specializes in placing disabled adults in nonsheltered work settings. Over a 5-year span the agency placed thirty-five individuals in nonsheltered jobs. Much of the success of this agency can be traced to the Madison secondary special education program, which trained students during adolescence in real work settings. This in situ training undoubtedly paved the way for successful adult employment.

Figure 10.1 Characteristics of a community vocational training program.

NONSCHOOL AND NONSHELTERED VOCATIONAL TRAINING ENVIRONMENTS UTILIZED BY SEVERELY HANDICAPPED STUDENTS IN THE MADISON METROPOLITAN SCHOOL DISTRICT DURING THE 1982–1983 SCHOOL YEAR

			Persons in Environment		
Environment	Type of Work	Days and Times	Approximate Percentage of Nonhandicapped Persons	Percentage of Severely Handicapped Students	Chronological Age of Students
Bittersweet Restaurant	Janitorial	Wed 9:00–10:30	9	2	14, 15
Chez Michel Restaurant	Food preparation	Wed 8:15–10:45	11	3	13, 13, 13
Ivy Inn Hotel	Housekeeping	Thur 9:30–11:00	35	2	13, 15
Ovens of Brittany Restaurant	Food preparation	Thur 9:00–10:45	45	2	12, 13
Concordance Natural Food Store	Packaging, weighing, pricing, and stocking grocery items	Thur 9:00–10:45	45	2	12, 15
L'Escargot Restaurant Office	Clerical	Wed 1:00–2:30	10	2	14, 15
University of Wisconsin Student Union	Clerical	Thur 1:00–2:30	115	2	15, 15
University of Wisconsin Student Union	Busing and setting tables, and refilling condiment containers	Tue 9:30–11:00	120	3	12, 13, 14
Hill Farms State Office Building	Clerical	Fri 1:00–2:30	35	3	13, 13, 15

Source: Adapted from L. Brown, B. Shiraga, A. Ford, P. VanDeventer, J. Nisbet, R. Loomis, and M. Sweet, Teaching severely handicapped students to perform meaningful work in nonsheltered vocational environments. Reprinted with permission.

Sensorimotor Programming: The Akron Program

Children and youth with severe handicaps also are educated by other professionals outside of school programs. These services have been referred to as *related services*. They include services such as physical therapy, speech therapy, occupational therapy, and adaptive physical education. The services have been termed "related" because they have not been deemed central to the educational process. Rather, education in academic, self-care, and vocational curricula has been viewed as primary, and the supplemental services in the motor and communication areas serve as adjuncts to the educational process.

The related services typically have been provided by therapists who are employed by the school district on a contractual basis. They conduct a fixed number of sessions in a week and usually "pull" the student to a therapy room to work on a one-to-one basis. The therapy service is supposed to be coordinated with activities in the classroom and the home.

Although related service programs have been successful in improving students' sensory, motor, and communicative development, certain problems have been associated with their administration. One problem deals with the amount of service time delivered to a student. Related services are costly because of the hourly fees that must be paid to therapists. Since the services are related to or supplementary to the educational program, school administrators have been wont to limit the amount of related services provided for students. Parents have been concerned that their children receive the necessary amount of therapeutic services to faciliate their optimal development. Many due process fair hearings have been initiated by parents opposing school administrators over the appropriate amount of related services. The explicit issue under consideration is the appropriate amount of educational services that will benefit the student, but the underlying issue is often the cost of the disputed service.

A second issue with related services deals with the way in which the therapy is delivered. Some critics have pointed to the shortcomings of the isolated therapy approach in which students work alone with therapists in separate sessions. The accusation is that therapy is not coordinated with extant efforts by teachers and parents. Furthermore, the latter people are not trained to implement the therapy techniques in the school and home settings. Therefore, it can be argued that the students' physical development is being therapeutically stimulated only 4 or 6 hours per week, i.e., the times when sessions are conducted. Some therapists counter that the specialized techniques of their profession should not be used spuriously by untrained persons; otherwise, harm could be done to the child.

Ms. Philippa Campbell (1977) and the personnel at the Akron (Ohio) Children's Hospital have developed a model for related services that has overcome many of these shortcomings. The *transdisciplinary* approach (Brackman, Fundakowski, Filler, and Peterson, 1977; Haynes, Patterson, D'Wolf, Hutchinson, Lowry, Schilling, and Siepp, 1976; McCormick and Goldman, 1979) has professionals learn the skills of disciplines outside their own fields. Thus, a physical therapist would learn the procedures of systematic instruction normally used by teachers. Teachers could learn handling, positioning, and stimulation practices used by physical therapists. Occupational therapists could learn the techniques of speech pathologists and use them in their sessions with their clients. The essence of the transdisciplinary model is that professionals acquire and utilize skills from other disciplines. There is not a rigid adherence to traditional professional roles; rather, there is a sharing of roles.

The main advantage of transdisciplinary service delivery is that the student receives a variety of related services for many hours of the day. Since the teacher has been trained in multiple disciplines, speech and physical therapy techniques can be used throughout a typical day. Thus, rather than receiving a designated number of hours of speech therapy, the student receives the impact of these procedures from a number of well-trained professionals throughout the school hours. Students with severe handicaps have difficulty generalizing skills to other people and settings. The traditional isolated therapy model presents a related service in a circumscribed context and is not likely to lead to generalization to settings outside the therapy context. In contrast, the transdisciplinary approach has the student practice the skills in multiple settings with different people, a condition that should promote their generalization to other settings and people.

In order to expedite transdisciplinary services, professionals must spend time training other professionals from different disciplines. The training relies heavily on role modeling and observational learning. The first step in training other professionals is to conduct therapy or instructional sessions in the natural settings of the classroom, gym, etc., rather than in an isolated therapy room. By conducting sessions in settings with the teacher and other professionals present, a speech therapist, for example, can model techniques for these professionals. Similarly, the teacher can model instructional programs to related service personnel. Thus, much learning occurs incidentally across professions as staff members mutually model their techniques in group settings.

Of course, it cannot be expected that a professional can learn another's procedures adequately purely through informal observations. There also must be meetings between professionals in which information related to the philosophy and methods of a discipline such as occupational therapy can be shared. Readings can be suggested and techniques described. Most important, the professionals can decide just which techniques can be used by different staff members. There may be certain techniques (e.g., range of motion) that a physical therapist does not want implemented by others. The thrust of the meetings is to plan strategies so that many professionals can use techniques of other disciplines on a daily basis.

One way to reach this goal is to have the teaching staff implement functional sequences in which chains of responses from related service prescriptions, e.g., stretching or vocalizing, are practiced. Transdisciplinary modeling and instruction is not an easy process to establish. As with segregated school programs, it is administratively easier to conduct therapy sessions in isolation. We feel there are greater potential benefits to the student through repeated varied practice with the transdisciplinary approach.

Another problem with related services is that particularly in integrated and rural programs, the therapist must travel large distances to serve students. The Akron Children's Hospital Occupational Physical Therapy (OT/PT) program has overcome this difficulty through implementing the transdisciplinary model. As a result of training teachers and other staff members on site in OT/PT procedures, a number of professionals can implement OT/PT practices when the therapists are not present. If students received these related services only when the therapist visited the school, they would be limited to a couple of hours of service per month.

We have summarized three model programs. These programs have been validated with a large number and variety of students with severe handicaps (e.g., Brown et al., 1984). The characteristics of these programs also have been replicated in a number of school districts. The ability of a model program to be replicated is critical, particularly when it has received substantial external funding and has the support of a university affiliation. There are obviously numerous other programs besides the ones cited here that could be deemed model. The common phrase running across the Madison and Akron programs is *integrated service delivery*. Vincent's preschool program integrated preschool special education with medical services as well as integrating handicapped and nonhandicapped students. Brown's secondary program employed a similar integration of students as well as a coordinated school and adult service program. Campbell's transdisciplinary program integrated the roles and responsibilities of professionals across a number of disciplines. The reader should be able to incorporate some of the characteristics of these model projects into his or her educational program.

Research

Besides the innovations in classroom practice that have been made in many model educational programs, other advances with regard to how persons with severe handicaps learn and behave have been developed through research investigations. Although there have been research efforts in numerous areas, we have selected two topics that are relevant with regard to how severely handicapped students perform in educational settings. These research reviews are not exhaustive. References to further readings on these topics are presented. The aim of the presentation is to enable the reader to learn more about these topics and get a feel for the research methods used in contemporary studies of persons with severe handicaps.

Behavior Modification and Instruction

As was stated in earlier chapters, the original educational and research efforts for severely handicapped persons in the 1950s and 1960s were most concerned with the remediation of problem behaviors. Little attention was given to learning constructive skills. Fortunately, some investigators turned

Figure 10.2 Behavior of two autistic children. The percentage of occurrence of self-stimulation and of correct trials is plotted on the ordinate for subject 1 and subject 2 when they engaged in self-stimulation (no suppression condition); and when self-stimulation was suppressed (suppression condition).

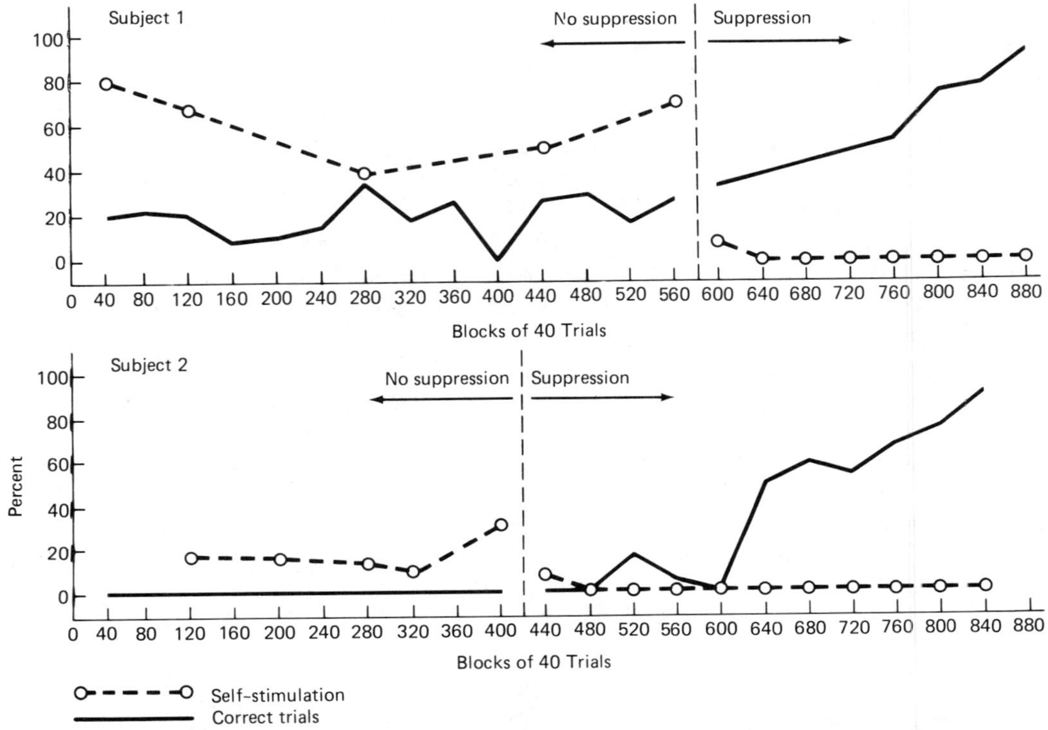

Source: Adapted from R. L. Koegel and A. Covert, The relationship of self-stimulation to learning in autistic children, *Journal of Applied Behavior Analysis* 5, 383. Reprinted with permission of the Society of Experimental Analysis of Behavior, Inc.

their attention to the relationship between learning curricular tasks and suppressing problem behaviors. Koegel and Covert (1972) were the first investigators to monitor how a problem behavior such as self-stimulation covaries with the learning of new behaviors. The researchers used single case designs (see Figure 10.2) to monitor the behavior of two autistic children.

Most research with humans uses group design methodology in which one or more groups (samples) of persons are compared to other groups of persons. Statistics are used to compare the group averages and to conclude, for instance, that one kind of instructional procedure is superior to another. Group designs have the advantage of drawing conclusions from large numbers of persons. Thus, the investigator is in a good position to conclude that the findings from the sample apply to the population at large. That is, what one finds from a sample of 100 second graders can be generalized as a characteristic of all second graders in the world.

Group designs do have a distinct disadvantage in regard to special populations. Since handicapped persons, particularly severely handicapped persons, are so different from individual to individual, it is difficult to generalize about a whole sample or population. Therefore, the alternative—single case design—has the advantage of monitoring the specific characteristics of individual handicapped persons. In single case studies a particular effect such as an instructional or behavior management procedure must be replicated over two to four individuals. When a set of individual graphs confirm an effect, the researchers may conclude that they have validated a particular procedure. The single case approach has the advantage of including a careful description of the way in which repeated measures have been taken on the behavior of individuals. Thus, the idiosyncratic patterns of responding are not hidden among the means or averages of a sample. The main disadvantage of the single case approach is that one is limited in generalization from the two to six persons under investigation to the whole population of, say, autistic children. In the remainder of this section we present findings from both single case and group design research.

To return to our discussion of learning and behavior management, Koegel and Covert (1972) had each of their autistic children attempt to learn different tasks before a behavior modification procedure was instituted. Thus, pretreatment baseline data were collected on how well they performed on the tasks and how often the self-stimulatory behaviors appeared. Figure 10.2 shows the rather high rates of self-stimulatory behavior and poor task acquisition. It appeared that the excessive appearance of the problem behaviors precluded the students' attending to and learning the tasks at hand.

After baseline, a behavioral intervention was implemented. The aversive stimulus of slapping the student's hand after every instance of self-stimulation was used. Figure 10.2 shows that the contingent punishment procedure reduced the problem behavior significantly. At the same time the curve of self-stimulatory behavior was descending, the curve of task acquisition was accelerating. Thus, it appears that it was necessary to suppress the problem behavior before the conditions were present in order to facilitate learning. With the problem behavior appearing at a low rate, the autistic children could attend to the task cues and be motivated by the reinforcers received for correct performance. In baseline, reinforcement (DRA) alone could not improve task performance while self-stimulation was still present.

It should not be concluded from this study that punishment is always necessary to ameliorate problem behaviors and facilitate learning. Rather, the main finding was that problem behaviors interfered with learning, and the behaviors had to be suppressed before effective instruction could proceed.

Figure 10.3 Percentage of occurrence of errors and self-injury for Mark across the four experimental conditions.

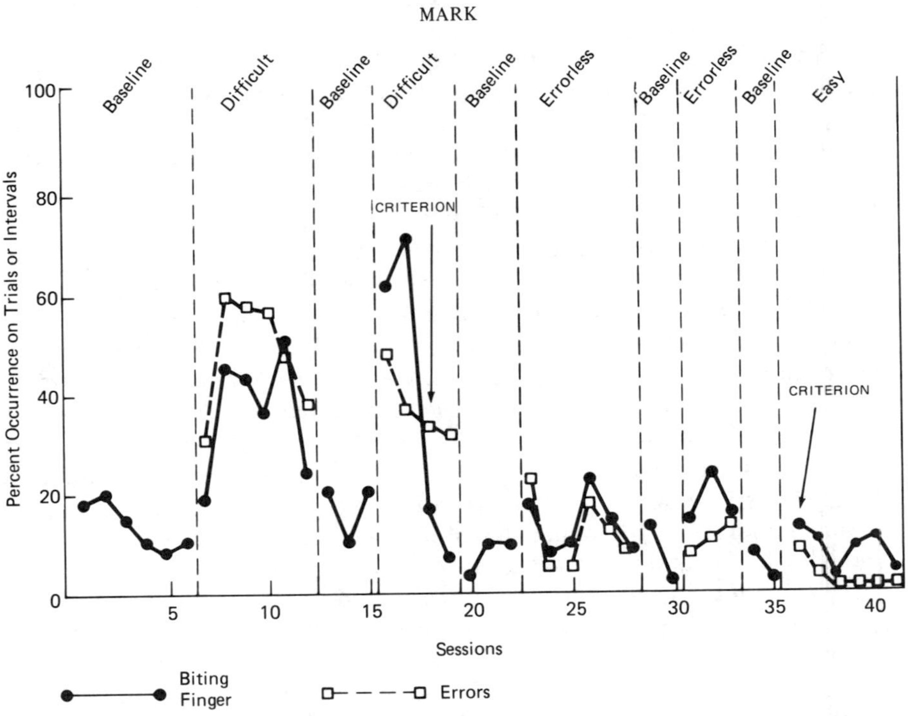

Source: Adapted from M. Weeks and R. Gaylord-Ross, Task difficulty and aberrant behavior in severely handicapped students, *Journal of Applied Behavior Analysis* 14, 456. Reprinted with permission of the Society of Experimental Analysis of Behavior, Inc.

With students with less severe behavior problems, milder behavior management procedures might have been successful. In Chapter 5, it was stated that ecological, reinforcement, or curricular procedures should be attempted prior to use of a punishment contingency. Possibly a curricular approach would have proved effective with the children in Keogel and Covert (1972) study.

Next, a study by Weeks and Gaylord-Ross (1981) demonstrated how curricular strategies can be used to reduce prcblem behavior. Three severely handicapped students were exposed to a series of conditions differing in their level of task difficulty. In these conditions the students' rate of problem behavior and performance in learning tasks was monitored. Figure 10.3 shows that in the baseline and the easy task conditions, there was little problem behavior. In baseline an instructor presented no tasks; in the easy condition rather simple discrimination and perceptual-motor tasks were presented. It was expected and found that the students made few errors on the

Figure 10.4 Example of a fading sequence in the errorless condition.

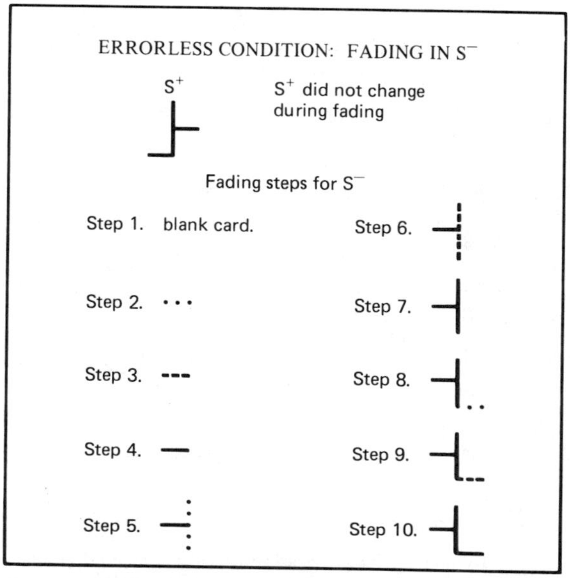

Source: Adapted from M. Weeks and R. Gaylord-Ross, Task difficulty and aberrant behavior in severely handicapped students, *Journal of Applied Behavior Analysis* 14 (1981): 453. Reprinted with permission of the Society of Experimental Analysis of Behavior, Inc.

easy tasks. It was also known that the students' problem behavior was under the control of negative reinforcement. It thus was predicted that difficult tasks would produce frustration and lead to the appearance of problem behaviors that in the past had led to escape from task performance. Conversely, easy tasks and no tasks (baseline) would produce no frustration and no concomitant aberrant behavior.

The results from Figure 10.3 show exactly these findings. Difficult discriminations (geometric figures and self-care tasks) led to the appearance of errors and problem behaviors at a substantial rate.

A final condition was introduced to demonstrate the power of curricular modifications. Difficult tasks were made easier by the application of errorless learning tactics. That is, the difficult discrimination was task-analyzed into a series of learning steps in which the incorrect (S^{Δ}) stimulus was faded in gradually. Figure 10.4 shows this series of steps. Ultimately the student could discriminate between S^D and S^{Δ}, whereas initially he had to distinguish only between S^D and a blank card. The data in Figure 10.3 show that the errorless procedure was successful in teaching difficult tasks with few errors. In addition, the errorless condition produced few problem behav-

Figure 10.5 Comparison of social bids involving severely handicapped students in integrated and segregated settings.

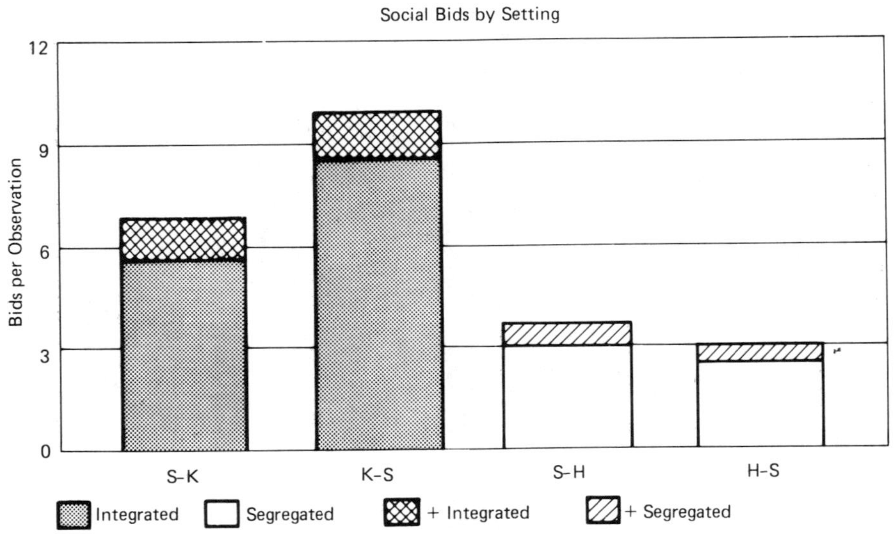

Source: R. P. Brinker and M. E. Thorpe, Evaluation of integration of severely handicapped students in regular education and community settings, *Research Report No. 84–11* (Princeton, N.J.: Educational Testing Service, 1984), p. 100. Reprinted with permission.

iors. The errorless procedure was also replicated successfully with self-care tasks. Thus, a curricular modification that reduces the difficulty of a task may effectively suppress problem behaviors that are under the control of negative reinforcement.

Social Integration

Much of this book has focused on the integration of students with severe handicaps with nonhandicapped persons in a variety of natural settings. A number of research questions emanate from the integration process. In what ways do handicapped and nonhandicapped persons interact on and off school campuses? How do the attitudes of nonhandicapped persons change as a function of exposure to persons with severe handicaps? These and other questions dealing with the social integration process have been addressed in a number of research studies. We shall describe two such studies. The interested reader should examine the chapter by Gaylord-Ross and Peck (1984) that thoroughly reviews the extant research dealing with the social integration of students with severe handicaps.

Brinker and Thorpe (1984) were interested in the social interaction patterns of severely handicapped students in integrated and segregated school settings. They designed a comprehensive study that examined these settings in twelve different school districts across the United States. The districts differed in size, ethnicity, density of population, and geographic locale. Brinker took observation samples of severely handicapped students interacting with staff persons, handicapped students, and nonhandicapped students. Measures were taken in 10-minute time samples at different times of the day and week during interactive periods such as recess. The primary measure was the number of bids or initiations (of an interaction) one person made toward another during an observational sample. The numbers of bids were tallied across hundreds of severely handicapped students in thousands of sessions in integrated and segregated school sites.

Figure 10.5 shows that in integrated settings there was a higher rate of bids from severely handicapped students to other students (S—K, to handicapped and nonhandicapped) than in segregated settings (S—H, bids to handicapped students). Also, in integrated settings there was a higher rate of bids from other students to severely handicapped students (K—S) than in segrated settings (H—S). Apparently, integrated schools better facilitate peer interactions, a process critical to the social development of children (Hartup, 1978). Segregated settings promote more adult-student interactions, and this does not permit the peer modeling process to promote social skills.

Another research question involving social integration deals with attitudes and attitude change. Voeltz (1980a, 1980b, 1982) conducted a longitudinal investigation of the attitudes of nonhandicapped fourth, fifth, and sixth graders toward their severely handicapped peers. She contrasted students in three kinds of public schools. One sample of students attended no-contact, or segregated, schools where no severely handicapped students were present. A second sample of students attended low-contact schools. Severely handicapped students enrolled in integrated, low-contact schools had no ongoing program to systematically encourage social interaction between handicapped and nonhandicapped students. A third high-contact school was integrated, and there were "special friends" programs that facilitated social interaction. The special friends program consisted of a slide-sound filmstrip of the integration process, discussion groups for participating regular education students, and structured play periods during which pairs of severely handicapped and nonhandicapped special friends could engage in leisure activities.

Children from these three types of schools were administered a social acceptance questionnaire during the fall and spring of each school year. The questionnaire contained twenty-one items that measured the person's attitude toward disabled persons (see Figure 10.6). The testee was required to agree, disagree, or indicate an undecided response on each item. The re-

Figure 10.6 The five factors of social acceptance of handicapped students.

THE ACCEPTANCE SCALE

	Factor-pattern coefficients				
	1	2	3	4	5
Social Contact Willingness:					
I wish I could make friends with a mentally retarded person.	.70				
If someone told me about a new TV show on Saturday morning about handicapped kids, I would watch it if I could.	.68				
I wish I could play with some mentally retarded students.	.67				
I think I could be good friends with a special education student.	.54				
I would like my class to go to camp the same week that a class of handicapped kids was there.	.52				
Deviance Consequation:					
Children who are retarded should not be in my room at school.		.57			
Kids who talk to themselves a lot are scary. I don't like to be close to them.		.45			
It doesn't make sense to have deaf kids in school with kids who can hear.		.42			
Kids who talk funny so I can't understand them very well shouldn't be in my group in school activities.		.42			
I don't say hello to kids who are retarded.		.41			
I get embarrassed when I talk to someone who is cross-eyed.		.37			
If I had a retarded brother or sister, I wouldn't tell anybody.		.32			
Actual Contact, Wheelchair:					
I have talked to some students in wheelchairs.			.77		
I have helped some students in wheelchairs.			.71		
Actual Contact, Mental Retardation:					
I have talked with some mentally retarded students at my school.				-.54	
I have played on the playground with some mentally retarded students.				-.44	
I have made friends with a mentally retarded student.	.39			-.36	
Mild Deviance Consequation:					
If another kid can't do something or does something wrong, he can expect to be called a dummy.					-.51
If there are too many kids in my room who have trouble with math and reading, my teacher won't have time for me and my friends.					-.38

Source: Adapted from L. Voeltz, Effects of structured interactions with severely handicapped peers on children's attitudes, *American Journal of Mental Deficiency* 82, 389. Reprinted with permission.

sponses were tallied so that scores ranged from 0 to 42, with 42 being the most positive score toward disabled persons.

Figure 10.7 shows the results of the study over a 2-year period (Voeltz 1980a). The initial administration of the questionnaire was done after the three types of programs were already in effect for at least 6 months. Thus, there was no "pure" pretest in which all schools were segregated or the special friends program had yet to be instituted. It can be seen that the high-contact program had more acceptant scores than the low-contact schools, which in turn had higher scores than the no-contact schools. Over the next two testing periods, the latter two groups had negligible changes whereas students in the high-contact group continued to increase their scores in the positive direction. These results attained statistical significance.

Thus, from the Voeltz research, it appears that integrating severely handicapped students on public school campuses without systematic programs for interaction will produce little effect on the attitudes of nonhandicapped students. Their attitudes toward accepting disabled persons will be roughly equivalent to those of students attending schools where no severely handicapped students are present. It is only when interaction programs such as special friends are instituted that substantial changes in attitudes occur. Furthermore, the desirable drift toward positive attitudes continued at the school as more nonhandicapped students participated in special friends programs from semester to semester.

We have described two research studies that examined the social integration process. Both studies used group statistical designs. One examined behavioral interactions and the other studied attitudes. Both investigations reported positive outcomes from the integration process. The studies did not examine the individuals in detail, as would be the case in single case designs. Although these rich descriptions of individual behavior were lacking, the findings in the large group studies built confidence that the integration process had substantial effects. That is, that positive attitudes and interactions are likely to develop among students who are not observed in the study but who are exposed to similar experiences.

Ambitious research efforts are usually the province of university professors with well-funded grants, but teachers can participate in the research process for their own programs. For example, all the measures taken in the four studies just described can be administered by a classroom teacher. Voeltz's questionnaire is easy to give to regular education students; the trial-by-trial measurement of aberrant behavior and skill acquisition by Koegel and Covert (1972) and Weeks and Gaylord-Ross (1981) could be done by school personnel; and the Brinker (1982) time sample observations of social interactions could be completed in a similar fashion. Educational personnel are not likely to carry out intensive investigations on the scale that researchers do, but teachers may want to obtain samples or indicators of student performance and attitudes. For these reasons, educational personnel should stay

Figure 10.7 Mean acceptance scale scores for grades 4 through 6. N = 39 classrooms.

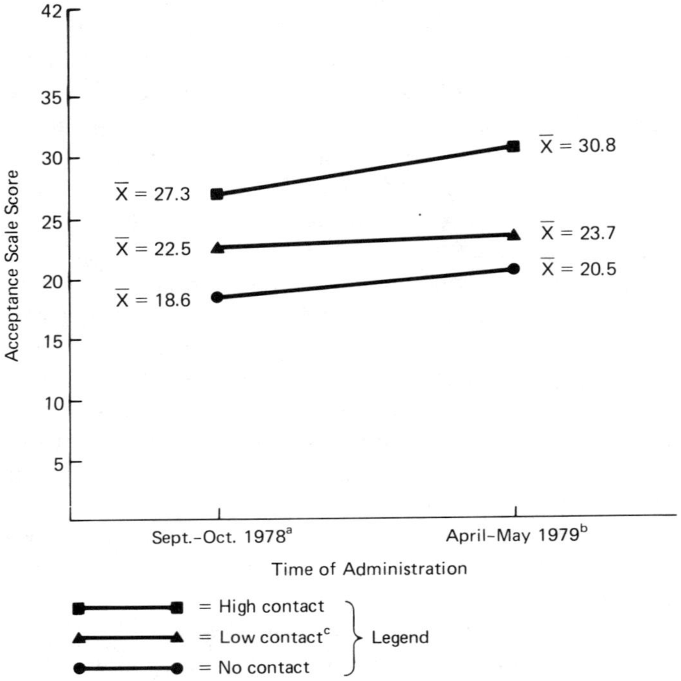

[a]Prior to this test date, the High Contact school experienced over 1 year of exposure and one semester of the interaction program; the Low Contact schools experienced over 1 year of exposure only; neither variable was present at the No Contact schools.

[b]Between the two administration dates, two additional semesters of the program occurred at the High Contact school; two additional semesters of exposure only occurred at the Low Contact schools; no change occurred at the No Contact schools.

[c]Note that the mean scale scores obtained at the Low Contact schools, grades 4 through 6 are virtually identical to the overall mean scale scores obtained for the total sample of children in grades 2 through 7; for all children, the fall mean was 22.3 (N = 2464) and the spring mean was 23.9 (N = 2476).

Source: Voeltz, L. M. 1980a. *Dimensions of Children's Acceptance of Handicapped Peers in Integrated Settings*. Paper presented at the Fifty Eighth Annual Convention of the Council for Exceptional Children, Philadelphia.

up to date on recent research in the field. New instructional techniques, curricula, and measurement procedures that can be used in the classroom are frequently presented in research monographs.

New Educational Developments

During the past 25 years there have been major developments that have advanced the services for students with severe handicaps. First, free educational programs have been provided for all disabled students. Second, school and residential programs are being located in normalized, least restrictive settings such as public schools. Third, an effective instructional technology has emerged that can be used to teach severely disabled students a wide range of useful skills. Fourth, a cadre of professional personnel has been trained to educate students with severe handicaps. With all these developments in place, the future outlook for services for this population can be viewed as promising and optimistic.

Microcomputers

Although the systematic presentation of cues, reinforcers, and task-analyzed curricula has produced a powerful instructional design, further advances in instruction may be made through the use of technological hardware. Increasing attention has been given to the use of microcomputers in education. Much of the curriculum in regular education has been put on computers so that the student can obtain repeated practice and drill in an autotutorial manner. More advanced computer programs that require problem-solving strategies also have been developed. For mildly handicapped students, similar curriculum efforts have been made (Turkel and Podell 1984).

The implications of using microcomputers for students with severe handicaps are less clear. Because of their serious intellectual delays, it may be hard to train students to be "literate" on microcomputers. However, some straightforward procedures have been used to establish a dialog between severely disabled individuals and microcomputers. Striking a key on the keyboard of a microcomputer can be considered an operant response. When the keyboard is struck, a variety of visual and auditory feedback can appear from the screen. A letter or number typically appears. More complex feedback may appear, such as flashing multicolored patterns or simple musical jingles. This feedback can be conceptualized as a reinforcing event. Thus, a starting point could be teaching the severely handicapped student to strike a single key that has been programmed to provide audio or visual feedback. The student initially can be prompted to strike the key (e.g., with manual guidance) and subsequently can be reinforced with teacher praise or edibles. With practice, prompts can be faded and external reinforcers thinned so that the student independently strikes the key at a substantial rate.

There are numerous keys on keyboards, and the keys are fairly small. Thus, a student with motor disabilities may have particular difficulty striking a designated key. Fortunately, adaptive devices have been developed (Casella, 1984) so that a large manipulandum can be fitted to extend from the keyboard. This adaptation would make it easy for the student to activate the system.

At this point, merely striking a key for positive reinforcement can serve an educational function. For example, Brinker and Lewis (1982) have taught severely disabled infants to respond operantly to a microcomputer with the assistance of adaptive devices. The infants thus learned a discriminated operant, took a first step toward becoming computer-literate, and developed operational causality with the ability to control the environment.

The presence of physical disabilities is a major limitation on extending the use of microcomputers for use by severely handicapped students. Fortunately, a number of adaptive devices have been developed that permit students with motor impairments to interface with computers.

Because keys on a keyboard are small and close to each other, it may be difficult for a child to strike the keys accurately. The Computer King Keyboard® increases the size of each key to 1¼ inches in diameter. In addition, the keys are recessed to permit easier control. The Extended Keyboard® has programmable function keys so that a student can operate the microcomputer with one hand. This adaptation is important because some microcomputer operations require the striking of two keys simultaneously, and the Extended Keyboard circumvents this requirement. With the Keyboard Guard®, a guard operates as a barrier to the keyboard; the student must place his or her hand over the guard. This required movement avoids multiple or repeated striking of keys, thus preventing error responses.

Adaptive Devices

There are students who have severe motor impairments that prevent them from striking a keyboard, no matter how extensive the adaptive device. The Voice Based Learning System® allows a person to speak into a microphone. The words then are processed by the system to trigger keyboard responses. Thus, vocal sounds are the manipulanda of the microcomputer. The Voice Based Learning System® will even transform grunts or sounds lacking traditional language meaning into specific operations on the microcomputer. Before the microcomputer is operable, each of the student's sounds must be coded in to represent particular keyboard operations.

There are other adaptive devices for students with particular physical disabilities. For instance, some students have no use of their hands for the operation of keyboard devices. The Sweda Card® permits input from multiple sources into the microcomputer. For example, the movement of the cheek or leg can activate a manipulandum on the Sweda Card that will de-

Figure 10.8 Names and manufacturers of adaptive devices for microcomputers.

ADAPTIVE DEVICES FOR MICROCOMPUTERS

Device:	Company:
Unicorn Keyboard	Unicorn Engineering 6201 Harwood Avenue Oakland, CA 94610 (415) 428-1626
Expanded Keyboard	Executive Peripheral Systems, Inc. 800 San Antonia Road Palo Alto, CA 94303
Echo II Speech Synthesizer	Street Electronics 1140 March Avenue Carpinteria, CA 93013 (805) 684-4593
Adaptive Firmware Card	Adaptive Peripherals 4529 Bagley Avenue North Seattle, WA 98103 (206) 633-2610
Micro-Switches	Zygo Industries, Inc. P.O. Box 1008 Portland, OR 97207 (503) 297-1724
Shadow/VET	Scott Instruments 1111 Wilbur Springs Drive Dentar, TX 76201 (817) 387-9514

liver input to the microcomputer. Thus, different body parts such as the cheek or leg can operate the computer. A device called the Light Sensor Pen® permits a student to write on the video screen of the microcomputer and deliver input to the microprocessor. Writing rather than striking a keyboard is another alternative means of providing input to the computer.

Figure 10.8 lists all these adaptive devices and the companies where they can be purchased. There obviously has been a revolution in technological devices like microcomputers. New adaptive and other devices are being developed at a rapid pace. In the case of microcomputers, adaptive devices are important because they allow students to provide input to computers in ways they would not normally be able to do. Once a student can deliver input, the computer can be used as a word processor or programmer. With a word processor, the student can write letters or messages to the population at large. With a programming device, the student can participate in video games, do drills for academic tasks, or engage in problem-solving programs.

Making students computer-literate opens up a number of worlds for the

Figure 10.9 Overall flow chart of a computer skills assessment inventory.

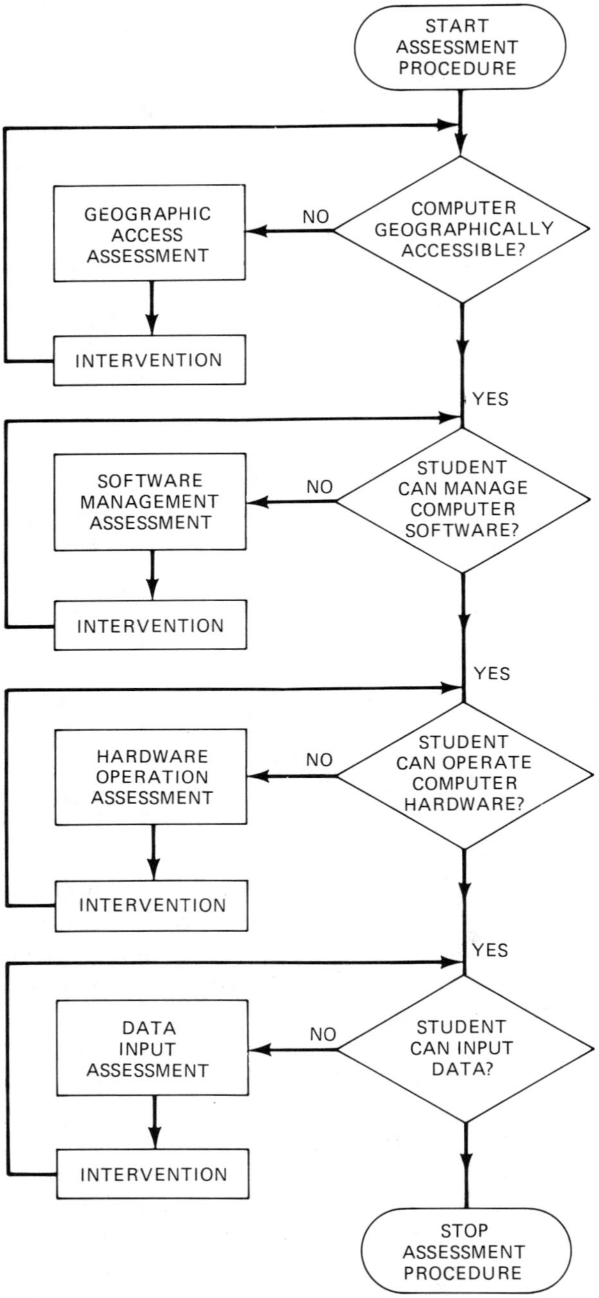

handicapped student. The word processing capabilities enable the student to communicate with other people in ways the language-limited or physically impaired student normally would not be capable of. The microcomputer also can serve as an instructional device since the student can participate in curricular strands placed on software in areas such as mathematics, language arts, and social studies.

There are also career opportunities involved with microcomputers, which are permeating office, industrial, and other work settings. When handicapped people become adept in using computers, they may obtain positions in business in which either all or part of the job involves the use of the computer. The range of possible occupations varies from lower-level positions such as generating mailing labels to higher-level positions such as computer operators or repairpersons. The possibilities appear endless, and the main objective is that the teaching profession keep up with the rapid changes in technology.

The true challenge for educators is to assure that adaptations will be made in the emerging high-technology field so that handicapped persons may participate with these devices in the fullest manner. In order to coordinate the technological requirements of the microcomputer with the particular disabilities of the student, Casella (1984) has developed a computer skills assessment inventory. The inventory (see Figure 10.9) takes into account the particular disabilities of the student and suggests adaptations to enable the student to operate the microcomputer effectively. Figure 10.10 shows how the problem of access to the computer may be resolved with seven possible adaptations. The possibilities for the extension of high technology into the lives of handicapped persons for purposes of instruction, communication, and vocation seem endless. It is the task of educators to guarantee that handicapped students are able to participate fully in this technological revolution.

Summary

We have seen how a more enlightened society can bring about changes in the education of persons with severe handicaps. The changes that have been made and those yet to be made will continue to enhance the quality of life for persons having handicapping conditions. The model programs we described should be emulated; also, new innovative efforts are likely to produce noteworthy results.

In addition to these developments, our field shows promise for other new breakthroughs in the forthcoming decades. Although the developments in the past two decades have been impressive, if our field is to grow in coming years there must be further breakthroughs in research and service delivery.

Figure 10.10

RESOLUTIONS TO COMPUTER ACCESS PROBLEMS.

Situation:

Lap tray of wheel chair interferes with access to computer.

Resolution:

1. Remove lap tray.
2. Adjust height of computer table legs.
3. Design wooden block lifts to raise table height.
4. Move computer to alternative location.
5. Move child to alternative chair.
6. Select computer with detachable keyboard.
7. Purchase detachable keyboard for existing equipment.

Source: Adapted from V. Casella, Utilization of microcomputers with the physically handicapped, in *Using Microcomputers in Special Education*, ed. A. E. Blackhurst (Boston: Little, Brown & Co., in press). Reprinted with permission.

Epilogue

We have attempted to describe educational practices that should be effective in teaching severely handicapped children and youth. An educational model has been presented that is comprehensive in emphasizing functional goals and objectives, systematic instruction, measurement, multiple-setting teaching, coordination of services, curriculum development, and the infusion of new technologies. It is important that practitioners gain experience in implementing this model. Just reading about teaching techniques will not guarantee that an instructor will be able to implement these procedures successfully. We have developed a series of field-based exercises that a student of the teaching profession can implement in school settings.

This list of exercises is by no means exhaustive. It should serve as a springboard for a fuller implementation of our educational model. The exercises may be done by a preservice student completing a practicum or student teaching course in a university program or by an in-service student who is a full-time instructor. The professor of a methods course in teaching students with severe handicaps probably will wish to expand our list in order to develop a comprehensive, field-based experience.

1. Complete a *screening* instrument with at least two students. Write up your findings and suggest what other instruments can be used to complete a comprehensive assessment.
2. Use at least two assessment instruments on at least three students to complete a comprehensive assessment. Conduct assessments that are based on both behavioral observations of the student and a checklist of performed skills. Establish interobserver agreement on at least one completed assessment device. Write a report of the assessment for each of the students. The report should summarize findings from the assessment and suggest educational goals and instructional strategies.
3. Conduct an environmental inventory with at least one student. List the skills needed to succeed in the residential and community environments for the student.
4. Write a set of long-term goals and short-term objectives for at least three

students. The IEP for each student should contain at least one goal from the major educational domains, i.e., personal management, vocational, social and leisure, community, academic, and domestic (other possible domains could be self-care, communication, fine and gross motor, etc.). The long-term goal would be an outcome predicted to be obtained in a year or longer. The goal should be written in behavioral terms (i.e., John will learn to vacuum and clean rooms). The short-term objective represents the intermediate steps needed to attain the long-term goal. For example, there could be a series of four short-term objectives spanning the quarterly periods of a year. The completion of the fourth objective would be equivalent to attaining the long-term goal. Thus, each goal should have at least one short-term objective. The short-term objective should state the behavior to be performed, the conditions under which it will be performed, the numerical criterion of performance, and when it will be obtained. An example would be: "John will be able to vacuum a room (living room or bedroom) so there are no particles of dirt present by October 1 at a criterion of five consecutive occasions." Thus, for your assignment each pupil should have five to fifteen goals and ten to forty objectives.

5. Design and implement at least four instructional programs. The programs should have an objective, a task-analyzed curriculum, an instructional methodology, a recording sheet, and a graph of the collected data.
6. Implement at least one instructional program on each of the following topics:
   a. Generalization of a skill to another setting, material, or person
   b. Maintenance of a skill at least 3 months after it has been taught
   c. Individualized functional sequence; demonstrate how a number of tasks can be taught in a distributed fashion in natural contexts
   d. Management of a problem behavior using a behavior modification problem that has followed the decision model for selecting a treatment procedure
7. Read and criticize at least one commercial curriculum program in a written report. Focus on how the curriculum can be adapted for individual students. Discuss how readable the curriculum is and how easily it can be put into practice by the classroom teacher.
8. Design a schedule for a school program. The schedule should list the sequence of activities for each of the students for each day of the week. Also, staff members, e.g., teacher, paraprofessional, or speech pathologist, should be listed with regard to which students and activities they are involved with at each time of the day (see Chapter 7). When the schedule is designed, attempt to implement it with an actual class of students. Make necessary changes in the schedule when the occasions arise.

9. Write an analysis of the physical and social environment of an educational program for students with severe handicaps. Describe both the special education classroom and the other settings on and off the school campus. Judge whether the students appear to be exposed to a wide array of persons and settings in their daily instruction. Next, make at least two recommendations to improve the social and physical environment of the program.
10. Institute at least one home-school program in which the parents of a student carry out instruction in the home or classroom. The instruction should be coordinated with the student's IEP. A communication, training, and data collection system should be established for the parents in conjunction with the home-school program.
11. Conduct a discussion group with other trainees in special education about the career decisions they made in deciding to enter this field. Next, interview at least two special education teachers with experience in the field. Discuss what they do to continue their professional development. Question them about their personal mechanisms for coping with teacher burnout. Finally, develop a list of recommendations for preventing the burnout of special education teachers.

References

Alexander, D. 1974. Comparison for mental retardates of non-choice, initial choice, and idiosyncratic-choice reward strategies. *Psychological Reports* 35:135–45.

Allen, V. L. (ed.). 1976. *Children as Teachers: Theory and Research on Tutoring*. New York: Academic Press.

Alpern, G. D., Boll, T. J., and Shearer, M. S. 1980. *Developmental Profile II*, rev. ed. Aspen, Colo.: Psychological Developmental Publications.

Association for the Severely Handicapped. 1981. Resolution on intrusive interventions. *TASH Newsletter* 11:1–2.

Ball, R. S., Merrifield, P., and Stott, L. H. 1978. *Extended Merrill-Palmer Scale*. Chicago: Stoelting.

Balthazar, E. E. 1973. *Balthazar Scales of Adaptive Behavior for the Profoundly and Severely Mentally Retarded, I and II*. Palo Alto, Calif.: Consulting Psychologists Press.

Bandura, A., and Walters, R. H. 1963. *Social Learning and Personality Development*. New York: Holt, Rinehart and Winston.

Baumeister, A. A., and Berry, M. 1976. Distribution of practice and specificity of learning in normals and retardates. *American Journal of Mental Deficiency* 72:227–31.

Baumgart, D., Brown, L., Pumpian, J., Nisbet, J., Ford, A., Sweet, M., Ranieri, L., Hansen, L., and Schroeder, J. 1980. The principle of partial participation and individualized adaptations in educational programs for severely handicapped students. In L. Brown, M. Falvey, J. Pumpian, D. Baumgart, J. Nisbet, A. Ford, J. Schroeder, and R. Loomis (eds.), *Curricular Strategies for Teaching Severely Handicapped Students Functional Skills in School and Nonschool Environments*, vol. 10. Madison, Wis.: Madison Metropolitan School District.

Bayley, N. 1969. *Bayley Scales of Infant Development*. New York: Psychological Corporation.

Becker, H., Schur, S., Paoletti, M., and Petty, D. M. 1982. *Basic Life Skills Screening Inventory*. Dallas, Tex.: South Central Regional Center for Services to Deaf-Blind Children.

Bellamy, G. T., Horner, R. H., and Inman, D. P. 1979. *Vocational Habilitation of Severely Retarded Adults*. Baltimore: University Park Press.

Bellamy, G. T., Rose, H. E., Boles, S. M., Wilson, D. J., and Clarke, J. Y. 1981. Final Report Contract No. 300-78-0346. The Vocational Opportunities Cooperative (Project VOC): *A Model Project for Severely Handicapped Youth.* Washington, D.C.: U.S. Department of Education.

Berk, R. A. 1976. Effects of choice of instructional methods on verbal learning tasks. *Psychological Reports* 38:867–70.

Blatt, B. 1973. *Souls in Extremis: An Anthology on Victims and Victimizers.* Boston: Allyn & Bacon.

Brackman, B., Fundakowski, G., Filler, J., and Peterson, C. 1977. The Chicago Early Childhood Education Program. In B. Wilcox, F. Kohl, and T. Volesburg (eds.), *The Severely and Profoundly Handicapped Child.* Proceedings from the Statewide Institute for Education of the Severely and Profoundly Handicapped. State Board of Education, Illinois Office of Education. Champaign, Ill.

Bradford, L. P. 1978. A dozen reasons some meetings bomb—and others work wonders. *Training* 15(5):47–51.

Brazelton, T. B. 1973. *Neonatal Behavioral Assessment Scale.* Philadelphia: J. B. Lippincott.

Bricker, D. 1976. Educational synthesizer. In A. Thomas (ed.), *Hey, Don't Forget About Me: New Directions for Serving the Severely Handicapped.* Reston, Va.: The Council for Exceptional Children.

Bricker, W. A., and Campbell, P. H. 1980. Interdisciplinary assessment and programming for multihandicapped students. In W. Sailor, B. Wilcox, and L. Brown (eds.), *Methods of Instruction for Severely Handicapped Learners.* Baltimore: Paul H. Brookes.

Brigance, A. H. 1982. *Brigance Diagnostic Inventory of Early Development.* North Billeria, Mass.: Curriculum Associates.

Brinker, R. P. 1982. *The Rate and Quality of Social Behavior of Severely Handicapped Students in Integrated and Nonintegrated Settings.* Paper presented at the Integration Evaluation Parent Conference, Educational Testing Service, Princeton, N.J.

Brinker, R. P., and Lewis, M. 1982. Making the world work with microcomputers: A learning prosthesis for handicapped infants. *Exceptional Children* 49:163–70.

Brinker, R. P., and Thorpe, M. E. 1984. *Evaluation of Integration of Severely Handicapped Students in Regular Education and Community Settings.* Research Report No. 34-11, Educational Testing Service, Princeton, N.J.

Brown, F., and Holvoet, J. 1982. The effect of systematic peer interaction on the incidential learning of two severely handicapped students. *Journal of the Association for the Severely Handicapped* 7:19–28.

Brown, F., Holvoet, J., Guess, D., and Mulligan, M. 1980. The individualized curriculum sequencing model (III): Small group instruction. *Journal of the Association for the Severely Handicapped* 5:352–67.

Brown, L., Branston, M. B., Hamre-Nietupski, S., Pumpian, J., Certo, N., and Gruenewald, L. 1979. A strategy for developing chronological age appropriate and functional curricular content to severely handicapped adolescents and young adults. *Journal of Special Education* 13:81–90.

Brown, L., Branston-McClean, M., Baumgart, D., Vincent, L., Falvey, M., and Schroeder, J. 1979. Using the characteristics of current and subsequent least restrictive environments as factors in the development of curricular content for severely handicapped students. *TASH Review* 4:407–24.

Brown, L., Nietupski, J., and Hamre-Nietupski, S. 1976. The criterion of ultimate functioning and public school services for severely handicapped students. In M. Thomas (ed.), *Hey, Don't Forget About Me: New Directions for Serving the Severely Handicapped.* Reston, Va.: Council for Exceptional Children.

Brown, L., Shiraga, B., Ford, A., VanDeventer, P., Nisbet, J., Loomis, R., and Sweet, M. 1984. Teaching severely handicapped students to perform meaningful work in nonsheltered vocational environments. In R. Morris and B. Blatt (eds.), *Perspectives in Special Education: State of the Art.* Glenview, Ill.: Scott, Foresman.

Burton, R., Balsamo, C., Carrington, E., Garozzo, D., Ierardi, M., Kailukaitis, M., Klaire, R., and Probert, G. 1978. *Priority Needs Assessment Scale.* Southbury, Conn.: Southbury Training School.

Cain, L. F., Levine, S., and Elzey, F. F. 1963. *Cain-Levine Social Competency Scales.* Palo Alto, Calif.: Consulting Psychologists Press.

Campbell, P. H. 1977. Approximating the norm through adaptive and prosthetic devices. In E. Sontag, J. Smith, and N. Certo (eds.), *Educational Programming for the Severely/Profoundly Handicapped.* Reston, Va.: Council for Exceptional Children.

Carey, W. B. 1972. Clinical applications of infant temperament measures. *Journal of Pediatrics* 81:323–28.

Casella, V. In press. Utilization of microcomputers with the physically handicapped. In A. E. Blackhurst (ed.), *Using Microcomputers in Special Education.* Boston: Little, Brown & Co.

Cassell, R. N. 1962. *The Child Behavior Rating Scale.* Los Angeles: Western Psychological Services.

Castello, K., Pinkney, P., and Scheffers, W. 1981. *Visual Functioning Assessment Tool (VFAT).* Chicago: Stoelting.

Cattell, P. 1940. *Infant Intelligence Scale.* New York: Psychological Corporation.

Cohen, H. 1983. *You Can Negotiate Anything.* New York: Bantam Books.

Cohen, M. A., Gross, P. J., and Haring, N. G. 1976. Developmental pinpoints. In L. Brown and N. Haring (eds.), *Teaching the Severely Handicapped,* vol. I. New York: Grune & Stratton.

Cohen, S. P. 1979. *Pre-school Screening Instrument (PSSI).* Chicago: Stoelting.

Collins, M. T., and Rudolph, J. M. 1975. *A Manual for the Assessment of a Deaf-Blind Multiply Handicapped Child,* rev. ed. Denver: Mountain Plains Regional Center for the Deaf-Blind.

Council for Exceptional Children. 1979. *We Can Help.* Reston, Va.: author.

Dallas County Mental Health/Mental Retardation Center. 1972. *The RADEA Program.* Dallas, Tex.: Melton Peninsula Company.

Dardig, J. C., and Heward, W. L. 1981. A systematic procedure for prioritizing IEP goals. *Directive Teacher* 3:6–7.

Dent, H., and Johnson, R. 1964. The effects of massed versus distributed practice on the learning of organic familial defectives. *American Journal of Mental Deficiency* 68:533–36.

DiGaetani, J. L. 1980. The business of listening. *Business Horizons* 23(5):40–46.

Doll, E. A. 1965. *Vineland Social Maturity Scale.* Circle Pines, Minn.: American Guidance Service.

Donahue, M., Montgomery, J., Keiser, A., Roecker, V., Smith, L., and Walden, M.

1978. *Marshalltown Behavior Developmental Profile*. Marshalltown, Pa.: Area Education Agency 6, Preschool Division.

Dreger, R. M., Lewis, P. M., Rich, T. A., Miller, K. S., Reid, M. P., Overlade, D. C., Taffel, C., and Fleming, E. L. 1964. Behavioral classification project. *Journal of Consulting Psychology* 28:1–13.

Ebbinghaus, H. 1964. *Memory*. (Translated by H. A. Ruger and C. E. Bussenius.) New York: Dover. (Originally published as *Uber das Gedachtnis*. 1885. Leipzig: Duncker und Humbolt.)

Efron, M., and Duboff, B. 1975. *A Vision Guide for Teachers of Deaf-Blind Children*. Raleigh, N.C.: South Atlantic Regional Center for Deaf-Blind Children.

Egel, A. L., and Neef, N. 1983. *Model Educational Services for Autistic Children and Youth: A Final Report*. College Park, Md.: University of Maryland, Department of Special Education.

Egel, A., Richman, G., and Koegel, R. 1981. Normal peer models and autistic children's learning. *Journal of Applied Behavior Analysis* 14:3–11.

Everington, C. (ed.). 1982. *Los Lunas Curricular Systems,* 4th ed. Los Lunas, N.M.: Education Department, Los Lunas Hospital and Training School.

Falvey, M., Brown, L., Lyon, S., Baumgart, P., and Schroeder, J. 1980. Strategies for using cues and correction procedures. In W. Sailor, B. Wilcox, and L. Brown (eds.), *Methods of Instruction for Severely Handicapped Students*. Baltimore: Paul H. Brookes.

Faules, D. F., and Alexander, D. C. 1978. *Communication and Social Behavior: A Symbolic Interaction Perspective*. Reading, Mass.: Addison-Wesley.

Felixbrod, J. J., and O'Leary, K. D. 1973. Effects of reinforcement on children's academic behavior as a function of self-determined and externally imposed contingencies. *Journal of Applied Behavior Analysis* 6:241–50.

Fieber, N. M. 1977. *Sensorimotor Cognitive Assessment and Curriculum for the Multi-Handicapped Child*. Omaha: Meyer Children's Rehabilitation Institute.

Finnie, N. 1975. *Handling the Young Cerebral Palsied Child at Home*. New York: E.P. Dutton.

Fisher, R., and Ury, W. 1983. *Getting to Yes: Negotiating Agreement Without Giving In*. New York: Penguin Books.

Foster, R. W. 1974. *Camelot Behavioral Checklist*. Lawrence, Kans.: Camelot Behavior Systems.

Foxx, R. M., and Azrin, N. H. 1973. The elimination of autistic self-stimulatory behavior by overcorrection. *Journal of Applied Behavior Analysis* 6:1–14.

Frankenberg, W. K. 1983. *Approaches to Prevention of Disabilities: The Role of the Primary Care Provider*. Paper presented at Pediatric Update. Developmental Disabilities: Prevention, Diagnosis, and Management. University of Kansas College of Health Sciences, Kansas City, Kans.

Frankenberg, W. K., Dodds, J. B., and Fandal, A. W. 1975. *Denver Developmental Screening Test*. Denver: Ladoca Project and Publishing Foundation.

Frankenberg, W. K., Fandal, A. W., Sciarillo, W., and Burgess, D. 1981. The newly abbreviated and revised Denver Developmental Screening Test. *Journal of Pediatrics* 99:995–99.

Freagon, S., Rotatori, A., Jr., and Fox, R. Evaluation criteria for curriculum for the severely and profoundly retarded. *Journal for Special Educators* 19(1983):39–43.

Fredericks, H.D.B., Baldwin, V., Grove, D., Moore, W., Riggs, C., and Lyons, B. 1978. Integrating the moderately and severely handicapped preschool child into a normal day care setting. In M. J. Geralnick (ed.), *Early Intervention and the Integration of Handicapped Children*. Baltimore: University Park Press.

Fuller, R. M. 1983. How to improve your listening. *Supervision* 45(7):8–10.

Fulton, R. T., Lloyd, L. L. (eds.). 1975. *Auditory Assessment of the Difficult-to-Test*. Baltimore: Williams & Wilkins.

Gardner, N.E.S. 1979. *Protection and Advocacy*. Lawrence, Kans.: Kansas Center for Mental Retardation and Human Development, University of Kansas.

Gaylord-Ross, C., Forte, J., and Gaylord-Ross, R. 1983. *The Community Classroom: Technological Vocational Training for Students with Serious Handicaps*. Paper presented at the annual convention for the Association of Persons with Severe Handicaps, San Francisco.

Gaylord-Ross, R. 1980. A decision model for the treatment of aberrant behavior in applied settings. In W. Sailor, B. Wilcox, and L. Brown (eds.), *Methods of Instruction for Severely Handicapped Students*. Baltimore: Paul H. Brookes.

Gaylord-Ross, R., Haring, T., Breen, C., and Pitts-Conway, V. 1984. The training and generalization of social interaction skills with autistic youth. *Journal of Applied Behavior Analysis* 17:229–47.

Gaylord-Ross, R., and Peck, C. A. 1984. Integration efforts for students with severe mental retardation. In D. Bricker and J. Filler (eds.), *Serving the Severely Retarded: From Research to Practice*. Reston, Va.: Council for Exceptional Children.

Gaylord-Ross, R. J., and Pitts-Conway, V. 1983. Social behavior development in integrated secondary autistic programs. In N. Certo, N. Haring, and R. York (eds.), *Public School Integration of Severely Handicapped Students*. Baltimore: Paul H. Brookes.

Goetz, L., Utley, B., Gee, K., Baldwin, M., and Sailor, W. 1981. *Auditory Assessment and Program Manual for Severely Handicapped Deaf-Blind Students*. Seattle: Association for the Severely Handicapped.

Gold, M. 1975. Vocational training. In J. Wortis (ed.), *Mental Retardation and Developmental Disabilities,* vol. 7. New York: Brunner Mazél.

———. 1980. *Try Another Way*. Chicago: Research Press.

Goodman, J. F. 1981. *Goodman Lock Box*. Chicago: Stoelting.

Gorham, K. A., Des Jardins, C., Page, R., Pettis, E., and Schreiber, B. 1975. Effect on parents. In N. Hobbs (ed.), *Issues in Classification of Children*. San Francisco: Jossey-Bass.

Griffin, P. M., and Sanford, A. R. 1981. *Learning Accomplishment Profile for Infants*. Chapel Hill, N.C.: Chapel Hill Training Outreach Project, 1974.

Grossman, H. J. (ed.). 1977. *Manual on Terminology and Classification in Mental Retardation*. Washington, D.C.: American Association on Mental Deficiency.

———. (ed.). 1983. *Classification in Mental Retardation*. Washington, D.C.: American Association on Mental Deficiency.

Guess, D., Horner, R., Utley, B., Holvoet, J., Maxon, D., Tucker, D., and Warren, S. 1978. A functional curriculum sequencing model for teaching the severely handicapped. *AAESPH Review* 3:202–15.

Guess, D., Sailor, W., and Baer, D. M. 1976. *Functional Speech and Language*

Training for the Severely Handicapped. Austin, Tex.: PRO-ED, Inc.

Halperin, M. 1979. *Helping Maltreated Children.* St. Louis: C.V. Mosby.

Hanson, M. J. 1978. *Teaching Your Down's Syndrome Infant: A Guide for Parents.* Baltimore: University Park Press.

Hartup, W. W. 1978. Peer interaction and the process of socialization. In M. J. Guralnick (ed.), *Early Intervention and the Integration of Handicapped and Nonhandicapped Children.* Baltimore: University Park Press.

Hassenstab, M. S., and Horner, J. S. 1982. *Comprehensive Intervention with Hearing-Impaired Infants and Preschool Children.* Rockville, Md.: Aspen Systems.

Haynes, U., Patterson, G., D'Wolf, N., Hutchinson, D., Lowry, W., Schilling, M., and Siepp, J. 1976. *Staff Development Handbook: A Resource for the Transdisciplinary Process.* New York: United Cerebral Palsy Association.

Hengel, G. W. 1979. Try this meeting planning guide. *Training.* 16(5):64–5.

Holvoet, J., Brewer, M., Mulligan, M., Guess, D., and Helmstetter, E. 1983. Influence of activity choice among adolescent, severely multiply handicapped students. In J. Holvoet and D. Guess (eds.), *The KICS Model: Evaluation Studies.* Lawrence, Kans.: Department of Special Education, University of Kansas.

Holvoet, J., Guess, D., Mulligan, M., and Brown, F. 1980. The individualized curriculum sequencing model (II): A teaching strategy for severely handicapped students. *Journal of the Association for the Severely Handicapped.* 5:337–51.

Holvoet, J., Mulligan, M., Schussler, N., Lacy, L., and Guess, D. 1982. *The KICS Model: Sequencing Learning Experiences for Severely Handicapped Children and Youth.* Lawrence, Kans.: Department of Special Education, University of Kansas.

Hovland, I. C. 1939. Experimental studies in rote-learning theory (V): Comparison of distribution of practice in serial and paired-associate learning. *Journal of Experimental Psychology* 26:622–33.

———. 1940a. Experimental studies in rote-learning theory (VI): Comparisons of retention following learning to same criterion by massed and distributed practice. *Journal of Experimental Psychology* 27:568–87.

———. 1940b. Experimental studies in rote-learning theory (VII): Distribution of practice with varying lengths of lists. *Journal of Experimental Psychology* 27:271–84.

Howell, D. A. 1977. The sensitive teacher. In M. A. Thomas (ed.), *Children Alone.* Reston, Va.: Council for Exceptional Children.

Hutton, W. O., and Talkington, L. W. 1974. *Developmental Record.* Portland, Oreg.: Continuing Education Publications.

Ilich, J. 1980. *Power Negotiating.* Reading, Mass.: Addison-Wesley.

Irvin, L. K., Gersten, R. M., Taylor, V. E., Heiry, T. J., Close, D. W., and Bellamy, G. T. 1982. *Trainee Performance Sample.* Milwaukee: Ideal Development Labs.

Johnson, L. 1981. *Individual Skill Priority Rating Sheet.* Winfield, Kans.: Department of Education, Winfield State Hospital and Training Center.

Karras, C. 1970. *The Negotiating Game: How to Get What You Want.* New York: Thomas Y. Crowell.

Kaufman, A. S., and Kaufman, N. L. 1983. *Kaufman Assessment Battery for Children (K-ABC).* Circle Pines, Minn.: American Guidance Service.

Kazdin, A. E. 1973. The effects of vicarious reinforcement on attentive behavior in the classroom. *Journal of Applied Behavior Analysis.* 6:71–78.

Kazdin, A. E., Silverman, N. A., and Sittler, J. L. 1975. The use of prompts to enhance vicarious effects of nonverbal approval. *Journal of Applied Behavior Analysis.* 8:279–86.

Kimble, G. A. 1949a. Performance and reminiscence in motor learning as a function of degrees of distribution of practice. *Journal of Experimental Psychology* 39:500–10.

———. 1949b. An experimental test of a two-factor theory of inhibition. *Journal of Experimental Psychology.* 39:15–23.

Kimble, G. A., and Bilodeau, E. A. 1949. Work and rest as variables in cyclical motor learning. *Journal of Experimental Psychology* 39:150–57.

Kline, D. F. 1977. *Child Abuse and Neglect.* Reston, Va.: Council for Exceptional Children.

Koegel, R. L., and Covert, A. 1972. The relationship of self-stimulation to learning in autistic children. *Journal of Applied Behavior Analysis* 5:381–87.

Koegel, R. L., Glahn, T. J., and Nieminen, G. S. 1978. Generalization of parent training results. *Journal of Applied Behavior Analysis* 11:95–109.

Koegel, R. L., Russo, D. C., and Rincover, A. 1977. Assessing and training teachers in the generalized use of behavior modification with autistic children. *Journal of Applied Behavior Analysis* 10:197–205.

Koegel, R. L., and Wilheim, H. 1973. Selective responding to the components of multiple visual cues by autistic children. *Journal of Experimental Child Psychology* 15:442–53.

Kohl, F. L., Moses, L. G., and Stettner-Eaton, B. A. 1983. The results of teaching fifth and sixth graders to be instructional trainers with students who are severely handicapped. *Journal of the Association for Persons with Severe Handicaps* 8:32–40.

Koontz, C. W. 1974. *Koontz Child Development Program: Training Activities for the First 48 Months.* Los Angeles: Western Psychological Services.

Krug, D. A., Arick, J. R., and Almond, P. J. 1980. *Autism Screening Instrument for Educational Planning (ASIEP).* Portland, Oreg.: ASIEP Education.

Kukla, D., and Connally, T. T. 1979. *Assessment of Auditory Functioning of Deaf-Blind/Multihandicapped Children.* Arlington, Va.: ERIC Document Reproduction Service.

Lambert, N., Windmiller, M., Cole, L., and Figueroa, R. 1975. *AAMD Adaptive Behavior Scale: Public School Version,* 1974 rev. Washington, D.C.: American Association of Mental Deficiency.

Langley, M. B. 1980. *Functional Vision Inventory for the Multiply and Severely Handicapped.* Chicago: Stoelting.

Laycock, V. K. 1980. Assessment and evaluation in the classroom. In M. I. W. Schefani, R. M. Anderson, and S. J. Odle (eds.), *Implementing Learning in the Least Restrictive Environment: Handicapped Children in the Mainstream.* Baltimore: University Park Press.

Lehr, D. H. 1982. Child abuse and neglect. In E. L. Meyen and D. H. Lehr (eds.), *Exceptional Children in Today's Schools: An Alternative Resource Book.* Denver: Love.

Lombardi, T. P. 1980. *Career Adaptive Behavior Inventory and Developmental Activities.* Monterey, Calif.: Publishers Test Service.

Lovaas, O. I., Schreibman, L., Koegel, R., and Kehm, R. 1971. Selective responding by autistic children to multiple sensory input. *Journal of Abnormal Psychology* 77:211–22.

Lovaas, O. I., and Simmons, J. Q. 1969. Manipulation of self-destruction in three retarded children. *Journal of Applied Behavior Analysis* 2:143–57.

Lyon, S., and Lyon, G. 1981. Roles and responsibilities of the transdisciplinary team members. In D. Guess, C. Jones, and S. Lyon (eds.), *Combining a Transdisciplinary Team Approach with an Individualized Curriculum Sequencing Model for Severely/Multiply Handicapped Children.* Lawrence, Kans.: University of Kansas, Department of Special Education.

Madsen, M. C. 1963. Distribution of practice and level of intelligence. *Psychological Reports* 13:39–42.

Malgady, R. G., Barcher, P. R., Davis, J., and Towner, C. 1980. *Vocational Adaptation Rating Scales (VARS).* Los Angeles: Western Psychological Services.

Mar, D., Mithaug, D., and Stewart, J. 1978. *Prevocational Assessment and Curriculum Guide.* Seattle: Exceptional Education.

McClennen, S. E., Hoekstra, R. R., and Bryan, J. E. 1980. *Social Skills for Severely Retarded Adults.* Champaign, Ill.: Research Press.

McCormick, L., and Goldman, R. 1979. The transdisciplinary model: Implications for service delivery and personnel preparation for the severely and profoundly handicapped. *AAESPH Review* 4:152–61.

McLean, J. E., Snyder-McLean, L., Jacobs, P., and Rowland, C. M. 1981. *Process-Oriented Educational Programs for the Severely/Profoundly Handicapped Adolescent.* Parsons, Kans.: Bureau of Child Research, University of Kansas.

Michaelis, C. T. 1980. *Home and School Partnerships in Exceptional Education.* Rockville, Md.: Aspen.

Montgomery, P., and Richter, E. 1977. *Sensorimotor Integration for Developmentally Disabled Children.* Los Angeles: Western Psychological Services.

Mulligan, M., Lacy, L., and Guess, D. Effects of massed, distributed, and spaced trial sequencing on severely handicapped students' performance. *Journal of the Association for the Severely Handicapped* 7(1982):48–61.

National Center on Child Abuse and Neglect. 1975. *Child Abuse and Neglect: The Problem and Its Management—An Overview of the Problem,* vol. 1. Washington, D.C.: U.S. Department of Health, Education and Welfare.

Neel, R. S., Billingsley, F. F., McCarty, F., Symonds, D., Lambert, C., Lewis-Smith, N., and Hanashiro, R. 1983. *Teaching Autistic Children: A Functional Curriculum Approach.* Seattle: Experimental Education Unit, University of Washington.

Nierenberg, G. 1981. *The Art of Negotiating.* New York: Cornerstone.

Nietupski, J., Schuetz, G., and Ockwood, L. 1980. The delivery of communication therapy services to severely handicapped students: A plan for change. *Journal of the Association for the Severely Handicapped* 5:13–23.

Parten, M. 1932. Social participation among preschool children. *Journal of Abnormal Social Psychology* 27:243–69.

Patterson, G. R., and Guillan, M. E. 1968. *Living with Children.* Champaign, Ill.: Research Press.

Peabody Model Vision Project. 1980. *Functional Vision Inventory*. Chicago: Stoelting.

Perlmutter, L. C., and Monty, R. A. 1977. The importance of perceived control: Fact or fantasy. *American Scientist*. 65:759–65.

Piaget, J. 1963. *The Origins of Intelligence in Children*. New York: W. W. Norton.

Popovich, D. 1977. *A Prescriptive Behavioral Checklist for the Severely and Profoundly Retarded,* vol. 1. Baltimore: University Park Press.

———. 1981a. *A Prescriptive Behavioral Checklist for the Severely and Profoundly Retarded,* vol. 2. Baltimore: University Park Press.

———. 1981b. *A Prescriptive Behavioral Checklist for the Severely and Profoundly Retarded,* vol. 3. Baltimore: University Park Press.

Popovich, D., and Laham, S. L. (eds.). 1981. *The Adaptive Behavior Curriculum: Prescriptive Behavioral Analysis for Moderately, Severely, and Profoundly Handicapped Students,* vol. 1. Baltimore: Paul H. Brookes.

Project RHISE. 1976. *Rockford Infant Developmental Evaluation Scales: RIDES*. Bensenville, Ill.: Scholastic Testing Service.

Public Law 94-142. 1977. *Federal Register* (Part IV). Washington, D.C.: U.S. Government Printing Office, August 23, 1977.

Quick, A. D., Little, T. L., and Campbell, A. A. 1974. *Project MEMPHIS Instruments for Individual Program Planning and Evaluation Comprehensive Developmental Scale*. Belmont, Calif.: Fearon.

Rago, W. V., Parker, R. M., and Cleland, C. 1978. Effect of increased space on the social behavior of institutional profoundly retarded male adults. *American Journal of Mental Deficiency* 82:554–58.

Raudsepp, E. 1983. How to make the most of meetings. *Supervision* 45(2):6–8.

Rea, J., Holvoet, J., and Schussler, N. 1983. Group instruction and incidental learning in learners with severe mental retardation. In J. Holvoet and D. Guess (eds.), *The KICS Model: Evaluation Studies*. Lawrence, Kans.: Department of Special Education, University of Kansas.

Richmond, B. O., and Kichlighter, R. H. 1982. *Children's Adaptive Behavior Report*. Atlanta: Humanics Limited.

———. 1979. *Childrens Adaptive Behavior Scale*. Special Child Publication. Seattle, Wash.

———. 1983. *Children's Adaptive Behavior Scale*. Atlanta: Humanics Limited.

Rock, K., Litchfield, D., Jans, C., Schulz, C., Ulrich, J., Pray, V., and Vedovatti, P. 1974. *Low-Functioning Vision Assessment Kit*. DeKalb, Ill.: Northwestern Illinois Association for Hearing, Vision, and Physically Handicapped Children.

Rogers, C. 1970. *Carl Rogers on Encounter Groups*. New York: Harrow.

Roman, B. 1978. *Infant Stimulation Training Skills*. Johnstown, Pa.: Mafex Associates.

Rosenthal, R. 1966. *Experimenter Effects in Behavioral Research*. New York: Appleton-Century Crofts.

Ruggles, T. R., and LeBlanc, J. M. 1979. *Variables Which Affect the Effectiveness of Group Training Procedures Designed for Children with Learning Problems*. Paper presented at the Twelfth Annual Gatlingburg Conference on Research in Mental Disabilities, Gulf Shores, Ala.

Ruttenberg, B. A., Kalish, B. I., Wenar, C., and Wolf, E. G. 1977. *Behavior Rating Instrument for Atypical Children (BRIAC)*. Chicago: Stoelting.

Sailor, W., and Mix, B. J. 1976. *The TARC Assessment System*. Lawrence, Kans.: H & H Enterprises.

Sanford, A. R. (ed.). 1974. *Learning Accomplishment Profile*. Chapel Hill, N.C.: Chapel Hill Training Outreach Project, 1974.

Santa Cruz Office of Education. 1973. *The Behavioral Characteristics Progression (BCP)*. Palo Alto, Calif.: Vort Corporation.

Sarason, S. B., and Doris, J. 1969. *Psychological Problems in Mental Deficiency*, 4th ed. New York: Harper & Row.

Schalock, R. 1978. *Competitive Employment*. Hastings, Nebr.: MidNebraska Mental Retardation Services.

Schalock, R., and Gadwood, L. 1980. *Community Living Skills*. Hastings, Nebr.: MidNebraska Mental Retardation Services.

Schalock, R. L., Ross, B. E., and Ross, I. 1976. *Basic Skills Screening Test*. Hastings, Nebr.: MidNebraska Mental Retardation Services.

Schreibman, L. 1975. Effects of within-stimulus and extra-stimulus prompting on discrimination learning in autistic children. *Journal of Applied Behavior Analysis* 8:91–112.

Schreibman, L., Keogel, R. L., and Craig, M. S. 1977. Reducing stimulus overselectivity in autistic children. *Journal of Abnormal Child Psychology* 5:425–36.

Seltz, D., and Modica, A. 1981. *Negotiate Your Way to Success*. New York: New American Library.

Shearer, D., Billingsley, J., Frohmann, A., Hilliard, J., Johnson, F., and Shearer, M. 1976. *Portage Guide to Early Education*. Portage, Wis.: CESA 12.

Shurager, H. C., and Shurager, P. S. 1964. *Haptic Intelligence Scale*. Chicago: Stoelting.

Sidman, M., and Stoddard, L. T. 1966. Programming perception and learning for retarded children. In N. R. Ellis (ed.), *International Review of Research in Mental Retardation*, vol. 2. New York: Academic Press.

Skinner, B. F. 1938. *The Behavior of Organisms: An Experimental Analysis*. New York: Appleton Century Crofts.

Somerton-Fair, M. E., and Turner, K. 1975. *Pennsylvania Training Model: Assessment Guide*. Harrisburg, Pa.: Pennstar.

Song, A., and Jones, S. 1979. *Wisconsin Behavior Rating Scale*. Madison, Wis.: Central Wisconsin Center for the Developmentally Disabled.

Sontag, E. 1977. *Educational Programming for the Severely and Profoundly Handicapped*. Reston, Va.: Council for Exceptional Children.

Sowers, J., Rusch, F. R., Connis, R. T., and Cummings, L. E. 1980. Teaching mentally retarded adults to time-manage in a vocational setting. *Journal of Applied Behavior Analysis* 13:119–28.

Spellman, C., and Cress, P. 1980. *Parsons Visual Acuity Kit*. Chicago: Burnell.

Stainback, S. B., Stainback, W. C., and Hatcher, C. W. 1983. Nonhandicapped peer involvement in the education of severely handicapped students. *Journal of the Association for the Severely Handicapped* 8:39–42.

Stillman, R. 1978. *Callier-Azusa Scale—Revised*. Dallas, Tex.: Callier Center for Communication Disorders.

Striefel, S. 1974. *Measuring Behavior 7: Teaching a Child to Imitate*. Lawrence, Kans.: H & H Enterprises.

Switzky, H. M., Woolsey-Hill, J., and Quoss, T. 1979. Habituation of visual fixation responses: An assessment tool to measure visual sensory-perceptual cognitive processes in nonverbal profoundly handicapped children in the classroom. *AAESP Review* 4:136–47.

Terman, L. M., and Merrill, M. A. 1973. *Stanford-Binet Intelligence Scale*. Boston: Houghton Mifflin.

Turkel, S. B., and Podell, D. M. 1984. Computer-assisted learning for mildly handicapped students. *Teaching Exceptional Children* 16:258–62.

Underwood, B. J., Kapelak, S. M., and Malmi, R. A. 1976. The spacing effect: Additions to the theoretical and empirical puzzles. *Memory and Cognition* 4:391–400.

Utley, B., Goetz, L., Gee, K., Baldwin, M., and Sailor, W. 1982. *Vision Assessment and Program Manual for Severely Handicapped and/or Deaf-Blind Students*. Seattle: Association for the Severely Handicapped.

Vincent, L., and Broome, K. 1977. A public school service delivery model for handicapped children between birth and five years of age. In E. Sontag, J. Smith, and N. Certo (eds.), *Educational Programming for the Severely/Profoundly Handicapped*. Reston, Va.: Council for Exceptional Children.

Vincent, L. J., Salisbury, C., Walter, G., Brown, P., Gruenewald, L. J., and Powers, M. 1980. Program evaluation and curriculum development in early childhood/special education: Criteria of the Next Environment. In W. Sailor, B. Wilcox, and L. Brown (eds.), *Methods of Instruction for Severely Handicapped Students*. Baltimore: Paul H. Brookes.

Vocational Opportunities Cooperative. 1982. *VOCSKILLS*. New Berlin, Wis.: Ideal Developmental Labs.

Voeltz, L. M. 1980a. *Dimensions of Children's Acceptance of Handicapped Peers in Integrated Settings*. Paper presented at the Fifty-eighth Annual Convention of the Council for Exceptional Children, Philadelphia.

———. 1980b. Children's attitudes toward handicapped peers. *American Journal of Mental Deficiency* 84:455–64.

———. 1982. Effects of structured interactions with severely handicapped peers on children's attitudes. *American Journal of Mental Deficiency* 86:380–90.

Voeltz, L. M., Evans, I. M., Derer, K. R., and Hanashiro, R. 1983. Targeting excess behavior for change: A clinical decision model for selecting priority goals in educational contexts. *Child and Family Behavior Therapy* 5:17–35.

Waldo, L., Hirsch, M., and Marshall, A. 1978. *Functional Sign Training for the Severely Multihandicapped*. Washington, D.C.: Handicapped Media Services and Captioned Films Program, Bureau of Education for the Handicapped (#446AH70146).

Wechsler, D. 1967. *Wechsler Preschool and Primary Scale of Intelligence (WPPSI)*. New York: Psychological Corporation.

———. 1974. *Weschler Intelligence Scale for Children—Revised*. New York: Psychological Corporation.

Weeks, M., and Gaylord-Ross, R. 1981. Task difficulty and aberrant behavior in severely handicapped students. *Journal of Applied Behavior Analysis*. 14:449–63.

Welch, R. J., O'Brian, J. J., and Ayers, F. 1974. *Cambridge Assessment Develop-*

mental Rating and Evaluation (C.A.D.R.E.). Cambridge, Minn.: CADRE Center, Cambridge-Isanti Public Schools.

White, O., Edgar, E., and Haring, N. G. 1982. *Uniform Performance Assessment System (UPAS).* Columbus, Ohio: Charles E. Merrill.

White, O. R., and Haring, N. G. 1976. *Exceptional Teaching: A Multimedia Training Package.* Columbus, Ohio: Charles E. Merrill.

White, O. R., and Liberty, K. A. 1976. Evaluation and measurement. In N. G. Haring and R. L. Schiefelbusch (eds.), *Teaching Special Children.* New York: McGraw-Hill.

Wolfe, V. F., and Cuvo, A. J. 1978. Effects of within-stimulus and extra-stimulus prompting on letter discrimination by mentally retarded persons. *American Journal of Mental Deficiency* 83:297–303.

Wolfensberger, W. 1972. *The Principle of Normalization in Human Services.* Downsview, Can.: National Institute of Mental Retardation.

Wuerch, B. B., and Voeltz, L. M. 1982. *Longitudinal Leisure Skills for Severely Handicapped Learners: The Ho'onanea Curriculum Component.* Baltimore: Paul H. Brookes.

Young, M. 1974. *Skills Achievement Profile.* Ladson, S.C.: Education and Training Department, SCDMR Coastal Regional Center.

Zeaman, D., and House, B. 1963. The role of attention in retardate discrimination learning. In N. Ellis (ed.), *Handbook of Mental Deficiency.* New York: McGraw-Hill.

Zehrback, R. R. 1975. *Comprehensive Identification Process (CIP).* Bensenville, Ill.: Scholastic Testing Service.

Index

Active listening, 301
Adaptive Behavior Curriculum, 207–209
Adaptive behavior tests
AAMD Adaptive Behavior Scale, 11, 12
Balthazar Scales of Adaptive Behavior for the Profoundly and Severely Retarded, 11
Basic Life Skills Screening Inventory, 12
Behavior Rating Scale for Atypical Children, 12
Brigance Diagnostic Inventory of Early Development, 12
Cain-Levine Social Competency Scale, 12
Callier-Azusa Scale, 12
Camelot Behavioral Checklist, 12
Child Behavior Rating Scale, 12
Children's Adaptive Behavior Report, 12
Children's Adaptive Behavior Scale, 12
Competitive Employment, 12
Developmental Pinpoints, 12
Developmental Record, 12
Marshalltown Behavior Development Profile, 13
Pennsylvania Training Model: Assessment Guide, 13
Priority Needs Assessment Scale, 13
Project MEMPHIS Instruments for Individual Program Planning and Evaluation, 13
TARC Assessment Inventory for Severely Handicapped Children, 12
Uniform Performance Assessment System, 13
Vineland Social Maturity Scale, 12
Vocational Adaptation Rating Scales, 13
Wisconsin Behavior Rating Scale—R, 12
Adaptive devices for computers, 328–331
Administrator, part of educational team, 291–292
Aim star procedure, 157–158
Akron program, 314–317
Alexander, D., 100
Almond, P. J., 27, 30
Alpern, G. D., 5
Arick, J. R., 27, 30
Assessment, 2
conducting, 36
developmental, 17, 19
diagnostic testing, 6–17
discussion with parents, 33–34
educational, 17–33, 94
criteria for, 18–19
environmental, 17, 20–22
interpreting results, 36–37
of learning styles, 22–31
making decisions after, 37–38
preparation for, 34–36
process of, 33–39
screening, 2–5
of sensorimotor defects, 31–33
Assessment of Auditory Functioning of Deaf-Blind/Multihandicapped Children, 32
Association for Persons with Severe Handicaps, 190
Attentional control, 23
Audiologist, part of educational team, 291

Auditory Assessment and Programming for Handicapped and Deaf-Blind Students, 32
Auditory Assessment of the Difficult-to-Test, 32
Aversive stimuli, 190–194
contingent restraint, 193
corporal punishment, 192
overcorrection, 193–194
parents as deliverers of, 269–270
timeout, 192
Ayers, F., 19
Azrin, N. H., 193, 222

Baer, D. M., 202–207, 208
Baldwin, M., 32
Baldwin, V., 243
Ball, R. S., 10
Balsamo, C., 13
Balthazar, E. E., 11
Bandura, A., 116
Barcher, P. R., 13
Baumeister, A. A., 91, 92
Baumgart, D., 20, 49, 79
Bayley, N., 10
Becker, H., 12
Behavior
adaptive, 167
maladaptive, 166–196
Behavior check, 114
Behavior management, in parenting, 267–271
Behavior modification, research in, 317–322
Behavioral assessment, 178–180
Behavioral programs, in functional curriculum, 112–115
Bellamy, G. T., 27, 75, 214
Berk, R. A., 100
Berry, M., 91, 92
Billingsley, F. F., 90
Billingsley, J., 19
Bilodeau, E. A., 91
Blatt, B., 227
Boll, T. J., 5
Brackman, B., 315
Bradford, L. P., 303
Branching, 219
Branston, M. B., 258
Branston-McClean, M., 20
Brazelton, T. B., 5
Breen, C., 247, 249
Brewer, M., 100
Bricker, D. D., 221, 293
Bricker, W. A., 13, 15
Brigance, A. H., 12
Brinker, R. P., 322, 323, 326, 328
Broome, K., 310
Brown, F., 116, 117, 118
Brown, L., 15, 20, 49, 79, 93, 198, 232, 234, 258, 312–313
Brown, P., 311
Bryan, J. E., 19, 31
Budd, C., 222
Burton, R., 13

Cadigan, E., 222
Cain, L. F., 12
Campbell, A. A., 13
Campbell, P., 13, 15, 315
Campbell, S., 221
Carey, W. B., 31
Carrington, E., 13
Casella, V., 328, 331, 332
Cassell, R. N., 12
Cattell, P., 10
Certo, N., 258
Chaining, 70
backward, 81–83
concurrent, 73, 75–77, 132–133
forward, 81–83
prompted serial, 83
serial, 73–74, 76
Child abuse and neglect, 296–297
Classroom design, 234–238
areas and zones, 234–237
decor, 237–238
Cleland, C., 180
Close, D. W., 27
Cohen, H., 305
Cohen, M. A., 12
Cohen, S. P., 5
Cole, L., 11
Collins, M. T., 12
Communication, 254
parent-professional, 254–258
Communication skills. *See* Language skills
Communications programs, in functional curriculum, 101–105
Community placement, 228–229
Comprehensive Intervention with Hearing-Impaired Infants and Preschool Children, 32
Concurrent chaining, 73, 75–77
Connally, T. T., 32

Consistency, 48–50
Contingent restraint, 193
Continuous reinforcement schedule, 64
Costello, K., 33
Council for Exceptional Children, 297
Covert, A., 318, 319, 320, 326
Cress, P., 33
Curricular factors in maladaptive behavior, 184–185
Curriculum. *See* Developmental curriculum; Functional curriculum
Curriculum, adapting, 218–223
 commercial availability of, 202–218, 221–222
 evaluating, 200–201
 guidelines for selecting, 199–202

Dallas County Mental Health/Mental Retardation Center, 19
Dardig, J. C., 37
Data
 collection of, by parents, 270–271
 graphing, 152–159
 interpretation of, 153–159
 management of, 159–163
 recording, 129–146
 reliability of, 146–153
Davis, J., 13
DeBriere, T., 221
Dent, H., 91, 92
Denver Developmental Screening Test, 3, 5
Derer, K. R., 172
Des Jardins, C., 7
Design
 classroom, 234–238
 instructional. *See* Instructional design
Developmental assessment, 17, 19
 Basic Skills Screening Test, 19
 Behavioral Characteristics Progression, 19
 Cambridge Assessment Development Rating and Evaluation, 19
 Career Adaptive Behavior Inventory and Developmental Activities, 19
 Community Living Skills, 19
 Infant Stimulation Training Skills, 19
 Koontz Child Development Program, 19
 Learning Accomplishment Profile, 19
 Los Lunas Curricular System, 19
 Portage Guide to Early Education, 19
 Prescriptive Behavioral Checklist for the Severely and Profoundly Retarded, 19
 RADEA program, 19
 Sensorimotor Cognitive Assessment and Curriculum for the Multihandicapped Child, 19
 Sensorimotor Integration for Developmentally Disabled Children, 19
 Skills Achievement Profile, 19
 Social Skills for Severely Retarded Adults, 19
Developmental curriculum, 93
Diagnostic assessment, 6–17
 adaptive behavior tests, 11
 components of, 6–7
 controversy over, 7–8
 criteria for, 8–9
 intelligence tests, 10–11
 types of, 9–15
Differential reinforcement, 52–53
DiGaetàni, J. L., 301, 399
Discrete-trial learning, 44–52, 140
 paradigm, 45
Discriminative stimulus (S^D), 45–46, 49–50, 51–78 passim
 consistency of, 49
 continuousness of, 49
Dodds, J. B., 3, 5
Doll, E. A., 12
Donahue, M., 13
Doris, J., 226
Dreger, R. M., 7
DuBoff, B., 33
Duration of responses, 145–146
D'Wolf, N., 315

Ebbinghaus, H., 91
Ecological factors in maladaptive behavior
 absence of engaging objects, 184
 crowding, 181–183
 environmental pollutants, 183–184
Edgar, E., 13
Educational assessment, 17–33, 94
Efron, M., 33
Egel, A. L., 90, 117
Elzey, F. F., 12
Environment, 224
 home, 228–229, 265–267
 physical, 226–238, 265–266
 school, 229–238
 segregated vs. integrated classes, 229–231

Environment [*cont.*]
social, 238–250
teaching, 225–226, 229–238
Environmental assessment, 17, 20–22
Environmental inventories, 94
Errorless learning, 62–64
Evans, I. M., 172
Everington, C., 19
Extinction, 187

Fading of stimulus, 61–64
Falvey, M., 20, 49, 50
Fandal, A. W., 3, 5
Felixbrod, J. J., 100
Fieber, N. M., 19
Figueroa, R., 11
Filler, J., 315
Finnie, N., 222, 275
Fisher, R., 305
Fleming, E. L., 7
Ford, A., 79, 232
Forte, J., 234
Foster, R. W., 12
Foxx, R. M., 193, 199, 201, 222
Frankenburg, W. K., 3, 5
Freagon, S., 199, 201, 221
Fredericks, H. D. B., 243, 244
Frequency, defined, 140
Frohman, A., 19
Fulton, R. T., 32
Functional analysis of maladaptive behavior, 176
Functional curriculum, 92–124
behavioral programs, 112–115
communication programs, 101–105
cues in, 96–98
educational assessment in, 94
environmental inventories in, 94
group instruction in, 115–124
materials, 95–96
students' choice of, 100–101
varying, 98–99
materials and activities, 93–96, 98–101
motor programs, 106–110
objectives, 94–95
sequencing skills, 110–112
setting, 96–98
Functional groups
intersequential, 122–124
intrasequential, 118–120
Functional skills sequences, recording of, 133–136
Functional Speech and Language Training for the Severely Handicapped, 202–207
Functional Vision Inventory for the Multiply and Severely Handicapped, 32
Fundakowski, G., 315

Gaddy, M., 222
Gadwood, L., 19
Gardner, N. E. S., 294, 299
Garozzo, D., 13
Gaylord-Ross, C., 234
Gaylord-Ross, R., 180, 185, 234, 235, 247, 248, 249, 250, 320–321, 322, 326
Gee, K., 32
Generalization, defined, 140
Generic skills, 99
Gersten, R. M., 27
Gillis, J., 222
Glahn, T. J., 49
Goetz, L., 32
Gold, M., 126
Goldman, R., 315
Goodman, J. F., 5
Gorham, K. A., 7
Griffin, P. M., 19
Gross, P. J., 12
Grossman, H. J., 11
Group instruction, 241–243
in functional curriculum, 115–124
Grove, D., 243
Gruenewald, L., 258, 311
Guess, A. R., 222
Guess, D., 89, 90, 91, 100, 107, 116, 202–207, 208
Guillan, M. E., 268, 275

Habituation, 108
Haffman, J., 222
Halperin, M., 296
Hamre-Nietupski, S., 93, 198, 258
Hanashiro, R., 90, 172
Hansen, L., 79
Hanson, M. J., 275
Haring, N. G., 12, 13
Haring, T., 247, 249
Harris, C., 221
Hasenstab, M. S., 32
Hatcher, C. W., 117
Haynes, U., 315
Heater, G., 222

Heiry, T. J., 27
Helmstetter, E., 100
Hengel, G. W., 303
Heward, W. L., 37
Hilliard, J., 19
Hirsch, M., 207
Hoekstra, R. R., 19, 31
Holvoet, J., 89, 90, 91, 100, 101, 107, 116, 117
Ho'onanea curriculum, 214–218
Horner, J. S., 32
Horner, R., 75, 107
House, B., 77
Hovland, I. C., 91
Howell, D. A., 296
Hutchinson, D., 315
Hutton, W. O., 12

Ierardi, M., 13
Ilich, J., 305
Impulsivity and reflectivity, 27–29
 inventory form, 28
Incidental learning, 226
Index of Qualification for Special Services, 13, 15
Individualized education plan (IEP), 22, 263–264, 295
Inman, D. P., 75
Institutionalization, 226–228
Instruction, multiple-setting, 225–226, 235
 integrated classes and, 230–231, 235
 off-campus activities, 231
 on-the-job vocational training, 231–232
Instructional design, 42–88
 model, 42–77
 program design, 86–88
Integrated classes, 230
Integrated service delivery, 317
Intelligence tests, 10–11
 Bayley Scales of Infant Development, 10
 Cattell Infant Intelligence Test, 10
 Extended Merrill-Palmer Scale, 10
 Haptic Intelligence Test, 10
 Kaufmann Assessment Battery for Children, 10
 Stanford-Binet Intelligence Test, 10
 Wechsler Intelligence Scale for Children—Revised, 10
 Wechsler Preschool and Primary Scale of Intelligence, 10
Interaction, social. *See* Social interaction
Interpersonal dynamics, 254–255
Intertrial interval (ITI), 45, 47–48, 50
Intervals, recording of, 142–143
Irvin, L. K., 27, 30
Isolation training, 75

Jacobs, P., 90
Jans, C., 32
Jarboe, D., 221
Johnson, F., 19
Johnson, L., 37
Johnson, R., 91, 92
Jones, S., 12

Kailukaitis, M., 13
Kalish, B. I., 12
Kapelak, S. M., 91
Karras, C., 305
Kaufman, A. S., 10
Kaufman, N. L., 10
Kazdin, A. E., 116
Kehm, R., 99
Keiser, A., 13
Kicklighter, R. H., 12
Kimble, G. A., 91
Klaire, R., 13
Kline, D. F., 296
Koegel, R. L., 49, 98, 99, 117, 318, 319, 320, 326
Kohl, F. L., 117
Koontz, C. W., 19
Krug, D. A., 27, 30
Kukla, D., 32

Lacy, L., 90
Laham, S. L., 207–208
Lambert, C., 90
Lambert, N., 11
Langley, M. B., 32
Language training, curricula for, 202–207, 221
Latency, 47, 146
Laycock, V. K., 22
Learning styles, 22–31
 tests of, 30–31
LeBlanc, J. M., 117
Lehr, D. H., 297
Leisure skills, curricula for, 214–218, 222
Level of processing, 25–27
Levine, S., 12

Lewis, M., 328
Lewis, P. M., 7
Lewis-Smith, N., 90
Liberty, K. A., 155–157
Listening, active and responsive, 300–303
Litchfield, D., 32
Little, T. L., 13
Lloyd, L. L., 32
Log, parent-teacher daily, 259–260
Lombardi, T. P., 19
Loomis, R., 232
Lovaas, O. I., 98, 193, 221
Low-Functioning Vision Assessment Kit, 32
Lowry, W., 315
Lundervold, D., 222
Lyon, G., 292
Lyon, S., 49, 292
Lyons, B., 243

Madison, WI
 preschool programs, 310–312
 secondary programs, 312–314
Madsen, M. C., 91, 92
Mainstreaming, 309–310
Maintenance, defined, 140
Maladaptive behavior, 166–172
 analyzing, 171–172, 176–186
 generic, 168–169
 levels, 171–172
 treating, 170–196
 types, 168–170, 171–172
Malgady, R. G., 13
Malmi, R. A., 91
Mar, D., 20
Marshall, A., 207
Martin-Petty, D., 12
Maxon, D., 107
McCarty, F., 90
McClennan, S. E., 19, 31
McCormick, L., 315
McLaughlin, P., 222
McLean, J. E., 90
Measurement, importance of, 126–129
 interpretation of, 153–159
 multiple-response, 131–137
 recording of, 129–146
 reliability of, 146–153
Merrifield, P., 10
Merrill, M. A., 10
Michaelis, C. T., 295
Microcomputers, 327–331
Mikalonis, L., 222
Miller, K. S., 7
Mithany, D. E., 222
Mithaug, D., 20
Mix, B. J., 12
Modality preference, 23–25
 inventory form, 25
Modica, A., 305
Montgomery, J., 13
Montgomery, P., 19
Monty, R. A., 100
Moore, W., 243
Moses, L. G., 117
Motivation, 116
Motor programs, in functional curriculum, 106–110
Mulligan, M., 90, 91, 100, 116
Multidisciplinary team, 289–293
Multiple-response measurement, 131–137
Multiple-setting instruction, 225–226, 235
 integrated classes and, 230–231, 235
 off-campus activities, 231
 on-the-job vocational training, 231–232

National Center on Child Abuse and Neglect, 296
Natural cues, 96
Neef, N., 90
Neel, R. S., 90, 96
Negative reinforcement. *See* Aversive stimuli
Nieminen, G. S., 49
Nierenberg, G., 305
Nietupski, J., 93, 101, 198
Nisbet, J., 79, 232
Norm-referenced measurement, 4
Normalization, 309
Nurse, part of educational team, 291

Object-specific skills, 99
O'Brien, J. J., 19
Observer agreement check, 147
Occupational therapist, part of educational team, 289
Occurrence agreement, 152
Ockwood, L., 101
Off-campus activities, 231
Off-task behavior, 168
O'Leary, K. D., 100
Operant conditioning, 43–46

Organizations, related to the handicapped, 275
Overcorrection, 193
Overlade, D. C., 7

P.L. 93-112 (Rehabilitation Act of 1973), 295
P.L. 94-142 (Education for All Handicapped Children Act of 1975), 8, 33, 229, 263, 295, 296, 310
Page, R., 7
Paoletti, M., 12
Paraprofessionals, in the classroom, 285–289
Parent involvement, 259–263
 daily log, 259–260
 in educational team, 292
 visits, 261–263
Parenting, 252–254
 behavior management, 267–271
 data collection in, 270–271
 demands of, 253
 parental involvement model, 271–276
 skills, 265–271
 support systems for, 274–276
Parker, R. M., 180
Parten, M., 244
Partial participation, 79, 80–81, 218, 220–221
Partition reliability, 150–152
Patterson, G. R., 268, 275, 315
Peabody Model Vision Project, 33
Peck, C. A., 322
Perlmutter, L. C., 100
Peterson, C., 315
Pettis, E., 7
Physical therapist, part of educational team, 290
Pica, 170
Pinkney, P., 33
Pitts-Conway, V., 247, 248, 249
Placement, 8
Play, social, 244
Podell, D. M., 327
Popovich, D., 19, 207–208
Positive reinforcement (S^{R+}), 47–48, 52, 53
 consistency of, 50
 contingency of, 49
 differential, 187–190
 parents as deliverers of, 268–269
 selection of, 50–52, 55
Powers, M., 311
Pray, V., 32
Primary reinforcement, 83
Probert, G., 13
Problem behavior. *See* Maladaptive behavior
Production, defined, 140
Project Rhise, 5
Prompt, 52
 observational, 57
 physical, 58
 recording of, 137–140
 sequence, 54–55
 sequencing, 58–59
 time delay in, 60–61
 verbal, 55–56
 within-stimulus, 63
Prosthetic devices, 79–80, 219–220
Psychologist, part of educational team, 290
Public Law 93-112. *See* P.L. 93-112
Public Law 94-142. *See* P.L. 94-142
Pumpian, J., 79, 258
Punishment, 190–194

Quarter-intersect line, 155–157
Quick, A. D., 13
Quoss, T., 108

Rago, W. V., 180
Ranieri, L., 79
Rate, recording of, 140–142
Raudsepp, E., 303
Rea, J., 117
Recording
 concurrent chains, 132–133
 duration, 145–146
 functional skills sequences, 133–136
 graphing, 152–159
 intervals, 142–143
 multiple-response measurement, 131–137
 prompts, 137–140
 rate, 140–142
 time sampling, 144–145
 trial-by-trial system, 129–131
Regression line, 155
Reid, M. P., 7
Reinforcement, 45, 46–47. *See also* Positive reinforcement
 primary, 83
 schedules of, 64, 189
  continuous, 64
  time-sample, 69

Reinforcement [*cont.*]
 variable ratio, 67
 secondary, 83–84
 thinning of, 64–70
Reinforcement preferences, 29–30
 inventory form, 30
Reinforcement variable, 187
Reinforcer preference test, 51, 53
Reliability
 observer agreement check to assure, 147–153
 occurrence agreement as measure of, 152
 partition agreement as measure of, 150–152
 total agreement as measure of, 150
Research, 317–327
 behavior modification, 317–322
 social integration, 322–327
Response, 44–45
Response adaptations, 78–80
Response chaining, 70
Response cost, 192
Response shaping, 70
Responsive listening, 301
Rich, T. A., 7
Richman, G., 117
Richmond, B. O., 12
Richter, E., 19
Riggs, C., 243
Rincover, A., 49
Rock, K., 32
Roecker, V., 13
Roman, B., 19
Rosenthal, R., 147
Ross, B. E., 19
Ross, I., 19
Rotatori, A., 199, 201
Rowland, C. M., 90
Rudolph, J. M., 12
Ruggles, T. R., 117
Rusch, F. R., 222
Russo, D. C., 49
Ruttenberg, B. A., 12

Sailor, W., 12, 15, 32, 202–207, 208
Salisbury, C., 311
Sanford, A. R., 19
Sarason, S. B., 226
Satiation, 51
Schalock, R., 12, 19
Schedule of reinforcement, 64
Scheduling, 239–241
Scheffers, W., 33
Schilling, M., 315
Schreiber, B., 7
Schreibman, L., 63, 98, 99
Schroeder, J., 20, 49, 79
Schuetz, G., 101
Schultz, C., 32
Schur, S., 12
Schussler, N., 90, 117
Screening, 2–5
 teacher's role in, 5
Screening tests, 3–4
 Brazelton Neonatal Behavioral Assessment Scale, 5
 Comprehensive Identification Process, 5
 Denver Developmental Screening Test, 5
 Developmental Profile II, 5
 Goodman Lock Box, 5
 parameters, 4–5
 Pre-school Screening Instrument, 5
 Rockford Infant Developmental Scales, 5
 validity of, 4
Secondary reinforcement, 83–84
Segregated classes, 229
Self-care skills, curricula for, 207–209, 222
Self-injury, 169
Self-stimulation, 168
Seltz, D., 305
Sensorimotor defects, 31–33
 instruments for measuring, 32–33
Sensorimotor programming, Akron program, 314–317
Sequencing skills, in functional curriculum, 110–112
Serial chaining, 73–74, 76
Shearer, D., 19
Shearer, M., 5, 19
Shiraga, B., 232
Shurager, H. C., 10
Shurager, P. S., 10
Siepp, J., 315
Silverman, N. A., 116
Simmons, J. Q., 193
Sittler, J. L., 116
Skills
 generic, 99
 object-specific, 99
Skinner, B. F., 43
Smith, L., 13

Snell, M. E., 221
Snyder-McLean, L., 90
Social awareness, 244
Social environment, 238–250
 group instruction, 241–243
 in the home, 266–267
 play, 244
 scheduling, 239–241
 social integration, 243–250, 322–327
 social interaction, 245–250
Social integration, research in, 322–327
Social interaction, 244, 245–250
 contexts, 248–250
 peer tutoring, 248–249
 special friends, 249–250
 student-centered, 249
 types of, 245–248
Somerton-Fair, M. E., 13
Song, A., 12
Sowers, J., 179, 222
Special education
 developments in, 327–331
 history, 308–310
 model programs, 310–317
 research, 317–327
Special Education Information Management System, 19
Speech therapist, part of educational team, 290
Spellman, C., 33, 221
Stainbeck, S. B., 117
Stainbeck, W. C., 117
Standardized tests, 9
Stettner-Eaton, B. A., 117
Stewart, J., 20
Stillman, R., 12
Stimulation, in home environment, 265–267
Stimulus, discriminative. *See* Discriminative stimulus
Stimulus control, 52
Stimulus overselectivity, 98–99
Stimulus-response paradigm, 45
Stott, L. H., 10
Striefel, S., 31
Swanson, M., 222
Sweet, M., 79, 232
Switzky, H. M., 108
Symonds, D., 90

Taffel, C., 7
Talkington, L. W., 12
Task analysis, 72. *See also* Curriculum
Tawney, J. W., 222
Taylor, V. E., 27
Teacher
 as advocate for the handicapped, 294–300
 as educator, 283–284
 as member of multidisciplinary team, 289–293
 as negotiator, 305–306
 as parent liaison, 284–285
 as supervisor of aide or paraprofessional, 285–289, 303
 skills for, 300–306
Terman, L. M., 10
Thorpe, M. E., 322, 323
Time sampling, 144–145
Timeout (aversive stimulus), 192
Token economy, 83–86
Total task instruction. *See* Concurrent chaining
Towner, C., 13
Trial and error learning, 52
Tucker, D., 107
Turkel, S. B., 327
Turner, K., 13

Ulrich, J., 32
Underwood, B. J., 91
Ury, W., 305
Utley, B., 32, 33, 107

Van Deventer, P., 232
Vedovatti, P., 32
Verbal cues, 97
Vincent, L. J., 20, 310, 311
Vocational Opportunities Cooperative, 210–213
Vocational training, 209–214, 222, 231–232
VOCSKILLS program, 210–214
Voeltz, L. M., 53, 172, 214–217, 219, 323–325, 326

Walden, M., 13
Waldo, L., 207
Walter, G., 311
Walters, R. H., 116
Warren, S., 107
Wechsler, D., 10
Weeks, M., 180, 185, 320, 326
Wehman, P., 222
Welch, R. J., 19
Wenar, C., 12

White, O. R., 13, 155–157
Wilcox, B., 15
Wilheim, H., 98
Windmiller, M., 11
Wolf, E. A., 12
Wolfensberger, W., 226, 229, 308
Woolsey-Hill, J., 108
Work skills, 209
Wuerch, B. B., 53, 214–217, 219

Young, M., 19

Zeaman, D., 77
Zehrbach, R. R., 5